287 ⋆⋆ 299

The local org;
argument
{ 76-77
87-91
98-104

5-116

44

156

81
84

320

main

a movement of prayers, a parish class

325 How coalition building
destroys militancy.

339 a bit of fine indignation here

354 real income cut in half!

357 the Crisis

POOR PEOPLE'S MOVEMENTS
Why They Succeed,
How They Fail

By the same authors:

REGULATING THE POOR: The Functions of Public Welfare

THE POLITICS OF TURMOIL: Essays on Poverty, Race, and the Urban Crisis

POOR PEOPLE'S MOVEMENTS

Why They Succeed, How They Fail

by

FRANCES FOX PIVEN
and RICHARD A. CLOWARD

PANTHEON BOOKS, New York

Library of Congress Cataloging in Publication Data

Piven, Frances Fox, 1932–
 Poor People's Movements.

 Includes bibliographies and index.
 1. Labor and laboring classes—United States—Political activity—History. 2. Afro-Americans—Civil rights—History.
 3. Welfare rights movement—United States—History.
 I. Cloward, Richard A., 1926–, joint author. II. Title.
 HD8076.P55   322.4′4′0973   77–5298
 ISBN 0–394–48840–7

Manufactured in the United States of America

First Edition

Grateful acknowledgment is made to the following for permission to reprint previously published material:

The Antioch Press: Excerpts from "Kennedy in History: An Early Appraisal" by William G. Carleton in *The Antioch Review*, vol. 24, no. 3. Reprinted by permission of the editors.

Delacorte Press: Excerpted verse from *Toil and Trouble* by Thomas R. Brooks. Copyright © 1964 by Thomas R. Brooks. Reprinted by permission of Delacorte Press.

Fortune: Quotation from *Fortune*, Fall 1931.

Greenwood Press, Inc.: Excerpt from *World Revolutionary Propaganda* by Harold D. Lasswell and Dorothy Blumenstock. Used with the agreement of the reprint publisher, Greenwood Press, Inc.

Lexington Books: *Bread or Justice* by Lawrence Neil Bailis. Reprinted by permission of Lexington Books, D. C. Heath and Company, Lexington, Mass., 1974.

Lexington Books and The Rand Corporation: *Protests by the Poor* by Larry R. Jackson and William A. Johnson. Reprinted by permission of Lexington Books, D. C. Heath and Company, Lexington, Mass., 1974, and The Rand Corporation.

George T. Martin, Jr.: Excerpts from "The Emergence and Development of a Social Movement Organization Among the Underclass: A Case Study of the National Welfare Rights Organization" by George T. Martin, Jr., Ph.D. dissertation, Department of Sociology, University of Chicago, 1972. Reprinted by permission.

Monthly Review Press: Excerpts from Rosa Luxemburg's *Selected Writings*, edited by Dick Howard. Copyright © 1971 by Monthly Review Press. Reprinted by permission of Monthly Review Press.

The Nation: "No Rent Money . . . 1931" by Horace Cayton in the September 9, 1931, issue and "Labor 1975: The Triumph of Business Unionism" by B. J. Widick in the September 6, 1975, issue.

National Welfare Rights Organization: Excerpt from the "National Welfare Rights Organization Newsletter." Reprinted by permission.

The New American Library, Inc.: Excerpts from *Lyndon B. Johnson: The Exercise of Power* by Rowland Evans and Robert Novak. Copyright © 1966 by Rowland Evans and Robert Novak. Reprinted by arrangement with The New American Library, Inc., New York, N.Y.

The New York Times Company: Excerpt from March 6, 1930, February 2, 1932, and June 16, 1963, issues. Copyright © 1930, 1932, 1963 by The New York Times Company. Reprinted by permission.

Radical America: "Personal Histories of the Early CIO" by Staughton Lynd from the May–June 1969 issue, vol. 5, no. 3. Copyright © 1969 by *Radical America*.

United Auto Workers: Four lines of lyrics attributed to Maurice Sugar, counsel for United Auto Workers.

ACKNOWLEDGMENTS

We would like to thank Bert DeLeeuw, Murray Edelman, Mark Naison, Bill Pastreich, and Howard Zinn for reading and commenting on this manuscript at various stages in its preparation.

CONTENTS

Introduction

This book is about several protest movements that erupted among lower-class groups in the United States during the middle years of the twentieth century. We first examine the protests that arose during the years of the Great Depression, both among the unemployed and among industrial workers. Then we turn to the black protests that arose after World War II, starting in the South and spreading to the northern cities.

It is not our purpose, however, to present a comprehensive historical account of these events. We have tried to rely whenever we could on the historical research done by others.[1] Our purpose is rather to probe for the political meaning of the extraordinary struggles which occurred during these two tumultuous periods in recent American history. We have tried to understand the features of the American political economy which explain why these eruptions occurred when they did, why the eruptions took the forms they did, and why elites responded to them as they did. And we have tried to understand these events because we think they reveal much about both the limitations and the possibilities for power by the poor in the electoral-representative political institutions of the United States.

There is, of course, a considerable literature on protest movements. It is our opinion, however, that the most important question to be asked about protest movements is not dealt with in this literature. As forms of political struggle, protest movements sometimes succeed and sometimes fail. Sometimes they force concessions from the state that help to relieve the condition of life of the lower classes,

---

[1] The chapters on the movement of industrial workers and the civil rights movement are based on secondary sources because a great deal of historical work has been done on these movements. Less has been done on the movement of the unemployed in the Great Depression, and in that chapter we rely on both secondary and primary sources. The chapter on the welfare rights movement is based on our direct knowledge of and involvement in this movement, supplemented by the relatively few studies that have been done.

and sometimes they are ignored or repressed. Once protest is acknowledged as a form of political struggle the chief question to be examined must inevitably be the relationship between what the protestors
do, the context in which they do it, and the varying responses of the
state. It is this kind of analysis of past protest movements that hardly
exists. As a consequence lower-class groups, and those who align
themselves with lower-class groups, have been denied the political
wisdom that historical analysis of their own struggles might provide.

One result of this denial of history is the persistence of certain
doctrines among the activists and agitators who, from time to time
in the twentieth-century United States, have tried to mobilize the
lower classes for political action. Some of these activists, like the
cadres of the civil rights movement, were simply brave reformers,
committed not to the total transformation of American society but
to reforms consistent with American doctrines. Others, like many of
the organizers in the depression movements, were socialists of one
kind or another who saw particular protests as only a first step in
a longer-term revolutionary struggle.

But whatever their overarching ideology, activists have usually
concentrated their efforts on developing formally structured organizations with a mass membership drawn from the lower classes. What
underlies such efforts is the conviction that formal organization is a
vehicle of power. This conviction is based on several assumptions.
First, formal organization presumably makes possible the coordination of the economic and political resources of large numbers of
people who separately have few such resources. Second, formal
organization presumably permits the intelligent and strategic use of
these resources in political conflict. And third, formal organization
presumably ensures the continuity of lower-class political mobilization over time. This, in brief, is the model of mass-based, permanent
organization which has dominated efforts to build political power
among the lower classes.

Since the essence of this model of political action is that formal
organization will ensure regular, disciplined, and continuing contributions and participation from its members, the model depends
for its success on the ability of organizations to secure incentives
or sanctions that will command and sustain the required contributions and participation from masses of people. The presumption of
most reformers and revolutionaries who have tried to organize the
lower classes is that once the economic and political resources of at
least modest numbers of people are combined in disciplined action,

public or private elites will be forced to yield up the concessions necessary to sustain and enlarge mass affiliation.

The model has not succeeded in practice, as the studies in this book reveal. The model has not succeeded because it contains a grave flaw. The flaw is, quite simply, that it is not possible to compel concessions from elites that can be used as resources to sustain oppositional organizations over time.

In part, activists do not recognize the flaw inherent in the mass-based permanent organization model because they are attracted to the possibility of organizing the lower classes at extraordinary times, at moments when large numbers of lower-class people are roused to indignation and defiance and thus when a great deal seems possible. Organizers do not create such moments, as we will be at some pains to explain later, but they are excited by them, and the signs of the moment conspire to support the organizer's faith. One such sign is the sheer excess of political energy among the masses, which itself breathes life into the belief that large organizations can be developed and sustained. Another is that, in the face of the threat of popular insurgency, elites may offer up concessions that would otherwise have seemed improbable; the victories needed to sustain organization thus seem ready to be won. Most important of all in affirming the viability of the model, elites are likely at times of mass disturbance to seek out whatever organizations have emerged among the insurgents, soliciting their views and encouraging them to air grievances before formal bodies of the state. While these symbolic gestures give the appearance of influence to formal organizations composed of lower-class people, elites are not actually responding to the organizations; they are responding to the underlying force of insurgency. But insurgency is always short-lived. Once it subsides and the people leave the streets, most of the organizations which it temporarily threw up and which elites helped to nurture simply fade away. As for the few organizations which survive, it is because they become more useful to those who control the resources on which they depend than to the lower-class groups which the organizations claim to represent. Organizations endure, in short, by abandoning their oppositional politics.

Our main point, however, is not simply that efforts to build organizations are futile. The more important point is that by endeavoring to do what they cannot do, organizers fail to do what they can do. During those brief periods in which people are roused to indignation, when they are prepared to defy the authorities to whom they ordinarily defer, during those brief moments when lower-class groups exert some force against the state, those who call themselves leaders do not usually escalate the momentum of the people's protests. They do not because they are preoccupied with trying to build and sustain embryonic formal organizations in the sure conviction that these organizations will enlarge and become powerful. Thus the studies that follow show that, all too often, when workers erupted in strikes, organizers collected dues cards; when tenants refused to pay rent and stood off marshals, organizers formed building committees; when people were burning and looting, organizers used that "moment of madness" to draft constitutions.

The study of past movements reveals another point of equal importance. Organizers not only failed to seize the opportunity presented by the rise of unrest, they typically acted in ways that blunted or curbed the disruptive force which lower-class people were sometimes able to mobilize. In small part, this resulted from the doctrinal commitment to the development of mass-based, permanent organization, for organization-building activities tended to draw people away from the streets and into the meeting rooms. In part it resulted from the preoccupation with internal leadership prerogatives that organization-building seems to induce. But in the largest part organizers tended to work against disruption because, in their search for resources to maintain their organizations, they were driven inexorably to elites, and to the tangible and symbolic supports that elites could provide. Elites conferred these resources because they understood that it was organization-building, not disruption, that organizers were about.

Ordinarily, of course, elites do not support efforts to form organizations of lower-class people. But when insurgency wells up, apparently uncontrollable, elites respond. And one of their responses is to cultivate those lower-class organizations which begin to emerge in such periods, for they have little to fear from organizations, especially from organizations which come to depend upon them for support. Thus, however unwittingly, leaders and organizers of the lower classes act in the end to facilitate the efforts of elites to channel the insurgent masses into normal politics, believing all the while that they are taking the long and arduous but certain path to power. When the tumult is over, these organizations usually fade, no longer useful to those who provided the resources necessary to their survival. Or the organization persists by becoming increasingly subservient to those on whom it depends.

Either way, no lesson seems to be learned. Each generation of leaders and organizers acts as if there were no political moral to be derived from the history of failed organizing efforts, nor from the obvious fact that whatever the people won was a response to their turbulence and not to their organized numbers. Consequently, when new institutional dislocations once again set people free from prevailing systems of social control, with the result that protest erupts for another moment in time, leaders and organizers attempt again to do what they cannot do, and forfeit the chance to do what they might do.

We wrote this book as a step toward culling the historical wisdom that might inform lower-class political mobilizations in the future. The first chapter is a theoretical overview of the societal forces which structure protest movements by the lower classes in the United States. We consider this overview essential, for the forces which structure mass insurgency also define the boundaries within which organizers and leaders act, however much they might suppose otherwise. It is our belief that many past organizing efforts foundered because they failed to take account of the profound ways in which the social structure restricts the forms of political action in which the lower classes can engage, and having failed to recognize these limitations, organizers and leaders also failed to exploit the opportunities afforded by lower-class mobilizations when they did occur.

Then we turn to the movements of the Great Depression and of the post–World War II period. Our studies of insurgency during the years of the Great Depression include the movement of the unemployed that gave rise to the Workers' Alliance of America and the movement of industrial workers that produced the Congress of Industrial Organizations. The postwar studies include the southern civil rights movement and the protest organizations it spawned, and the movement of welfare recipients that generated the National Welfare Rights Organization. The industrial workers' movement and the civil rights movement gained more than the others; it is our central concern to show how differences in the strategies of organizers and leaders help to explain variations in what was won.

Before we go on to the body of our argument we ought to explain our use of the words "lower class" or "poor." We do not use the terms in the contemporary sociological sense of a stratum beneath the working class, but rather as a stratum within the working class that is poor by standards prevailing in society at the time. Although the specific social origins of the participants in the movements examined here varied greatly—some were white men, some were black women; some were displaced southern agricultural workers, some were urban immigrant industrial workers—we consider that all of the protest movements we analyze arose among sectors of the working class, including the protest of welfare mothers in the 1960s. Our usage deviates from sociological custom but it is consistent with classical Marxist definitions of the working class. Our usage also deviates from the current fashion on the left of referring to impoverished and underemployed working-class groups as "lumpen proletarians," a fashion we find not only offensive for its denigrating implications but also an abuse of Marx, who meant the term to refer to deviant and criminal elements from all classes.

F.F.P.
R.A.C.

March 1977

POOR PEOPLE'S MOVEMENTS
Why They Succeed,
How They Fail

CHAPTER

1

The Structuring
of Protest

Common sense and historical experience combine to suggest a simple but compelling view of the roots of power in any society. Crudely but clearly stated, those who control the means of physical coercion, and those who control the means of producing wealth, have power over those who do not. This much is true whether the means of coercion consists in the primitive force of a warrior caste or the technological force of a modern army. And it is true whether the control of production consists in control by priests of the mysteries of the calendar on which agriculture depends, or control by financiers of the large-scale capital on which industrial production depends. Since coercive force can be used to gain control of the means of producing wealth, and since control of wealth can be used to gain coercive force, these two sources of power tend over time to be drawn together within one ruling class.

Common sense and historical experience also combine to suggest that these sources of power are protected and enlarged by the use of that power not only to control the actions of men and women, but also to control their beliefs. What some call superstructure, and what others call culture, includes an elaborate system of beliefs and ritual behaviors which defines for people what is right and what is wrong and why; what is possible and what is impossible; and the behavioral imperatives that follow from these beliefs. Because this superstructure of beliefs and rituals is evolved in the context of unequal power, it is inevitable that beliefs and rituals reinforce inequality, by rendering the powerful divine and the challengers evil. Thus the class struggles that might otherwise be inevitable in sharply unequal societies ordinarily do not seem either possible or right from the perspective of those who live within the structure of belief and ritual fashioned by those societies. People whose only possible recourse in struggle is to defy the beliefs and rituals laid down by their rulers ordinarily do not.

What common sense and historical experience suggest has been true of many societies is no less true of modern capitalist societies, the United States among them. Power is rooted in the control of coercive force and in the control of the means of production. However, in capitalist societies this reality is not legitimated by rendering the powerful divine, but by obscuring their existence. Thus electoral-representative arrangements proclaim the franchise, not force and wealth, as the basis for the accumulation and use of power. Wealth is, to be sure, unequally distributed, but the franchise is widely and nearly equally distributed, and by exercising the franchise men and women presumably determine who their rulers will be, and therefore what their rulers presumably must do if they are to remain rulers.

Since analysts of power also live within the boundaries of ritual and belief of their society, they have contributed to this obfuscation by arguing that electoral arrangements offset other bases of power. Even the most sophisticated American political scientists have begun with the assumption that there are in fact two systems of power, one based on wealth and one based on votes, and they have devoted themselves to deciphering the relative influence of these two systems. This question has been regarded as intricate and complicated, demanding assiduous investigations in a variety of political settings, and by methods subject to the most rigorous empirical strictures. ("Nothing categorical can be assumed about power in any community" was Polsby's famous dictum.) The answer that emerged from these investigations was that electoral-representative procedures accomplished a substantial dispersal of power in a less-than-perfect world. It followed that those who struggled against their rulers by defying the procedures of the liberal democratic state were dangerous troublemakers, or simply fools.

In the 1960s the dominant pluralist tradition was discredited, at least among those on the ideological left who were prodded by outbreaks of defiance among minorities and students to question this perspective. In the critique that emerged it was argued that there were not two systems of power, but that the power rooted in wealth and force overwhelmed the power of the franchise. The pluralists had erred, the critics said, by failing to recognize the manifold ways in which wealth and its concomitants engulfed electoral-representative procedures, effectively barring many people from participation while deluding and entrapping others into predetermined electoral "choices." The pluralists had also erred by ignoring the consistent bias toward the interests of elites inherent in presumably neutral governing structures, no matter what the mandate of the electorate.

We do not wish to summarize the critique, which was by no means simple, or all of a piece. We wish only to make the point that the challenge rested in large part on the insight that modes of participation and nonparticipation in electoral-representative procedures were not, as the pluralists had implied by their narrow empirical strictures, the freely made political choices of free men and women. Rather, modes of participation, and the degree of influence that resulted, were consistently determined by location in the class structure. It was an important insight, and once it had been achieved the conclusion followed not far behind that so long as lower-class groups abided by the norms governing the electoral-representative system, they would have little influence. It therefore became clear, at least to some of us, that protest tactics which defied political norms were not simply the recourse of troublemakers and fools. For the poor, they were the only recourse.

But having come this far, we have gone no further. The insights that illuminated the critiques of electoral-representative processes have been entirely overlooked in the few studies that have been done of the nature of protest itself. From an intellectual perspective, it is a startling oversight; from a political perspective, it is all too easily explained by the overwhelming biases of our traditions. Briefly stated, the main argument of this chapter is that protest is *also* not a matter of free choice; it is not freely available to all groups at all times, and much of the time it is not available to lower-class groups at all. *The occasions when protest is possible among the poor, the forms that it must take, and the impact it can have are all delimited by the social structure in ways which usually diminish its extent and diminish its force.* Before we go on to explain these points, we need to define what we mean by a protest movement, for customary definitions have led both analysts and activists to ignore or discredit much protest that does occur.

The emergence of a protest movement entails a transformation both of consciousness and of behavior. The change in consciousness has at least three distinct aspects. First, "the system"—or those aspects of the system that people experience and perceive—loses legitimacy. Large numbers of men and women who ordinarily accept the authority of their rulers and the legitimacy of institutional arrangements come to believe in some measure that these rulers and these arrangements are unjust and wrong.[1] Second, people who are ordinarily fatalistic, who believe that existing arrangements are inevitable, begin to assert "rights" that imply demands for change. Third, there is a new sense of efficacy; people who ordinarily consider themselves helpless come to believe that they have some capacity to alter their lot.

The change in behavior is equally striking, and usually more easily recognized, at least when it takes the form of mass strikes or marches or riots. Such behavior seems to us to involve two distinguishing elements. First, masses of people become defiant; they violate the traditions and laws to which they ordinarily acquiesce, and they flaunt the authorities to whom they ordinarily defer. And second, their defiance is acted out collectively, as members of a group, and not as isolated individuals. Strikes and riots are clearly forms of collective action, but even some forms of defiance which appear to be individual acts, such as crime or school truancy or incendiarism, while more ambiguous, may have a collective dimension, for those who engage in these acts may consider themselves to be part of a larger movement. Such apparently atomized acts of defiance can be considered movement events when those involved perceive themselves to be acting as members of a group, and when they share a common set of protest beliefs.

Prevailing definitions, by stressing articulated social change goals as the defining feature of social movements, have had the effect of denying political meaning to many forms of protest. Thus while the impulse to proliferate idiosyncratic usages ought ordinarily to be resisted, we believe that the difference between our definition and those generally found in the fairly extensive sociological literature on social movements is no mere definitional quibble. Joseph Gusfield,

---

[1] In this connection Max Weber writes: "The degree in which 'communal action' and possibly 'societal action,' emerges from the 'mass actions' of the members of a class is linked to general cultural conditions, especially to those of an intellectual sort. It is also linked to the extent of the contrasts that have already evolved, and is especially linked to the *transparency* of the connections between the causes and the consequences of the 'class situation.' For however different life chances may be, this fact in itself, according to all experience, by no means gives birth to 'class action . . .' " (184, emphasis in the original).

for example, defines a social movement as "socially shared activities and beliefs directed toward the demand for change in some aspect of the social order. . . . What characterizes a social movement as a particular kind of change agent is its quality as an articulated and organized group" (2, 453). Similarly John Wilson says: "A social movement is a conscious, collective, organized attempt to bring about or resist large-scale change in the social order by noninstitutionalized means" (8).

The stress on conscious intentions in these usages reflects a confusion in the literature between the mass movement on the one hand, and the formalized organizations which tend to emerge on the crest of the movement on the other hand—two intertwined but distinct phenomena.[2] Thus formalized organizations do put forward articulated and agreed-upon social change goals, as suggested by these definitions, but such goals may not be apparent in mass uprisings (although others, including ourselves as observers and analysts, may well impute goals to uprisings). Furthermore our emphasis is on collective defiance as the key and distinguishing feature of a protest movement, but defiance tends to be omitted or understated in standard definitions simply because defiance does not usually characterize the activities of formal organizations that arise on the crest of protest movements.

Whatever the intellectual sources of error, the effect of equating movements with movement organizations—and thus requiring that protests have a leader, a constitution, a legislative program, or at least a banner before they are recognized as such—is to divert attention from many forms of political unrest and to consign them by definition to the more shadowy realms of social problems and deviant behavior. As a result such events as massive school truancy or rising worker absenteeism or mounting applications for public welfare or spreading rent defaults rarely attract the attention of political analysts. Having decided by definitional fiat that nothing political has occurred, nothing has to be explained, at least not in the terms of political protest. And having contrived in this way not to recognize protest or to study it, we cannot ask certain rather obvious and important questions about it.

---

[2] Thus, Zald and Ash use the term "social movement organizations" to encompass both forms of social action. Roberta Ash does, in her later work, distinguish between movements and movement organizations, but she continues to stress articulated goals as a defining feature of a movement.

Institutional Limits on the Incidence
of Mass Insurgency

Aristotle believed that the chief cause of internal warfare was inequality, that the lesser rebel in order to be equal. But human experience has proved him wrong, most of the time. Sharp inequality has been constant, but rebellion infrequent. Aristotle underestimated the controlling force of the social structure on political life. However hard their lot may be, people usually remain acquiescent, conforming to the accustomed patterns of daily life in their community, and believing those patterns to be both inevitable and just. Men and women till the fields each day, or stoke the furnaces, or tend the looms, obeying the rules and rhythms of earning a livelihood; they mate and bear children hopefully, and mutely watch them die; they abide by the laws of church and community and defer to their rulers, striving to earn a little grace and esteem. In other words most of the time people conform to the institutional arrangements which enmesh them, which regulate the rewards and penalties of daily life, and which appear to be the only possible reality.

Those for whom the rewards are most meager, who are the most oppressed by inequality, are also acquiescent. Sometimes they are the most acquiescent, for they have little defense against the penalties that can be imposed for defiance. Moreover, at most times and in most places, and especially in the United States, the poor are led to believe that their destitution is deserved, and that the riches and power that others command are also deserved. In more traditional societies sharp inequalities are thought to be divinely ordained, or to be a part of the natural order of things. In more modern societies, such as the United States, riches and power are ascribed to personal qualities of industry or talent; it follows that those who have little or nothing have only what they deserve. As Edelman observes in his study of American political beliefs:

> The American poor have required less coercion and less in social security guarantees to maintain their quiescence than has been true in other developed countries, even authoritarian ones like Germany and notably poor ones like Italy; for the guilt and self-concepts of the poor have kept them docile (1971, 56).

Ordinarily, in short, the lower classes accept their lot, and that acceptance can be taken for granted; it need not be bargained for by their rulers. This capacity of the institutions of a society to enforce political docility is the most obvious way in which protest is socially structured, in the sense that it is structurally precluded most of the time.

Sometimes, however, the poor do become defiant. They challenge traditional authorities, and the rules laid down by those authorities. They demand redress for their grievances. American history is punctuated by such events, from the first uprisings by freeholders, tenants, and slaves in colonial America, to the postrevolutionary debtor rebellions, through the periodic eruptions of strikes and riots by industrial workers, to the ghetto riots of the twentieth century. In each instance, masses of the poor were somehow able, if only briefly, to overcome the shame bred by a culture which blames them for their plight; somehow they were able to break the bonds of conformity enforced by work, by family, by community, by every strand of institutional life; somehow they were able to overcome the fears induced by police, by militia, by company guards.

When protest does arise, when masses of those who are ordinarily docile become defiant, a major transformation has occurred. Most of the literature on popular insurgency has been devoted to identifying the preconditions of this transformation (often out of a concern for preventing or curbing the resulting political disturbances). Whatever the disagreements among different schools of thought, and they are substantial, there is general agreement that the emergence of popular uprisings reflects profound changes in the larger society. This area of agreement is itself important, for it is another way of stating our proposition that protest is usually structurally precluded. The agreement is that only under exceptional conditions will the lower classes become defiant—and thus, in our terms, *only under exceptional conditions are the lower classes afforded the socially determined opportunity to press for their own class interests.*

The validity of this point follows from any of the major theories of civil disorder considered alone. When the several theoretical perspectives are considered concurrently and examined in the light of the historical events analyzed in this book, the conclusion is suggested that while different theories emphasize different kinds of social dislocations, most of these dislocations occurred simultaneously in the 1930s and 1960s. One does not have to believe that the various major theoretical perspectives are equally valid to agree that they may all cast at least some light on the series of dislocations that preceded the eruption of protest, at least in the periods we study. This

an undefined "anger" is the conceptual limit here.

argues that it not only requires a major social dislocation before protest can emerge, but that a sequence or combination of dislocations probably must occur before the anger that underlies protest builds to a high pitch, and before that anger can find expression in collective defiance.

It seems useful to divide perspectives on insurgency according to whether the emphasis is on pressures that force eruptions, or whether the emphasis is on the breakdown of the regulatory capacity of the society, a breakdown that permits eruptions to occur and to take form in political protest. Thus among the "pressure" theorists one might include those who emphasize economic change as a precondition for civil disorder, whether economic improvement or immiseration. Sharp economic change obviously disturbs the relationship between what men and women have been led to expect, and the conditions they actually experience. If people have been led to expect more than they receive, they are likely to feel frustration and anger.[3] Some analysts, following de Tocqueville, emphasize the frustration produced by periods of economic improvement which may generate expectations that outpace the rate of actual economic gain.[4] Others, following more closely in the tradition of Marx and Engels,[5] emphasize that it is new and unexpected hardships that generate frustration and anger, and the potential for civil strife. However, this disagreement, as others have noted, is not theoretically irreconcilable.

all very vague

vague

---

[3] Perhaps the best known exponent of this widely held "relative deprivation" theory of civil strife is Ted Robert Gurr (1968, 1970). See also Feierabend, Feierabend, and Nesvold. For an excellent critique of the political theorists who base their work on this theory, see Lupsha.

[4] Both de Tocqueville and his followers include conditions of political liberalization, and the rising political expectations that result, as possible precursors of civil strife. Probably the most well-known of the contemporary "rising expectations" theorists is James C. Davies, who, however, argues a variant of the theory known as the "J-Curve." According to Davies, it is only when long periods of improvement are followed by economic downturns or political repression that civil strife results (1962).

[5] The views of Marx and Engels are, however, both more historically specific and comprehensive than the relative deprivation theory, and might be better described as not inconsistent with that theory. Economic crises, and the attendant hardships, activate proletarian struggles not only because of the extreme immiseration of the proletariat at such times, and not only because of the expansion of the reserve army of the unemployed at such times, but because periods of economic crisis reveal the contradictions of capitalism, and particularly the contradiction between socialized productive forces and the anarchy of private ownership and exchange. In Engels' words, "The mode of production rises in rebellion against the form of exchange. The bourgeoisie are convicted of incapacity further to manage their own social productive forces" (1967). Deprivation, in other words, is only a symptom of a far more profound conflict which cannot be resolved within the existing social formation.

Whether one stresses that it is good times or bad times that account for turmoil among the lower orders may be more a reflection of the empirical cases the author deals with, and perhaps of the author's class sympathies, than of serious conceptual differences.[6] Both the theorists of rising expectations and those of immiseration agree that when the expectations of men and women are disappointed, they may react with anger. And while sudden hardship, rather than rising expectations, is probably the historically more important precondition for mass turmoil, both types of change preceded the eruptions noted in the pages that follow.[7]

Still other pressure theorists focus not on the stresses generated by inconsistencies between economic circumstance and expectation, but follow Parsons (1951) in broadening this sort of model to include stresses created by structural changes generally, by inconsistencies between different "components of action" leading to outbreaks of what Parsons labels "irrational behavior" (1965). The breadth and vagueness of this model, however, probably make it less than useful. As Charles Tilly comments, "there is enough ambiguity in concepts like 'structural change,' 'stress' and 'disorder' to keep a whole flotilla of philologists at sea for life" (1964, 100).

The major flaw, in our view, in the work of all pressure theorists is their reliance on an unstated and incorrect assumption that economic change or structural change is extraordinary, that stability and the willing consensus it fosters are the usual state of affairs. Economic change, and presumably also structural change, if one were clear as to what that meant, are more the usual than the occasional features of capitalist societies. Nevertheless, historical evidence suggests that extremely rapid economic change adds to the frustration and anger that many people may experience much of the time.

The other major set of theoretical perspectives on popular uprising emphasizes the breakdown of the regulatory capacity of social institutions as the principle factor leading to civil strife. These explanations also range broadly from social disorganization theorists

---

[6] Geshwender points out that rising expectations and relative deprivation hypotheses (as well as status inconsistency hypotheses) are theoretically reconcilable.

[7] Barrington Moore asserts bluntly that the main urban revolutionary movements in the nineteenth and twentieth centuries "were all revolutions of desperation, certainly not of rising expectations, as some liberal theorists of revolution might lead one to anticipate." Snyder and Tilly, however, seem to disagree, and report that at least short-term fluctuations in prices and industrial production did not predict the incidence of collective violence in nineteenth- and twentieth-century France (1972).

such as Hobsbawm, who emphasizes the breakdown of the regulatory controls implicit in the structures and routines of daily life; to those such as Kohnhauser, who argues that major societal changes—depression, industrialization, urbanization—break the ties that bind people to the multiple secondary associations that ordinarily control political behavior (1959); to those who focus on divisions among elites as the trigger that releases popular discontents. Taken together, these social disorganization perspectives provide a major insight, however general, into the links between societal change, the breakdown of social controls—what Ash calls the "deroutinization" of life (164–167)—and the eruption of protest.[8] The disorganization theories suggest that periods of rapid change tend, at the same time as they build frustration, to weaken the regulatory controls inherent in the structures of institutional life.

More specifically, economic change may be so jarring as to virtually destroy the structures and routines of daily life. Hobsbawm points to the impact of just such conditions in accounting for the rise of "social banditry" among the Italian peasantry in the nineteenth century:

> [Social banditry] is most likely to become a major phenomenon when their traditional equilibrium is upset: during and after periods of abnormal hardship, such as famines and wars, or at the moments when the jaws of the dynamic modern world seize the static communities in order to destroy and transform them (1963, 24).

Barrington Moore stresses a similar theme:

> The main factors that create a revolutionary mass are a sudden increase in hardship coming on top of quite serious deprivations,

---

[8] Just as the relative deprivation theories are not inconsistent with a Marxist interpretation of the origins of working- and lower-class protest, neither is the emphasis on social disorganization necessarily inconsistent (although most of the proponents of that perspective are clearly not Marxists). Thus a Marxist interpretation of protest would acknowledge the significance of both relative deprivation and social disorganization, treating these however not as historically generalizable causes of uprisings, but as symptoms of historically specific contradictions in capitalist society. Bertell Ollman's work on character structure as inhibiting class consciousness and class action contributes to making explicit the link between social disorganization and mass uprisings from a Marxist perspective. Ollman argues that the "proletariat's 'fear of freedom' and their submissiveness before authority . . . are, after all, simply attempts to repeat in the future what has been done in the past" (42). But clearly, periods of major social dislocation may force a break in these character patterns, if only by precluding the possibility of repeating in the future what has been done in the past.

together with the breakdown of the routines of daily life—getting
food, going to work, etc.—that tie people to the prevailing order.

The significance of economic change is, in other words, not simply
that people find their expectations frustrated and so feel anger. It
is also that when the structures of daily life weaken, the regulatory
capacities of these structures, too, are weakened. "A revolution takes
place" says Lefebvre "when and only when, in such a society, people
can no longer lead their everyday lives; so long as they can live their
ordinary lives relations are constantly re-established" (32).

   Ordinary life for most people is regulated by the rules of work
and the rewards of work which pattern each day and week and
season. Once cast out of that routine, people are cast out of the
regulatory framework that it imposes. Work and the rewards of work
underpin the stability of other social institutions as well. When men
cannot earn enough to support families, they may desert their wives
and children, or fail to marry the women with whom they mate.
And if unemployment is longlasting entire communities may dis-
integrate as the able-bodied migrate elsewhere in search of work. In
effect daily life becomes progressively deregulated as what Edelman
calls the "comforting banalities" of everyday existence are destroyed
(95). The first signs of the resulting demoralization and uncertainty
are usually rising indices of crime, family breakdown, vagrancy, and
vandalism.[9] Barred from conforming to the social roles they have
been reared to live through, men and women continue to stumble
and struggle somehow to live, within or without the rules.

   Thus it is not only that catastrophic depression in the 1930s and
modernization and migration in the 1960s led to unexpected hardships; massive unemployment and the forced uprooting of people
and communities had other, perhaps equally traumatic effects on
the lives of people. The loss of work and the disintegration of communities meant the loss of the regulating activities, resources, and
relationships on which the structure of everyday life depends, and
thus the erosion of the structures that bound people to existing social

---

[9] It ought to be noted that Charles Tilly, in his influential work on collective violence
in nineteenth-century France, does not confirm the generally accepted view that there
is a relationship between crime and collective violence, or between either of these variables and the presumably disorganizing impact of urban growth. However, the evidence
suggests that these relationships did hold in the periods which we investigate in the
twentieth-century United States, and we do not consider the issue yet settled. In other
respects, as we will note, we agree with Tilly's alternative emphasis on resource shifts
as a precondition for collective struggle. See Tilly (1964), and Lodhi and Tilly (1973).

arrangements. Still, neither the frustrations generated by the economic change, nor the breakdown of daily life, may be sufficient to
lead people to protest their travails. Ordinarily, when people suffer
such hardships, they blame God, or they blame themselves.

For a protest movement to arise out of these traumas of daily life,
people have to perceive the deprivation and disorganization they
experience as both wrong, and subject to redress.[10] The social arrangements that are ordinarily perceived as just and immutable must come
to seem both unjust and mutable. One condition favoring this
transvaluation is the scale of distress. Thus in the 1930s, and again
in the postwar years, unemployment reached calamitous proportions.
Large numbers of people lost their means of earning a livelihood at
the same time. This was clearly the case in the 1930s when unemployment affected one-third of the work force. But among blacks the
experience in the post–World War II period was equally devastating,
for millions were forced off the land and concentrated in the ghettos
of the cities. Within these central city ghettos, unemployment rates
in the 1950s and 1960s reached depression levels. The sheer scale
of these dislocations helped to mute the sense of self-blame, pre-
disposing men and women to view their plight as a collective one,
and to blame their rulers for the destitution and disorganization they
experienced.

This transvaluation is even more likely to take place, or to take
place more rapidly, when the dislocations suffered by particular
groups occur in a context of wider changes and instability, at times
when the dominant institutional arrangements of the society, as
people understand them, are self-evidently not functioning. When
the mammoth industrial empires of the United States virtually
ground to a halt in the early 1930s and the banks of the country
simply closed their doors, the "American Way" could not be so fully
taken for granted by the masses of impoverished workers and the
unemployed. Similarly, while the institutional disturbances that preceded the black movements of the 1960s were not dramatically visible
to the society as a whole, they were to the people who were uprooted
by them. For blacks, changes in the southern economy meant nothing

---

[10] "The classical mob," writes Hobsbawm, "did not merely riot as protest, but because it
expected to achieve something by its riot. It assumed that the authorities would be
sensitive to its movements, and probably also that they would make some sort of
immediate concession . . ." (111). Rudé's account of the food riots among the urban
poor in the eighteenth century makes the same point (1964).

less than the disintegration of the *ancien régime* of the feudal plantation, just as the subsequent migratory trek to the cities meant their
wrenching removal into an unknown society.

Finally, as these objective institutional upheavals lead people to
reappraise their situation, elites may contribute to that reappraisal,
thus helping to stimulate mass arousal—a process that has often been
noted by social theorists. Clearly, the vested interest of the ruling
class is usually in preserving the status quo, and in preserving the
docility of the lower orders within the status quo. But rapid institutional change and upheaval may affect elite groups differently, undermining the power of some segments of the ruling class and enlarging
the power of other segments, so that elites divide among themselves. This dissonance may erode their authority, and erode the
authority of the institutional norms they uphold. If, in the ensuing
competition for dominance, some among the elite seek to enlist the
support of the impoverished by naming their grievances as just, then
the hopes of the lower classes for change will be nourished and the
legitimacy of the institutions which oppress them further weakened.[11]

Indeed, even when elites play no actual role in encouraging protest, the masses may invent a role for them. Hobsbawm describes how
peasants in the Ukraine pillaged the gentry and Jews during the
tumultuous year 1905. They did so, however, in the firm conviction
that a new imperial manifesto had directed them to take what they
wanted. An account by a landowner makes the point:

> "Why have you come?" I asked them.
> "To demand corn, to make you give us your corn," said several
> voices simultaneously. . . .
> I could not refrain from recalling how I had treated them for
> so long.
> "But what are we to do?" several voices answered me.
> "We aren't doing this in our name, but in the name of the Tsar."
> "It is the Tsar's order," said one voice in the crowd.
> "A general has distributed this order of the Tsar throughout the
> districts," said another (187).[12]

---

[11] Roberta Ash ascribes the politicization of Boston mobs during the revolutionary
period to this process. As the discontented wealthy sought allies among the poor, street
gangs were transformed into organized militants in the political struggle (70–73).

[12] Hobsbawm and Rudé make the same point about the English farm laborers' protests
against enclosure: "[T]hey were reluctant to believe . . . that the King's government
and Parliament were against them. For how could the format of justice be against
justice?" (65).

Nor is this tendency only observable among Russian peasants. Crowds of welfare recipients demonstrating for special grants in New York City in May 1968 employed a similar justification, inciting each other with the news that a rich woman had died and left instructions that her wealth be distributed through the welfare centers. These events suggest that people seek to legitimate what they do, even when they are defiant, and the authority of elites to define what is legitimate remains powerful, even during periods of stress and disorder.

Our main point, however, is that whatever position one takes on the "causes" of mass unrest, there is general agreement that extraordinary disturbances in the larger society are required to transform the poor from apathy to hope, from quiescence to indignation.[13] On this point, if no other, theorists of the most diverse persuasions agree. Moreover, there is reason to think that a series of concurrent dislocations underlay the mass protests of the 1930s and 1960s. And with that said, the implication for an understanding of the potential for political influence among the poor becomes virtually self-evident: *since periods of profound social dislocations are infrequent, so too are opportunities for protest among the lower classes.*

The Patterning of Insurgency

Just as quiescence is enforced by institutional life, and just as the eruption of discontent is determined by changes in institutional life, the forms of political protest are also determined by the institutional context in which people live and work. This point seems self-evident to us, but it is usually ignored, in part because the pluralist tradition defines political action as essentially a matter of choice. Political actors, whoever they may be, are treated as if they are not con-

---

[13] Rosa Luxemburg's discussion of the profound and complex social upheavals that lead to mass strikes makes the same point: "[I]t is extremely difficult for any leading organ of the proletarian movement to foresee and to calculate which occasions and moments can lead to explosions and which cannot . . . because in each individual act of the struggle so many important economic, political, and social, general and local, material and psychological moments are brought into play that no single act can be arranged and resolved like a mathematical problem. . . . The revolution is not a maneuver executed by the proletariat in the open field; rather, it is a struggle in the midst of the unceasing crashing, crumbling, and displacing of all the social foundations" (245).

stricted by a social environment in deciding upon one political strategy or another; it is as if the strategies employed by different groups were freely elected, rather than the result of constraints imposed by their location in the social structure. In this section, we turn, in the most preliminary way, to a discussion of the ways in which the expression of defiance is patterned by features of institutional life.

THE ELECTORAL SYSTEM AS A STRUCTURING INSTITUTION

In the United States the principal structuring institution, at least in the early phases of protest, is the electoral-representative system. The significance of this assertion is not that the electoral system provides an avenue of influence under normal circumstances. To the contrary, we shall demonstrate that it is usually when unrest among the lower classes breaks out of the confines of electoral procedures that the poor may have some influence, for the instability and polarization they then threaten to create by their actions in the factories or in the streets may force some response from electoral leaders. But whether action emerges in the factories or the streets may depend on the course of the early phase of protest at the polls.

Ordinarily defiance is first expressed in the voting booth simply because, whether defiant or not, people have been socialized within a political culture that defines voting as the mechanism through which political change can and should properly occur. The vitality of this political culture, the controlling force of the norms that guide political discontent into electoral channels, is not understood merely by asserting the pervasiveness of liberal political ideology in the United States and the absence of competing ideologies, for that is precisely what has to be explained. Some illumination is provided by certain features of the electoral system itself, by its rituals and celebrations and rewards, for these practices help to ensure the persistence of confidence in electoral procedures. Thus it is significant that the franchise was extended to white working-class men at a very early period in the history of the United States, and that a vigorous system of local government developed. Through these mechanisms, large proportions of the population were embraced by the rituals of electoral campaigns, and shared in the symbolic rewards of the electoral system, while some also shared in the tangible rewards of a relatively freely dispensed government patronage. Beliefs thus nurtured do not erode readily.

Accordingly, one of the first signs of popular discontent in the contemporary United States is usually a sharp shift in traditional voting patterns.[14] In a sense, the electoral system serves to measure and register the extent of the emerging disaffection. Thus, the urban working class reacted to economic catastrophe in the landslide election of 1932 by turning against the Republican Party to which it had given its allegiance more or less since 1896.[15] Similarly, the political impact of the forces of modernization and migration was first evident in the crucial presidential elections of 1956 and 1960. Urban blacks, who had voted Democratic in successively larger proportions since

---

[14] The tendency for popular discontent to lead to third-party efforts is of course also evidence of the force of electoral norms. Thus as early as the depression of 1828–1831, labor unrest was expressed in the rise of numerous workingman's political parties, and late in the nineteenth century as the industrial working class grew, much labor discontent was channeled into socialist political parties, some of which achieved modest success at the local level. In 1901 the Socialist Party came together as a coalition of many of these groups, and by 1912 it had elected 1,200 party members to local public office in some 340 cities and towns, including the mayor's office in 73 cities (Weinstein, 7). Similarly the agrarian movements of the late nineteenth century were primarily oriented toward the electoral system. Nor is this tendency only evident in the United States. In Europe, for example, with the disillusionment of the failed revolution of 1848, and with the gradual extension of the franchise to workers, socialist parties also began to emphasize parliamentary tactics. The classical justification for this emphasis became Engels' introduction to *Class Struggles in France*, in which Engels writes of the successes achieved by the German party through the parliamentary vote: "It has been discovered that the political institutions in which the domination of the bourgeoisie is organized offer a fulcrum by means of which the proletariat can combat these very political institutions. The Social Democrats have participated in the elections to the various Diets, to municipal councils, and to industrial courts. Wherever the proletariat could secure an effective voice, the occupation of these electoral strongholds by the bourgeoisie has been contested. Consequently, the bourgeoisie and the government have become much more alarmed at the legal than at the illegal activities of the labor party, dreading the results of elections far more than they dread the results of rebellion." Some years later, Kautsky published a letter from Engels disavowing the preface and blaming it on the "timid legalism" of the leaders of the German Social Democratic Party who were committed to the parliamentary activities through which the party was thriving, and fearful of the threatened passage of antisocialist laws by the Reichstag (see Howard, 383; Michels, 370 fn 6).

[15] Burnham's well-known theory of "critical elections" resulting from the cumulative tension between socio-economic developments and the political system is similar to this argument (1965, 1970). The relationship betwen economic conditions and voter responses has been subjected to extensive empirical study by American political scientists. These studies generally tend to confirm the proposition that deteriorating economic conditions result in voter defections from incumbent parties. See for example Bloom and Price; Kramer; and Campbell, Converse, Miller, and Stokes.

the election of 1936, began to defect to Republican columns or to stay away from the polls.

These early signs of political instability ordinarily prompt efforts by contending political leaders to placate the defecting groups, usually at this stage with conciliatory pronouncements. The more serious the electoral defections, or the keener the competition among political elites, the more likely that such symbolic appeasements will be offered. But if the sources of disturbance and anger are severe—and only if they are severe and persistent—conciliations are likely merely to fuel mass arousal, for in effect they imply that some of the highest leaders of the land identify with the indignation of the lowly masses.

Moreover, just as political leaders play an influential role in stimulating mass arousal, so do they play an important role in shaping the demands of the aroused.[16] What are intended to serve as merely symbolic appeasements may instead provide a focus for the still inchoate anxieties and diffuse anger that drive the masses. Thus early rhetorical pronouncements by liberal political leaders, including presidents of the United States, about the "rights" of workers and the "rights" of blacks not only helped to fuel the discontents of workers and blacks, but helped to concentrate those discontents on demands articulated by leading officials of the nation.[17]

---

[16] Edelman ascribes the influence of public officials as "powerful shapers of perceptions" to their virtual monopoly on certain kinds of information, to the legitimacy of the regime with which they are identified, and to the intense identification of people with the state (101–102).

[17] Our conviction that the demands of the protestors, at least for the periods we examine, are shaped as much by their interaction with elites as by the structural factors (or contradictions) which produced the movements is one difference between this analysis and some Marxist interpretations. Thus if one explains the origins of protest not by the breakdown of social controls, or by relative deprivation, but by the basic and irreconcilable contradictions that characterize capitalist institutions, then the political agenda the movement evolves ought to reflect those basic and irreconcilable contradictions. Hence it would follow that working-class and lower-class movements arising in a corporate capitalist society are democratic and egalitarian or, in an older terminology, progressive, and not ultimately cooptable. Manuel Castells, for example, who has done some of the best work on social movements from a Marxist perspective, defines a movement as "a certain type of organization of social practices, the logic of whose development contradicts the institutionally dominant social logic" (93). By his definition Castells thus minimizes a host of problems in evaluating the political directions of social movements that historical experience unfortunately does not minimize. See also Useem (1975, 27–35). Or, in another terminology, we do not take it for granted that conscious (or subjective) orientations of action approximate objective class interests (see Dahrendorf (174–176) and Balbus for a discussion of this distinction).

But when people are thus encouraged in spirit without being appeased in fact, their defiance may escape the boundaries of electoral rituals, and escape the boundaries established by the political norms of the electoral-representative system in general. They may indeed become rebellious, but while their rebellion often appears chaotic from the perspective of conventional American politics, or from the perspective of some organizers, it is not chaotic at all; it is structured political behavior. When people riot in the streets, their behavior is socially patterned, and within those patterns, their actions are to some extent deliberate and purposeful.

SOCIAL LOCATION AND FORMS OF DEFIANCE

In contrast to the effort expended in accounting for the sources of insurgency, relatively little attention has been given to the question of why insurgency, when it does occur, takes one form and not another. Why, in other words, do people sometimes strike and at other times boycott, loot, or burn? Perhaps this question is seldom dealt with because defiant behavior released often appears inchoate to analysts, and therefore not susceptible to explanation, as in the nineteenth-century view of mental illness. Thus Parsons characterizes reactions to strain as "irrational" (1965); Neil Smelser describes collective behavior as "primitive" and "magical"; and Kornhauser attributes unstable, extremist, and antidemocratic tendencies to mass movements. Many defiant forms of mass action that fall short of armed uprisings are thus often simply not recognized as intelligent political behavior at all.

The common but false association of lower-class protest with violence may also be a residue of this tradition and its view of the mob as normless and dangerous, the barbarian unchained. Mass violence is, to be sure, one of many forms of defiance, and perhaps a very elemental form, for it violates the very ground rules of civil society. And lower-class groups do on occasion resort to violence—to the destruction of property and persons—and perhaps this is more likely to be the case when they are deprived by their institutional location of the opportunity to use other forms of defiance. More typically, however, they are not violent, although they may be militant. They are usually not violent simply because the risks are too great; the penalties attached to the use of violence by the poor are too fearsome and too overwhelming.[18] (Of course, defiance by the lower class frequently *results* in violence when more powerful groups, discomfited or alarmed by the unruliness of the poor, use force to coerce them into docility. The substantial record of violence associated with protest movements in the United States is a record composed overwhelmingly of the casualties suffered by protestors at the hands of public or private armies.)

Such perspectives have left us with images which serve to discredit lower-class movements by denying them meaning and legitimacy, instead of providing explanations. While the weakening of social controls that accompanies ruptures in social life may be an important precondition for popular uprisings, it does not follow either that the infrastructure of social life simply collapses, or that those who react to these disturbances by protesting are those who suffer the sharpest personal disorientation and alienation. To the contrary it may well be those whose lives are rooted in some institutional context, who are in regular relationships with others in similar straits, who are best able to redefine their travails as the fault of their rulers and not of themselves, and are best able to join together in collective protest.[19] Thus while many of the southern blacks who participated in the civil rights movement were poor, recent migrants to the southern cities, or were unemployed, they were also linked together in the

---

[18] Gamson argues convincingly that rational calculations of the chances of success underlie the use of violence: "Violence should be viewed as an instrumental act, aimed at furthering the purpose of the group that uses it when they have some reason to think it will help their cause. . . . [It] grows from an impatience born of confidence and rising efficacy rather than the opposite. It occurs when hostility toward the victim renders it a relatively safe and costless strategy" (81).

[19] It may be for this reason that the extensive data collected after the ghetto riots of the 1960s on the characteristics of rioters and nonrioters provided little evidence that the rioters themselves were more likely to be recent migrants or less educated or suffer higher rates of unemployment than the ghetto population as a whole. But while there are data to indicate that the rioters did not suffer higher indices of "rootlessness," little is known about the networks or structures through which their defiance was mobilized. Tilly speculates interestingly on the relation between integration and deprivation by suggesting that the more integrated shopkeepers and artisans of Paris may have led the great outburst of the French Revolution precisely because they were in a better position to do so, and because they had a kind of leadership role, and were therefore responsive to the misery of the hordes of more impoverished Parisians (1964). Hobsbawm and Rudé ascribe a similar role to local artisans in the English farm laborers' protests of the early nineteenth century (1968, 63–64).

southern black church, which became the mobilizing node of movement actions.[20]

Just as electoral political institutions channel protest into voter activity in the United States, and may even confine it within these spheres if the disturbance is not severe and the electoral system appears responsive, so do other features of institutional life determine the forms that protest takes when it breaks out of the boundaries of electoral politics. Thus, it is no accident that some people strike, others riot, or loot the granaries, or burn the machines, for just as the patterns of daily life ordinarily assure mass quiescence, so do these same patterns influence the form defiance will take when it erupts.

First, people experience deprivation and oppression within a concrete setting, not as the end product of large and abstract processes, and it is the concrete experience that molds their discontent into specific grievances against specific targets. Workers experience the factory, the speeding rhythm of the assembly line, the foreman, the spies and the guards, the owner and the paycheck. They do not experience monopoly capitalism. People on relief experience the shabby waiting rooms, the overseer or the caseworker, and the dole. They do not experience American social welfare policy. Tenants experience the leaking ceilings and cold radiators, and they recognize the landlord. They do not recognize the banking, real estate, and construction systems. No small wonder, therefore, that when the poor rebel they so often rebel against the overseer of the poor, or the slumlord, or the middling merchant, and not against the banks or the governing elites to whom the overseer, the slumlord, and the merchant also defer.[21] In other words, it is the daily experience of

---

[20] Tilly, reviewing the literature on the French Revolution, makes a similar argument about the structuring of the great outbursts of collective violence among the sans-culottes: "[T]he insurrection was a continuation, in an extreme form, of their everyday politics" (1964, 114). See also the account by Hobsbawm and Rudé of the role of the "village parliaments" and churches in English agricultural uprisings (1968, 59–60).

[21] Max Weber makes the similar point "that the class antagonisms that are conditioned through the market situation are usually most bitter between those who actually and directly participate as opponents in price wars. It is not the *rentier*, the share-holder, and the banker who suffer the ill will of the worker, but almost exclusively the manufacturer and the business executives who are the direct opponents of workers in price wars. This is so in spite of the fact that it is precisely the cash boxes of the *rentier*, the share-holder, and the banker into which the more or less 'unearned' gains flow, rather

Schwartz

people that shapes their grievances, establishes the measure of their demands, and points out the targets of their anger.

Second, institutional patterns shape mass movements by shaping the collectivity out of which protest can arise. Institutional life aggregates people or disperses them, molds group identities, and draws people into the settings within which collective action can erupt. Thus factory work gathers men and women together, educates them in a common experience, and educates them to the possibilities of cooperation and collective action.[22] Casual laborers or petty entrepreneurs, by contrast, are dispersed by their occupations, and are therefore less likely to perceive their commonalities of position, and less likely to join together in collective action.[23]

Third, and most important, institutional roles determine the strategic opportunities for defiance, for it is typically by rebelling against the rules and authorities associated with their everyday activities that people protest. Thus workers protest by striking. They are able to do so because they are drawn together in the factory setting, and their protests consist mainly in defying the rules and authorities associated with the workplace. The unemployed do not and cannot strike, even when they perceive that those who own the factories and businesses are to blame for their troubles. Instead, they riot in the

---

than into the pockets of the manufacturers or the business executives" (186). Michael Schwartz illustrates this point in a study of the Southern Farmers' Alliance. The Texas members of the alliance singled out landlords and merchants as the target of their demands, and not the banks, speculators, and railroads who were ultimately responsible for their plight, because the tenant farmers had direct experience with the landlords and merchants.

[22] Marx and Engels made a similar argument about the conditions for the development of a revolutionary proletariat: "But with the development of industry, the proletariat not only increases in number; it becomes concentrated in greater masses, its strength grows, and it feels its strength more. The various interests and conditions of life within the ranks of the proletariat are more and more equalized, in proportion as machinery obliterates all distinctions of labour, and nearly everywhere reduces wages to the same low level" (1948, 17–18). By contrast, peasants were not likely to be mobilized to enforce their own class interest, for their "mode of production isolates them from one another instead of bringing them into mutual intercourse . . ." (1963, 123–124). This view of the revolutionary potential of the proletariat did not anticipate the ability of employers to manipulate the institutional context of factory work, to divide those they had brought together by, for example, elaborating job titles and hierarchies within the work place so as to "balkanize" the proletariat. See Gordon, Edwards, and Reich for a discussion of the significance of this development.

[23] Useem, in his study of the draft-resistance movement that arose during the Vietnam War, concludes that the absence of an institutional setting that united the men subject to the draft severely hampered The Resistance in mobilizing its constituency (1973).

streets where they are forced to linger, or storm the relief centers, and it is difficult to imagine them doing otherwise.

That they should do otherwise, however, is constantly asserted, and it is in such statements that the influence (as well as the absurdity) of the pluralist view becomes so evident. By denying the constraints which are imposed by institutional location, protest is readily discredited, as when insurgents are denounced for having ignored the true centers of power by attacking the wrong target by the wrong means. Thus welfare administrators admonish recipients for disrupting relief offices and propose instead that they learn how to lobby in the state legislature or Congress. But welfare clients cannot easily go to the state or national capital, and when a few do, they are of course ignored. Sometimes, however, they can disrupt relief offices, and that is harder to ignore.

In the same vein, a favorite criticism of the student peace movement, often made by erstwhile sympathizers, was that it was foolish of the students to protest the Vietnam War by demonstrating at the universities and attacking blameless administrators and faculties. It was obviously not the universities that were waging the war, critics argued, but the military-industrial complex. The students were not so foolish, however. The exigencies of mass action are such that they were constrained to act out their defiance within the universities where they were physically located and could thus act collectively, and where they played a role on which an institution depended, so that their defiance mattered.

Since our examples might suggest otherwise, we should note at this juncture that the tendency to impute freedom of choice in the evolution of political strategies is not peculiar to those who have large stakes in the preservation of some institution, whether welfare administrators or university professors. Nor is the tendency peculiar to those of more conservative political persuasion. Radical organizers make precisely the same assumption when they call upon the working class to organize in one way or another and to pursue one political strategy or another, even in the face of overwhelming evidence that social conditions preclude the exercise of such options. Opportunities for defiance are not created by analyses of power structures. If there is a genius in organizing, it is the capacity to sense what it is possible for people to do under given conditions, and to then help them do it. In point of fact, however, most organizing ventures ask that people do what they cannot do, and the result is failure.

Important

It is our second general point, then, that the opportunities for defiance are structured by features of institutional life.[24] *Simply put, people cannot defy institutions to which they have no access, and to which they make no contribution.*

The Limited Impact of Mass Defiance

If mass defiance is neither freely available nor the forms it takes freely determined, it must also be said that it is generally of limited political impact. Still, some forms of protest appear to have more impact than others, thus posing an analytical question of considerable importance. It is a question, however, that analysts of movements, especially analysts of contemporary American movements, have not generally asked. The literature abounds with studies of the social origins of protestors, the determinants of leadership styles, the struggles to cope with problems of organizational maintenance. Thus protest seems to be wondered about mainly for the many and fascinating aspects of social life which it exposes, but least of all for its chief significance: namely, that it is the means by which the least-privileged seek to wrest concessions from their rulers.[25]

---

[24] This is perhaps what C. L. R. James means when he writes: "Workers are at their very best in collective action in the circumstances of their daily activity or crises arising from it" (95). Richard Flacks has also made a related argument regarding the importance of what he calls "everyday life" in shaping popular movements.

[25] Michael Lipsky's work is in a way an exception to these assertions, for he sets out specifically to evaluate protest as a strategy for achieving political goals (1968, 1970). The flaw in Lipsky's work is not in his intellectual objective, which is important, but in his understanding of what it is that he is evaluating. Protest strategies, in Lipsky's view, consist primarily of "showmanship" by powerless groups to gain the attention of potential sympathizers or "reference publics." But by this definition, Lipsky rules out the historically most important forms of lower-class protest, such as strikes and riots. Lipsky was led to define protest so narrowly by the New York City rent strike on which his analysis is based, for that particular event, as Lipsky clearly shows, did consist primarily of speeches and press releases, and very little rent striking. Small wonder, therefore, that the outcome of the rent strike was determined by a scattering of liberal reform groups, provoked as they always have been by scandalous stories of slum housing, and appeased as they always have been by purely symbolic if not sentimental gestures. And small wonder that the slums remained and worsened. Lipsky concludes from this experience that protest is a weak and unstable resource, and that whatever responses are made by government will depend wholly on whether significant third parties share the protestors' objectives. But this conclusion, while valid for the particular case Lipsky studied, seems to us unwarranted as a generalization about protest. In our view, protest

It is our judgment that *the most useful way to think about the effectiveness of protest is to examine the disruptive effects on institutions of different forms of mass defiance, and then to examine the political reverberations of those disruptions.* The impact of mass defiance is, in other words, not so much directly as indirectly felt. Protest is more likely to have a seriously disruptive impact when the protestors play a central role in an institution, and it is more likely to evoke wider political reverberations when powerful groups have large stakes in the disrupted institution. These relationships are almost totally ignored in the literature on social movements; there are no studies that catalogue and examine forms of defiance, the settings in which defiance is acted out, the institutional disruptions that do or do not result, and the varying political reverberations of these institutional disruptions.

THE LIMITS OF INSTITUTIONAL DISRUPTION

To refer to an institutional disruption is simply to note the obvious fact that institutional life depends upon conformity with established roles and compliance with established rules. Defiance may thus obstruct the normal operations of institutions. Factories are shut down when workers walk out or sit down; welfare bureaucracies are thrown into chaos when crowds demand relief; landlords may be bankrupted when tenants refuse to pay rent. In each of these cases, *people cease to conform to accustomed institutional roles; they withhold their accustomed cooperation, and by doing so, cause institutional disruptions.*

By our definition, disruption is simply the application of a negative sanction, the withdrawal of a crucial contribution on which others depend, and it is therefore a natural resource for exerting power over others. This form of power is, in fact, regularly employed by individuals and groups linked together in many kinds of coopera-

that consists merely of what Lipsky calls "noise" is hardly a resource at all, because it is hardly protest at all. Moreover, the responses that reference publics make to showmanship are of course weak and tokenistic. Reference publics do play a crucial role in determining responses to protest, not when they are provoked by "noise," but when they are provoked by the serious institutional disruptions attendant upon mass defiance.

tive interaction, and particularly by producer groups. Farmers, for example, keep their products off the market in order to force up the price offered by buyers; doctors refuse to provide treatment unless their price is met; oil companies withhold supplies until price concessions are made.[26]

But the amount of leverage that a group gains by applying such negative sanctions is widely variable. Influence depends, first of all, on whether or not the contribution withheld is crucial to others; second, on whether or not those who have been affected by the disruption have resources to be conceded; and third, on whether the obstructionist group can protect itself adequately from reprisals. Once these criteria are stated, it becomes evident that the poor are usually in the least strategic position to benefit from defiance.

Thus, in comparison with most producer groups, the lower classes are often in weak institutional locations to use disruption as a tactic for influence. Many among the lower class are in locations that make their cooperation less than crucial to the operation of major institutions. Those who work in economically marginal enterprises, or who perform marginally necessary functions in major enterprises, or those who are unemployed, do not perform roles on which major institutions depend. Indeed, some of the poor are sometimes so isolated from significant institutional participation that the only "contribution" they can withhold is that of quiescence in civil life: they can riot.

Moreover, those who manage the institutions in which many of the lower classes find themselves often have little to concede to disruptors. When lower-class groups do play an important role in an institution, as they do in sweatshops or in slum tenements, these institutions—operated as they often are by marginal entrepreneurs—may be incapable of yielding very much in response to disruptive pressure.

Finally, lower-class groups have little ability to protect themselves against reprisals that can be employed by institutional managers.

---

[26] Spencer, McLoughlin, and Lawson, in their historical study of New York City tenant movements, provide an interesting example of the use of disruption, not by the tenants, but by the banks. Thus when Langdon Post, the Tenement House Commissioner under LaGuardia, tried to initiate a campaign to force compliance with the housing codes, "five savings banks owning 400 buildings on the Lower East Side threatened to vacate rather than comply. The president of the New York City Taxpayers' Union warned that 40,000 tenements would be abandoned." Post withdrew his threat (10).

The poor do not have to be historians of the occasions when protestors have been jailed or shot down to understand this point. The
lesson of their vulnerability is engraved in everyday life; it is evident
in every police beating, in every eviction, in every lost job, in every
relief termination. The very labels used to describe defiance by the
lower classes—the pejorative labels of illegality and violence—testify
to this vulnerability and serve to justify severe reprisals when they
are imposed. By taking such labels for granted, we fail to recognize
what these events really represent: a structure of political coercion
inherent in the everyday life of the lower classes.

We can now comment on the association of disruption with spontaneity, perhaps another relic of traditional ways of thinking about
lower-class uprisings, although here the issue is a little more complicated. Disruption itself is not necessarily spontaneous, but lower-
class disruptions often are, in the sense that they are not planned
and executed by formal organizations. In part, this testifies to the
paucity of stable organizational resources among the poor, as well
as to the cautious and moderate character of such organizations as
are able to survive. But even if formal organizations existed, and
even if they were not committed by the exigencies of their own survival to more cautious tactics, the circumstances that lead to mass
defiance by the lower class are extremely difficult to predict; and
once defiance erupts, its direction is difficult for leaders to control.
Rosa Luxemburg's discussion of the mass strike is pertinent:

> . . . the mass strike is not artificially "made," not "decided" out
> of the blue, not "propagated," but rather it is an historical phe-
> nomenon which at a certain moment follows with historical neces-
> sity from the social relations. . . . If anyone were to undertake
> to make the mass strike in general, as one form of proletarian
> action, the object of methodical agitation, and to go house to
> house peddling this "idea" in order gradually to win the working
> class to it, it would be as idle, as profitless, and as crazy an occupa-
> tion as it would be to seek to make the idea of the revolution
> or of the barricade struggle into the object of a particular agita-
> tion . . . (231–245).

Still, if the lower classes do not ordinarily have great disruptive
power, and if the use of even that kind of power is not planned, it
is the only power they do have. Their use of that power, the weigh-
ing of gains and risks, is not calculated in board rooms; it wells up
out of the terrible travails that people experience at times of rupture

and stress.[27] And at such times, disruptions by the poor may have reverberations that go beyond the institutions in which the disruption is acted out.

THE LIMITS OF POLITICAL DISRUPTION

It is not the impact of disruptions on particular institutions that finally tests the power of the poor; it is the political impact of these disruptions. At this level, however, a new set of structuring mechanisms intervenes, for the political impact of institutional disruptions is mediated by the electoral-representative system.

Responses to disruption vary depending on electoral conditions. Ordinarily, during periods of stability, governmental leaders have three rather obvious options when an institutional disruption occurs. They may ignore it; they may employ punitive measures against the disruptors; or they may attempt to conciliate them. If the disruptive group has little political leverage in its own right, as is true of lower-class groups, it will either be ignored or repressed. It is more likely to be ignored when the disrupted institution is not central to the society as a whole, or to other more important groups. Thus if men and women run amok, disrupting the fabric of their own communities, as in the immigrant slums of the nineteenth century, the spectacle may be frightening, but it can be contained within the slums; it will not necessarily have much impact on the society as a whole, or on the well-being of other important groups. Similarly, when impoverished mobs demand relief, they may cause havoc in the relief offices, but chaotic relief offices are not a large problem for the society as a whole, or for important groups. Repression is more likely to be employed when central institutions are affected, as when railroad workers struck and rioted in the late nineteenth century, or

---

[27] Rosa Luxemburg's comments are again persuasive: "At the moment that a real, earnest period of mass strikes begins all these 'calculations of costs' change into the project of draining the ocean with a water glass. And it is an ocean of frightful privations and sufferings which the proletarian masses buy with every revolution. The solution which a revolutionary period gives to these seemingly invincible difficulties is that along with them such an immense amount of mass idealism is let loose that the masses are insensitive to the sharpest sufferings. Neither revolution nor mass strikes can be made with the psychology of a trade unionist who will not cease work on May Day unless he is assured in advance of a determined support in the case of measures being taken against him" (246).

when the police struck in Boston after the First World War. Either way, to be ignored or punished is what the poor ordinarily expect from government, because these are the responses they ordinarily evoke.[28]

But protest movements do not arise during ordinary periods; they arise when large-scale changes undermine political stability. It is this context, as we said earlier, that gives the poor hope and makes insurgency possible in the first place. It is this context that also makes political leaders somewhat vulnerable to protests by the poor.

At times of rapid economic and social change, political leaders are far less free either to ignore disturbances or to employ punitive measures. At such times, the relationship of political leaders to their constituents is likely to become uncertain.[29] This unsettled state of political affairs makes the regime far more sensitive to disturbances, for it is not only more likely that previously uninvolved groups will be activated—the scope of conflict will be widened, in Schattschneider's terminology—but that the scope of conflict will be widened at a time when political alignments have already become unpredictable.[30]

When a political leadership becomes unsure of its support, even disturbances that are isolated within peripheral institutions cannot be so safely ignored, for the mere appearance of trouble and disorder is more threatening when political alignments are unstable. And when the disrupted institutions are central to economic production or to the stability of social life, it becomes imperative that normal operations be restored if the regime is to maintain support

---

[28] Disruptions confined within institutions have the characteristics that Schattschneider attributes to small conflicts: "It is one of the qualities of extremely small conflicts that the relative strengths of the contestants are likely to be known in advance. In this case the stronger side may impose its will on the weaker without an overt test of strength because people are not apt to fight if they are sure to lose" (4).

[29] Lodhi and Tilly, in arguing against the social disorganization perspective, suggest that the amount of collective violence should be related to "the structure of power, the capacity of deprived groups for collective action, the forms of repression employed by the authorities, and the disparities between the weak and the powerful in shared understandings about collective rights to action and to use of valued resources . . ." (316). It is our point that each of these factors changes, at least temporarily, during periods of serious and widespread instability. Most importantly, the resources available to the regime decline (316).

[30] "To understand any conflict it is necessary, therefore, to keep constantly in mind the relations between the combatants and the audience because the audience is likely to do the kinds of things that determine the outcome of the fight. . . . The stronger contestant may hesitate to use his strength because he does not know whether or not he is going to be able to isolate his antagonist" (2).

among its constituents. Thus when industrial workers joined in massive strikes during the 1930s, they threatened the entire economy of the nation and, given the electoral instability of the times, threatened the future of the nation's political leadership. Under these circumstances, government could hardly ignore the disturbances.

Yet neither could government run the risks entailed by using massive force to subdue the strikers in the 1930s. It could not, in other words, simply avail itself of the option of repression. For one thing the striking workers, like the civil rights demonstrators in the 1960s, had aroused strong sympathy among groups that were crucial supporters of the regime. For another, unless insurgent groups are virtually of outcast status, permitting leaders of the regime to mobilize popular hatred against them, politically unstable conditions make the use of force risky, since the reactions of other aroused groups cannot be safely predicted. When government is unable to ignore the insurgents, and is unwilling to risk the uncertain repercussions of the use of force, it will make efforts to conciliate and disarm the protestors.

These placating efforts will usually take several forms. First and most obviously, political leaders will offer concessions, or press elites in the private sector to offer concessions, to remedy some of the immediate grievances, both symbolic and tangible, of the disruptive group. Thus mobs of unemployed workers were granted relief in the 1930s; striking industrial workers won higher pay and shorter hours; and angry civil rights demonstrators were granted the right to desegregated public accommodations in the 1960s.

Whether one takes such measures as evidence of the capacity of American political institutions for reform, or brushes them aside as mere tokenism, such concessions were not offered readily by government leaders. In each case, and in some cases more than in others, reform required a break with an established pattern of government accommodation to private elites. Thus the New Deal's liberal relief policy was maintained despite widespread opposition from the business community. Striking workers in the mid-1930s succeeded in obtaining wage concessions from private industry only because state and national political leaders abandoned the age-old policy of using the coercive power of the state to curb strikes. The granting of desegregated public accommodations required that national Democratic leaders turn against their traditional allies among southern plantation elites. In such instances concessions were won by the protestors only when political leaders were finally forced, out of a concern for their own survival, to act in ways which aroused the fierce opposition of economic elites. In short, under conditions of severe electoral instability, the alliance of public and private power is sometimes weakened, if only briefly, and at these moments a defiant poor may make gains.[31]

Second, political leaders, or elites allied with them, will try to quiet disturbances not only by dealing with immediate grievances, but by making efforts to channel the energies and angers of the protestors into more legitimate and less disruptive forms of political behavior, in part by offering incentives to movement leaders or, in other words, by coopting them. Thus relief demonstrators in both the 1930s and the 1960s were encouraged to learn to use administrative grievance procedures as an alternative to "merely" disrupting relief offices, while their leaders were offered positions as advisors to relief administrators. In the 1960s civil rights organizers left the streets to take jobs in the Great Society programs; and as rioting spread in the northern cities, street leaders in the ghettos were encouraged to join in "dialogues" with municipal officials, and some were offered positions in municipal agencies.[32]

Third, the measures promulgated by government at times of disturbance may be designed not to conciliate the protestors, but to undermine whatever sympathy the protesting group has been able to command from a wider public. Usually this is achieved through new

---

[31] The rapidly growing Marxist literature on the theory of the capitalist state stresses legitimation or social cohesion as one of the two primary functions of the state (the other being the maintenance of the conditions for capitalist accumulation). The interpretation of electoral-representative institutions presented here is consistent with that general perspective. As noted earlier, we view the wide distribution and exercise of the franchise as an important source of the legitimacy of state authority. Electoral activities generate a belief in government as the instrument of a broad majority rather than of particular interests or a particular class. It is this phenomenon which Marx defined as the false universality of the state. (See also Poulantzas and Bridges for a discussion of suffrage, and political parties based on suffrage, from this perspective.) We argue further that the franchise plays a major role in protecting the legitimacy of the state against periodic challenges. Electoral contests serve as a signal or barometer of discontent and disaffection, and the threat of electoral defeat constrains state officials to promulgate measures that will quiet discontent and restore legitimacy.

[32] The newcomers to officialdom were by and large absorbed into local agencies that made relatively insignificant decisions about service delivery to the insurgent population. The analogy to the use of natives by colonial administrations is obvious. Anderson and Friedland say in general of such agencies and their activities that they "encourage citizen participation at a local level insulated from national politics . . . " (21). See also Katznelson for a discussion of "state-sponsored creation of client-patron/broker links" (227).

programs that appear to meet the moral demands of the movement, and thus rob it of support without actually yielding much by way of tangible gains. A striking example was the passage of the pension provisions of the Social Security Act. The organized aged in the Townsend Movement were demanding pensions of $200 a month, with no strings attached, and they had managed to induce some 25 million people to sign supporting petitions. As it turned out, the Social Security Act, while it provided a measure of security for many of the future aged, did nothing for the members of the Townsend Movement, none of whom would be covered by a work-related insurance scheme since they were no longer working, and most of whom would in any case be dead when the payments were to begin some seven years later. But the pension provisions of the Social Security Act answered the *moral* claims of the movement. In principle, government had acted to protect America's aged, thus severing any identification between those who would be old in the future and those who were already old. The Social Security Act effectively dampened public support for the Townsend Plan while yielding the old people nothing. Other examples of responses which undermine public support abound. The widely heralded federal programs for the ghettos in the 1960s were neither designed nor funded in a way that made it possible for them to have substantial impact on poverty or on the traumas of ghetto life. But the publicity attached to the programs—the din and blare about a "war on poverty" and the development of "model cities"—did much to appease the liberal sympathizers with urban blacks.

Finally, these apparently conciliatory measures make it possible for government to safely employ repressive measures as well. Typically, leaders and groups who are more disruptive, or who spurn the concessions offered, are singled out for arbitrary police action or for more formal legal harassment through congressional investigations or through the courts. In the context of much-publicized efforts by government to ease the grievances of disaffected groups, coercive measures of this kind are not likely to arouse indignation among sympathetic publics. Indeed, this dual strategy is useful in another way, for it serves to cast an aura of balance and judiciousness over government action.

The main point, however, is simply that *the political impact of institutional disruptions depends upon electoral conditions*. Even serious disruptions, such as industrial strikes, will force concessions only when the calculus of electoral instability favors the protestors. And even then, when the protestors succeed in forcing government to respond, they do not dictate the content of those responses. As to the variety of specific circumstances which determine how much the protestors will gain and how much they will lose, we still have a great deal to learn.

THE DEMISE OF PROTEST

It is not surprising that, taken together, these efforts to conciliate and disarm usually lead to the demise of the protest movement, partly by transforming the movement itself, and partly by transforming the political climate which nourishes protest. With these changes, the array of institutional controls which ordinarily restrain protest is restored, and political influence is once more denied to the lower class.

We said that one form of government response was to make concessions to the protestors, yielding them something of what they demanded, either symbolic or material. But the mere granting of such concessions is probably not very important in accounting for the demise of a movement. For one thing, whatever is yielded is usually modest if not meager; for another, even modest concessions demonstrate that protest "works," a circumstance that might as easily be expected to fuel a movement as to pacify it.

But concessions are rarely unencumbered. If they are given at all, they are usually part and parcel of measures to reintegrate the movement into normal political channels and to absorb its leaders into stable institutional roles. Thus the right of industrial workers to unionize, won in response to massive and disruptive strikes in the 1930s, meant that workers were encouraged to use newly established grievance procedures in place of the sit-down or the wildcat strike; and the new union leaders, now absorbed in relations with factory management and in the councils of the Democratic Party, became the ideological proponents and organizational leaders of this strategy of normalcy and moderation. Similarly, when blacks won the vote in the South and a share of patronage in the municipalities of the North in response to the disturbances of the 1960s, black leaders were absorbed into electoral and bureaucratic politics and became the ideological proponents of the shift "from protest to politics" (Rustin).[33]

This feature of government action deserves some explanation because the main reintegrative measures—the right to organize, the right to vote, black representation in city government—were also responses to specific demands made by the protestors themselves. To all appearances, government simply acted to redress felt grievances. But the process was by no means as straightforward as that. As we suggested earlier, the movements had arisen through interaction with elites, and had been led to make the demands they made in response to early encouragement by political leaders. Nor was it fortuitous that political leaders came to proclaim as just such causes as the right to organize or the right to vote or the right to "citizen participation." In each case, elites responded to discontent by proposing reforms with which they had experience, and which consisted mainly of extending established procedures to new groups or to new institutional arenas. Collective bargaining was not invented in the 1930s, nor the franchise in the 1960s. Driven by turmoil, political leaders proposed reforms that were in a sense prefigured by institutional arrangements that already existed, that were drawn from a repertoire provided by existing traditions. And an aroused people responded by demanding simply what political leaders had said they should have. If through some accident of history they had done otherwise, if industrial workers had demanded public ownership of factories, they would probably have still gotten unionism, if they got anything at all; and if impoverished southern blacks had demanded land reform, they would probably have still gotten the vote.

At the same time that government makes efforts to reintegrate disaffected groups, and to guide them into less politically disturbing forms of behavior, it also moves to isolate them from potential supporters and, by doing so, diminishes the morale of the movement. Finally, while the movement is eroding under these influences, its

---

[33] James Q. Wilson seems to us to miss the point when he ascribes the demise of SNCC and CORE to failure and rebuff, and the intolerable strain this exerted on these "redemptive" organizations which required a total transformation of society on the one hand, and extraordinary commitments from their members on the other hand. First, and most important, by no stretch of the reasonable imagination can SNCC and CORE be said to have failed, as we will explain in chapter 4. Second, while these may have been redemptive organizations, their demise was most specifically the result of the impact of government measures on both cadres and constituency. It was government responses that generated factionalism and disillusionment, and not simply "the disillusionment that inevitably afflicts a redemptive organization" (180–182).

leaders attracted by new opportunities, its followers conciliated, confused, or discouraged, the show of repressive force against recalcitrant elements demolishes the few who are left.

However, the more far-reaching changes do not occur within the movement, but in the political context which nourished the movement in the first place. The agitated and defiant people who compose the movement are but a small proportion of the discontented population on which it draws. Presumably if some leaders were coopted, new leaders would arise; if some participants were appeased or discouraged, others would take their place. But this does not happen, because government's responses not only destroy the movement, they also transform the political climate which makes protest possible. The concessions to the protestors, the efforts to "bring them into the system," and in particular the measures aimed at potential supporters, all work to create a powerful image of a benevolent and responsive government that answers grievances and solves problems. As a result, whatever support might have existed among the larger population dwindles. Moreover, the display of government benevolence stimulates antagonist groups, and triggers the antagonistic sentiments of more neutral sectors. The "tide of public opinion" begins to turn—against labor in the late 1930s, against blacks in the late 1960s. And as it does, the definitions put forward by political leaders also change, particularly when prodded by contenders for political office who sense the shift in popular mood, and the weaknesses it reveals in an incumbent's support. Thus in the late 1960s, Republican leaders took advantage of white resentment against blacks to attract Democratic voters, raising cries of "law and order" and "workfare not welfare"—the code words for racial antagonism. Such a change is ominous. Where once the powerful voices of the land enunciated a rhetoric that gave courage to the poor, now they enunciate a rhetoric that erases hope, and implants fear. The point should be evident that as these various circumstances combine, defiance is no longer possible.

THE RESIDUE OF REFORM

When protest subsides, concessions may be withdrawn. Thus when the unemployed become docile, the relief rolls are cut even though many are still unemployed; when the ghetto becomes quiescent,

evictions are resumed. The reason is simple enough. Since the poor
no longer pose the threat of disruption, they no longer exert leverage on political leaders; there is no need for conciliation. This is
particularly the case in a climate of growing political hostility, for
the concessions granted are likely to become the focus of resentment
by other groups.

But some concessions are not withdrawn. As the tide of turbulence
recedes, major institutional changes sometimes remain. Thus the
right of workers to join unions was not rescinded when turmoil subsided (although some of the rights ceded to unions were withdrawn).
And it is not likely that the franchise granted to blacks in the South
will be taken back (although just that happened in the post-Reconstruction period). Why, then, are some concessions withdrawn while
others become permanent institutional reforms?

The answer, perhaps, is that while some of the reforms granted
during periods of turmoil are costly or repugnant to various groups
in the society, and are therefore suffered only under duress, other
innovations turn out to be compatible (or at least not incompatible)
with the interests of more powerful groups, most importantly with
the interests of dominant economic groups. Such an assertion has the
aura of a conspiracy theory, but in fact the process is not conspira-
torial at all. Major industrialists had resisted unionization, but once
forced to concede it as the price of industrial peace, they gradually
discovered that labor unions constituted a useful mechanism to
regulate the labor force. The problem of disciplining industrial
labor had been developing over the course of a century. The depression produced the political turmoil through which a solution was
forged. Nor was the solution simply snatched from the air. As noted
earlier, collective bargaining was a tried and tested method of dealing with labor disturbances. The tumult of the 1930s made the use
of this method imperative; once implemented, the reforms were
institutionalized because they continued to prove useful.

Similarly, southern economic elites had no interest in ceding
southern blacks the franchise. But their stakes in disfranchising
blacks had diminished. The old plantation economy was losing
ground to new industrial enterprises; plantation-based elites were
losing ground to economic dominants based in industry. The feudal
political arrangements on which a plantation economy had relied
were no longer of central importance, and certainly they were not of
central importance to the new economic elites. Black uprisings, by
forcing the extension of the franchise and the modernization of

southern politics, thus helped seal a fissure in the institutional fabric of American society, a fissure resulting from the growing inconsistency between the economic and political institutions of the South. What these examples suggest is that *protesters win, if they win at all, what historical circumstances has already made ready to be conceded.* Still, as Alan Wolfe has said, governments do not change magically through some "historical radical transformation," but only through the actual struggles of the time (154). When people are finally roused to protest against great odds, they take the only options available to them within the limits imposed by their social circumstances. Those who refuse to recognize these limits not only blindly consign lower-class protests to the realm of the semirational, but also blindly continue to pretend that other, more regular options for political influence are widely available in the American political system.

A Note on the Role
of Protest Leadership

The main point of this chapter is that both the limitations and opportunities for mass protest are shaped by social conditions. The implications for the role of leadership in protest movements can be briefly summarized.

Protest wells up in response to momentous changes in the institutional order. It is not created by organizers and leaders.

Once protest erupts, the specific forms it takes are largely determined by features of social structure. Organizers and leaders who contrive strategies that ignore the social location of the people they seek to mobilize can only fail.

Elites respond to the institutional disruptions that protest causes, as well as to other powerful institutional imperatives. Elite responses are not significantly shaped by the demands of leaders and organizers. Nor are elite responses significantly shaped by formally structured organizations of the poor. Whatever influence lower-class groups occasionally exert in American politics does not result from organization, but from mass protest and the disruptive consequences of protest.

Finally, protest in the United States has been episodic and transient, for as it gains momentum, so too do various forms of institutional accommodation and coercion that have the effect of restoring quiescence. Organizers and leaders cannot prevent the ebbing of protest, nor the erosion of whatever influence protest yielded the lower class. They can only try to win whatever can be won while it can be won.

In these major ways protest movements are shaped by institutional conditions, and not by the purposive efforts of leaders and organizers. The limitations are large and unyielding. Yet within the boundaries created by these limitations, some latitude for purposive effort remains. Organizers and leaders choose to do one thing, or they choose to do another, and what they choose to do affects to some degree the course of the protest movement. If the area of latitude is less than leaders and organizers would prefer, it is also not enlarged when they proceed as if institutional limitations did not in fact exist by undertaking strategies which fly in the face of these constraints. The wiser course is to understand these limitations, and to exploit whatever latitude remains to enlarge the potential influence of the lower class. And if our conclusions are correct, what this means is that strategies must be pursued that escalate the momentum and impact of disruptive protest at each stage in its emergence and evolution.

With these propositions in mind, we now turn to an analysis of recent protest movements.

References

Anderson, Gosta Esping, and Friedland, Roger. "Class Structure, Class Politics and the Capitalist State." Madison: University of Wisconsin, September 1974, mimeographed.

Ash, Roberta. *Social Movements in America*. Chicago: Markham Publishing Co., 1972.

Balbus, Isaac D. "The Concept of Interest in Pluralist and Marxian Analysis." *Politics and Society* 1 (1971).

Bloom, Howard S., and Price, Douglas H. "Voter Response to Short-Run Economic Conditions: The Asymmetric Effect of Prosperity and Recession." *American Political Science Review* 69 (December 1975).

Bridges, Amy. "Nicos Poulantzas and the Marxist Theory of the State." *Politics and Society* 4 (Winter 1974).

Burnham, Walter Dean. "The Changing Shape of the American Political Universe." *American Political Science Review* 59 (1965).

————. *Critical Elections and the Mainsprings of American Politics.* New York: W. W. Norton and Co., 1970.

Campbell, Angus; Converse, Philip E.; Miller, Warren E.; and Stokes, Donald E. *The American Voter.* New York: John Wiley and Sons, 1960.

Castells, Manuel. "L' Analyse Interdisciplinaire de la Croissance Urbaine." Paper presented at a colloquium of the Centre National de la Recherche Scientifique, June 1–4, 1971, in Toulouse.

Dahrendorf, Ralf. *Class and Class Conflict in Industrial Society.* Stanford: Stanford University Press, 1959.

Davies, James C. "Toward a Theory of Revolution." *American Sociological Review* 27 (1962).

Dollard, John, et al. *Frustration and Aggression.* New Haven: Yale University Press, 1939.

Edelman, Murray. *Politics as Symbolic Action.* New Haven: Yale University Press, 1971.

Engels, Frederick. "Socialism: Utopian and Scientific." In *Engels: Selected Writings,* edited by W. O. Henderson. Baltimore: Penguin Books, 1967.

————. "Introduction to Karl Marx's 'The Class Struggles in France, 1848–1850.' " In *Selected Works,* Vol. 1, by Karl Marx and Frederick Engels. New York: International Publishers, 1970.

Feierabend, Ivo; Feierabend, Rosalind L.; and Nesvold, Betty A. "Social Change and Political Violence: Cross National Patterns." In *Violence in America: A Staff Report,* edited by Hugh Davis Graham and Ted Robert Gurr. Washington, D.C.: U. S. Government Printing Office, 1969.

Flacks, Richard. "Making History vs. Making Life: Dilemmas of an American Left." *Working Papers for a New Society* 2 (Summer 1974).

Gamson, William A. *The Strategy of Social Protest.* Homewood, Illinois: Dorsey Press, 1975.

Geschwender, James. "Social Structure and the Negro Revolt: An Examination of Some Hypotheses." *Social Forces* 3 (December 1964).

Gordon, David M.; Edwards, Richard C.; and Reich, Michael. "Labor Market Segmentation in American Capitalism." Paper presented at the Conference on Labor Market Segmentation, March 16–17, 1973, at Harvard University.

Gurr, Ted Robert. "Psychological Factors in Civil Violence." *World Politics* 20 (January 1968).

————. *Why Men Rebel.* Princeton, N.J.: Princeton University Press, 1970.

Gusfield, Joseph R., ed. *Protest, Reform and Revolt: A Reader in Social Movements.* New York: John Wiley and Sons, 1970.

Hobsbawm, Eric. *Primitive Rebels*. New York: W. W. Norton and Co., 1963.

————, and Rudé, George. *Captain Swing*. New York: Pantheon Books, 1968.

Howard, Dick, ed. *Selected Writings of Rosa Luxemburg*. New York: Monthly Review Press, 1971.

Huntington, Samuel P. *Political Order in Changing Societies*. New Haven: Yale University Press, 1968.

James, C. L. R.; Lee, Grace C.; and Chaulieu, Pierre. *Facing Reality*. Detroit: Bewick Editions, 1974.

Katznelson, Ira. "The Crisis of the Capitalist City: Urban Politics and Social Control." In *Theoretical Perspectives in Urban Politics*, edited by W. D. Hawley and Michael Lipsky. New York: Prentice-Hall, 1976.

Kornhauser, William. *The Politics of Mass Society*. New York: The Free Press, 1959.

Kramer, Gerald H. "Short-Term Fluctuations in U. S. Voting Behavior, 1896–1964." *American Political Science Review* 65 (March 1971).

Lefebvre, Henry. *Everyday Life in the Modern World*. London: Allen Lane, The Penguin Press, 1971.

Lipsky, Michael. "Protest as a Political Resource." *American Political Science Review* 62 (December 1968).

————. *Protest in City Politics*. Chicago: Rand McNally, 1970.

Lodhi, Abdul Qaiyum, and Tilly, Charles. "Urbanization, Crime, and Collective Violence in 19th Century France." *American Journal of Sociology* 79 (September 1973).

Lupsha, Peter A. "Explanation of Political Violence: Some Psychological Theories Versus Indignation." *Politics and Society* 2 (Fall 1971).

Luxemburg, Rosa. "Mass Strike Party and Trade Unions." In *Selected Writings of Rosa Luxemburg*, edited by Dick Howard. New York: Monthly Review Press, 1971.

Marx, Karl. *The Eighteenth Brumaire of Louis Bonaparte*. New York: International Publishers, 1963.

————, and Engels, Frederick. *Manifesto of the Communist Party*. New York: International Publishers, 1948.

Michels, Robert. *Political Parties*. Glencoe: The Free Press, 1949.

Moore, Barrington. "Revolution in America?" *New York Review of Books*, January 30, 1969.

Ollman, Bertell. "Toward Class Consciousness Next Time: Marx and the Working Class." *Politics and Society* 3 (Fall 1972).

Parsons, Talcott. *The Social System*. New York: The Free Press, 1951.

————. "An Outline of the Social System." In *Theories of Society: Foundations of Modern Sociological Thought*, edited by Talcott Parsons, Edward Shils, Kaspar D. Naegele, and Jesse R. Pitts. New York: The Free Press, 1965.

Poulantzas, Nicos. *Political Power and Social Classes*. London: New Left Books and Sheed and Ward, Ltd., 1973.

Rudé, George. *The Crowd in History*. New York: John Wiley and Sons, 1964.

Rustin, Bayard. "From Protest to Politics." *Commentary* 39 (February 1965).

Schattschneider, E. E. *The Semi-Sovereign People*. New York: Holt, Rinehart, and Winston, 1960.

Schwartz, Michael. "The Southern Farmers' Alliance: The Organizational Forms of Radical Protest." Unpublished Ph.D. dissertation, Department of Sociology, Harvard University, 1971.

Smelser, Neil J. *Theory of Collective Behavior*. New York: The Free Press, 1962.

Snyder, David, and Tilly, Charles. "Hardship and Collective Violence in France, 1830–1960." *American Sociological Review* 37 (October 1972).

Spencer, Joseph; McLoughlin, John; and Lawson, Ronald. "New York City Tenant Organizations and the Formation of Urban Housing Policy, 1919 to 1933." Unpublished paper of The Tenant Movement Study, New York, Center for Policy Research, 1975.

Tilly, Charles. "Reflections on the Revolution of Paris: A Review of Recent Historical Writing." *Social Problems* 12 (Summer 1964).

Useem, Michael. *Conscription, Protest and Social Conflict: The Life and Death of a Draft Resistance Movement*. New York: John Wiley and Sons, 1973.

————. *Protest Movements In America*. Indianapolis: Bobbs-Merrill, 1975.

Weber, Max. *Essays in Sociology*. Translated, edited, and with an Introduction by H. H. Gerth and C. Wright Mills. New York: Oxford University Press, 1946.

Wilson, James Q. *Political Organizations*. New York: Basic Books, 1973.

Wilson, John. *Introduction to Social Movements*. New York: Basic Books, 1973.

Wolfe, Alan. "New Directions in the Marxist Theory of Politics." *Politics and Society* 4 (Winter 1974).

Zald, Mayer N., and Ash, Roberta. "Social Movement Organizations: Growth, Decay, and Change." *Social Forces* 44 (March 1966).

CHAPTER
2

The Unemployed
Workers' Movement

The depression movements of the unemployed and of industrial workers followed a period of economic breakdown that produced distress and confusion in the daily lives of millions of people, and produced contradiction and confusion in the posture of elites. For those still working, the discontents released by economic collapse during the 1930s were expressed in struggles within the factory system, which we will turn to in the next chapter. But the men and women for whom life had changed most drastically and immediately were no longer in the factories. They were among the masses of the unemployed, and their struggle had to take another form, in another institutional context. The depression saw the rise and fall of the largest movement of the unemployed this country has known, and the institution against which the movement was inevitably pitted was the relief system.

At the time of the Great Depression, formal arrangements for relief of the indigent were sparse and fragmented. In many places, including New York City and Philadelphia, there simply was no "outdoor" relief (the term used to describe aid given to people who were not institutionalized). Even where public relief agencies existed, what little was actually given was usually provided by private charities. But niggardly aid and fragmented adminstration did not signify an underdeveloped institution. To the contrary, a national relief system did exist. Despite the diversity of administrative auspices, the norms that guided the giving of relief were everywhere quite similar. The dole was anathema to the American spirit of work and self-sufficiency. Therefore, it should be dispensed to as few as possible and made as harsh as possible to discourage reliance upon it. Accordingly, very little was given, and then only to a handful of the aged and crippled, widowed and orphaned—to "deserving" people who clearly were not able to work.

These practices were not only a reflection of harshly individualistic American attitudes. They were also a reflection of American economic realities. Work and self-reliance meant grueling toil at low wages for many people. So long as that was so, the dole could not be dispensed permissively for fear some would choose it over work. Thus, most of the poor were simply excluded from aid, ensuring that they had no alternative but to search for whatever work they could find at whatever wage was offered. And if they found no work, then they would have to survive by whatever means they could.

But this much could have been achieved without any relief arrangements at all; the threat of starvation was sufficient. The more important function of the relief system was accomplished, not by refusing relief, but by degrading and making outcasts of those few who did get aid. At the time of the Great Depression the main legal arrangement for the care of the destitute was incarceration in almshouses or workhouses. In some places the care of paupers was still contracted to the lowest bidder, and destitute orphans were indentured to those who would feed them in exchange for whatever labor they could perform. The constitutions of fourteen states denied the franchise to paupers (Brown, 9–10; Woodroofe, 154). By such practices the relief system created a clearly demarcated and degraded class, a class of pariahs whose numbers were small but whose fate loomed large in the lives of those who lived close to indigence, warning them always of a life even worse than hard work and severe poverty.

The meaning of these relief practices was thus not only in their inhumanity but in the functions they performed in legitimating work in the face of the extreme inequalities generated by American capitalism. For many people work was hard and the rewards few, and the constraints of tradition weak in the face of the transformations wrought by industrial capitalism. The discontent these poor might have felt was muffled, in part, by the relief system and the image of the terrible humiliation inflicted on those who became paupers. The practices called charity were shaped, in short, by economic imperatives, by the need for cheap and docile labor on the farms and in the factories of a burgeoning capitalist society. For the practices of relief to change, this subordination of the institution of charity to the institution of profit had to be ruptured.

The wonder of this relief system, however, was that it generated such shame and fear as to lead the poor to acquiesce in its harsh and restrictive practices. In part the poor acquiesced simply because they shared American beliefs in the virtue of work and self-sufficiency, and in the possibility of work and self-sufficiency for those who were ambitious and deserving. But any doubts they might otherwise have felt about this judicious sorting out of the worthy by the American marketplace were dispelled by the spectacle of the degraded pauper displayed by the relief system. Even when unemployment was endemic, most people endured in silence, blaming themselves for their misfortunes. They did not demand relief, for to do so was to give up the struggle to remain above the despised pauper class. Most of the time, the unemployed poor obeyed the prohibition against going on the dole, and by doing so collaborated in their own misery and in the punitive practices of local relief officials.

Occasionally, however, unemployment reached calamitous levels and the jobless rebelled. At the depths of each of the recurrent depressions of the nineteenth and early twentieth centuries, people joined together and demanded some form of aid to ease their distress. In the slump of 1837 some 20,000 unemployed in Philadelphia assembled to demand, among other things, that the national government relieve distress among the unemployed by a public works program (Foner, 162), and in New York City, a crowd of thousands in City Hall Park protested against the "monopolies" and the high cost of food and rent. The crowd then paraded to the wholesale flour depot, and dumped flour and wheat in the streets (Gutman, 1976, 60–61). In the panic of 1857 protests of the unemployed emerged in several big cities. Ten thousand Philadelphians rallied "to stimulate their representatives in the State House to an appreciation of their troubles," and a system of ward associations was set up to issue food to the needy (Feder, 32). In New York a meeting of 15,000 in Tompkins Square to demand work culminated in the destruction of fences and benches and the seizure of food wagons, although in this instance the workers got neither jobs nor relief, and federal troops were called in (Feder, 35). The depression of 1873 stimulated new demonstrations. In New York City, rallies drew 10,000 to 15,000 people who were dispersed by mounted police, and in Chicago, mass meetings of the unemployed, organized by anarchists under the slogan "Bread or Blood," culminated in a march of 20,000 on the City Council (Feder, 52; Boyer and Morais, 86). Subsequently, unemployed workers stormed the offices of the Chicago Relief and Aid Society, swamping the Society with applications for aid. The Society surrendered, and about 10,000 were given relief over the next year (Feder, 52; Seymour, August 1937, 8).[1] In the depression of 1884 the unemployed in Chicago marched again, this time into better-off neighborhoods (Montgomery, 20), and in 1893 a new and bitter depression led to a series of marches on Washington by the unemployed, the best known of which was of course "Coxey's army." Coxey's marchers got nothing, but mass demonstrations in the big industrial cities did succeed at least in getting soup kitchens and, in some places, local public works projects as well.

These experiences suggest that when unemployment is severe and widespread, at least a partial transvaluation may occur among the poor. The prohibition against the dole may weaken, if only because the extent of distress belies the customary conviction that one's economic fortunes and misfortunes are a matter of personal responsibility, of individual failure. At such times large numbers of the poor demand relief, the relief of work or the relief of food and money. This transvaluation occurred again in the Great Depression, and just as the scale of the calamity in the 1930s was unparalleled, so too was the protest movement that arose among the unemployed.

The Great Depression:
Preconditions for Insurgency

The depression came suddenly, at a time when the American belief in unprecedented and unbroken prosperity had never been so fervent, earlier depressions notwithstanding. People were taken by surprise, the rulers as much as the ruled, and it took time for the political forces set in motion by the calamity to emerge. Then, as the depression continued and worsened, the harshening and disordering of a way of life began to take form in rising popular discontent. The actions of elites added momentum to this process, for they too were shaken and divided, and their cacaphonic accusations

---

[1] Gutman describes these 1873 protests and the organizations that led them in a number of industrial cities (1965).

and proposals heightened the sense of indignation that was spreading. In the period of general political uncertainty that ensued, protest movements emerged among different groups, focusing on different institutional grievances. The earliest uprisings occurred among the unemployed.

THE ECONOMIC COLLAPSE

The decade preceding the depression had been a boom time for American business. National income rose from about $60 billion in 1922 to $87 billion in 1929, and by June of 1929 the index of industrial production reached its highest point ever (Bernstein, 1970, 54, 251). For the nation as a whole prosperity had never seemed so assured.

These were not nearly such good years for many workers and farmers, however. Rising productivity and profits in the twenties were largely the result of increasing mechanization rather than the expansion of the labor force. Meanwhile depressed farm prices (the result of overproduction stimulated by heavy immigration earlier in the century, followed by the demand for food during World War I when the United States was feeding its allies) were forcing millions of people off the land and to the cities. The resulting labor surplus meant that for the first time in the American experience, prosperity was accompanied by continuing high unemployment throughout the decade (Lescohier and Brandeis, 137–151). The labor surplus also accounts for the fact that wages remained relatively fixed, while profits soared. Moreover, some industries, particularly mining and textiles, were in a slump throughout the decade, and these workers suffered sharp wage cuts. But the hardships of particular groups remained submerged, because the people who bore them were subdued by the aura of prosperity that symbolized the era. These were self-evidently good times in America; anyone who really wanted to work could ostensibly earn a livelihood.

Then, in 1929, the production index began to slip from its June high, and by October, after a dizzying burst of speculation, the stock market reacted in the panic known as Black Thursday. The impact on unemployment was immediate. One government official judged that the numbers out of work rose by 2.5 million within two weeks of the crash, and President Roosevelt's Committee on Economic

[margin annotation: even these authors go for it.]

Security later estimated that the number of unemployed jumped from 429,000 in October 1929 to 4,065,000 in January 1930 (Bernstein, 1970, 254). The number rose steadily to 8 million in January 1931, and to 9 million in October (Bernstein, 1970, 254–257).

Particular industries were devastated, as were the towns where they were located. Bernstein reports, for example, that by January 1930, 30 to 40 percent of the male labor force was out of work in Toledo, where Willys-Overland had cut its payroll from 20,000 to 4,000. In Detroit a personal loan company discovered in March that half its outstanding commitments were from people who had lost their jobs. By the end of that year almost half of New England's textile workers were unemployed, and the Metropolitan Life Insurance Company reported that 24 percent of its industrial policy holders in forty-six larger cities were jobless. The Ford Motor Company employed 130,000 workers in the spring of 1929; by the summer of 1931 there were only 37,000 left on the payroll (Bernstein, 1970, 255–256). Sidney Hillman reported that at the height of the season in January 1932 only 10 percent of his New York garment workers were employed (Bernstein, 1970, 317). The chronic unemployment of the 1920s had become catastrophic unemployment.

Most of the nation's public figures were stubbornly unwilling to recognize the disaster, at least at first. The White House issued messages of reassurance that "the fundamental strength of the Nation's economic life is unimpaired," that recovery is "just around the corner," and that in any case the temporary downturn was being stemmed by modest public works expenditures. Official refusal to recognize the disaster early in the depression also took form in White House denials that there was very much unemployment at all. If the 1930 census of unemployment did not support such contentions, Hoover argued that it was because the enumerators "had to list the shiftless citizen, who had no intention of living by work, as unemployed" (cited in Edelman, 184).[2] If there was not very much unemployment, it followed that there was not very much need for unusual measures to aid the unemployed. Hoover limited himself mainly to offering rhetorical encouragement of local charity efforts.

---

[2] When Congress required the Bureau of the Census to count unemployment in the census of 1930, the bureau reported some 3 million out of work or laid off, a figure that was treated as absurdly low by experts. Hoover found the need to further reduce the figure by explaining away 500,000 to 1 million as people who had no intention of seeking jobs, and another 500,000 to 1 million as people who were simply between jobs (Bernstein, 1970, 268).

In October 1930 he established an Emergency Committee for Employment, but ignored the recommendation of Colonel Arthur Woods, head of the committee, that the White House seek substantial appropriations from Congress for public works. A second committee, appointed in August 1931, was called the Organization on Employment Relief. But while its name revealed some dim acknowledgment of the problem, its activities, consisting of "coordinating" local efforts and exhorting American citizens to contribute to local charities, did not.

Nor, at first, were local officials much better attuned to the scale of the problem. City leaders in Buffalo, Cincinnati, Kansas City, Milwaukee, and Louisville initiated "make a job" or "man a block" campaigns, assigning the jobless to do snow removal or street cleaning while at the same time allowing them to canvass households for small donations. Philadelphia's mayor appointed a committee to organize the peddling of fruit (Colcord, 166), clubs and restaurants in some places began to participate in schemes for saving food leftovers for the unemployed, and some communities set aside plots of land so that the jobless could grow vegetables to ease their plight. The problem was defined as minor, and temporary, and so were the gestures made to deal with it. Until 1932 even the newspapers carried little news of the depression. Middletown newspapers made their first mention in April 1930 under the caption "Factories are Recovering from Bad Slump" (Lynd and Lynd, 17).

As the depression worsened in 1930 there were stirrings in Congress for federal action to alleviate unemployment by reviving and expanding the United States Employment Service and by expanding federal public works projects. The measures proposed were modest and the Congress elected in the fall of 1930 passed both bills. Hoover, ever staunch, vetoed the first and emasculated the second by appointing administrators hostile to federal public works. Nothing had been done to deal with the disaster except, perhaps, to begin to acknowledge it.

THE IMPACT ON DAILY LIFE

The habit of work, and the wages of work, underpin a way of life. As unemployment continued to grow, and the wages of those still employed shriveled, that way of life crumbled. Despite denials by the public figures of the nation, the evidence was there in the daily lives of the people. One dramatic sign was the spread of malnutrition and disease. Surveys of school children showed that one quarter suffered from malnutrition, new patients in tuberculosis clinics almost doubled, and a study by the U. S. Public Health Service revealed that the families of unemployed workers suffered 66 percent more illness than the families of employed workers. In 1931 New York City hospitals reported about one hundred cases of actual starvation (Bernstein, 1970, 331). Another sign was the weakening of family life as ties wore thin under the strains and humiliations of poverty. Desertions became common and divorce rates rose, while marriage rates and the birthrate dropped.[3] And as poverty deepened and morale weakened, the crime rate rose, as did drunkenness and sexual promiscuity, and the suicide rate (Bernstein, 1970, 332).

Without work, and with family life weakened, men and women, especially the young, took to the road. At first the movement was back to the farms. But soon farm income fell precipitously as well, and then there was no place to go except to move on, shunted from town to town. Just how many transients there were is not known, but the Southern Pacific Railroad reported that it had ejected 683,457 people from its trains in 1932 (Bernstein, 1970, 325). Everywhere shanty towns built of packing cases and junk sprang up. In Oklahoma City the vagrants lived in the river bottom; in Oakland, they lived in sewer pipes that a manufacturer could not sell; in New York they built shacks in the bed of an abandoned reservoir in Central Park and called it "Hoover Valley."

The Rise of Protest

Most of the people who were thrown out of work suffered quietly, especially at the start of the depression, when official denials helped to confuse the unemployed and to make them ashamed of their plight. Men and women haunted the employment offices, walked the streets, lined up for every job opening, and doubted themselves for

---

[3] See Bernstein, 1970, 327–328; Lynd and Lynd, 147, 544; Bakke, 1940, 17, 115. Several depression studies provide extensive evidence of the destructive impact of unemployment on family relations. See Cooley; Komarovsky; and Stouffer and Lazarsfeld.

not finding work. Families exhausted their savings, borrowed from relatives, sold their belongings, blaming themselves and each other for losing the struggle to remain self-reliant. But as the depression worsened, as the work forces of entire factories were laid off, as whole neighborhoods in industrial towns were devastated, and as at least some political leaders began to acknowledge that a disaster had occurred, attitudes toward what had happened and why, and who was to blame, began to change among some of the unemployed. They began to define their personal hardship not just as their own individual misfortune but as misfortune they shared with many of their own kind. And if so many people were in the same trouble, then maybe it wasn't they who were to blame, but "the system."[4]

MOB LOOTING, MARCHES, AND DEMONSTRATIONS

One of the earliest expressions of unrest among the unemployed was the rise of mob looting. As had happened so often before in history during periods of economic crisis, people banded together to demand food. By and large, the press refrained from reporting these events for fear of creating a contagion effect. In New York bands of thirty or forty men regularly descended upon markets, but the chain stores refused to call the police, in order to keep the events out of the papers. In March 1,100 men waiting on a Salvation Army bread line in New York City mobbed two trucks delivering baked goods to a nearby hotel. In Henryetta, Oklahoma, 300 jobless marched on storekeepers to demand food, insisting they were not begging and threatening to use force if necessary (Bernstein, 1970, 422; Brecher, 144). Indeed, Bernstein concludes that in the early years of the depression "organized looting of food was a nation-wide phenomenon" (1970, 421–423).

---

[4] Bakke provides vivid accounts of the demoralization and shame experienced by both unemployed American and English workers during this period. It was the sense of being *different*, if one was unemployed, that was so shameful: "And if you can't find any work to do, you have the feeling you're not human. You're out of place. You're so different from all the rest of the people around that you think something is wrong with you" (1934, 63). But clearly once people realized that by being out of work they were just the same as people around them, demoralization could more easily turn to indignation.

More consciously political demonstrations began as well. By early 1930, unemployed men and women in New York, Detroit, Cleveland, Philadelphia, Los Angeles, Chicago, Seattle, Boston, and Milwaukee were marching under such Communist banners as "Work or Wages" and "Fight—Don't Starve" (Karsh and Garman, 87; Leab, 300). Len de Caux, a labor journalist, was living in Cleveland at the time and described what was happening there:

> Marching columns of unemployed became a familiar sight. Public Square saw demonstrations running into tens of thousands. . . . The street-scene is etched in memory. It was in the heart of working-class Cleveland, during a communist-led demonstration. Police had attacked an earlier demonstration. In the street battle, several unemployed had been injured, and one had since died. In the same neighborhood, the Unemployed Councils had called a mass protest, a solemn occasion that brought out thousands. The authorities, under criticism and on the defensive, withdrew every cop from the area, many blocks wide . . . (163–164).

The crowds did not always stay in their own neighborhoods, and the authorities were not always judicious. On February 11, 1930, for example, some 2,000 unemployed workers stormed the Cleveland City Hall, dispersing only when the police threatened to turn fire hoses on them. A few days later the unemployed demonstrated at City Hall in Philadelphia, and had to be driven off by the police. A week later mounted police with nightsticks dispersed a crowd of 1,200 jobless men and women in Chicago. On February 26 a crowd of 3,000 was broken up by tear gas before the Los Angeles City Hall (Bernstein, 1970, 426–427).

In March the demonstrations became a national event. The Communists declared March 6, 1930, International Unemployment Day, and rallies and marches took place in most major cities. Many of the demonstrations were orderly, as in San Francisco where the chief of police joined the 2,000 marchers and the mayor addressed them, or in Chicago where some 4,000 people marched down Halsted and Lake Streets, and then dispatched a committee to petition the mayor (Lasswell and Blumenstock, 196). But in other places, including Washington, D.C., and Seattle, local officials grew alarmed and ordered the police to disperse the crowds with tear gas. In Detroit, Cleveland, Milwaukee, and Boston, the crowds resisted, and fierce battles broke out between the demonstrators and the police (Keeran,

72–73; Leab, 306–307).[5] The worst clash occurred in New York City,[6] an event which was reported by the *New York Times*:

> The unemployment demonstration staged by the Communist Party in Union Square broke up in the worst riot New York has seen in recent years when 35,000 people attending the demonstration were transformed in a few moments from an orderly, and at times a bored, crowd into a fighting mob. The outbreak came after communist leaders, defying warnings and orders of the police, exhorted their followers to march on City Hall and demand a hearing from Mayor Walker. Hundreds of policemen and detectives, swinging night sticks, blackjacks and bare fists, rushed into the crowd, hitting out at all with whom they came into contact, chasing many across the street and into adjacent thoroughfares and rushing hundreds off their feet. . . . From all parts of the scene of battle came the screams of women and cries of men, with bloody heads and faces. A score of men were sprawled over the square with policemen pummeling them. The pounding continued as the men, and some women, sought refuge in flight.

The demonstration was sufficiently threatening to prod the mayor to agree to form a committee to collect funds to be distributed to the unemployed.[7] In October 1930 the unemployed gathered again in a mass rally at City Hall plaza to demand that the Board of Estimate appropriate twenty-five dollars a week for each unemployed person. The police again attacked the demonstrators, and two of the organizers were injured, but the Board of Estimate appropriated one million dollars for relief (Naison, 72–73).

---

[5] "In Detroit, despite police warnings to avoid the area, between 50,000 and 100,000 people gathered in the streets and on the sidewalks of the downtown district. Police Commissioner Harold Emmons mobilized the entire Detroit police force of 3,600. . . . For two hours the fighting raged, until in desperation the police ordered city buses and street cars to drive through the protesters in order to clear the streets. . . . A riot comparable to Detroit's disturbance took place in Cleveland after the mayor informed 10,000 to 25,000 demonstrators that he was powerless to adjust their grievances. A three hour riot in Milwaukee led to forty-seven arrests and four injuries" (Keeran, 72–73).

[6] The *Daily Worker* reported 37 arrested and 130 injured in New York; 45 arrested and 25 injured in Detroit; 60 arrested and 20 injured in Los Angeles; 12 arrested and 16 injured in Seattle; 11 arrested and 6 injured in Washington (Rosenzweig, 1976a).

[7] The Communist organizers of the demonstration, however, were charged with "unlawful assembly" and "creating a public nuisance," and served six months on Blackwell's Island (Leab, 310). The demonstrations on March 6 also sparked enough concern in the Congress to justify the creation of what was to become the House Un-American Activities Committee (Bernstein, 1970, 427–428).

The demonstrations were branded as riots by the press; it was the Communist and Socialist organizers who misnamed them unemployment demonstrations, said the *New York Times* (October 17, 1930, 1). But the unemployed came, whatever the labels of the leaders, and despite the castigation of the press. Len de Caux suggests why:

> The communists brought misery out of hiding in the workers' neighborhoods. They paraded it with angry demands. . . . In hundreds of jobless meetings, I heard no objections to the points the communists made, and much applause for them. Sometimes, I'd hear a communist speaker say something so bitter and extreme, I'd feel embarrassed. Then I'd look around at the unemployed audience —shabby clothes, expressions worried and sour. Faces would start to glow, heads to nod, hands to clap (162–163).

For some people at least, distress was turning to indignation, an indignation strong enough to withstand official scorn or state force.

Communist agitators were helping in that transformation, but the unemployed were ready to respond to any leader who articulated their grievances. When Father James R. Cox, a Pittsburgh priest known as the Mayor of Shantytown, called a rally at Pitt Stadium to protest unemployment and demand public works and relief measures, some 60,000 people turned out, and 12,000 followed him on to Washington where he presented their demands to Hoover (Bernstein, 1970, 432).[8] And later, in the spring of 1932, thousands of unemployed veterans and their families descended on Washington, D.C. Their songs expressed their disaffection:

> Mellon pulled the whistle
> Hoover rang the bell
> Wall Street gave the signal
> And the country went to Hell

The veterans had in fact not come in a revolutionary or even in a very belligerent spirit. They had come only to plead with the Congress for early payment of pensions due them by law in 1945. The Congress turned them down, Hoover refused to meet with their

---

[8] It should be noted, because much is often made of it, that two Communist-led hunger marches on Washington, D.C., in 1931 and 1932 failed to attract many followers. However, Herbert Benjamin, who organized the marches, argued in a talk given in April 1976 in New York City that the marches were not intended to be large, but recruited only delegates from local groups, and that the marches themselves were executed with "careful military planning." In any case, there is no denying the successful mobilizations by the Communists in the big cities.

leaders, and when they still did not leave, he sent the Army to rout them. "What a pitiable spectacle," said the *Washington News,* "is that of the great American Government, mightiest in the world, chasing men, women and children with Army tanks. . . . If the Army must be called out to make war on unarmed citizens, this is no longer America" (Schlesinger, 1957, 265).

RENT RIOTS

The rising anger among the unemployed took other forms than street marches and riots. Jobless men and women began to defy the local authorities—and the rules upheld by these authorities— associated with specific hardships. One such kind of defiance was mass resistance to evictions. As unemployment rose, large numbers of families in many places could not pay their rents, and the number of evictions increased daily.[9] In 1930 and 1931 small bands of people, often led by Communists, began to use strong-arm tactics to prevent marshals from putting furniture on the street. Sometimes they were successful. Even when they were not, physical resistance was the only resort for people forced from their homes. The rent riots began on the Lower East Side and in Harlem,[10] but quickly spread to other parts of the city. The *New York Times* described an eviction of three families in the Bronx on February 2, 1932:

> Probably because of the cold, the crowd numbered only 1,000 although in unruliness it equalled the throng of 4,000 that stormed the police in the first disorder of a similar nature on January 22. On Thursday a dozen more families are to be evicted unless they pay back rents.
>
> Inspector Joseph Leonary deployed a force of fifty detectives and mounted and foot patrolmen through the street as Marshal

---

[9] In New York City some 186,000 families were served dispossess notices during eight months ending in June 1932 (Boyer and Morais, 261). Bernstein reports a Philadelphia study published in 1933 that found 63 percent of the white families and 66 percent of the black were in rent arrears (1966, 289). A study conducted at about the same time in the San Francisco area also found widespread rent defaults (Huntington). In five industrial cities in Ohio eviction orders were issued against nearly 100,000 families between January 1930 and June 1932 (Boyer and Morais, 261).

[10] The *Daily Worker* carried numerous accounts of apparently successful eviction resistance actions, beginning in the fall of 1930.

Novick led ten furniture movers into the building. . . . Women
shrieked from the windows, the different sections of the crowd
hissed and booed and shouted invectives. Fighting began simultaneously in the house and the street. The marshal's men were rushed
on the stairs and got to work after the policemen had driven the
tenants back into their apartments.

Boyer and Morais claim that such tactics succeeded in restoring
77,000 evicted families to their homes in New York City (261).

Chicago was also the scene of frequent "rent riots," especially in
the black neighborhoods where unemployment reached catastrophic
proportions and evictions were frequent. In the brief period from
August 11 to October 31, 1931 there were 2,185 cases before Renter's
Court, 38 percent of which involved blacks (Gosnell, 1967, 321–329).
Small groups known as "black bugs" marched through the streets
to mobilize large crowds to reinstall evicted familes, sometimes even
when the family was not present.[11] Police repression in Chicago was
so thorough[12] that these actions of necessity were virtually spontaneous:

> During the last part of 1930 the Unemployed Councils had estab-
> lished headquarters in many of the poorer sections of the city.
> The meeting-halls served as clubhouses where jobless men tired
> of tramping the streets in search of work came to rest and talk
> rather than face the trying tensions of the home. These men, estab-
> lishing mutual relations of identification on the basis of their
> common misfortune, began to act together to prevent evictions.
> The demonstrations were entirely unplanned and could not be
> throttled at the source because the men themselves never knew in
> advance when or where they would next demonstrate. Someone
> might come into the hall and tell of a person blocks away who
> was at that moment being evicted. Their indignation aroused, the
> men would march in a group down the street, adding the sympathe-
> tic and the curious to their number as they marched, until by the
> time they reached the scene of the eviction, the crowd would have
> grown in size and temper. The furniture of the unfortunate family
> would be replaced and the crowd, delighted with its success, would
> disperse gradually, in small groups (Lasswell and Blumenstock, 170–
> 171).

---

[11] For descriptions of the Chicago rent riots see Abbott, Chapter 14; Bernstein, 1970, 428;
Hofstadter and Wallace, 172–175; Lasswell and Blumenstock, 196–201.

[12] With one exception—a funeral procession—every outdoor demonstration planned by
the Communists in 1930 in Chicago was cut short by the police (Lasswell and Blumenstock, 168–169) .

Horace Cayton describes a Chicago rent riot in which he participated. One day in 1931 Cayton was sitting in a restaurant on the South Side and saw through the window a long file of black people, marching in deadly earnest. He joined them and later described what happened:

> We were met at the street by two squad cars of police who asked us where we were going. The black crowd swarmed around the officers. . . . No one moved. Everyone simply stood and stared at them. One officer lost his head and drew his gun, levelling it at the crowd. . . . No threats, no murmurs, no disorder; the crowd just looked at him. There the officer stood. Just then a siren was heard—the whisper went around—the riot squad was coming! . . . four cars full of blue-coated officers and a patrol wagon. They jumped out before the cars came to a stop and charged down upon the crowd. Night sticks and "billies" played a tattoo on black heads. "Hold your places!" shouted the woman. "Act like men!" answered the crowd. They stood like dumb beasts—no one ran, no one fought or offered resistance, just stood, an immovable black mass.

These tactics frequently culminated in beatings, arrests, and even killings,[13] but they also forced relief officials to give out money for rent payments (Seymour, December 1937, 14). A rent riot in August 1931 left three people dead and three policemen injured: "News of the riot screamed in the headlines of the evening press. The realization of the extent of unrest in the Negro district threw Chicago into panic" (Lasswell and Blumenstock, 197). Mayor Anton Cermak responded by promptly ordering a moratorium on evictions, and some of the rioters got work relief.[14]

Karsh and Garman report that in many places the Communists organized gas squads to turn the gas back on in people's houses and electric squads to string wires around the meter after it was shut off by the local utility (88). In Detroit, it took one hundred policemen to evict a resisting family, and later two Detroit families who protected their premises by shooting the landlord were acquitted by sympathetic juries (Bernstein, 1970, 428).

---

[13] The American Civil Liberties Union reported fourteen dead as a result of protests by the jobless (cited in Rosenzweig, 1976a).

[14] As one official tells the story, the riot ". . . flared up the whole community. I spent the next forty-eight hours in the streets down there, trying to quiet things down. I went to see Ryerson and the Committee of leading businessmen. . . . I said the only way to stop this business is to put these evicted men back to work at once. This was on a Saturday. They said, 'We don't have the money.' I said, 'You better get some.' By Monday morning, they had the money, and we put three hundred of those men to work in the parks that day" (Terkel, 396).

RELIEF INSURGENCY

There is surely reason to think that it is easier for people to defend their homes against the authorities than to demand relief, simply because Americans are more likely to believe they have a right to their homes than to believe they have a right to handouts, no matter how overwhelming the economic disaster that confronts them. Most of the unemployed resisted the final degradation of asking for relief for as long as they could. A study of those who applied for aid in 1932 in San Francisco and Alameda counties, for example, reported:

> Nearly two-thirds did not apply for relief until at least a year had elapsed after the chief breadwinner had lost his regular employment, and nearly one-third of these families had managed to get along for two years or longer. . . . By the time they applied for relief, many of these families were in debt to the grocer and the landlord; they had used their pitifully small savings; they had borrowed sums which though small, could probably never be repaid. Finally, they were defeated in their valiant struggle to maintain their independence . . . (Huntington, 66, 74).[15]

For many, sheer desperation finally forced violation of the prohibition against the dole. For others, it was more than desperation; it was anger. Some people came to believe that if there were no jobs —if the factories and offices and workshops turned them away—then they had a right to the income they needed to survive anyway. Fired by this new indignation, crowds of jobless men and women descended on relief offices, cornered and harassed administrators, and even took over the offices until their demands were met—until money or goods were distributed to them.[16] Lasswell and Blumenstock describe these early relief actions in Chicago:

> Hearing that some family had been refused relief or that some particularly needy case was being denied immediate attention,

---

[15] Bakke in his survey of New Haven also reported that three-quarters of the unemployed had not applied for relief until after two or more years of unemployment (1940, 363).

[16] Just how many people participated in unemployed actions remains a matter of speculation. Rosenzweig, who has done extensive work on the movement, says that "easily two million workers joined in some form of unemployed activity at some point in the thirties" but he does not give the evidence for this estimate (1974, 43).

groups would gather and march on the relief stations, demanding action. Social workers in many of the offices, having intimate knowledge of the misery behind such demands, hesitated to call the police. . . . Hence at first the relief offices met the demands of the demonstrators, giving Mrs. Jones the food basket which she should have had a week earlier. With success, demonstrations of this sort increased in number and size. The relief stations found themselves unable to deal with this type of mass pressure. For example, on the afternoon of August 31, 1931, a group of 400 persons began to march on the United Charities offices located at 4500 Prairie Avenue. By the time they reached the relief station, the number had grown to fifteen or sixteen hundred. A speaker addressed them in front of the station, and the tension grew so high that when Joel Hunter, Chief Administrator of the Charities, asked for the selection of a committee to present the grievances of the crowd, there was a move to storm the station. A police squad arrived, and a general riot ensued (171).

A study published by the American Public Welfare Association later in 1937 described similar demonstrations across the nation:

> Relief offices were approached by large committees, numbering ten, fifteen, twenty, and sometimes more persons, which demanded immediate audience, without previous appointment and regardless of staff members' schedules. . . . Frequently these large committees were buttressed by neighborhood crowds which gathered outside the relief office and waited while committees within presented "demands" (Seymour, December 1937, 15).

Relief officials, who were accustomed to discretionary giving to a meek clientele and were not much governed by any fixed set of regulations, usually acquiesced in the face of aggressive protests. With each abrasive encounter, officials in local and private charities gradually forfeited the discretion to give or withhold aid. Mark Naison reports some of the incidents: "I stood in the rain for three days and the Home Relief Bureau paid no attention to me," a woman declared at a neighborhood meeting in New York City. "Then I found out about the Unemployed Council. . . . We went in there as a body and they came across right quick." "The woman at the desk said I was rejected," another woman added. "I was crying when Comrade Minns told me to come to the meeting of the Unemployed Council. One week later I got my rent check" (152).[17]

---

[17] Even in dealing with cases of individual hardship, the contrast between the approach of the Unemployed Councils and that of private charity agencies was striking. As late as

As the unemployed became more disruptive, even cherished procedures of investigation and surveillance of recipients were relinquished. A news sheet put out by an unemployed group in Port
Angeles, Washington, exemplified the new spirit:

> "Home Visitors" or "snoopers" are only relief workers on a cash
> basis. They are picked for their ability as snoopers and stool pigeons
> only. They ask you so damn many questions that there is nothing
> personal left to you anyway (cited in Seymour, December 1937, 15).

As indignation mounted, in other words, some people not only
defied the prohibition against going on the dole, but some even
began to defy the apparatus of ritualized humiliation that had made
that prohibition so effective. And as they did, the movement gathered
momentum.

Naison describes the unemployed movement in Harlem (where
unemployment affected 80 percent of heads of household) during
this period:

> To force the relief system to function more effectively, the unem-
> ployed movement settled on a strategy of stimulating disorder.
> Harlem Council activists organized large groups of jobless workers,
> took them to the local relief station, and demanded that they
> receive aid. If the relief bureau officials refused to see them or
> claimed they were out of aid, the demonstrators camped in the
> bureau offices and remained there until they received aid or were
> removed by the police. If police tried to remove the demonstrators
> or prevent them from entering the bureaus, Council tactics became
> more violent. At one demonstration in late June of 1932, the Amster-
> dam News reported a group from the Harlem Council broke down
> the bureau's doors and "overturned desks and chairs" before the
> police could arrest them. Other demonstrations ended in pitched
> battles between police and Council activists that resulted in bloodied
> heads and numerous arrests (137).

In Chicago, "spontaneous outbreaks grew in size and frequency,
and through them the accumulated tensions and effects resulting
from economic deprivation and from newspaper neglect or criticism
and police repression became 'collectivised.' " The number of demon-

---

December 1932, an official of the Urban League explained how the league dealt with
relief problems as follows: "We find that we are able to settle about 75 percent of the
complaints which come to us without even calling the district office. This is done by
patiently explaining to the complainant the situation as we see it after listening to him"
(quoted in Prickett, 234).

strations increased, from 408 in 1931 to 566 in 1932 (Lasswell and Blumenstock, 172–173). The demonstrations were also becoming more massive and well-organized. On January 11, 1932, simultaneous demonstrations were held at all the relief stations of Chicago.[18] Later that year, some 5,000 men who had been forced to take refuge in municipal lodging houses marched on relief headquarters to demand three meals a day, free medical attention, tobacco twice a week, the right to hold Council meetings in the lodging houses, and the assurance of no discrimination against Unemployed Council members. Their demands were granted. Later in 1932, when relief funds were cut 50 percent by a financially strangled city administration, some 25,000 of the unemployed marched again, this time through the Chicago Loop in a cold, driving rain. The authorities quickly managed to borrow funds from the Reconstruction Finance Corporation, and the cut was rescinded.

In Detroit hundreds of people organized by the Unemployed Councils gathered at City Hall in August 1931 to demand better food and better treatment from the police at the municipal lodging houses. Just a few months later, the Young Communist League led a march of several thousand on one of the Briggs auto plants to demand jobs and unemployment insurance (Keeran, 77). Then in March 1932, after the severe winter, unemployed workers in Detroit who had been assembled by Communist organizers to march on the Ford River Rouge plant were fired on by Dearborn police. Four of the marchers were killed, many more were wounded. The press was divided: the *Detroit Mirror* savagely attacked the "riotous" marchers, but the *Detroit Times* accused the police of having "changed an orderly demonstration into a riot with death and bloodshed as its toll" (Keeran, 82–83; Prickett, 119). Two days later, some sixty thousand Detroit workers marched behind the coffins to the tune of the Internationale.

In Atlanta in June 1932 city and county authorities decided to drop 23,000 families from the relief rolls, claiming there were no funds. To maintain a degree of order in the face of this decision, local authorities proceeded to arrest hundreds of farm workers (who had come to Atlanta in search of work) on charges of vagrancy, in order to send them back to the countryside. But when a thousand of

---

[18] Lasswell and Blumenstock provide a blow-by-blow account of this and other demonstrations, many of which resulted in arrests, injuries, and killings (204–210).

the unemployed rallied at the courthouse, the order to cut the families was rescinded, and additional money was appropriated for relief (Herndon, 188–192).[19] In St. Louis 3,000 of the jobless marched and forced the passage at City Hall of two relief bills (Boyer and Morais, 263). Each such protest that succeeded in getting people money added morale and momentum to the movement, and further undermined the doctrine that being "on the county" was a confession of personal failure, a badge of shame.

Local Fiscal Breakdown

The number of jobless continued to rise. In the big industrial cities, where unemployment was especially severe, the unemployed sometimes comprised voting majorities. Faced with mounting protests, local officials could not remain indifferent. Clearly the private agencies which had in many places handled whatever relief was given could not meet the surging demand, and various *ad hoc* arrangements were quickly invented, often with the cooperation of local businessmen and philanthropists. Committees were set up, local citizens were exhorted to contribute to charity drives, and in some places city employees found their wages reduced for contributions to the relief fund. By these methods, expenditures for relief rose from $71 million in 1929 to $171 million in 1931 (Chandler, 192).

But this amount of relief in cities like New York, Chicago, Detroit, and Philadelphia barely scratched the surface of the need. The city manager of Cincinnati reported on the relief methods used there at the end of 1931, when about one-quarter of the city's workers were unemployed, and another quarter worked only part-time:

> Relief is given to a family one week and then they are pushed off for a week in the hope that somehow or other the breadwinner may find some kind of work. . . . We are paying no rent at all. That, of course, is a very difficult problem because we are continually having evictions, and social workers . . . are hard put to find places

---

[19] Subsequently Angelo Herndon, one of the Communist organizers of the Atlanta demonstration, was indicted and convicted for inciting insurrection under a century-old Georgia statute. His sentence to a twenty-year term by the Georgia courts was finally overturned by the Supreme Court in 1937.

for people whose furniture has been put out on the streets (quoted in Chandler, 43).

In New York City, where the charter of 1898 prohibited "outdoor" relief as distinct from relief in workhouses or poor houses, disruptions by the unemployed had led to the creation of an arrangement whereby the police precincts distributed direct relief to the most destitute from funds contributed by city employees. In 1931, on Governor Roosevelt's initiative, New York State established an emergency program which supplemented local relief funds with an initial outlay of $20 million. Even so, by 1932, the lucky among the unemployed in New York City were receiving an average grant of $2.39 per week, and only one-quarter were getting that (Schlesinger, 1957, 253). Testimony before the Senate Committee on Manufactures in the summer of 1932 reported that 20,000 children in New York had been placed in institutions because parents could not provide for them.

In Chicago in October 1931 40 percent of the work force was unemployed, but help was being given only to the completely destitute. A local official reported:

> In the city of Chicago there are 1,000 men eating in the breadlines food that costs 4½ cents a day, and these men are from the so-called Gold Coast of Chicago. These resources are about to end, and they are confronted with one meal a day within, say 30 days after the city funds will become exhausted (quoted in Chandler, 45).

Since Chicago was a railway hub, officials also had to deal with large numbers of transients, some of whom lived in a shanty town at the foot of Randolph Street, scavenging garbage for a living. Others were crowded in asylums and poor houses. Bernstein reports that the Oak Forest poor house, having filled its corridors, turned away 19,000 people in 1931 (1970, 297–298). By June 1932, Mayor Cermak told a House committee that if the federal government didn't send $150 million for relief immediately, they should be prepared to send troops later. And Chicago's leading industrialists and bankers joined in an appeal to Hoover for federal relief funds (Bernstein, 1970, 467).

In Philadelphia, public relief had been abolished in 1879,[20] and

---

[20] The Pennsylvania constitution explicitly forbade appropriations for "charitable purposes" but eventually the pressure was so great that the legislature made an appropriation anyway under the "general welfare" clause (Bernstein, 1970, 459).

so it fell to a committee of leading philanthropists and businessmen
to deal with the problem. They inaugurated a diversified program
of work relief, shelters, and loans, but their efforts were dwarfed by
the need. Some 250,000 were out of work in Philadelphia. "We have
unemployment in every third house," the executive director of the
Philadelphia Children's Bureau told the Senate Subcommittee on
Manufactures. "It is almost like the visitation of death to the households of the Egyptians at the time of the escape of the Jews from
Egypt" (Bernstein, 1970, 299–300).

In Detroit, Frank Murphy had won the mayoralty in 1930 with a
campaign that pledged aid to the unemployed, and a public relief
program was established with the result that the costs of relief rose
from $116,000 in February 1929 to $1,582,000 two years later. But
even so, Detroit provided only $3.60 for two adults per week, and
a study in 1931 of those dropped from the rolls showed that average
total income per person was $1.56 a week. Not surprisingly, Mayor
Murphy reversed his belief in local responsibility, and told the
Senate Manufactures Subcommittee that there ought to be federal
help.

These cities were actually the more liberal ones. In most places,
people got only a little food: Baltimore, for example, provided an
average weekly relief allotment of eighty cents in commodities
(Greenstein). In Atlanta, white recipients received sixty cents a
week, while blacks got less, when they got anything at all (Herndon,
188). *Fortune* summed up local relief efforts in the fall of 1931:

> The theory was that private charitable organizations and semi-
> public welfare groups . . . were capable of caring for the casualties
> of a world-wide economic disaster. And the theory in application
> meant that social agencies manned for the service of a few hundred
> families, and city shelters set up to house and feed a handful of
> homeless men, were compelled by the brutal necessities of hunger
> to care for hundreds of thousands of families and whole armies
> of the displaced and jobless. . . . The result was the picture now
> presented in city after city . . . heterogeneous groups of official and
> unofficial relief agencies struggling under the earnest and untrained
> leadership of the local men of affairs against an inertia of misery
> and suffering and want they are powerless to overcome (cited in
> Bernstein, 1970, 301).

In November 1932 a distinguished group of California citizens
serving on the State Unemployment Commission published a report
of its findings:

Unemployment and loss of income have ravaged numerous homes. It has broken the spirits of their members, undermined their health, robbed them of self-respect, destroyed their efficiency and employability. . . . Many households have been dissolved; little children parcelled out to friends, relatives or charitable homes; husbands and wives, parents and children separated, temporarily or permanently. Homes in which life savings were invested and hopes bound up have been lost never to be recovered. Men, young and old, have taken to the road . . . the army of homeless grows alarmingly. . . . Precarious ways of existing, questionable methods of "getting by" rapidly develop (cited in Bernstein, 1970, 321).

And in 1932 the New York *Evening Graphic* ran a series on starvation cases that year. The depression was no longer being denied.

However pathetic local relief programs were compared to the scale of the need, the cost of even that puny effort had brought many cities close to bankruptcy, and other municipal services were taking the brunt of the fiscal squeeze. A Detroit official reported that essential public services had been reduced "beyond the minimum point absolutely essential to the health and safety of the city," and this despite the fact that municipal salaries had been sharply cut. Chicago (whose finances had been in a shambles even before the depression) owed its school teachers $20 million dollars in back pay (Hopkins, 92–93). Boston had not paid its police for months (Bird, 108).

With local disturbances increasing, and local finances on the verge of collapse, other urban states followed New York's example. New Jersey, Pennsylvania, Ohio, and Wisconsin provided emergency outlays of relief funds, and other states began to underwrite municipal borrowing for relief. As a result of state and local efforts, total expenditures for relief rose by another $71 million between 1931 and 1932, to reach a total of $317 million. This amount of relief provided less than $27 that year for each of the 12 million unemployed. Even so, the effort was taking a heavy toll from local governments; to meet relief debts in the face of sharply declining tax revenues, spending on other programs fell by $966 million between 1931 and 1932. Increasingly, local governments turned to borrowing, but they found fewer purchasers for their bonds, partly because many municipalities were no longer credit-worthy. On April 15 *Survey* magazine published reports from thirty-seven large cities and concluded that "the industrial cities of the Middle West and the large cities of Pennsylvania are in desperate plight. . . . Complete breakdown is imminent."

By early 1933 nearly one thousand local governments had defaulted on their debts (Chandler, 48–50).

In February 1932, as part of a campaign for his bill to provide federal loans for unemployment relief, Senator La Follette sent out a questionnaire to mayors all over the country asking about current numbers of people on relief, anticipated increases, the amounts of relief aid being given, whether the city was in a position to float bond issues to meet relief needs, and whether the mayors favored federal appropriations to "aid in providing more adequate relief for the needy or in lessening the burden on local taxpayers." In their replies, the mayors described widespread distress and clamored for federal aid. Not only were they administering relief on a starvation basis, but virtually every municipality claimed to be close to bankruptcy and faced the prospect of having to cut off relief altogether.[21]

Unable to resist the political pressures of the unemployed, local elites had brought their cities to the brink of fiscal collapse. But even so, city budgets could not handle the demand for relief, and so the pressure was not abated, but worsened as unemployment rose. Driven by the protests of the masses of unemployed and the threat of financial ruin, mayors of the biggest cities of the United States, joined by business and banking leaders, had become lobbyists for the poor.

Electoral Instability and Federal Response

By November 1932 the political unrest that had spurred local leaders to try to respond to the unemployed spread upward to produce a national political disturbance—the electoral upheaval of 1932. In the avalanche of new legislation that followed, concessions were made to each group in a volatile constituency. What the unemployed got was federal relief.

---

[21] Senator La Follette had these replies read into the *Congressional Record*, 1932, 3099–3260. La Follette was head of the Senate Subcommittee on Manufactures that held hearings on proposals for federal relief early in 1932. The testimony at these hearings provided overwhelming evidence of the devastating effects of unemployment. Nevertheless, the bill that emerged from the committee was defeated by a coalition of Republicans and conservative Democrats. Later that year, as the pressure mounted, Congress finally authorized federal loans to the states for relief through the Reconstruction Finance Corporation. Hoover reluctantly supported the measure as not interfering with private and local responsibilities for relief. In a way, he was right; the loans that resulted were too minuscule to be called interference.

The Republican Party had been in power since the toppling of the Wilson Administration in the election of 1920, when Harding carried every major nonsouthern city. With eastern businessmen at the helm, the Republicans ruled securely thereafter, receiving substantial majorities in each election until 1930, their strength concentrated particularly in the urban North. Hoover had won the presidency with a majority of 6.5 million votes.

As for the Democratic Party, after the debacle of 1924 during which the agrarian wing had been defeated, it too had come firmly under the control of eastern conservatives, businessmen like Bernard Baruch and John J. Raskob, and machine politicians like Alfred E. Smith. But the depression created the shifting currents that would bring new leaders to the forefront of the Democratic Party, and would then force the massive realignment of voters that brought these leaders to national power. The realignment was first signaled in the election of 1928 when big city wage earners began to switch to the Democratic Party and the candidacy of Al Smith.[22] The shift of urban working-class voters became more evident as the depression worsened; the Republicans suffered reversals in the congressional elections of 1930. But it was the presidential election of 1932 that produced one of the most sweeping political realignments in American history, and it was the election of 1936 that confirmed it.

The man who rose to power through these dislocations was, of course, Franklin Delano Roosevelt; he won the Democratic nomination from a divided and uncertain Democratic Party on the fourth ballot, and then went on to campaign by making promises to everyone who would listen.[23] What working people listened to were the promises to "build from the bottom up and not from the top down, that put their faith once more in the forgotten man at the bottom of the economic pyramid" (Roosevelt, 159–206, 625). Roosevelt won with a plurality of almost seven million votes, capturing the largest electoral majority since 1864, and sweeping in an overwhelmingly

---

[22] In some cities—Boston, New York, Milwaukee, and San Francisco—the shift in 1928 was dramatic; the Democratic percentage of the vote doubled in these places (Bernstein, 1970, 78–79).

[23] Raymond Moley writes of the campaign as follows: "I was charged in 1932 with mobilizing personnel and ideas to promote the presidential ambitions of Governor Roosevelt. I welcomed all points of view, planners, trustbusters, and money wizards. I expanded the so-called Brain Trust very considerably and maintained contact with a great variety of people from Bernard Baruch to Huey Long. The task was to win an election in an electorate comprising many ideologies, and mostly no ideology. The issue was recovery, and the therapy used was a combination of many prescriptions" (559–560).

Democratic Congress. And much of Roosevelt's majority was concentrated in the big cities of the country, where unemployment and hardship were also concentrated. Economic catastrophe had resulted in a mass rejection of the party in power.

In the interim between the election and Roosevelt's inauguration, the index of industrial production sank to its lowest point ever, and the number of unemployed was increasing at the rate of about 200,000 a month (Lescohier and Brandeis, 163), to reach at least 12 million by March 1933. The clamor for federal relief was virtually irresistible. A Social Science Research Council Bulletin characterized the situation this way:

> By the time the new federal administration came into power in 1933, the pressure for more money had become so nearly unanimous that it was politically desirable for congressmen and senators to favor large appropriations for relief; candidates were elected often on a platform which predicated adequate relief appropriations by Congress (White and White, 84).

In a message to Congress three weeks after the inauguration, Franklin Delano Roosevelt called for a Civilian Conservation Corps, a public works program, and a massive program of federal emergency relief. The Civilian Conservation Corps provided jobs at subsistence wages for a mere 250,000 men. The Public Works Administration was slow in getting started, and in any case it was designed not so much to provide jobs for the unemployed as to stimulate the economy, so that most of the jobs went to skilled workers. By contrast the Federal Emergency Relief Act, drawn up by Senators Edward P. Costigan, Robert F. Wagner, and Robert N. La Follette, Jr., allocated $500 million for immediate grants to the states for relief of the unemployed, half of which was to be spent on a matching basis. The act was signed on May 12, Harry Hopkins was sworn in as administrator on May 22, and by the evening of that day, he made the first grants to the states. By early June, forty-five states had received federal grants for relief, and total expenditures on relief rose to $794 million in 1933, to $1,489 million in 1934, and to $1,834 million in 1935 (Brown, 204). When the program was terminated in June 1936 the federal government had spent $3 billion as its share of relief expenditures.[24]

---

[24] On May 23, the day after he took office, Hopkins notified the states that the federal government would make grants-in-aid equal to one-third of the relief expenditure in

It had taken protest and the ensuing fiscal and electoral disturbances to produce federal relief legislation, and it took continued protest to get the legislation implemented. By 1934 many people had been without work a long time—an estimated 6 million for more than a year (Karsh and Garman, 86). And during 1933, 1934, and 1935, groups of the unemployed continued to agitate, and were at least partly responsible for the fact that many states and localities participated in federal emergency relief programs at all. In August 1933, when state appropriations were needed in Ohio, 7,000 jobless marched on the state capitol (Rosenzweig, 1975, 58). In Colorado, when the federal relief funds were discontinued in the winter of 1934 because the state had repeatedly failed to appropriate its share of costs, mobs of the unemployed rioted in relief centers, looted food stores, and stormed the state legislature, driving the frightened senators from the chamber. Two weeks later, the General Assembly sent a relief bill to the governor, and federal funding was resumed (Cross). An attempt in Chicago to cut food allowances by 10 percent in November 1934 led to a large demonstration by the unemployed, and the city council restored that cut. In the spring of 1935 the federal government withheld relief after Illinois failed to provide its share of funding. When relief offices closed down, the unemployed marched and demonstrated in Chicago and Springfield until the state legislature appropriated funds. Relief was cut in Kansas City, Kansas, later that year and 2,000 of the unemployed assembled in front of the courthouse where they remained and prayed and sang hymns until a new relief appropriation was voted (Gilpin).

These were only the publicized protests. A survey conducted in New York City revealed that almost all of the forty-two district relief administrators in New York City reported frequent dealings with unemployed groups, most of them led by Communists. These groups were disruptive—shouting, picketing, refusing to leave the relief offices—and the groups frequently won their demands. Five of the relief offices were observed continuously over a thirty-day period during which 196 demands by unemployed groups were recorded, of which 107 were granted (Brophy and Hallowitz, 63–65).

By the winter of 1934 20 million people were on the dole, and

---

the state during the first quarter of the year. But this ratio was disregarded as time went on, and the proportion of relief paid by the federal government increased until it was as much as three-quarters of the relief expenditure in some states (White and White, 82).

monthly grant levels had risen from an average of $15.15 per family in May 1933 to an average of $24.53 in May 1934, and to $29.33 in May 1935. Harry Hopkins explained the new government posture toward the unemployed:

> For a long time those who did not require relief entertained the illusion that those being aided were in need through some fault of their own. It is now pretty clear in the national mind that the unemployed are a cross-section of the workers, the finest people in the land (Kurzman, 85).

From Disruption to Organization

From the onset of the depression, the potential for unrest among the unemployed attracted organizers and activists from the left. Their approaches to work with the unemployed varied. But they all deplored the loose and chaotic character of the movement, and they all strove to build organization.

The Communists were first in the field—indeed, they had been in the field as early as 1921, trying to organize the unemployed into "Councils of Action," but without much success. In 1929 they began a new campaign to form "Unemployed Councils."[25] During the winter of 1929–1930, Communist organizers worked vigorously, on the breadlines, in the flop houses, among the men waiting at factory gates, and in the relief offices. By mid-1930 the unemployed had become the chief focus of party activity. The party's theoretical journal, *The Communist*, asserted that those out of work were "the tactical key to the present state of the class struggle" (cited in Rosenzweig, 1976a).

During this early period, Communist activists concentrated on direct action rather than on organization, and the actions they led in the streets and in the relief offices were generally more militant and disruptive than those of other unemployed groups. Communists, many of whom were unemployed workers,[26] seized upon every griev-

---

[25] The Unemployed Councils were officially launched under that name at a National Conference of the Unemployed in Chicago on July 4, 1930 (Bernstein, 1970, 428). The Councils were renamed Unemployment Councils in 1934.

[26] A high proportion of party members were unemployed during the early depression years, and relatively few of them were in basic industry. For this reason, much of the party's emphasis at this stage was on the work of street nuclei among the unemployed. That was to change later in the depression.

ance as an opportunity for inciting mass actions, and channeled their formidable self-discipline and energy into the extensive pamphleteering and agitation that helped bring the unemployed together, and helped raise the pitch of anger to defiance. Moreover, Communists themselves often took the lead in confrontations with police; comrades were exhorted to stand firm and defend other unemployed workers when the police attacked, as they often did (Seymour, August 1937, 9–11; Leab, 300–303; Lasswell and Blumenstock, 165–213).

At this stage, there were few membership meetings, little formal structure within each group, and very little effort to establish formal linkages among the different groups. The Councils sprang alive at mass meetings and demonstrations; in between, only a cadre group constituted the organization. "But because of the temper of the times," says Leab, "this hard core managed to bring out ever-increasing numbers of people for the various protest demonstrations" (304).

Early in the depression most Socialists had been opposed to organizing the unemployed. Instead, the National Executive Committee of the Socialist Party had, in May 1929, urged the creation of Emergency Conferences on Unemployment that would lobby for the Socialist program of old age benefits, unemployment insurance, and the abolition of child labor. Little came of the Emergency Conferences, but groups of Socialists in some localities, many of them associated with the League for Industrial Democracy, began to organize committees or unions of the unemployed despite the absence of a national mandate. They used grievance procedures and mass pressure tactics not very different from the Communist unemployed groups.[27] The most successful of these was the Chicago Workers' Committee on Unemployment which was credited with raising Cook County relief payments to one of the highest in the nation (Rosenzweig, 1974, 12). By February 1932, prodded by the success of the Communist Unemployed Councils, and by the local Socialist-led organizations that had already emerged, the National Executive Committee of the Socialist Party finally endorsed direct organizing of the unemployed (Rosenzweig, 1974, 14), with the result

---

[27] There is some evidence that the Socialist groups tended to attract a more middle-class constituency than the Communists, perhaps because of their emphasis on educational programs and their more conservative tactics, and perhaps because they lacked the Communists' zeal in mobilizing the working class.

that Socialists in other places, most importantly in New York and Baltimore, began organizing on the model of the Chicago Workers' Committee. These groups later initiated the Workers' Alliance of America, the culmination of the organizational efforts among the unemployed.

Other radicals were also active, many of them affiliated with the Conference for Progressive Labor Action formed in May 1929 by Socialists and trade unionists who were opposed both to the conservative leadership of the AFL and to the dual union approach of the Communist Trade Union Unity League. The CPLA began as a propaganda and education organization but by 1931 it began to move to the left and A. J. Muste, who had run the Brookwood Labor College in the 1920s, emerged as the leading figure, with a program to build local organizations of the unemployed. The Muste groups, usually called Unemployed Leagues, flourished particularly in the rural areas and small towns of Ohio, West Virginia, Kentucky, North Carolina, and Pennsylvania, where the approach taken by the Muste radicals, at least at the beginning, was nondoctrinaire and oriented toward the immediate needs of the unemployed. The Seattle Unemployment League, a kind of model for many of these efforts (although it was not actually affiliated with the CPLA), was a particular success, at least briefly. It claimed 12,000 members in Seattle itself by the end of 1931 and a statewide membership of 80,000 by the end of 1932. At first the Seattle group emphasized barter, working for farmers in exchange for produce. But when the harvest season of 1931 was over, and self-help came to an end, the league turned to the city for help. The city council, uneasy about the growing numbers of league supporters, voted an appropriation of half a million dollars for relief, and turned the fund over to the league to administer. During the spring elections of 1932, when an estimated one-third of Seattle's voters were league members, the league supported a slate headed by John F. Dore, who campaigned with talk of taking huge fortunes away "from those who stole them from the American workers," and won with the largest plurality in Seattle history. Once in office, however, Dore took the administration of relief away from the league and threatened to use machine guns on the unemployed demonstrations, earning himself the name "Revolving Dore" (Bernstein, 1970, 416–418).

Many of the Unemployed Leagues, like the Seattle League, did not last long as self-help efforts, if only because self-help programs could not cope with extensive and lasting unemployment. By 1933 the leagues became more political and abrasive in outlook and tactics, joining in the general demand for public relief. Some fell under the leadership of the Communists, and later some of the leaders of the leagues, Louis Budenz among them, joined the Communist Party.

Other groups appeared in many towns, sometimes under auspices which had nothing to do with radical politics. Local politicians, for example, set up clubs in their wards to handle relief grievances on behalf of individual constituents, particularly before elections,[28] and in many rural or partially rural areas, groups organized around self-help and barter programs.[29] In Dayton, Ralph Borsodi, a utopian thinker who believed in a return to the land, was engaged by the Council of Social Agencies to organize groups that undertook to produce their own goods (Bernstein, 1970, 420). Arthur Moyer, the president of Antioch College, established the Midwest Exchange, Inc., which encouraged self-help and barter among independent groups (Glick, 13–14). In Harlem, self-help took the form of food collections and rent parties often organized by the churches or by the disciples of Father Divine.[30]

In some places, particularly in the coal regions where unemployment was endemic, trade unions helped and even joined with the unemployed. Locals of the United Mine Workers led two hunger marches in Charleston, West Virginia, for example, and joined with the Unemployed Council in Gallup, New Mexico, in leading mass resistance against evictions of unemployed miners from homes built on land owned by mining companies. In Pennsylvania, some locals of the UMW affiliated with and gave financial support to the unemployed groups (Seymour, December 1937, 6). Elsewhere, unemployed groups occasionally provided support for striking workers. In the Toledo Auto-Lite strike and the Milwaukee Streetcar strike in

---

[28] Gosnell describes such ward activity in Chicago (1937).

[29] Clark Kerr provides an exhaustive description of these self-help groups, whose active membership he estimates at 75,000 in 1932.

[30] In Harlem even the Unemployed Councils undertook food collections to meet the immediate needs of the destitute (*Daily Worker*, April 24, 1931). In general, however, the more radical leaders of the unemployed scorned the self-help approach, as is suggested by an article entitled "Organized Looking into Garbage Cans" in the March 1st, 1933, issue of the *Detroit Hunger Fighter*, a news sheet of the Detroit Unemployed Council: "The procedure is to go to all kinds of food establishments and trade the labor of unemployed workers for unsaleable food, to gather old clothing, etc., as a means of lightening the burden of maintaining the unemployed for the bosses and evading the issue of struggle . . . 55 percent of the population cannot live on what the other 45 percent throws away. . . . "

1934, it was the support of thousands of the unemployed that finally broke employer resistance. And in Minneapolis, unemployed workers were included in the militant local 574 of the Teamsters (Glick, 13). By and large, however, the trade unions avoided the unemployed, who were dropped from the union membership rolls as their dues lapsed.[31] Subsequently William Green and John L. Lewis sent messages of greetings to meetings of the unemployed (Seymour, December 1937, 10), but the CIO refused to permit the request of the organization of the unemployed to affiliate.

Because of the variegated character of the unemployed movement, membership cannot be accurately estimated, and in any case it probably fluctuated widely. People were attracted by the chances of getting relief, and many dropped out once the needed aid was received. Until February 1934 the Unemployed Councils did not have either dues or members; adherents were simply called supporters (Seymour, August 1937, 11–13). Still, if any gauge is provided by the groups' own claims, the numbers were impressive for a grassroots organization. By 1933 the Ohio Unemployed League claimed a membership of 100,000 distributed among 187 locals throughout the state; the Pennsylvania Unemployed League in 1935 claimed 25,000 members in twelve counties; the Pennsylvania Security League reported some 70,000 members (Seymour, December 1937); the Pittsburgh Unemployed Citizens' League claimed 50,000 dues-paying members in fifty locals (Karsh and Garman, 92). In Chicago the Unemployed Councils alone claimed a membership of 22,000 in forty-five local branches (Karsh and Garman, 90) while the Socialist-led groups had organized 25,000 jobless by mid-1932 (Rosenzweig, 1976a).

THE FORMATION OF A NATIONAL ORGANIZATION

The movement of the unemployed had originated in local communities, in sporadic street demonstrations, in rent riots, and in the disruption of relief centers. Many of the local organizations were loosely structured, held together more by the periodic demonstrations

---

31 Consistent with its historic emphasis on voluntarism, the AFL had opposed government measures to aid the unemployed until mid–1932, by which time its ranks had broken on the issue, and even some employers were pressing the federation to reverse itself.

than by regular and formal affiliations; they gathered momentum from direct action victories which yielded money or food or a halt to evictions. But most of the radical leaders of the different groups felt that the looseness of these local groups was a drawback. As early as November 1930 the Communist Party political committee criticized the absence of "organizational crystallization" in the Unemployed Councils, and a party official complained that "despite millions of leaflets and hundreds of meetings, not to speak of the half dozen demonstrations in every city, organized unemployed councils are almost nonexistent" (Rosenzweig, 1976b, 42).[32]

However bitterly the Communists, the Socialists, and the Musteites disagreed about issues of international socialism, they shared the view that the victories won by the unemployed in the early depression were mere handouts. A significant political movement capable of winning major victories depended, they thought, on firmly structured local and state organizations knit together in a national body and with a national program.[33] Instead of disparate local groups disrupting relief offices or leading marches on mayors for handouts, a nationwide poor people's organization should be formed, an organization representing such massive voting numbers as to compel the Congress to enact more fundamental economic reforms. The coming of the New Deal, with a more sympathetic president and Congress, of course, encouraged this approach, for the time seemed propitious to achieve far-reaching change through the electoral system.

Moreover, a major shift in Comintern policy in 1935 (prompted by belated realization of the seriousness of the fascist threat and the menace it posed to world communism) encouraged this emphasis on organization and electoral strategies among the Communists, who had led the most militant and disruptive of the unemployed groups.[34]

---

[32] Herbert Benjamin, leader of the Unemployed Councils, commented later on directives by the party leadership to overcome these failings that "down below people weren't concerned . . . [They were] just concerned with finding any means they could of acting" (quoted in Rosenzweig, 1976b, 40).

[33] David Lasser, a Socialist and leader of a New York unemployed group who later became head of the Workers' Alliance, argued in 1934 that the demands of the unemployed had become national in scope, and that the unemployed themselves had matured so that they would not be satisfied with short run concessions, but wanted a reordering of society (*New Leader*, December 12, 1934, 1).

[34] The widely held assumption that the policies of the American Communist Party were simply reflexive responses to the dictates of the International has recently been disputed by a number of young historians who argue that the Popular Front was, at least in part, an authentic—if perhaps mistaken—response of American Communists to domestic political developments. See for example Buhle, Keeran, and Prickett.

The "Popular Front" line called upon Communists to seek alliances with the liberal and socialist groups they had previously denounced as "social fascists." This quite clearly meant seeking alliances within the New Deal coalition and with the New Deal itself.[35]

In fact, there were attempts to form a national organization almost from the start. Stimulated by the successful demonstrations of March 6, 1930, the Communists held a meeting in New York City at the end of March, reportedly drawing together 215 delegates from thirteen states, and calling for the formation of an autonomous national unemployment organization.[36] In July a larger meeting attracting 1,320 delegates was held in Chicago to declare the formation of the Unemployed Councils of the U.S.A. A platform calling for federal unemployment insurance and federal appropriations for relief was adopted, and a formal structure describing the relationship between local, city, county, state, and national groups was elaborated. By 1934 the Unemployed Councils also adopted a written constitution (Leab, 308–311). Finally the shift in Comintern policy in 1935 set the stage not only for the development of an organization, but for the development of an organization that would embrace all of the unemployed groups.

In the fall of 1932, prompted by the upcoming election, the Socialists had also taken steps toward the development of a national organization.[37] The Chicago Workers Committee called a meeting of "all Unemployed Leagues that we know of except the Communist Party's 'Unemployed Councils' " (Seymour, December 1937, 7). The result was the formation of the Federation of Unemployed Workers Leagues of America, which called on the incoming president and the Congress to enact legislation for direct relief, public works and slum clearance, unemployment and old-age insurance, a shorter work day, and the prohibition of child labor. The federation itself was shortlived, but the conviction that a nationwide organization would

---

[35] Earl Browder later recalled that the party had begun working with New Deal relief agencies in 1935 (Buhle, 231).

[36] Prior to this, the Unemployed Councils were considered part of the Trade Union Unity League but this affiliation did not much affect the strictly local activities of the early groups (Seymour, December 1937, 3).

[37] Aside from this conference activity, Norman Thomas' campaign for the presidency in 1932 brought a halt to whatever direct organizing of the jobless the Socialists were doing. The election campaign was apparently considered more important (Rosenzweig, 1974, 15).

be a powerful force persisted, and the Socialist groups moved to consolidate into state federations during 1934.

Meanwhile, in July 1933, 800 delegates from thirteen states showed up in Columbus, Ohio, for the first national conference of the Unemployed Leagues. By this time, the radical intellectual leaders of the Conference for Progressive Labor Action, who had organized the Leagues, had become ardent believers in a "mass labor party" whose goal would be the "complete abolition of planless, profiteering capitalism, and the building of a workers' republic" (Karsh and Garman, 91).[38]

Efforts to weld together a national organization continued throughout 1934. In March leaders from Socialist-led organizations in Baltimore, New York City, Westchester, Pittsburgh, Reading, and Hartford formed the Eastern Federation of Unemployed and Emergency Workers. During the summer and fall of 1934 the groups represented in the Eastern Federation met with the Socialist-led state federations from Illinois, Wisconsin, and Florida and with the Muste groups to plan a demonstration, out of which emerged a Provisional National Committee to plan for the establishment of a nationwide organization of the unemployed.[39]

Finally, at a conference held in Washington in early 1935, a "permanent nonpartisan federation" of most of the large unemployed organizations in the United States was formed, called the Workers' Alliance of America. Delegates attended from unemployed organizations in sixteen states.[40] A constitution was adopted, a dues system and a National Executive Committee were established, and the Executive Committe was directed by the conference to negotiate unification with the Communist Unemployed Councils. A second National Workers' Alliance Convention in April 1936 drew 900

---

[38] Shortly afterwards the Unemployed Leagues became affiliated with the American Workers Party, which in 1934 joined with the Trotskyist Communist League of America to form the Workers Party of the United States, which in turn merged with the Socialist Party in 1936, until the Trotskyists were expelled in 1937 (Rogg, 14; Glick). Under the aegis of the Workers Party, issues of revolutionary strategy became preeminent, factional fighting was endemic, and the Unemployed Leagues lost most of their followers (Rosenzweig, 1975, 69–73).

[39] The demonstration on November 24 was claimed by its organizers to have turned out 350,000 people in 22 states (Rosenzweig, 1974, 24).

[40] As is usual in these matters, estimates of affiliation varied wildly. The groups at this convention claimed 450,000 members, but the Communist Unemployed Councils, who were not yet affiliated, estimated active affiliation at 40–50,000 (Rosenzweig, 1974, 26).

delegates representing organizations from thirty-six states, including the Unemployed Councils. By the end of the year the alliance claimed 1,600 locals with a membership of 600,000 in forty-three states.[41] It was this convention that marked the merging of most major groups of the unemployed: the Workers' Alliance, the Unemployed Councils, the National Unemployment League, the American Workers Union, and several independent state groups. David Lasser, the Socialist who headed the New York Workers' Committee on Unemployment and who had been chairman of the first alliance, was again named chairman, and Herbert Benjamin, a Communist who had been national secretary of the Unemployed Councils, was named organizational secretary. The Communists in the Unemployed Councils, by now well into their Popular Front phase, deferred to the Socialists by settling for half as many seats on the new National Executive Board. With these matters resolved, a Washington headquarters was established, and the office and field staff expanded. State "unity" conventions followed the national meeting and new local organizations began to write the alliance for charters. To all appearances, a great deal had been achieved. A national poor people's organization had been born.

THE DECLINE OF LOCAL PROTEST

David Lasser, during his early efforts to forge what became the Workers' Alliance, had argued that a national organization would both stimulate local organizations and give them permanence (*New Leader*, December 22, 1934, 1). In fact, while the leaders of the unemployed groups had been concentrating on forming a national organization complete with a constitution and a bureaucratic structure, the local groups across the country were declining. They were declining largely as a result of the Roosevelt Administration's more liberal relief machinery, which diverted local groups from disruptive tactics and absorbed local leaders in bureaucratic roles. And once

---

[41] Rosenzweig reports 791 delegates at this convention (1974, 33), and Seymour (December 1937, 8) and Brophy and Hallowitz (9) estimate membership in the alliance to have been only about 300,000.

the movement weakened, and the instability of which it was one expression subsided, relief was cut back. That this happened speaks mainly to the resiliency of the American political system. That it happened so quickly, however, and at so cheap a price, speaks to the role played by leaders of the unemployed themselves. For by seeking to achieve more substantial reform through organization and electoral pressure, they forfeited local disruptions and became, however inadvertently, collaborators in the process that emasculated the movement.

The ability of the local groups to attract followers had depended on their concrete victories in the relief centers. But the expanded administrative machinery, the readier funds, and the new aura of sympathy provided under the Roosevelt Administration made it possible for relief officials to regularize their agency procedures and to regain control over relief-giving. These officials often took the view that there was no true dichotomy of interest between themselves and the unemployed, but rather that conflict had been fostered by group leaders who capitalized on inadequacies to incite conflict and to exploit and manipulate the unemployed for political purposes. What was needed were standardized procedures for dealing with grievances according to "merit," rather than in response to "pressure." (Pressure, they argued, should be exerted on legislators, not on well-meaning relief administrators.) Accordingly, they began to develop precise criteria to determine who should get how much relief. At the same time, they introduced elaborate formalized procedures for negotiating with organized groups of the unemployed. In New York City, for example, guidelines for negotiations specified that unemployed delegations should be limited to three to five persons; meetings were to be held no more than every two weeks and then only with a designated staff member; unemployed delegations and the clients they represented were never to be seen simultaneously; written answers were forbidden; and finally, *no relief was to be given while the delegation was on the premises* (emphasis added, Brophy and Hallowitz, 50–53).

Throughout the country, similar rules were laid down, often through negotiations with the unemployed groups themselves. Excerpts from one, prepared by the Pennsylvania State Office of the Consultant on Community Contracts, illustrate the intricacy of the new procedures as well as the benign language in which they were couched:

OUTLINE OF PROCEDURE for the RECOGNITION of
Unemployed and Labor Organizations and
Handling Their Complaints

Representatives of the Unemployed Organization in each district will be given forms supplied by the Relief Office on which each inquiry will be clearly set down. (One complaint only on each blank.) The forms are to be made out in duplicate. . . .

When the client, having made application, has failed to get what he believes he really *needs* and is entitled to, after talking it over with his visitor, he may, if he chooses, state the case to the chosen representative of his organization, who will clearly and legibly set down the necessary information on the form supplied by the Relief Office. No inquiry will be answered if the client has not first taken the matter up with the visitor. . . . The chosen representative will . . . seek to persuade the client to *omit impossible demands*, or those involving the change of rules and regulations governing relief over which the local relief office has no control.

Each complaint, in duplicate on the form specified, will be submitted to the District Supervisor of the Relief Board at the regular meeting scheduled for this purpose. . . .

The meeting in each relief district will take place once a week with a Committee not exceeding five from the Unemployed Organization. . . .

Such cases as still appear to the Committee of the Unemployed Organization to be unsatisfactorily adjusted may be submitted to the County Executive Committee of the Unemployed Organization, and if on examination of these cases, the County Committee feels that further action is necessary, they may submit to the Executive Director for final decision. . . . *The Executive Director will receive no complaints which have not conformed to this requirement.*

The representatives of the Unemployed Organization . . . will earnestly endeavor to gain a thorough knowledge of policies and regulations and will cooperate in interpreting these to their general membership (emphasis in original, quoted in Seymour, December 1937, Appendix).

Within a short time, the presentation of complaints by committees had replaced mass demonstrations in Pennsylvania. A composite of the typical relief official's view of the benefits of such procedures was presented in the *Survey* magazine of September 1936:

We used to receive whatever sized groups the leaders sent in, rarely less than twenty-five. The result was just a mass meeting with everybody out-talking everybody else. Specific charges or grievances were completely lost in speechmaking against the general organization of society. Sometimes we'd have half a dozen delegates in a day, keeping the office in a turmoil. There just wasn't time to keep our work going and sit in on all the speechmaking. So we insisted that delegations be limited. We now . . . are able to get somewhere (quoted in Seymour, December 1937, 16).

Some relief agencies not only formalized their dealings with the unemployed groups, but saw to it that those dealings took place in a separate complaint office or public relations office, far from the relief centers. Chicago was one of the first places to establish such a system. The unemployed groups there were numerous, the Workers Committee on Unemployment alone claiming some sixty-three locals by 1933 (Karsh and Garman, 89). Repeated local demonstrations, climaxing in several injuries, inspired the county bureau of public welfare to establish a public relations office in January 1933, at the same time denying the unemployed groups access to local relief stations. At first the Chicago groups boycotted the new office, complaining of its remoteness and asserting that it had been set up to avoid pressure from the unemployed. The bureau held firm, however, and the groups gave in. The director could then report that the new office

has been and is thoroughly successful in this respect; it has relieved one of the most vexatious problems of district relief administration. Individual complaints, both from the justly aggrieved and the unsatisfiable, continue to be received at the local office but representative committees are no longer recognized there. Insomuch as some of these committees were previously disruptive of all orderly procedure, the situation is vastly improved (quoted in Seymour, December 1937, 22).

The introduction of a centralized grievance office stripped the Chicago unemployed groups of their main weapon against the relief centers. As a result, their membership declined, and internal dissension among the groups increased (Seymour, August 1937, 81). Meanwhile, the two top leaders of the Chicago Workers Committee on Unemployment took jobs with the Federal Emergency Relief Administration (Rosenzweig, 1974, 35).

In some places, relief administrators went so far as to induct leaders of the unemployed into the relief bureaucracy on the grounds that "organized client groups meet a need," and that "some process should be developed to make group 'vocalization' possible. Fair hearings and similar procedures in client group representation at advisory committee meetings should prove to be effective in relation to special situations" (quoted in Seymour, December 1937, 20). A report distributed by the Family Welfare Association elaborated the new empathy of relief officialdom: "It is only as the community understands and participates in the work that the needs of the client can be satisfactorily met" (Seymour, August 1937, 66).[42] Indeed, as unemployed groups were inducted in these ways, they came to be more "seasoned" and "reasonable," and functioned as a kind of auxiliary staff, even undertaking investigations which the agency itself did not have the facilities to perform (Seymour, August 1937, 68). Clearly, when the unemployed acceded to these new procedures, they did not pose much difficulty for local officials. A Chicago relief administrator could tell a reporter that the unemployed groups were a good thing because "They gave the men a chance to blow off steam" (Rosenzweig, 1976a).

Similar procedures were developed under the work relief program. They, too, were a stabilizing force. Beginning under the Civil Works Administration established in 1933, and later under the Works Progress Administration, the unemployed began to form associations modeled on trade unions. At the beginning, they staged strikes, often successfully, for higher wages and better working conditions. In West Virginia, for example, CWA strikers won an increase in their hourly wages from thirty-five to forty-five cents; in Illinois, they won an increase from forty to fifty cents. Strikes could also result in severe penalties. Frequently the men who participated were declared "voluntarily separated." But with the vast expansion of federal work relief in 1935, a new and more conciliatory federal policy began to evolve. Workers were conceded the right to organize and to select representatives to negotiate with relief officials; grievance procedures and appeals boards were established; state administrators were instructed in the maintenance of fair and friendly relations with workers. With these arrangements in place, the president himself declared work relief strikes illegal and authorized administrators to replace striking men.

Some leaders of the unemployed, it should be acknowledged, feared

---

42 In line with these new views on community participation, black advisory commissions were set up in the Harlem Emergency Relief Bureau and the WPA, and a substantial number of blacks were promoted to administrative positions (Naison, 403).

entanglement with the bureaucracies which administered direct relief or work relief, and urged resistance. The Communist Party organizers, schooled in the militancy of the early 1930s, were especially inclined to ignore grievance procedures, at least at first.[43] (The Socialists had never explicitly endorsed riot-like tactics.) But when relief officials held firm, Communist leaders sometimes found that urging more abrasive tactics imperiled their standing with their members (Brophy and Hallowitz, 8). Most local leaders, believing cooperation would yield them significant influence over relief policies, hailed the bureaucratic reforms, and relinquished the use of confrontation tactics. They acceded to the new grievance procedures, agreed to the elaborate rules on how negotiations should be conducted, and allowed themselves to become "client participants" or "consultants" on agency policy (on occasion to find themselves being lectured on the more constructive uses of their leisure time). The whole development appeared to be a forward-looking one, certainly in the view of relief administrators, the more progressive of whom prided themselves on cooperating with the movement's leadership by helping to "educate" the poor so that they could move from primitive "pressure tactics" to a more sophisticated level of political action—by which they meant lobbying with legislatures and negotiating with administrators, instead of disrupting relief offices.

The irony was not that relief administrators held these views, but that many of the leaders of the unemployed did as well. The earlier successes of the unemployed movement in obtaining benefits for people had not been won by lobbying or negotiating, or by using standardized complaint procedures. (If there was an effective lobby at work, it was composed of local political officials who were extremely hard pressed by rising relief costs. The United States Conference of Mayors, for example, was formed during this period expressly for the purpose of persuading the federal government to provide financial assistance to localities for relief expenditures.) What leverage these groups had exerted on local relief officials resulted from the very disturbances, the "pressure tactics," which both leaders and administrators later scorned as primitive. Victories in obtaining relief had

---

[43] The ban on relief station demonstrations in Chicago, for example, was bitterly denounced by the Communists, who continued for awhile to demonstrate in defiance of the ruling. And Herbert Benjamin defined the tendency to employ "more or less friendly" negotiations with relief officials as "right opportunism" (Rosenzweig, 1976a).

been won by mobilizing people for abrasive demonstrations and by demanding benefits on the spot for hundreds of people. By abandoning disruptive tactics in favor of bureaucratic procedures, the movement lost the ability to influence relief decisions in the local offices. No longer able to produce tangible benefits, the alliance also lost the main inducement by which it had activated great numbers of people. There was in the end no mass constituency, however impermanent, in whose name and with whose support it could negotiate. With the force of the movement lost, with its local leaders engaged in bureaucratic minuets, and with its national leaders concentrating on legislative reform through the electoral system, relief officials soon regained control over the relief centers, and the national administration regained control of relief policy.

THE CONTRACTION OF RELIEF

Even as radical leaders exerted themselves to form a national organization, dramatic changes had taken place in relief policy. In October 1934 Roosevelt declared that direct relief should be terminated. His message was familiar, echoing as it did age-old beliefs: "Continued dependence upon relief induces a spiritual and moral disintegration fundamentally destructive to the national fiber. . . . We must preserve not only the bodies of the unemployed from destitution but also their self-respect, their self-reliance and courage and determination." Accordingly, "The Federal Government must quit this business of [direct] relief" (Schlesinger, 1960, 267–268).

Instead of direct relief, the president called for a public works program to provide a job for every able-bodied person, and to that end requested an unprecedented $4 billion appropriation, to be supplemented by $880 million unspent under previous emergency relief appropriations. As for those who could not work, which included some 1.5 million families or individuals currently receiving federal emergency assistance, they would be turned over to the states and localities, as before the New Deal. Under the Social Security Act of 1935, however, the federal government would pay for a share of these state and local relief costs.

At first glance, the president's new programs seemed a bold reform, bolder by far than the federal relief program, and a victory for the

good old Texas

unemployed. The jobless workers of the country would no longer need to subsist on the degrading dole. Government would put them to work, and put them to work at rebuilding America.[44]

Meanwhile, those who could not work would be cared for by the states and localities, affirming America's tradition of local responsibility for the indigent. But while the new federal programs might have been equal to the imagination of reformers persuaded by promises of massive federal action to help the unemployed, they were to turn out in reality to be far from equal to the magnitude of need, or indeed even to the magnitude of the president's promises. Instead of 3.5 million jobs, the Works Progress Administration actually provided an average of about 2 million durings its first five years of operation. Moreover, job quotas fluctuated wildly from month to month, in no apparent relation to unemployment, so that project workers never knew when they might be laid off. In any case, those who got on were the lucky ones. At its peak, WPA accounted for only about one in four of the estimated unemployed (Howard, 854–857).[45] Thus, in 1936, when WPA provided about 2.5 million jobs, nearly 10 million were still unemployed.

With direct federal relief abolished, the great mass of the unemployed, together with the old, the infirm, and the orphaned, were once again forced to turn to state and local relief agencies, which as a practical matter could not handle the burden, and which as a political matter no longer had to. Some localities scaled down their grants; others simply abolished relief. Distress was especially severe in some industrial states, such as Ohio, Pennsylvania, and Illinois. In New Jersey licenses to beg were issued instead of relief (Seymour, December 1937, 9). Texas simply refused relief to the able-bodied (*Washington Post*, February 6, 1936). Early in 1936 FERA and WPA initiated several local surveys to ascertain what had happened to former recipients of direct federal relief who did not subsequently get on the WPA rolls. In one area after another they found large numbers of people in dire need, without food or fuel. Some were

---

[44] Hopkins probably echoed liberal sentiment when he wrote in 1936 that the work relief program signaled that the United States would never again let its poor live in destitution, and never again allow its communities to settle for the shabbiness of public life before the WPA programs (69).

[45] A count made by the Bureau of the Census in 1937 showed that all federal emergency workers (including those employed by the Civilian Conservation Corps and the National Youth Administration, as well as the WPA) accounted for only 18 percent of the total number unemployed that year (Howard, 554).

struggling to live on the pittance granted by local relief agencies; less lucky ones begged, or searched through garbage cans.[46] And in February 1936 Dr. Harry Ward, a professor at Union Theological Seminary, made a nationwide tour and reported to the press that people were slowly starving to death as a result of relief cuts (*New York Post*, February 13, 1936).

These hardships provoked some new protests. In Fall River, Massachusetts, men cut off the WPA rolls stormed the City Hall (*Boston Globe*, January 26, 1936). In New York City some 200 relief recipients demonstrated at City Hall (*New York Times*, June 27, 1936). In May 1936, a month after the alliance convention, 5,000 marchers organized by the New Jersey Workers Alliance descended on the state house when relief funds ran out. Later that summer, a similar march took place at the Pennsylvania state house. In the fall of 1936 alliance leaders conducted work stoppages and demonstrations on WPA projects to demand more adequate security wages and to protest layoffs (Karsh and Garman, 93–94).

While in a few instances demonstrators got promises from state and local officials, none of this much moved Washington. One reason was that the almost unanimous support for relief measures in 1933 had evaporated. Business was improving (although unemployment was hardly diminishing); local finances were no longer in a shambles; and what sentiment remained in favor of relief had been assuaged by the bold new programs of 1935. Meanwhile, with the worst of the national crisis apparently passed, opposition to relief in all its forms was rising, especially in the business community. A sample of press opinion at the time provides some inkling of that opposition, and the historically familiar reasons for it. The *Chicago Tribune*, on November 23, 1935, ran a story headlined "Relief Clients Refuse to Work as Corn Pickers" followed by an account of a survey of nine counties and the excuses that relief clients used to avoid working in the corn fields. The *Los Angeles Examiner*, on November 5, 1935, under the headline "Farm Loss in Millions" also explained to its readers that people on the dole refused to work. The *New Mexican* had a similar complaint on March 6, 1936, telling its readers that sheepmen could not get herders because they were on relief at forty

---

[46] Similar reports on the situation were issued by the American Association of Social Workers in 1936 and 1937. For a summary of these various findings, see Howard, 77–85.

dollars a month. The next day the *Indianapolis News* editorialized about the waste of relief, and especially about the inability of private employers to compete with the pay and working conditions provided by WPA. And on March 30, 1936, the *New York Times* summed up press opinion with an editorial explaining the importance of cutting work relief costs. There is no right to work, pontificated the editors; the protests merely indicate the "demoralization wrought by ill-advised schemes of relief."

But it was not only that the political climate had changed. The unemployed themselves were less of a threat, and so less had to be done for them. They were less of a threat partly because their numbers had been divided. Many of the most competent and able had been absorbed into the new work projects; some had even been hired to work in the relief centers. Many others had been shunted to the residual state and local direct relief programs. The remainder were left with nowhere to turn, but their numbers were reduced and their sense of indignation blunted by New Deal reforms. All of this was made easier, however, by the directions local affiliates of the Workers' Alliance had taken in the local centers. It remained to be seen what the alliance would achieve as a national lobbying force.

Organization and Electoral Influence

The Workers' Alliance of America, committed from the start to obtaining reform through lobbying, reacted to the administration's new programs by attacking the White House for its empty promises and drafting a relief bill of its own. The bill did not brook compromise. It called for a $6 billion relief appropriation for the seventeen-month period from February 1, 1936, to June 30, 1937; for relief at decent standards; and for "security wages" on work projects equal to trade union scales. The alliance used its network to deluge the White House with postcards, telegrams, and petitions. But the bill failed by overwhelming margins in the Congress.

This did not deter the alliance leaders from the strategy of persuasion and coalition on which they had embarked. If anything, Roosevelt's initiatives in other areas during 1935—the Wagner Act, the Wealth Tax Act, and the Social Security Act, for example—had the consequence of moderating whatever abrasiveness their earlier rhetoric had contained. The second alliance convention was held in the Department of Labor auditorium, and Roosevelt himself was invited to address the delegates (Rosenzweig, 1974, 35). Roosevelt declined, but Nels Anderson, Director of Labor Relations for the WPA, addressed the friendly convention instead. David Lasser subsequently described himself as the New Deal's spur on the left: "We had an agreement with Harry Hopkins always to ask for more" (Rosenzweig, 1974, 33).

But the agreement was to ask, not to get. Aubrey Williams, Hopkins' deputy, scolded an alliance delegation that demanded an increase in WPA wages, instructing them to "lay your problems before Congress when it comes back. Don't embarrass your friends" (Rosenzweig, 1974, 34). And, in April 1937, when alliance leaders met with Harry Hopkins to again demand an increase in WPA wages, Hopkins simply turned them down.

As if following the instructions of New Deal officials, leaders of the alliance, now based in Washington, D.C., began to cultivate relations with several friendly senators and congressmen during the spring of 1937, and regularized its cordial relationship with WPA officials. The alliance had been recognized as the official bargaining agent for WPA workers, and alliance leaders now corresponded frequently with WPA administrators, communicating a host of complaints, and discussing innumerable procedural questions regarding WPA administrative regulations. Some of the complaints were major, having to do with pay cuts and arbitrary layoffs. Much of the correspondence, however, had to do with minute questions of procedure, and especially with the question of whether WPA workers were being allowed to make up the time lost while attending alliance meetings.

Alliance leaders also wrote regularly to the president, reviewing the economic situation for him, deploring cuts in WPA, and calling for an expansion of the program (correspondence between David Lasser, Herbert A. Benjamin, Aubrey Williams, David Niles, Colonel F. C. Harrington, and Franklin Delano Roosevelt, WPA files).

In June 1937 the third annual convention of the Workers' Alliance, meeting in Milwaukee, called for an appropriation of $3 billion for work relief and $1 billion for direct relief, as well as the establishment of a national planning commission to plan permanent public works programs. The alliance also sponsored the Schwellenbach-Allen Resolution, which provided that no WPA worker could be discharged who was unable to find suitable private employment. The resolution never reached the floor of the Congress. In fact, Congress adjourned two days before an alliance-sponsored national march reached Washington to lobby for the measure, despite the presence of an advance contingent of hundreds of marchers (Benjamin).[47] Instead, Harry Hopkins agreed to establish another joint committee with the alliance to develop plans for a WPA labor relations board.

When a new and severe recession hit in the winter of 1937–1938, there was a wave of small demonstrations by the unemployed across the country. But there is no evidence that the national alliance called for them, or that its local organizers mobilized them. The protests appear to have occurred in cities where the unemployed had not been previously organized; not much happened in New York or Chicago, for example, which had been former strongholds of alliance

---

[47] In a personal communication to one of us, Benjamin takes strong exception to our views of the alliance activities. It is worth quoting his opinions at length: "You seem unaware that our 'lobbying' activities differed very greatly from what is generally termed mass lobbying. We engaged in mass lobbying; angry delegations besieging reactionary members of Congress in their offices. We marched and picketed and were arrested. We appeared before legislative committees not to plead but to demand. And we engaged in electoral activities that demonstrated, to some members of Congress at least, that we did have political clout that they would disregard only at their peril. (The WAA, contrary to your thesis, was credited with among others defeating the supposedly unshakable chairman of the powerful Rules Committee.) In your opinion, it was more important to disrupt some local relief office over some petty grievance of an individual. We found that it was more important to establish decent standards *and* regulations through mass actions and then handle routine matters in the way a shop chairman handles grievances. And our Executive Board and conventions, speaking for our membership, approved our policies. So we prepared and fought for the (Marcantonio) Relief and Work Standards Act and helped our local organizations prepare local ordinances modelled on this bill. We fought for higher relief appropriations to provide more WPA jobs and higher wage scales. . . . Your basic error, my good friend, is that you start with an incorrect premise. . . . The struggle of the unemployed is a political struggle. It is directed against the political institutions, the agencies of government who make policies and appropriate funds. Our job was to make this clear to backward workers who did not understand that they had a right and therefore should not plead but demand and fight. It was easy to get them to raise hell with a social worker about their own immediate grievances. We taught them to go beyond this to a higher level of political action. *And this was the most important contribution we made to the political education and development of the American workers*" (underlining in the original, August 8, 1976). We are grateful for the opportunities to cite Benjamin's disagreements with our analysis in his own words. We think his comments help to make clear that the alliance leaders were neither weak nor opportunistic. But we believe that they were mistaken in restricting their understanding of "political institutions" to legislative and executive bodies; the relief system was also a political institution, and in the midst of the depression, an important one. We think they were also mistaken in failing to recognize the relationship between massive local disruptions and the actions taken by legislative and executive bodies.

tell, he is closer to the truth than they are.

groups.[48] Only in Detroit did large numbers gather, and then at a rally sponsored by the newly formed United Auto Workers to protest inadequate relief after layoffs in the auto industry (*State Journal*, Lansing, Michigan, February 5, 1938).[49]

Undaunted by its earlier legislative failures,[50] the alliance continued to propose legislative programs, and to cement its relations with the administration. In March 1938 the alliance called a National Conference on Work and Security to "hammer out a real program" of social reconstruction (Rodman). To ensure receptivity to its proposals, the alliance mobilized itself to support the national Democratic ticket in the fall elections. The lead story in an issue of its newspaper *WORK* dated October 22, 1938, emblazoned with the headline ALLIANCE SWINGS FORCES INTO NOVEMBER ELECTION CAMPAIGN, provides a description of these efforts:

> Acting immediately on the political action program for the Workers Alliance outlined by 500 delegates at the fourth annual convention in Cleveland, Alliance locals and State organizations from coast to coast sent in reports of feverish activity on behalf of New Deal, labor and progressive candidates for governors' chairs, State Legislatures and Congress.
>
> Leaflets outlining the stake of the nation's jobless and WPA workers in the November elections; mass rallies called jointly by the Alliance and the progressive trade unions, at which pro-labor candi-

---

[48] In St. Louis, the *Globe Democrat* reported that a crowd of 750 people had demanded relief at once for the unemployed (December 17, 1937). In Grand Rapids, 500 relief and WPA clients rallied (*Grand Rapids Herald*, February 10, 1938), and in Kalamazoo a crowd of jobless workers marched to the courthouse (*Detroit Free Press*, February 22, 1938) . The *San Francisco Chronicle* reported a mass demonstration in Marshall Square to protest inadequate relief (February 27, 1938). And in Spokane, some 800 protested against cuts in the rolls (*Spokane Review*, April 1, 1938), while in Seattle, 300 jobless workers occupied the relief offices, demanding lodging and feeding (*Seattle Times*, April 2, 1938).

[49] Montgomery and Schatz report that locals of the United Electrical Workers and of the Steel Workers Organizing Committee also undertook relief battles for their unemployed members during the collapse of 1937–1938. Moreover, in Minneapolis where the Trotskyist-led Local 574 of the Teamsters was influential, a number of unions joined together in the summer of 1939 to lead a strike against WPA projects to protest cutbacks imposed by Congress.

[50] Benjamin again takes exception to our views, citing the "billions that have been spent since for unemployment insurance, public welfare, social security and the many other such measures" as gains won by the Workers' Alliance (personal communication, August 20, 1976). But all of the measures cited by Benjamin were enacted in 1935, before the Workers' Alliance had been launched. In our view, the credit for these reforms ought to go to the movement of the unemployed rather than to the organization that emerged out of it.

dates outlined their programs; house-to-house canvassing; radio programs—through every medium the Workers Alliance, speaking in
the name of 400,000 organized unemployed men and women in the
nation, is calling out its members to march to the polls on Nov.
8th. and cast ballots for progress.

New York City Alliance will climax months of strenuous political
activity with a huge and novel parade in which they will demonstrate to the public just how much WPA means to the 175,000
workers and their families on work programs in that city.

Pennsylvania Workers Alliance has rallied the entire state organization in a campaign to expose the phoney "liberalism" behind
which the Republican Party is masking in the Keystone State primaries, and calling upon the unemployed on relief and WPA to vote
for the New Deal, Governor Earle slate to the man.

Minnesota Alliance has begun carrying on a vigorous campaign
for Governor Benson and the election of progressive Farmer-Labor
Party candidates. . . .

Out West, in Montana, the Workers Alliance has thrown the
full weight of its powerful organization behind the campaign to
re-elect one of Congress' foremost progressives, Jerry O'Connell. . . .

Events would soon demonstrate how powerful the organization was.
The electoral efforts of the alliance were not sufficient to command
even token responses from the National Administration. When the
alliance invited Aubrey Williams, deputy administrator of WPA
to speak at its September 1938 convention, he turned them down.
When they substituted Father Francis J. Haas, a New Deal official,
he cancelled at the last minute, but not before some 100,000 leaflets
had been distributed which carried his name.

More important, WPA funds were cut in 1939 after Congress had
introduced provisions that both reduced WPA wages and compelled
workers to be terminated who had been on the WPA rolls for
eighteen continuous months. The leadership of the alliance, as was
its wont, called a National Right-to-Work Congress, and on June 13
Lasser and Benjamin respectfully submitted the opinions of the
assembled delegates of the unemployed to the president. The unemployed, they said, had called for public works and government
measures to stimulate the economy, but assured the president that
"It is the conviction of the people represented in our Congress that
the failure to achieve recovery to date could not be laid at the door
of your administration." They concluded with this mild reproach:

The congress also asked us to convey to you the feeling of disappointment at the inadequate request for funds for work for the unem-

ployed for the coming 12 months. This disappointment was especially keen because the delegates could not reconcile your request with your generous and sound philosophy on this question, so enthusiastically endorsed by them . . . and expressed the hope that your administration could see fit, before it is too late, to reconsider its estimate in the light of present day economic and business conditions. . . . The delegates wished us to convey to you their heartfelt appreciation for your wise and courageous leadership, and to express our earnest hope for a program which will make it possible for them to do their part as Americans to help achieve recovery, security and plenty for our country and its people.

A few weeks later Lasser followed the letter with a telegram. The tone was more urgent, ending with a request for permission to release the telegram to the press. Lasser was informed by the White House to do as he pleased (WPA files).

In fact, the alliance was of no political consequence. The end had already come, and was evident by the fourth annual convention in September 1938, which drew only five hundred delegates. The long succession of legislative defeats, and the bureaucratic envelopment which caused a decline of grassroots protests, had taken their toll. Membership and militancy had ebbed. Cleavages among the various factions widened; embittered and frustrated, the disparate groups that remained began to fall out. In 1940 David Lasser resigned to take a job with the WPA, and a year later the Workers' Alliance of America was quietly dissolved.

The Workers' Alliance of America had lofty aspirations. Until 1937 its constitution called for "abolition of the profit system," although its language became more moderate as its commitment to the New Deal became more ardent. Its legislative proposals included, among other things, all-inclusive unemployment insurance to be paid for by individual and corporate income taxes, and to be administered by workers and farmers. Communists, Socialists, Musteites, Trotskyites, and other unaffiliated radicals had agreed on the importance of building a national organization to exert electoral pressure for these reforms.[51] But even while the alliance leaders were

---

[51] Brendan Sexton, who was head of the New York Alliance, blames the demise of the organization on the Communist Party activists who became so committed to New Deal mayors, governors, and other public officials, including Roosevelt, that they were unwilling to confront them. "We couldn't keep the organization alive if we were unwilling to

taking pride in their organizational structure and their dues-paying membership, and were inventing far-reaching legislative reforms, their local affiliates had become entangled in bureaucratic procedures and were declining. That leadership failed to understand that government does not need to meet the demands of an organized vanguard in order to assuage mass unrest, although it does have to deal with the unrest itself. One way that government deals with unrest is through the vanguard. By creating a political climate that encouraged faith in the possibility of national electoral influence, the New Deal destroyed the incentive of the leaders of the unemployed to exacerbate disorder.[52] And by instituting procedures on the local level that subverted the use of disruptive tactics, the New Deal undermined the ability of the leaders of the unemployed to exacerbate disorder. Once that process had unfolded, the Workers' Alliance of America no longer mattered, one way or the other.

The particular tragedy of the Workers' Alliance is not that it failed to achieve the fundamental reforms to which it was committed. Achievements of that order are the result of forces larger than leaders alone can muster, and the alliance was neither the first to try nor the last to fail. Rather, if there is a tragedy, it is in the role the alliance played during the brief and tumultuous period when people were ready to act against the authorities and against the norms that ordinarily bind them. Instead of exploiting the possibilities of the time by pushing turbulence to its outer limits, the leaders of the unemployed set about to build organization and to press for legislation, and in so doing, they virtually echoed the credo of officialdom itself.

For a brief time, there were twenty million people on the relief rolls, but millions more badly needed relief and never got it. And when the alliance abandoned the relief centers to lobby for lofty programs of basic change, those millions on relief were abandoned

---

demonstrate against the very people who were refusing to expand WPA and to improve the relief system" (personal correspondence, February 4, 1970). While we agree with Sexton's evaluation of the outcome of alliance strategies, we see little evidence that nonparty leaders of the alliance took a different stance. We should also note that Sexton disagrees with our interpretation in other respects, arguing that the alliance flourished under the bureaucratization of relief, and the bureaucratization of its own internal structure, and was destroyed only by its unwillingness to demonstrate against New Deal officialdom, a policy that Sexton apparently considers unrelated to these organizational developments.

[52] Brian Glick draws conclusions broadly similar to ours regarding the effects of New Deal programs on the orientation of the alliance leadership on the national level.

too: the rolls were cut back and millions who were still unemployed were once again left destitute. The tragedy, in sum, is that the alliance did not win as much as it could, while it could.

References

Abbott, Edith. *The Tenements of Chicago, 1908–1935*. Chicago: University of Chicago Press, 1936.

Bakke, E. Wight. *The Unemployed Man: A Social Study*. New York: E. P. Dutton and Co., 1934.

———. *Citizens Without Work: A Study of the Effects of Unemployment Upon the Workers' Social Relations and Practices*. New Haven: Yale University Press, 1940.

Benjamin, Herbert. "Why We Marched." *Social Work Today*, October 1937.

Bernstein, Irving. *The Lean Years: A History of the American Worker, 1920–1933*. Baltimore: Penguin Books, 1970.

———. *The Turbulent Years: A History of the American Worker, 1933–1941*. Boston: Houghton Mifflin Co., 1971.

Bird, Caroline. *The Invisible Scar*. New York: David McKay Co., 1966.

Boyer, Richard O., and Morais, Herbert M. *Labor's Untold Story*. New York: United Electrical Radio and Machine Workers of America, 1972.

Brecher, Jeremy. *Strike!* Greenwich, Connecticut: Fawcett Publication, 1974.

Brophy, Alice, and Hallowitz, George. "Pressure Groups and the Relief Administration in New York City." Unpublished professional project. New York: New York School of Social Work, April 8, 1937.

Brown, Josephine C. *Public Relief, 1929–1939*. New York: Henry Holt and Co., 1940.

Buhle, Paul Merlyn. "Marxism in the United States, 1900–1940." Unpublished Ph.D. dissertation, University of Wisconsin, Madison, 1975.

Cayton, Horace. "No Rent Money . . . 1931." *The Nation*, September 9, 1931.

Chandler, Lester V. *America's Greatest Depression, 1929–1941*. New York: Harper and Row, 1970.

Colcord, Joanna C., et al. *Emergency Work Relief As Carried Out in Twenty-six American Communities, 1930–1931, with Suggestions for Setting Up a Program*. New York: Russell Sage Foundation, 1932.

Cooley, Robert Angell. *The Family Encounters the Depression*. New York: Charles Scribner's Sons, 1936.

Cross, Frank Clay, "Revolution in Colorado." *The Nation,* February 7, 1934.

De Caux, Len. *Labor Radical From the Wobblies to CIO: A Personal History.* Boston: Beacon Press, 1970.

Edelman, Murray. "Growth and Expansion." In *Labor and the New Deal,* edited by Milton Derber and Edwin Young. Madison: University of Wisconsin Press, 1957.

Feder, Leah H. *Unemployment Relief in Periods of Depression.* New York: Russell Sage Foundation, 1936.

Foner, Philip. *History of the Labor Movement in the United States.* New York: International Publishers, 1947.

Gilpin, DeWitt. "Fired for Inefficiency." *Social Work Today* 3 (November 1935).

Glick, Brian. "The Thirties: Organizing the Unemployed." *Liberation,* September-October 1967.

Gosnell, Harold. *Machine Politics: Chicago Model.* Chicago: University of Chicago Press, 1937.

———. *The Rise of Negro Politics in Chicago.* Chicago: University of Chicago Press, 1967.

Greenstein, Harry. "The Maryland Emergency Relief Program—Past and Future." Address delivered before the Maryland Conference of Social Work, February 25, 1935.

Gutman, Herbert G. "The Failure of the Movement by the Unemployed for Public Works in 1873." *Political Science Quarterly* 80 (June 1965).

———. *Work, Culture and Society in Industrializing America.* New York: Alfred A. Knopf, 1976.

Herndon, Angelo. *Let Me Live.* New York: Arno Press and The New York Times, 1969.

Hofstadter, Richard, and Wallace, Michael, eds. *American Violence: A Documentary History.* New York: Vintage Books, 1971.

Hopkins, Harry L. *Spending to Save: The Complete Story of Relief.* New York: W. W. Norton and Co., 1936.

Howard, Donald C. *The WPA and Federal Relief Policy.* New York: Russell Sage Foundation, 1943.

Huntington, Emily H. *Unemployment Relief and the Unemployed in the San Francisco Bay Region, 1929–1934.* Berkeley: University of California Press, 1939.

Karsh, Bernard, and Garman, Phillip L. "The Impact of the Political Left." In *Labor and the New Deal,* edited by Milton Derber and Edwin Young. Madison: University of Wisconsin Press, 1957.

Keeran, Roger Roy. "Communists and Auto Workers: The Struggle for a Union, 1919–1941." Unpublished Ph. D. dissertation, University of Wisconsin, 1974.

Kerr, Clark, "Productive Self-Help Enterprises of the Unemployed." Unpublished Ph. D. dissertation, University of California, Berkeley, 1939.

Komarovsky, Mirra. *The Unemployed Man and His Family.* New York: Dryden Press, 1940.

Kurzman, Paul. *Harry Hopkins and the New Deal.* Fairlawn, New Jersey: R. E. Burdick Publishers, 1974.

Lasswell, Harold D., and Blumenstock, Dorothy. *World Revolutionary Propaganda.* 1939. Reprint. Plainview, N.Y.: Books for Libraries Press, 1970.

Leab, Daniel. " 'United We Eat': The Creation and Organization of the Unemployed Councils in 1930." *Labor History* 8 (Fall 1967).

Lescohier, Don D., and Brandeis, Elizabeth. *History of Labor in the United States, 1896–1932* (in the 4-volume series *The History of Labor in the United States,* compiled by John R. Commons and his associates). New York: Macmillan Co., 1935.

Lynd, Robert S., and Lynd, Helen Merrell. *Middletown in Transition: A Study in Cultural Conflicts.* New York: Harcourt, Brace and Co., 1937.

Moley, Raymond. "Comment." *Political Science Quarterly* 87 (December 1972).

Montgomery, David, and Schatz, Ronald. "Facing Layoffs." *Radical America* 10 (March–April 1976).

Naison, Mark. "The Communist Party in Harlem, 1928–1936." Unpublished Ph. D. dissertation, Columbia University, 1975.

Prickett, James Robert. "Communists and the Communist Issue in the American Labor Movement." Unpublished Ph. D. dissertation, University of California, Los Angeles, 1975.

Rodman, Selden. "Lasser and the Workers' Alliance." *The Nation,* September 10, 1938.

Rogg, Nathan. "The Unemployed Unite." *Social Work Today* 3 (June 1936).

Roosevelt, Franklin D. *The Public Papers and Addresses of Franklin D. Roosevelt,* Vol. 1, compiled by Samuel I. Roseman. New York: Random House, 1938.

Rosenzweig, Roy. "Radicals in the Great Depression: Socialists and the Unemployed, 1929–1936." Unpublished paper, January 24, 1974.

———. "Radicals and the Jobless: The Musteites and the Unemployed Leagues, 1932–1936." *Labor History* 16 (Winter 1975).

————. "Organizations of the Unemployed in the 1930's." Unpublished paper, January 1976.

————. "Organizing the Unemployed: The Early Years of the Great Depression, 1929–1933." *Radical America* 10 (July–August 1976).

Schlesinger, Arthur M., Jr. *The Age of Roosevelt*, Vol. 1: *The Crisis of the Old Order, 1919–1933*. Boston: Houghton Mifflin Co., 1957.

————. *The Age of Roosevelt*, Vol. 3: *The Politics of Upheaval*. Boston: Houghton Mifflin Co., 1960.

Seymour, Helen. "The Organized Unemployed." Unpublished Ph.D. dissertation, University of Chicago, August 1937.

————. Unpublished report to the Committee on Social Security of the Social Science Research Council, December 1, 1937.

Stouffer, Samuel, and Lazarsfeld, Paul. *Research Memorandum on the Family in the Depression*. Social Science Research Council Bulletin No. 29.

Terkel, Studs. *Hard Times: An Oral History of the Great Depression.* New York: Pantheon Books, 1970.

White, Clyde R., and White, Mary K. *Relief Policies in the Depression.* Social Science Research Council Bulletin No. 38.

Woodroofe, Kathleen. *From Charity to Social Welfare.* Toronto: University of Toronto Press, 1966.

WPA General Files 040, National Archives and Record Service.

CHAPTER
3

The Industrial Workers' Movement

The experience of labor unions in the United States is the historical bedrock on which the organizer's credo is grounded. As organizers recount this history, factory workers finally organized into large, stable organizations after many bloody travails, and were then able to exert influence in the factory. Moreover, organization was said to have yielded influence in politics as well. The large voting numbers and financial resources which the unions accumulated presumably gave working people a measure of political power. To be sure, some believers in the credo are disappointed in the way unions have used their power, blaming an oligarchical leadership for a narrow preoccupation with wages and hours and for the avoidance of more fundamental economic and political issues. However, the belief that working people were able to gain both economic and electoral power through organization still holds firm. It is this belief that suggests to organizers the model other powerless groups should follow.

But on closer historical scrutiny, the bedrock turns out to be sand. Factory workers had their greatest influence and were able to extract their most substantial concessions from government during the early years of the Great Depression *before they were organized into unions*. Their power was not rooted in organization, but in their capacity to disrupt the economy. For the most part strikes, demonstrations, and sit-downs spread during the mid-1930s despite existing unions rather than because of them. Since these disorders occurred at a time of widespread political instability, threatened political leaders were forced to respond with placating concessions. One of these concessions was protection by government of the right to

96

organize. Afterwards, union membership rose, largely because government supported unionization. But once organized, the political influence of workers declined. The unions not only failed to win new victories from government commensurate with the victories of unorganized workers during the 1930s, but those already won were whittled away. Before we go on to offer our explanation of why industrial workers became a political force during the depression, we need to say a little about their lack of force before the depression.

The State Against Labor

When industrial workers band together they have power in their dealings with capital, or so it would seem. Their power is of course the disruptive power of the strike. If workers withhold their labor, production is halted and profits dwindle, and employers are pressured into making concessions. Moreover, as economic concentration proceeds, and the scale of enterprises and their interpenetration increases, the power of labor ought to increase as well. Not only do large-scale enterprises facilitate collective action among workers, but the impact of strikes is more severe, reverberating throughout an interdependent and concentrated economy.

All this may seem to be true in principle, but in historical fact it has not been. Between the onset of rapid industrialization at the end of the nineteenth century and the Great Depression, the history of strikes in mass production industries was largely a history of failure.[1] The explanation of this failure has preoccupied students of labor history. The interpretations which have resulted tend to fasten on divisions in the American working class which inhibited the solidarity necessary for effective strike action:[2] the corrosive effect of the business cycle on labor unity; deep status and ethnic conflicts among

---

[1] Gutman points out that not all strikes were defeated, and he cites information collected by the New Jersey Bureau of Labor Statistics on 890 New Jersey industrial disputes between 1881 and 1887 showing that strikers won over half the recorded disputes (48). But during these and succeeding years, the largest industrial confrontations were defeated, as in the major railroad, mining, and steel strikes.

[2] One of the most influential of these interpretations can be found in Selig Perlman. More radical analysts score Perlman for his defense of the bread-and-butter trade unionism that has emerged in the United States, but they do not take major exception to his analysis of the factors accounting for the historic lack of class consciousness.

workers; the divisive effects of the promise and reality of upward mobility; and the oligarchical and exclusionary character of such unions as did exist.

We will briefly review each of these explanations, for we think they help to explain the weakness of strike power. There can be no doubt that solidarity was essential to the effectiveness of strikes, for without it striking workers were easily replaced and production was easily continued. And there can be no doubt that American workers were divided. These divisions had their roots in features of the American economy and in the characteristics of the American working population, as well as in deliberate practices of employers designed to exacerbate divisions in order to turn workers against each other. With this review made, however, we will go on to argue that divisiveness among American workers fails to account adequately for the defeat of labor struggles. In instance after instance, worker struggles did not collapse from lack of internal unity; they were smashed by the coercive power of the state.

First and most obviously worker solidarity was influenced by market conditions. Workers could join together in strikes and slow-downs more readily when business prospered and when the demand for labor was strong. But during periods of depression, men and women were laid off, wages were cut, and hours were lengthened. Defensive strikes and riots sometimes erupted during depressions, but they usually had little effect. Not only did employers find it easier to resist strikes when trade was slow and there was less to be lost by halting production, but with jobs scarce, workers were forced to undersell each other in the scramble for employment. Workers' associations which emerged during boom times were unable to resist these forces; they were usually simply wiped out when the market fell.[3]

Second, solidarity was also inhibited because the American working population was fragmented by intense divisions determined by occupational status, by race, and by ethnicity. The result was a commensurately weak recognition of class commonalities. To some extent, these divisions were a natural and inevitable result of the heterogeneous origins of the American working population. But it was also the policy of employers to take advantage of such distinc-

---

[3] Boyer and Morais report, for example, that of the thirty national unions in existence before the depression of 1873, only eight or nine remained by 1877 (40).

tions, to elaborate them, and by doing so, to weaken working-class solidarity.

Thus it is well known that the status-conscious artisans of the nineteenth century looked down upon the growing stratum of unskilled workers created by industrialization. This sense of themselves as a class apart was strengthened when industrialists agreed to bargain only with skilled workers during mass strikes. By the end of the nineteenth century, as advancing mechanization drove many skilled workers into the ranks of the unskilled, and as a series of large-scale industrial strikes were defeated, status anxieties and simple fear combined to heighten craft exclusiveness among the remaining skilled workers.[4] Even as this leveling process went forward, the advantages of occupational and status distinctions appear to have been recognized by industrialists, and under the banner of "scientific management" some industries adopted the deliberate policy of elaborating job distinctions, both hierarchically and horizontally, thus multiplying divisions among workers.[5]

Status and job distinctions were often aggravated by racial and ethnic differences, and race and ethnicity also became the basis on which employers divided workers who were similarly situated. The expanded need for unskilled labor was filled by a vast increase in immigration, first from Ireland and Northern Europe, later from Southern Europe, then from Eastern Europe (and in the West, from the Orient). The immigrants provided a virtually bottomless reservoir of helpless and poverty-stricken workers on which employers could draw. The regular flow of immigrants was assured by powerful industrial lobbies which opposed any restrictions on "free labor" (while protecting fervently the tariff restrictions on free commerce).[6] Between 1860 and 1920, 28.5 million immigrants came to the United

---

[4] Leon Fink argues that in the 1880s skilled workers were at the heart of working-class mobilizations, and that they received support from a broad range of groups. He attributes the subsequent general rebuff of new immigrants and blacks by skilled workers to the collapse of the Knights of Labor and the defeat of a series of industrial strikes (67–68).

[5] Recent work by radical economists provides evidence that at the end of the nineteenth century, large corporations were restructuring job titles so as to elaborate status divisions among their workers, and to thereby inhibit solidarity and depress wages. See for example Stone; and Gordon, Edwards, and Reich. The rationale and methods for such fragmentation of natural worker groupings were provided by the doctrines of scientific management (Davis).

[6] The labor was "free" only from the employers' perspective. In 1864 Congress authorized employers to import foreign workers under contracts which indentured them to work for their employers until their passage was paid off (Brecher, xiii).

States (Brecher, xiii). As low-paid foreigners began to squeeze out higher-paid native American workers in many occupations, ethnic antagonisms were added to the antagonism between the skilled and the unskilled, further dissipating any sense of a common fate among workers. Nor were employers innocent in promoting these effects. Different immigrant groups were regularly pitted against each other, one group being used to underbid the wages of the other. Commons wrote of a visit he paid to a Chicago employment office in 1904:

> I saw, seated on benches around the office, a sturdy group of blond-haired Nordics. I asked the employment agent, "How comes it you are employing only Swedes?" He answered, "Well, you see, it is only for this week. Last week we employed Slovaks. We change about among different nationalities and languages. It prevents them from getting together. We have the thing systematized" (Lescohier and Brandeis, xxv).

Brecher cites a Carnegie plant manager writing in 1875: "My experience has been that Germans and Irish, Swedes and what I denominate 'buckwheats' (young American country boys), judiciously mixed, make the most effective and tractable force you can find" (120). As late as 1937, the Jones and McLaughlin Steel Corporation maintained rigid segregation between nationality groups, skillfully playing one off against the other (Bernstein, 1971, 475).[7] Such practices were, of course, far more likely to be resorted to during strikes, when immigrants and native blacks were used as strikebreakers.[8]

Third, in comparison with Europe, workers in America had greater opportunities for both economic and geographic mobility, at least until the end of the nineteenth century. Wages in the new

---

[7] Ethnic consciousness, by isolating foreign-language groups, also created an insular environment which made possible the development of militant protest among some of these groups. Thus Gutman reports that immigrant workers in the mid-1880s joined trade unions in far greater numbers than their proportion in the work force, acting out of what he defines as a proclivity to seek self-protection and continuity of culture and tradition (48–49). Fink argues similarly that ethnic solidarity played an important role in the upheavals of the 1880s, and gives examples of both Polish and Irish worker mobilizations in which ethnic nationalism and working-class assertiveness seemed to energize each other (66). Many years later, the Communist Party "found comparative difficulty in establishing roots among native-born English-speaking workers," and "relied heavily for support on the foreign language federations . . ." (Aronowitz, 142).

[8] Aronowitz reports that in the Homestead steel mill in 1907, English-speaking immigrants earned $16 a week, native-born whites $22, blacks were earnings $17, and Slavs who had been brought in with blacks to break the Homestead strike fifteen years earlier were earning $12 (150).

country were higher; as manufacturing expanded, opportunities seemed to abound, at least for the lucky, the skilled, the ambitious, and at least during periods of prosperity.[9] Moreover, for those who were not destitute, there was the opportunity for free land and free mining in the west.[10] Commons noted that the leaders of defeated labor struggles in the East could often be found on the free land of the West (Lescohier and Brandeis, xiii). Indeed, the Homestead Act which opened up the public domain in the West is generally regarded as a concession to labor, a concession which did not improve the lot of factory workers, but which gave a few of them the alternative of not being factory workers. Opportunity for advancement or for land thus drained off some of the more discontented and perhaps the more able, and also helped to sustain among those left behind the hope that they too could move upward, that their future lay not with collective struggles of the present, but with the individual opportunities of a future day.

Still another factor inhibiting and weakening industrial struggles was the status-conscious and oligarchical character of those workers' organizations that did develop. These were usually local unions of artisans whose ability to organize owed much to a tradition of brotherhood and pride in craft, as well as to the leverage that such organized craftsmen could exert in industries where they controlled entry into their occupations. These sources of strength, however, encouraged them to ignore and even to scorn the growing mass of unskilled workers. Moreover, the inevitable tendencies toward oligarchy, noted by Michels in Europe, seem to have been stronger within the craft unions in the United States, perhaps because class consciousness was weaker, mobility strivings sharper, and the business ethos more widely shared by workers and their leaders.[11] Over time, the leaders of craft unions came to function more as labor contractors than as labor leaders, depending more on collusive arrangements with employers for the maintenance of their leadership

---

[9] Gutman argues that developing industries did in fact offer unusual opportunities for mobility to skilled craftsmen and mechanics in the early stages of American industrialization (211–233).

[10] Roberta Ash points out that by the late nineteenth century, most urban workers were too impoverished to undertake the move west (36).

[11] The custom of paying union leaders salaries comparable to business executives, a practice not nearly so marked in Europe, is one evidence of these tendencies; the practice of investing union funds in various business ventures is another.

positions than on a united and militant following.[12] The result was a leadership that was less and less inclined to engage in strikes or agitation, and less and less interested in recruiting a mass following. When mass strikes did occur, they were often opposed by established union leaders, some of whom went so far in the big strikes of the late nineteenth and early twentieth centuries as to encourage their members to engage in strikebreaking.

In the preceding paragraphs, we have tried to summarize the prevailing explanations of American labor's inability to make much progress before the Great Depression. It is our view, however, that explanations pointing to divisions among industrial workers miss the main point. Mass strikes did occur, and the strikers often held fast, obdurate in the face of overwhelming economic necessity. The ultimate enfeeblement of workers was not just their lack of solidarity, and their consequent lack of economic power, but their lack of political power. Whatever force workers mounted against their bosses, whatever their determination and their unity, they could not withstand the legal and military power of the state, and that power was regularly used against them. During the colonial period, industrial codes established maximum wages, declared work compulsory, and forbade the combination of workmen for the purpose of raising wages (Raybeck, 12). The courts continued to view unions as criminal conspiracies until 1842 (Fleming, 123). As time went on, the laws regulating labor softened, but the practices of government did not. Until the Great Depression, striking workers were regularly subject to court injunctions and criminal prosecutions.[13] And what could not be done by law was done by military force. Company troops, deputized for the occasion by local sheriffs, state militia, and federal troops, were all deployed time and again to attack strikers and to protect strikebreakers. In the face of this kind of opposition, strikes were bound to fail, no matter whether the workers were united or not.

Some of the bitterest examples of the use of force by government

---

[12] These exchanges between labor leaders and employers were often mediated by local political machine leaders. For an interesting discussion of the links between union leaders and machine leaders, see Rogin.

[13] Some 1,845 labor injunctions were issued by federal and state courts from 1880 to 1930 (Bernstein, 1970, 200). The courts were also used to frame the leaders of workers' struggles on such charges as murder or insurrection or anarchy, as illustrated by the cases of the Molly McGuires, Joe Hill, the Haymarket anarchists, Big Bill Haywood, and Sacco and Vanzetti, to name only a few of the most notorious instances.

against strikers occurred during the severe depressions of the late nineteenth century when unemployment and wage cuts made people desperate, and the scale of the calamity forged a unity among workers which led to epidemics of protests. In 1877, when four years of severe depression had led to sharp wage cuts and left perhaps one million industrial workers unemployed, a strike on the Pennsylvania and Baltimore and Ohio railroads led to riots that swept through a dozen major rail centers, escalating to open conflict between workers and troops. When local police and state militia were unable to handle the disturbances—in Pittsburgh, for example, police and militia were openly sympathetic with the mob that was burning railroad property to the ground—3,000 federal troops were rushed from city to city under the direction of the War Department. Order was finally restored, leaving twenty-six dead in Pittsburgh, where the mob openly resisted; thirteen dead and forty-three wounded in Reading, Pennsylvania; nineteen dead and more than one hundred wounded in Chicago (Brecher, 1–23). Property damage reached about $5 million (Walsh, 20). It was subsequent to these upheavals that the huge National Guard Armories were constructed in the heart of America's big cities (Josephson, 365). A decade later, a new depression triggered another, even greater, uprising of workers, and again the strikes were broken with the aid of police and militia, justified this time by the Haymarket bombing incident.

The scenario was reenacted again in the depression of the 1890s when wage cuts and rising unemployment in manufacturing and transportation precipitated strikes involving some 750,000 workers, primarily in steel, in mining, and in the railroad industry. In Pennsylvania, the governor called out 7,000 troops to deal with the Homestead steel workers; in Idaho, in the Coeur d'Alene region, National Guard and federal troops rounded up all union miners and put them in a stockade where they were held for months without charges. The Pullman railroad strike of 1894 brought thousands of federal troops to Chicago, with the result that an estimated thirty-four people were killed, and Eugene Debs was imprisoned. Subsequently, the federal government stationed marshals in numerous railroad centers to protect railroad property, at a cost of at least $400,000 (Taft and Ross, 290–299; Greenstone, 21).[14]

---

[14] In the period from 1880–1904 the governors of Colorado spent over one million dollars for such military actions against workers, financed by the issuance of "insurrection" bonds (Boyer and Morais, 142 fn).

These statistics almost surely fail to suggest the true magnitude of violence by government against workers during this period. One contemporary writer, for example, estimated that in the years 1902–1904 alone, 198 persons were killed and 1,986 injured (cited in Taft and Ross, 380). Overall, Taft and Ross were able to identify 160 occasions on which state and federal troops were called out to deal with labor agitations. As Eugene Debs said after the strike by his American Railway Union was crushed by the federal government in 1894:

> We have only got a number, and a limited number, of poorly paid men in our organization, and when their income ceases they are starving. We have no power of the Government behind us. We have no recognized influence in society on our side. . . . On the other side, the corporations are in perfect alliance; they have all the things that money can command, and that means a subsidized press, that they are able to control the newspapers, and means a false or vitiated public opinion. The clergy almost steadily united in thundering their denunciations; then the courts, then the State militia, then the Federal troops; everything and all things on the side of the corporations (cited in Brecher, 94).

When the steel strike of 1919 was defeated by United States Steel, a report of the Interchurch Commission echoed the judgments of Eugene Debs twenty-five years earlier:

> The United States Steel Corporation was too big to be beaten by 300,000 working men. It had too large a cash surplus, too many allies among other businesses, too much support from government officers, local and national, too strong influence with social institutions such as the press and the pulpit, it spread over too much of the earth—still retaining absolutely centralized control—to be defeated by widely scattered workers of many minds, many fears, varying states of pocketbook and under a comparatively improvised leadership (quoted in Walsh, 56).

In a handful of instances, government remained neutral or supportive, and that spelled the difference between the success or failure of strikes. For example, during the uprisings of the 1890s, while federal and state troops were being used to break strikes elsewhere, the UMW called a national strike in an effort to organize the central competitive coalfields. When two recalcitrant companies in Illinois imported scabs whom the striking miners prevented from entering the mining areas, Governor John B. Tanner of Illinois sent National Guardsmen to avert the threat of violence, but with instructions not

American business led the way in Western repression.

to assist the mine owners. Both companies eventually signed with the UMW (Taft and Ross, 300–302).

It is often said that employers in the United States were exceptional for the virulence of their opposition to the demands of workers.[15] Their opposition is not difficult to understand. But who is to say that they would have been successful in the face of large-scale strikes had not government on all levels regularly come to their aid?[16] In other words, without the power to restrain their presidents, their governors, and often their mayors[17] from using troops against them, workers remained helpless, stripped of the economic power of the strike by the coercive power of government.[18]

That this was so in the nineteenth century was perhaps partly because the political power of employers, based on economic power, was not yet tempered by the mass numbers of a large industrial class. The United States remained predominantly a country of independent farmers and proprietors until the Civil War. Moreover, even after industrialization had advanced, and even after the number of wage workers grew, a rural, small proprietor view of American life, and of the role of private property in American life, continued to dominate the political culture. By 1880, wage and salaried employees accounted for 62 percent of the labor force, and farmers and small proprietors accounted for only 37 percent (Reich, Table 4–J, 175). But these numbers were still submerged by a political ideology that, by denying the realities of economic concentration, may have thwarted the popular emergence of urban, working-class interests, at least on the national and state levels.

[15] Nowhere else was the use of blacklists and the employment of private armies, as well as the elaborate network of employer espionage and blacklisting services, so highly developed. By the end of the nineteenth century, the ranks of Pinkerton agents and "reservists" outnumbered the standing army of the nation (Brecher, 55).

[16] In the Homestead strike of 1889, for example, strikers successfully battled Pinkertons and strikebreakers, only then to confront the Pennsylvania National Guard as well as legal proceedings which broke the strike (Ash, 122).

[17] Gutman argues persuasively that this pattern did not always hold in medium-sized industrial cities—in contrast to the large metropolises. In the context of rapid and disruptive industrialization, working people in industrial cities were sometimes able to mobilize sufficient community support to at least neutralize local government officials in industrial conflicts (234–260).

[18] "Employers in no other country," writes Lewis Lorwin, "with the possible exception of those in the metal and machine trades of France, have so persistently, so vigorously, at such costs, and with such a conviction of serving a cause, opposed and fought trade unions as the American employing class. *In no other Western country have employers been so much aided in their opposition to unions by civil authorities, the armed forces of government and their courts*" (emphasis ours, 355).

Perhaps a more important factor than American political culture in accounting for the absence of class-oriented politics was the development of political institutions that created the illusion of popular participation and influence. Long before an industrial working class had developed, American workers were given the franchise, in most states by the 1820s. One result was that the political alienation to which Bendix ascribes the European working-class movements of the nineteenth century did not emerge so acutely in the United States, for workers were at least granted the vote, the symbol of political influence, and they were included in the rituals of political participation as well. Thus artisans reacted to the depression of 1828–1831 by forming workingmen's parties, particularly in New York and Philadelphia.[19] They created a stir sufficient to produce some concessions, such as the end of imprisonment for debt and free public schools. Meanwhile, leaders of the workingmen's party in New York City were inducted into Tammany (Pelling, 32–33). These precedents were to be repeated and expanded as the working class enlarged. Big city machines were able to win and hold the allegiance of workers by absorbing their leaders and by conferring favors and symbols that sustained the loyalties of workers on individual, neighborhood, and ethnic bases. This not only prevented the emergence of industrial workers as a political force directed to class issues, but it actually freed political leaders on all levels of government to use police, militia, and troops against striking workers without jeopardizing working-class electoral support.

In the 1930s, this pattern was broken and government was forced to make accommodations to industrial workers, as industrial workers. Staughton Lynd puts the change succinctly: "Not only in the 1890s but equally in the period after World War I, the national government smashed emerging industrial unions. In the 1930s the national government sponsored them" (Lynd, 1974, 30).

The structural changes that presaged this new accommodation had been proceeding rapidly as industrialization increasingly dominated American life. The transformation was complete and precipitate. In 1860 the United States ranked behind England, France, and Germany in the value of its manufacturing products; by 1894 the United States was not only in the lead, but its manufacturing products nearly equaled those of England, Germany, and France to-

[19] Ash reports sixty-one workingmen's parties during this period.

gether (Gutman, 33). In the next few years, concentration proceeded apace, as mergers and consolidation resulted in the creation of corporations with billions of dollars in assets. By 1904 the top 4 percent of American concerns produced 57 percent of the total value of industrial products (Weinstein, 1). And by 1910 overall investment in manufacturing had increased twelve-fold over 1860 (Brecher, xii).

As a result, the number of workers employed in industry also increased to about 40 percent of the labor force (Reich, Table 4–L, 178), and these workers were concentrated in ever-larger industrial empires.[20] Taken together, these changes set the stage for the successful struggles of the 1930s. The advance of industrialization meant that when the economic collapse of the 1930s occurred, no sector of the economy was insulated, and no sector of the population spared. The discontents which galvanized workers also affected virtually the entire population, with the result that worker agitations were more threatening to political leaders. At the same time the industrial working class itself had enlarged, and its role in the economy had become more central, so that workers themselves were more menacing when insurgent. But if these structural changes created the preconditions for a political accommodation by government to industrial workers, the change was not to come until the workers themselves rose up in defiance with such disruptive effects that they forced the hand of the state.

Depression and the Preconditions
for Insurgency

Publicly the White House responded to the crash of 1929 and to rapidly mounting unemployment by issuing a steady stream of good cheer, declaring that the economy was fundamentally sound and that employment was picking up. Privately, however, Hoover was apparently less sanguine. In late November he called a conference of leading industrialists at which he described the situation as serious, and urged industry to help minimize panic by maintaining the

---

[20] After 1920 the proportion of factory workers in the labor force stabilized, and the number of retailing, service, professional, and government workers rose much faster (Bernstein, 1970, 55–63).

existing level of wages. For the first year, at least, most of the nation's big corporations cooperated, and wages held relatively firm for those still working.

But the depression rapidly worsened to the point that industry approached collapse. By 1932 half of all manufacturing units had closed down; production fell by 48 percent; reported corporate income fell from $11 billion to $2 billion; the value of industrial and railroad stock fell by 80 percent; and the numbers out of work continued to rise.[21] An estimated 8 million were jobless by the spring of 1931, 13.5 million by the end of 1932, and over 15 million, or one-third of the work force, in 1933.

With declining production and widespread unemployment, the policy of maintaining wage levels was doomed. Smaller companies began to cut wages first. By the fall of 1931, when the net income of the nation's 550 largest industrial corporations had declined by 68 percent, United States Steel announced a 10 percent wage cut, and the rush to cut wages was on. Those still working in the summer of 1932 suffered a drop in average weekly earnings from $25.03 to $16.73.[22] Wage cuts were more severe in mining and manufacturing where unemployment was also worse and less severe among railroad workers, but the overall drop in wages, together with unemployment and the spread of part-time employment, meant that the income of the labor force had been cut in half, from $51 billion in 1929 to $26 billion in 1933 (Raybeck, 321).[23]

During these first years of the depression, the distress produced by rapidly declining wages remained mainly within private spheres; most workers bore the hardships quietly, perhaps made fearful by the masses of unemployed at the factory gates. The reluctance of elites to acknowledge that much was amiss helped to turn distress inward, to keep the disorder of private lives from becoming a public issue. But as business conditions worsened, as unemployment spread, and as local relief efforts broke down, that began to change. By mid–1931, the depression was being acknowledged, helping the grievances in private lives to acquire a public meaning and releasing public

---

[21] U.S. Bureau of the Census, 1941.

[22] U. S. Bureau of the Census, 1941, 340 and 346.

[23] Some groups of workers were especially hard hit. Bernstein cites wage rates in Pennsylvania sawmills of five cents an hour, auto companies that paid women four cents an hour, and Connecticut sweatshops that paid sixty cents for a fifty-five hour week (1970, 319–320).

indignation. In September 1931, the American Legion announced that "the crisis could not be promptly and efficiently met by existing political methods." Theodore Bilbo told an interviewer: "Folks are restless. Communism is gaining a foothold. Right here in Mississippi, some people are about ready to lead a mob. In fact, I'm getting a little pink myself" (Schlesinger, 1957, 204–205). The Republican governor of Washington declared: "We cannot endure another winter of hardship such as we are now passing through" (Rees, 224). Edward F. McGrady of the AFL told the Senate Subcommittee on Manufactures: "I say to you gentlemen, advisedly, that if something is not done . . . the doors of revolt in this country are going to be thrown open" (Bernstein, 1970, 354). Somewhat later, in February 1933, Ernest T. Weir, Chairman of the National Steel Corporation, testified before the Senate Finance Committee: "Practically all the people have suffered severely and are worn out not only in their resources, but in their patience." John L. Lewis went further, pronouncing: "The political stability of the Republic is imperiled" (Bernstein, 1971, 15).

Signs of a pending worker revolt began to appear as well. Desperation strikes to resist wage cuts erupted among textile workers in Massachusetts, New Jersey, and Pennsylvania. In Harlan County, miners revolted as bad conditions grew worse, precipitating a sniping war between guards and strikers that left several dead. Similar outbreaks accompanied by violence followed among miners in Arkansas, Ohio, Indiana, and West Virginia. In April 1932, 150,000 miners in southern Illinois went on strike, and by summer the coal-mining counties of southern Illinois had become a battleground between armies of miners and deputies as thousands of miners descended on the still-operating mines to shut them down.[24] In the summer of 1932, after an outbreak of strikes by unorganized workers in the hosiery mills, Governor O. Max Gardner of North Carolina wrote a friend:

> This outburst at High Point and Thomasville was almost spontaneous and spread like the plague. It only confirms my general feeling that the spirit of revolt is widespread. . . . This thing burst forth from the nervous tension of the people who have lost and

---

[24] When the UMW negotiated a contract accepting a cut in wages, the Illinois miners simply turned it down. By late summer 1932 the National Guard established martial law in the area (Rees).

lost and many of whom are now engaged in the battle for the bare necessities of life (quoted in Bernstein, 1970, 421–422).

That summer, hard-pressed farmers in North Dakota, Michigan, Indiana, Ohio, New York, and Tennessee armed themselves with clubs and pitchforks to prevent the delivery of farm products to towns where the prices paid frequently did not cover the costs of production. These outbreaks were dangerous portents.

Still, considering the scale of the calamity that had overtaken them, most workers had remained relatively quiescent. Their first large-scale expression of discontent was to occur not in the streets, but at the polls, in the dramatic electoral realignment of 1932 when masses of urban working-class voters turned against the Republican Party to vote for a president of "the forgotten man."

When Roosevelt took office in the spring of 1933, the scale of the catastrophe was apparent to all. Industrial production had sunk to a new low and, by the day of the inauguration, every bank in America had closed its doors. Once in office, the new administration took the initiative, and there was little resistance from a stunned nation or a stunned Congress. Clearly the election was a mandate to attempt recovery, but economic panic and the electoral upset gave Roosevelt a relatively free hand in fashioning his early legislation. He proceeded to launch a series of measures, each to deal with a different facet of the breakdown, and each to cultivate and solidify a different constituency: farmers and workers, bankers and businessmen. Farmers got the Agricultural Adjustment Act, rewarding their half-century struggle for price supports, cheap credit, and inflated currency. The unemployed got the Emergency Relief Act. Business and organized labor got the National Industrial Recovery Act (NIRA). For business, the NIRA meant the right to limit production and fix prices. For working people, the NIRA included codes governing wages and hours, and the right to bargain collectively. Those provisions were to have an unprecedented impact on the unorganized working people of the country, not so much for what they gave, as for what they promised. The promises were not to be kept, at least not at first. But that the federal government had made such promises at such a time gave a new spirit and righteousness, and a new direction, to the struggles of unorganized workers.

The Rise of Protest

Franklin Delano Roosevelt was no brinksman; he was trying to build and conserve support wherever possible. The NIRA was designed to promote economic recovery, and this purpose was as much political as economic, for continuing depression spelled continuing political disaffection and uncertainty. Moreover the method for recovery was also political. The NIRA created a mechanism by which industry could regulate production and prices without the constraints of antitrust legislation. This was precisely what business leaders themselves had been asking for. As early as November 1930 Bernard Baruch had called for modification of the antitrust laws and the abatement of "uneconomic competition" through business self-regulation under government supervision. In October 1931, the Committee on Continuity of Business and Employment of the Chamber of Commerce had endorsed proposals for industrial planning under government sanction.[25] Even the National Association of Manufacturers approved.

THE PROMISE OF THE NIRA

But while the NIRA was designed and implemented to conciliate business, it was not meant to offend anyone either, and three passages were included to provide reassurance to organized labor. Section 7(a), written in consultation with the American Federation of Labor, required that every industry code or agreement promulgated under the statute provide "that employees shall have the right to organize and bargain collectively through representatives of their own choosing, and shall be free from the interference, restraint or coercion of employers. . . ." Business was by no means happy with this provision; the National Association of Manufacturers and the Iron and Steel Institute made their opposition clear from the outset. But the Chamber of Commerce took a different tack and privately agreed with the AFL on an exchange of support (Bernstein, 1971, 32). In

---

[25] Accounts of these developments can be found in Schlesinger, 1957, 182–183, and Bernstein, 1971, 19–20.

other words, some business leaders were reluctantly prepared to allow the NIRA to proclaim "the right to organize and bargain collectively" in exchange for the very large concessions that business gained under the act. In addition, labor was granted sections 7 (b) and (c), providing for the regulation of minimum wages and maximum working hours (to be fixed by collective bargaining agreements where these existed, and by industry codes where they did not), and prohibiting the employment of children.[26]

There was in fact considerable precedent for the principles enunciated in the NIRA. The desirability of collective bargaining had been endorsed by all twentieth century presidents of the United States (Taft and Ross, 387). As early as 1900, a collective bargaining arrangement was made between mine workers and owners in the bituminous coalfields, to be followed two years later by a similar agreement with the anthracite mine owners, under the prodding of their financier-backers and President Theodore Roosevelt (Lescohier and Brandeis, xiv–xv). The Railway Labor Act had provided similar protections to the Railway Brotherhoods in 1926. These earlier gains had, however, turned out to be ephemeral: collective bargaining in the coalfields did not last, and the Railway Labor Act turned out to be unenforceable in the face of resistance by the carriers.

But by the early 1930s, as unemployment rose and the destitution of the nation's workers began to seep through to national consciousness, opportunities for more substantial and lasting reform of labor law seemed at hand: the Supreme Court handed down a decision that overturned decades of court opposition to unionism; the Senate refused to confirm the appointment of John J. Parker to the Supreme Court because of his earlier support of yellow dog contracts; the Norris-LaGuardia Act was passed curbing the right of the courts to issue injunctions in labor disputes. The NIRA provisions seemed to complete these advances, and William Green, president of the American Federation of Labor, announced that millions of workers

---

[26] The AFL had broken with its traditional opposition to government regulation of wages and hours, which it feared would undermine the role of unions, to support a thirty-hour bill introduced by Senator Hugo L. Black of Alabama. The Black Bill had substantial support in the Congress, but the administration, concerned to win industry endorsement, threw its weight behind a substitute calling for a sliding scale, which was ultimately incorporated in the National Industrial Recovery Act (Bernstein, 1971, 22–29). Bernstein points out that in 1929, only 19 percent of manufacturing workers were scheduled for less than forty-eight hours a week, a practice which made the United States uniquely regressive among industrialized nations (1971, 24).

throughout the nation had received a "charter of industrial freedom" (Raybeck, 328). But charters are one thing, practical support quite another, and there is no evidence at all that the Roosevelt Administration intended more than the charter. "This is not a law to foment discord," Roosevelt told the public; it was rather the occasion "for mutual confidence and help" (quoted in Bernstein, 1971, 172). In the context of the dislocations of the depression, however, the charter not only fomented discord, it triggered an industrial war.

THE SURGE TOWARD UNIONIZATION

Even before Franklin Delano Roosevelt's inauguration, there were premonitions that sharp wage cuts and lengthening working hours would produce worker protests, as had often happened before. The first signs were spreading strikes in the textile mills and the mines, industries that had been depressed throughout the 1920s and then slumped further with the onset of bad times.[27] It was, however, the inauguration of a president who promised to look to the forgotten man and the passage of legislation which promised to protect the forgotten industrial worker that gave the discontented an élan, a righteousness, that they had not had before.

The impact on workers was electrifying. It was as if incipient struggles had now been crowned with an aura of what Rudé called "natural justice." Felt grievances became public grievances, for the federal government itself had declared the workers' cause to be just. There is, for example, the story of a group of workers at the Philco radio plant who organized a Walking, Hunting, and Fishing Club under the leadership of a twenty-one year old named James Carey, and then went to the president of Philco to demand a contract, insisting the NIRA had made collective bargaining a matter of national policy. When the Philco official disagreed, the workers promptly climbed in a couple of old automobiles and went off to Washington, absolutely convinced they would be proven right.[28] In industries

---

[27] For an account of the battles in the textile mills of the Piedmont, see Bernstein, 1970, 1–43; for an account of some of the miners' strikes, see Nyden, 403–468.

[28] As the story is told, they were proven right in this case. The workers hunted down Hugh Johnson, head of the National Recovery Administration, established under the NIRA, in the Commerce Building, brought back his affirmation in writing, and Philco accepted it. But the story is an exception.

that had already been organized, somnolent unions sprang to life. The ranks of the United Mine Workers had dwindled in the twenties as a result of the decade-long slump in the coal industry, and then were almost decimated by the depression. After passage of NIRA, John L. Lewis, head of the mine workers, moved into action, committing the entire UMW treasury and one hundred organizers. Sound trucks were dispatched into the coalfields blaring the message, "The President wants *you* to unionize." Bernstein quotes a UMW organizer in June 1933: "These people have been so starved out that they are flocking into the Union by the thousands. . . . I organized 9 Locals Tuesday" (1971, 37, 41–42). Within two months, UMW membership jumped from 60,000 to 300,000 (Thomas Brooks, 163; Levinson, 20–21), and paid-up memberships reached 528,685 in July 1934 (Derber, 8); the International Ladies Garment Workers Union quadrupled its membership, reaching 200,000 in 1934 (Derber, 9); the Amalgamated Clothing Workers, which had reported 7,000 dues-paying members at its low in 1932, added 125,000 new members (Bernstein, 1970, 335). And the Oil Field, Gas Well and Refinery Workers Union, which in 1933 claimed only 300 members in an industry employing 275,000, established 125 new locals by May 1934 (Bernstein, 1971, 109–111).

In nonunionized industries "there was a virtual uprising of workers for union membership," the executive council of the AFL reported to its 1934 convention; "workers held mass meetings and sent word they wanted to be organized" (Levinson, 52). The result was that almost two hundred local unions with 100,000 members sprang up in the automobile industry; about 70,000 joined unions in the Akron rubber plants; about 300,000 textile workers joined the United Textile Workers of America; and an estimated 50,000 clamored to join the steel union, organizing themselves in lodges named for the promise: "New Deal," "NRA," or "Blue Eagle" (Levinson, 51–78; Bernstein, 1971, 92–94). Harvey O'Connor, a labor newspaperman and former Wobbly, tells how it happened in the steel mills:

> So in 1933 along came the New Deal, and then came the NRA, and the effect was electric all up and down those valleys. The mills began reopening somewhat, and the steel workers read in the newspapers about this NRA section 7 (a) that guaranteed you the right to organize. That was true, and that's about as far as it went; you had the right to organize, but what happened after that was another matter. All over the country steel union locals sprang up spon-

taneously. . . . These locals sprang up at Duquesne, Homestead and
Braddock. You name the mill town and there was a Local there,
carrying a name like the "Blue Eagle" or the "New Deal" Local. . . .
There was even an "FDR" Local, I think. These people had never
had any experience with unionism. All they knew was that, by golly,
the time had come when they could organize and the Government
guaranteed them the right to organize (Lynd, 1969, 58).

But the guarantee was not to be kept. Interestingly enough, the first
obstacles were created by the existing unions themselves, for their
role at this stage was virtually to destroy the surge toward unionism
among the mass of unorganized industrial workers.

THE UNIONS IMPEDE UNIONIZATION

When the depression struck, the AFL was nearly half a century old.
It had been formed in the 1880s as a federation of national craft
unions, and its dominant leaders (aside from William Green, a
former UMW official) were the presidents of the large craft unions:
Bill Hutcheson, boss of 300,000 carpenters, who had once hired
strikebreakers to preserve his rule; Dan Tobin, $20,000-a-year presi-
dent of the teamsters;[29] John Frey, aging head of the aging molders;
Matthew Woll, of the photoengravers. The membership of the AFL
reached a peak of about 5 million in 1920, when the unions could
claim to represent 17 percent of the American work force (Mills,
53), then fell off during the depression of 1921, and stood still during the apparent prosperity of the twenties. The oligarchs, their
positions well-secured, were not much perturbed. At the turn of the
century the AFL had become closely allied with the National Civic
Federation, representing the big financiers and businessmen who
sought a "reasonable" cooperation of labor and capital. During the
1920s, this rapprochment with industry became virtually complete.
Matthew Woll, an AFL vice-president, became the acting president
of the National Civic Federation, and the AFL reversed its historic
opposition to scientific management, resolved that increases in wages
should be linked to increases in productivity, stressed union-manage-

---

[29] David Dubinsky was notable among AFL chieftains because his salary remained a
relatively modest $7,500 a year.

ment cooperation,[30] and undertook a campaign to purge communist influences in its member unions. Strike activities virtually ceased. Meanwhile, the mass of industrial workers remained unorganized.

With the depression, however, union membership sank to a new low of 2,126,000 or about 9 percent of the work force,[31] and at first the clamor of rank-and-file industrial workers begging for unionization seemed to arouse the enthusiasm of the AFL leadership. President William Green described section 7(a) as a "Magna Charta" for labor and boasted that membership would reach 10 million, and then 25 million. The AFL slogan would be, he proclaimed, "Organize the Unorganized in the Mass Production Industries."

But this was not to happen, and there were several reasons why. One was the predominance in the AFL structure of the large craft unions, for whom jurisdictional preoccupations were paramount. The workers who, with good faith and enthusiasm, were rushing to join unions, were assigned to what were called federal locals in the AFL structure. In the second half of 1933, after the passage of the NIRA, the AFL received 1,205 applications for federal local charters and granted 1,006 (Bernstein, 1971, 355). In deference to the jurisdictional claims of the craft unions, these locals were considered temporary bodies, and were denied voting rights in AFL councils (although the dues of the federal locals went far toward supporting the central AFL organs, for they were not siphoned off by the big affiliated unions). Moreover, ostensibly because they were organized on a plant basis and not by craft,[32] it was understood that the members of federal locals would ultimately be divided up among the craft unions who staked out their jurisdictional claims, sometimes splitting the newly organized workers in a factory among as many as fifteen or twenty different unions, with the result that they were hopelessly divided among competing organizations and incapable of action.

Whatever the difficulties it caused, the effort of the big craft unions to claim the new unionists for themselves was natural enough. But even this was done half-heartedly; to the oligarchs of the AFL, the

[30] A few union-management cooperation schemes to raise productivity were introduced but the main significance of this posture was rhetorical. See Nadworny.

[31] Union membership figures are necessarily estimates. For a discussion of difficulties in estimation see Derber, 3–7.

[32] The craft basis of AFL union organization had in fact resulted in a convoluted jurisdictional maze determined not so much by craft as by power struggles among the member unions.

new members spelled trouble. These leaders maintained their pre-eminence on the basis of the members whose allegiance they claimed and on whose apathy they could count. It was one thing to boast of organizing ten million of the unorganized, but quite another to welcome masses of unsettling newcomers either into existing organizations made secure by stasis, or even worse, into new and competitive unions within the AFL structure. In October 1933 a convention of the AFL Metal Trades Department denounced the AFL leadership for chartering federal unions, asserting that "this condition, if allowed to continue, will completely demoralize, if not actually destroy, the various international unions' charter and jurisdictional rights" (Levinson, 54).

Moreover, the oligarchs were accustomed not only to internal stability, but to external conciliation, and the signs of militancy among the unorganized suggested a mode of conflict that had become distasteful to many of the AFL leaders. Bill Collins, an AFL representative, sent to win the auto workers to the AFL banner in the face of a trend toward independent unionism, told the auto manufacturers, "I never voted for a strike in my life" (Fine, 69). Finally, there was the age-old contempt for the unskilled, which served to justify the organizational preoccupations of the AFL leadership. Collins is said to have confided to Norman Thomas, "My wife can always tell from the smell of my clothes what breed of foreigners I've been hanging out with" (Levinson, 60).[33] Tobin, leader of the teamsters, wrote during the crest of the NIRA agitations: "The scramble for admittance to the union is on. We do not want to charter the riff-raff or good-for nothings, or those for whom we cannot make wages or conditions. . . . We do not want the men today if they are going on strike tomorrow (Levinson, 13–14).

The actions of Michael F. Tighe, president of the Amalgamated Association of Iron, Steel, and Tin Workers, representing in 1933 some 50,000 skilled men in a steel industry employing some half million workers, are an example. Tighe had helped to break the 1919 steel strike by signing an agreement for his handful of skilled workers while the bulk of the steel workers were still out on strike.

---

[33] In a similar spirit, Harry McLauglin, executive secretary of the Cleveland Federation of Labor, told a group of auto workers who came to seek help in organizing the White Motors Company in Cleveland in 1932 that "no one can organize that bunch of hunkies out there" (Prickett, 159). One of those auto workers was Wyndham Mortimer, who became one of the key organizers of the United Automobile Workers.

Now, as men rushed to join his union, he seemed at first more confused than anything else, then condemned the walkouts by new unionists at two steel works, denounced a committee set up by the rank and file to organize strike machinery, and finally simply expelled 75 percent of his new members. Meanwhile, to show his good intentions, Tighe sent a letter to the steel mill owners asking them to lend an ear to the workers asking for recognition, assuring them he had "only one purpose, that of advancing the interests of both employer and employee." The letter was not answered (Levinson, 68–72). By the summer of 1935, Tighe reported a total membership of 8,600 in the entire steel industry.

Similarly, the new rubber unions, concentrated in Akron, found their members divided between nineteen craft locals (Schlesinger, 1958, 355). Demoralized, their membership fell from a peak of about 70,000 in 1934 to 22,000. The ranks of the auto unions shrank from an estimated 100,000 to 20,000, or 5 percent of the more than 400,000 workers in the industry. The United Textile Workers of America, having reached a membership of 300,000 in the summer of 1934, claimed only 79,200 members by August 1935. The Union of Mine, Mill, and Smelter Workers, a descendant of the militant Western Federation of Miners, had gained 49,000 recruits under a new young leadership. With no AFL organizers in sight, they called a strike in May 1934 and 6,600 men walked out at the Anaconda Copper Mine Company in Butte and Great Falls. The AFL Buildings and Metal Trades Department arrived on the scene and negotiated a settlement for 600 craftsmen, soon to be divided among sixteen craft unions, and the strike was scuttled (Bernstein, 1971, 106–109). By summer 1935, membership in the Mine, Mill, and Smelter Workers was down to 14,000 (Levinson, 78).

After a debacle at the AFL convention in the fall of 1935 over the issue of the industrial unionism, John L. Lewis and several other union leaders withdrew to form the Committee for Industrial Organization—later to split with the AFL and declare itself the Congress of Industrial Organizations. It included the small federal auto and rubber worker locals which had reluctantly been granted industrial charters by the AFL in 1934, but charters so hedged in as to protect the claims of the craft unions and the authority of the AFL leadership. Like the AFL, the CIO leaders announced they would "encourage and promote organization of the workers in the mass-production and unorganized industries of the nation" (Levinson, 119). What they would do, however, still remained to be seen.

Men and women had flocked to the unions, to the promise of labor power through organization. They had handed over the high dues that the AFL demanded of its federal locals and then found themselves confused by the jurisdictional tangles their leaders imposed on them, and discouraged by the moderation and conciliation their leaders demanded of them. At this stage, organization failed, and perhaps for that reason, the workers' movement grew.

Curious / the strength / and anger / of this / bias.

INDUSTRY RESISTS UNIONIZATION

Whatever the reluctance the AFL leadership showed in dealing with the mass of unorganized industrial workers, they at least applauded the promises the NIRA made to labor. Employers took a different view. They had allowed the promises to be made grudgingly, in return for the concessions that the NIRA provided to business, and they had no intention of seeing the promises fulfilled.

The less controversial of the legislative concessions to labor had been the provisions governing wages and hours but, since employers dominated the code authorities that fixed minimum wages and maximum hours for each industry, these provisions were also the more easily undermined in practice. Some codes simply neglected to mention minimum wages. Where the codes did specify wages and hours, particular manufacturers easily gained exemptions by pointing out the peculiar conditions obtaining in their industry or business, while others used the "stretch-out" to evade standards. Nevertheless, there were some improvements overall after the passage of the legislation and the establishment of the National Recovery Administration;[34] average hours of labor per week declined from 43.3 to 37.8, and average annual earnings in manufacturing, mining, and construction increased from $874 in 1933 to $1,068 in 1935 (Rayback, 332).

From the outset industry had viewed section 7 (a), which presumably gave workers the right to organize and bargain collectively, as the more serious threat, and industry leaders moved quickly to emasculate the provision. Some corporations flatly prohibited unioni-

---

[34] In some industries, notably textiles, the codes provided a vehicle through which the industry could place a floor under intense competitive wage-slashing and price-slashing. And in textiles, the codes were more effective; average weekly earnings rose from $10.90 to $13.03, and hours dropped sharply, from forty-six to thirty-three (Walsh, 145).

zation; many more began to set up "employee representation" plans. These plans, or company unions, had become popular in the 1920s, and by 1928 an estimated 1.5 million workers were included (Pelling, 146). But between 1933 and 1935, new company plans proliferated.[35] As the demand for unionization escalated despite these devices, companies began to maintain blacklists and simply fired known union members by the thousands, despite the ostensible protections afforded by section 7 (a). And increasingly, in the face of the upsurge of worker militancy, employers resorted to the techniques of violence and espionage, to barbed-wire fences and sandbag fortifications, to well-armed and well-financed "Citizen Associations," to special deputies and the massive use of labor spies.[36] Subsequent testimony before a subcommitte of the Senate Committee on Education and Labor, chaired by Senator La Follette, indicated that American industry had hired 3,781 labor spies between 1933–1937 (Raybeck, 344);[37] the cost of anti-union agents in 1936 alone was put at $80 million (Thomas Brooks, 164).

THE STRUGGLE ESCALATES

If industry leaders were not satisfied with the compromises of the New Deal, neither were the rank and file of labor. The right to organize and join a union had given the workers hope, and un-

---

[35] A National Industrial Conference Board sample found that of 623 company union plans in effect in November 1933 in manufacturing and mining, some 400 had been instituted after the passage of the NIRA. A broader industry survey by the Bureau of Labor Statistics found a similar percentage (Bernstein, 1971, 39–40).

[36] These practices had been popularized by industry in the early 1920s under the official designation of the "American Plan." The "Plan" included the systematic use of blacklists, labor spies, injunctions, and propaganda. In 1936 the "Mohawk Valley Formula," developed by Remington Rand to successfully break a strike, further systematized employer techniques by including denunciation of labor leaders as dangerous radicals, use of police to break up labor meetings, massive propaganda in the local community, and the organization of vigilante "citizen" committees to protect strikebreakers (Bernstein, 1970, 148–151; 1971, 478–479; Raybeck, 343–344; Walsh, 216–228).

[37] Walsh lists some of the corporations known to employ labor spy agencies: Chrysler, General Motors, Quaker Oats, Wheeling Steel, Great Lakes Steel, Firestone Tire and Rubber, Post Telegraph and Cable, Radio Corporation of America, Bethlehem Steel, Campbell Soup, Curtis Publishing Company, Baldwin Locomotive Works, Montgomery Ward, Pennsylvania Railroad, Goodrich Rubber, Aluminum Company of America, Consolidated Gas, Frigidaire, Carnegie Steel, National Dairy Products, and Western Union (206–207).

leashed their discontent.[38] But unionization had so far been a failed cause, resisted by employers, fumbled by AFL leaders, and worn away in government procedures that led nowhere. The number of unionized workers again plummeted to a historic low by 1935, accounting for only 9.5 percent of the labor force (Mills, 53). However, while union membership was falling, worker militancy was rising. During the spring and summer of 1934 strikes spread and, as they escaped the control of established union leaders, became more unpredictable. Three times as many workers struck in 1933 after NIRA as in 1932; the number of industrial disputes reported by the U. S. Bureau of Labor Statistics rose from 841 in 1932 to 1,695 in 1933,[39] and then to 1,856 in 1934 when a million and a half workers were involved in strikes (Millis and Montgomery, 692, 700–701). With employer resistance also mounting, many of the strikes culminated in large-scale battles.

The first of these was the "Battle of Toledo." Toledo had been devastated by the depression. Its main plant was Willys-Overland, which produced 42,000 cars in March 1929 and employed 28,000 people. In a matter of months, production was cut back; by spring of 1932, Willys employed only 3,000 people (Keeran, 63). Meanwhile the auto parts industry in Toledo was also hard hit, with the result that unemployment in the city was high, and the wages of those still working were below the NIRA code minimum. Early in 1934, demands for union recognition at the Electric Auto-Lite Company and several smaller firms were rejected, and 4,000 workers walked out. The workers returned to the plants after federal officials secured a commitment from the employers to "set up a machinery" for negotiations. But Auto-Lite then refused to negotiate, and a second strike was called on April 11. Only a minority of the workers joined the walkout this time, however, and the company determined to keep its plant open, hiring strikebreakers to reach full production.

Toledo was a stronghold of A. J. Muste's radical Unemployed Leagues, and the Musteites rapidly mobilized large numbers of un-

---

[38] The proportion of strikes involving the issue of union recognition rose from 19 percent in 1932 to 45.9 percent in 1934. Union recognition continued to be an issue in about half the reported work stoppages until 1942, according to Bureau of Labor Statistics sources cited by Bernstein (1950, 143, 144).

[39] Measured another way, the man-days lost due to strikes increased from a maximum of 603,000 in any month in 1933 before the NIRA became law in June, to 1,375,000 in July, and to 2,378,000 in August, so that 1933 ended with more labor stoppages than had occurred at any time since 1921 (Bernstein, 1971, 173).

employed workers to reinforce the picket lines. On April 17 the company responded by obtaining a court order limiting picketing and prohibiting league members from picketing altogether. But the Musteites decided to violate the restraining order, and some local Communists joined in with the slogan "Smash the Injunction by Mass Picketing" (Keeran, 168). A handful of militants then began picketing. They were quickly arrested, but upon their release, they returned to the picket lines, their numbers now enlarged by workers emboldened by the militants' example. More arrests and further court injunctions seemed to only galvanize the strikers, and the numbers of people on the picket lines grew larger day by day. Sympathy for the strikers in Toledo was such that the sheriff could not use the local police to protect the strikebreakers and instead deputized special police, paid for by Auto-Lite.

By May 23, the crowd massed outside the plant had grown to some 10,000 people, effectively imprisoning the 1,500 strikebreakers inside the factory. The sheriff then decided to take the initiative, and the deputies attacked. The crowd fought back, several people were seriously wounded, and a contingent of the Ohio National Guard was called in. Armed with machine guns and bayonetted rifles, the Guardsmen marched into the Auto-Lite plant in the quiet of dawn and succeeded in evacuating the strikebreaking workers. But the next day, the crowd gathered again, advanced on the Guardsmen, showering them with bricks and bottles. On the third advance, the Guard fired into the crowd, killing two and wounding many more. The crowd still did not disperse. Four more companies of Guardsmen were called up, and Auto-Lite agreed to close the plant. Then, with the threat of a general strike in the air, the employers finally agreed to federal mediation which resulted in a 22 percent wage increase and limited recognition for the union.[40]

The next scene of battle was Minneapolis. The city had always been a stronghold of the open shop, vigilantly enforced by an employers' "Citizens' Alliance" formed in 1908 to prevent unionization by means of stool pigeons, espionage, propaganda, and thugs. During 1933, when a third of the work force in Minneapolis was unemployed and the wages of those still working had been cut, a handful of local Trotskyist militants—members of the Socialist Workers Party—gained control of Teamsters Local 574 and began to sign

---

[40] Accounts of the Toledo events can be found in Keeran, 164–172; Bernstein, 1971, 218–228; Brecher, 158–161; and Taft and Ross, 252.

workers up. After an initial victory in the coal yards, the local began to organize the truck drivers and helpers. But Minneapolis businessmen, alerted by worker agitation elsewhere in the country, were prepared for a showdown. When Local 574 presented its demands to the trucking employers, the Citizens' Alliance stepped in and promised to smash the strike. The union's demands were summarily rejected.

Mediation efforts by the Regional Labor Board were fruitless and, on May 15, 1934, the strike was on. The alliance promptly swore in 155 "special officers," prompting workers in Minneapolis to rally behind the truck drivers, many of them by going on strike themselves. Both sides established military headquarters and armed their men. Pickets roved through the city in bands, some on motorcycles, seeing to it that no trucks moved. On May 21, after the police threatened to move trucks, the first battle broke out between the two armies. Thirty of the vastly outnumbered police were injured in the hand-to-hand fighting that ensued. The next day, a crowd of 20,000 gathered, fighting broke out again, and two special deputies were killed, some fifty wounded. With workers virtually in control of the city, and with the first families of Minneapolis in panic, the sense of impending class war grew.

At this point, Governor Olson managed to force a temporary truce. Negotiations proceeded, but the ambiguously worded agreement which resulted soon broke down, and both sides again began preparations for battle. After mediation efforts by federal representatives were rejected by the employers, who apparently hoped to force the Governor to bring in the National Guard to break the strike, the workers struck again. At the next confrontation between the two camps, police wounded sixty-seven workers and killed two. Governor Olson then intervened in earnest, declaring martial law and raiding the headquarters of both camps. The trucking employers finally accepted a federal plan that, within two years, led to collective bargaining agreements with 500 Minneapolis employers (Bernstein, 1971, 229–252; Schlesinger, 1958, 385–389). Meanwhile, Daniel Tobin, international president of the Teamsters, had refused his support to the workers, denouncing the strike leadership as "reds" (Karsh and Garman, 99).[41]

---

[41] Seven years later Tobin instigated the government prosecution of leaders of the Socialist Workers Party under the Smith Act in an effort to destroy the leadership of the Minneapolis local of the Teamsters (Lens, 230–231).

In San Francisco, longshoremen encouraged by section 7(a) were flocking into the International Longshoremen's Association. Their special grievance was the "shape-up" hiring system which left them at the mercy of the foremen, never able to count on a day's work. But the ILA leaders made no effort to challenge the shape-up, and a rank-and-file movement developed, led by a small caucus of Communists and other radicals, including Harry Bridges.[42] At a meeting in February 1934 the rank and file forced union officials to demand a union hiring hall or threaten to strike in two weeks. Roosevelt had been warned that the waterfront bosses wanted a showdown, that any money they might lose in a dock strike would be more than worth it if the union was destroyed (Schlesinger, 1958, 390). A federal mediating team worked out a compromise that provided some degree of union recognition, but did not give the union control of the hiring hall. Joseph Ryan, president of the ILA, accepted. But local leaders, pressed by the rank and file, spurned the plan, and the strike was on.

Employers imported large numbers of strikebreakers, but rank-and-file teamsters refused to haul goods to and from the docks and some even joined the picket lines. On May 10 the Communist-led Maritime Workers Industrial Union joined the strike, prodding AFL maritime unions to do the same, so that the strike soon spread to include most maritime workers (Weinstein, 64–67). From the first day the police tried to break the strike by force, and the pickets fought back. After forty-five days, the San Francisco business community decided that the port had to be opened and 700 policemen prepared to storm the picket lines. When the battle was over, twenty-five people were hospitalized. Several days later, on July 5, the police again charged crowds of pickets who had gathered to stop strikebreakers. This time, 115 people were hospitalized, two strikers were killed, and 1,700 National Guardsmen marched into San Francisco to restore order. The funeral procession for the slain strikers was transformed into an awesome political statement by the working people of San Francisco. A writer who observed the occasion described it:

---

[42] This group was really a spin-off of the small and militant Maritime Workers Industrial Union, organized by Communists. The MWIU began to organize San Francisco longshoremen in 1932, but after section 7 (a) was enacted, and the rush to join the union was on, it was the old International Longshoremen's Association into which longshoremen flooded, and with them went the group of radicals from the MWIU (Weinstein, 64–66).

In solid ranks, eight to ten abreast, thousands of strike sympathizers. . . . Tramp-tramp-tramp. No noise except that. The band with its muffled drums and somber music. . . . On the marchers came— hour after hour—ten, twenty, thirty thousand of them. . . . A solid river of men and women who believed they had a grievance and who were expressing their resentment in this gigantic demonstration (Charles G. Norris, quoted by Bernstein, 1971, 281–282).

In the upswell of anger and sympathy, the momentum for a general strike grew. By July 12 some twenty unions had voted to strike, and Hugh Johnson announced a "civil war" in San Francisco. But the strike folded after four days, undermined by the local AFL Central Labor Council that had been forced to take on the leadership of a general strike of which it wanted no part. Once the general strike collapsed, the longshoremen had no choice but to accept arbitration, with the result that hiring halls jointly operated by the union and employers were established. In the interim William Green of the AFL had himself denounced the San Francisco general strike (Brecher, 154–157).

The textile strike that erupted across the nation in the summer of 1934 took on the character of a crusade as "flying squadrons" of men and women marched from one southern mill town to another, calling out the workers from the mills to join the strike. By September, 375,000 textile workers were on strike. Employers imported armed guards who, together with the National Guard, kept the mills open in Alabama, Mississippi, Georgia, and the Carolinas (Bernstein, 1971, 298–311). Before it was over, the head of a local union in Alabama had been shot, his aides beaten; Governor Talmadge of Georgia declared martial law and set up a detention camp for an estimated 2,000 strikers; fifteen strikers were killed, six of them when the sheriff's deputies clashed with a flying squadron in Honea Path, South Carolina; riots broke out in Rhode Island, Connecticut, and Massachusetts and National Guardsmen were on duty across New England; and the trade journal *Fibre and Fabric* pontificated that "a few hundred funerals will have a quieting influence."[43]

During that same summer, deputies killed two strikers and injured thirty-five others when the Kohler Company in the "model" com-

---

[43] These outbreaks are described in Schlesinger, 1958, 394; Brecher, 168–176; Levinson, 73–74; Taft and Ross, 354.

pany town of Kohler Village, Wisconsin, refused to bargain with the union (Taft and Ross, 352). All in all, a minimum of fifteen strikers were killed in 1933, and at least forty more were killed in 1934. In a period of eighteen months, troops had been called out in sixteen states (Levinson, 56–57).

The State on the Horns of the Industrial Dilemma

As worker demands escalated, industry resistance escalated to match, and each side repeatedly called on federal authorities to mediate. At first, the policy of conciliating business prevailed, but conciliation grew more and more difficult as workers became more militant.

The automobile industry is an example. Before the NIRA went into effect, there was virtually no union organization among automobile workers.[44] After the NIRA, workers joined the AFL federal locals, independent unions began to appear, and a series of strikes broke out in the summer of 1933. Meanwhile, the National Industrial Recovery Administration had, as in other industries, ceded the initiative in formulating automobile codes to the owners of the industry.[45] The National Automobile Chamber of Commerce in effect became the auto industry code authority (Levinson, 57). The wages and hours code which auto industrialists submitted and which the president signed called for hourly rates ranging between forty-one and forty-three cents and a work week ranging from thirty-five

---

[44] A small Communist-led union did exist, the Auto Workers Union. The AWU had claimed some 23,000 members in 1918, but it was ejected from the AFL for refusing to drop its jurisdictional claims to all the workers in the auto industry, and then was decimated by the open shop drive in the early 1920s. It was at that point that Communist activity in the union began and, while the union never gained many members, it did serve an important agitational and supportive role in the defensive strikes of the late 1920s and again in 1932–1933 (Keeran, 4–17; 43–48; 89–103).

[45] Edelman points out: "Industry enjoyed the huge advantage of initiative as well as economic power in code formulation. Trade associations usually prepared the first drafts of codes and were highly influential in the discussion of adjustments in them at hearings. NRA deputy administrators who presided at the hearings were largely drawn from industry, giving management a further advantage when its position conflicted with that of unions or workers. Some NRA officials and unions tried to secure equal representation for labor representatives on code authorities, but voting membership for labor representatives was granted in only twenty-three cases and non-voting membership in twenty-eight" (166).

to forty-eight hours, but labor leaders claimed those standards were widely violated. The provision designed by the industry to demonstrate observance of section 7 (a) came to be known as the "merit clause." It specified that "employers in this industry may exercise their right to select, retain, or advance employees on the basis of individual merit, without regard to their membership or non-membership in any organization" (Levinson, 57–58). Under this clause companies began to discharge unionists in the fall of 1933. At the same time General Motors rushed through a series of company union elections and announced that it would not recognize or enter into a contract with any independent union on behalf of its employees. Each time the code was extended—in December 1933, in September 1934, and in February 1935—labor leaders protested vehemently, but to little avail, excepting that the president appointed a labor advisory board and also ordered a survey of wages and unemployment in the automobile industry.

Agitation among the auto workers continued. In March 1934, when workers in several GM plants were threatening to strike, President Roosevelt called industry and labor representatives to a meeting at the White House. The resulting peace agreement established the principle of proportional representation. Employees in a plant would be divided among company unions and various independent unions for collective bargaining purposes. Roosevelt called the plan "the framework for a new structure of industrial relations"; the president of General Motors, Alfred P. Sloan, said, "All's well that ends well"; and William Green concurred, heralding a labor victory. But experience suggested that it was a plan for dividing workers against each other. The *New York Times* correspondent wrote that "organized labor's drive for a greater equality of bargaining power with industry has been nullified."[46]

Similar stratagems were followed in the textile industry. Codes governing wages and hours were undermined by stretchouts that greatly increased the workload. Despite the supposed protections of section 7(a), thousands of unionists were fired, and the Cotton National Textile Industrial Relations Board disposed of worker complaints simply by referring them to the industry's Textile Institute. Meanwhile the NRA sanctioned an industry-wide cut in produc-

---

46 New Deal efforts to keep peace in the auto industry are described in Fine, 31; Levinson, 57–62; Bernstein, 1971, 182–185.

tion which reduced employment and wages still further. The inevitable strike was temporarily averted when the NRA promised a survey and a seat on the Textile Board for the United Textile Workers. When the strike finally erupted in the summer of 1934 the president intervened by appointing a new Textile Labor Relations Board to study workloads in the industry, while the Department of Labor would survey wages, and the Federal Trade Commission would assess the capacity of the industry to increase hours and employment (Brecher, 176). United Textile Workers leaders called off the walkout, claiming a victory.[47] The strikers returned to the mills only to find that thousands of their numbers were barred from reemployment and evicted from their company houses by the mill owners.[48]

In the steel industry, the National Labor Board, pressed by strikes in Weirton and Clairton, finally ordered an employee election but the employers refused to abide by the order. When handed the case, the Department of Justice refused to act. Later, when the companies were laying in supplies of tear gas, bullets, and submachine guns to defend against unionists, rank and filers went to Washington to see the president, who was away on a cruise. This time the workers rejected the offer of the NRA chief, General Hugh Johnson (who proposed the appointment of a board to hear their grievances), and instead wrote the president that they thought it "useless to waste any more time in Washington on the 'National Run Around' " (Levinson, 70).

But while the federal government was conciliating businessmen through this period, it was also showing an unprecedented concern and restraint in dealing with labor. "To an extraordinary extent at this time," writes Bernstein, "the laboring people of the United States looked to the federal government and especially to Roosevelt for leadership and comfort" (1971, 170). In the uncertain climate of the time, however, labor support could not simply be taken for granted. Accordingly, Roosevelt attempted to appease demands by workers; even the unfilled promises and evasive studies of the NRA were an effort at appeasement and a sharp contrast with the court

[47] This was the second outbreak in the mills in only four years, and the second sellout by the AFL. In 1929, when a spontaneous strike spread across the Piedmont, the AFL had responded with a speaking tour by President Green in which he appealed to the mill owners to deal with organized labor (Bernstein, 1970, 11–43).
[48] New Deal maneuverings in textiles are described in Levinson, 73–76; Raybeck, 331; Bernstein, 1971, 300–304.

injunctions and federal troops of an earlier era. As complaints from
labor leaders over violations of 7 (a) became more bitter, the National
Labor Board was established to settle employer-worker disputes.
Senator Robert F. Wagner, an ally of labor, was appointed chairman
and the NLB became an advocate of the right to organize and of
the principle of collective bargaining. Despite some initial successes,
the NLB lacked legal authority and could do nothing when employers
simply defied it, as happened in several major cases in late 1933. In
February 1934 the NLB, which had been authorized mainly to hold
discussions, was empowered to conduct employee elections and, later
in 1934, a resolution sponsored by Wagner led to the reorganization
of the board into the National Labor Relations Board. None of these
changes proved very effective in the face of employer resistance,
particularly since the Department of Justice showed considerable
reluctance to prosecute cases referred to it by the board. Even in
election cases, where the NLRB had clear authority, employers
delayed compliance and stalled in the courts. By March 1935 none
of the cases referred to the Department of Justice had resulted in a
judgment (Bernstein, 1971, 320–322).

But with industrial war escalating, the policies of conciliating business while placating labor could not last. The administration could
not ignore the battles that were raging between industry and labor,
if only because industrial peace was essential for recovery. And once
entangled, it could not take sides without alienating one camp or
the other. When strikes and riots broke out in the coal mines controlled by the steel companies (known as the "captive" mines) in
the summer of 1933, Hugh Johnson forced a settlement to which
Lewis agreed but which the miners themselves rejected. The steel
industry and the UMW were soon locked in conflict, the *New York
Times* reported 100,000 miners on strike, and negotiations under the
auspices of the NRA were leading nowhere. With coke stocks danger-
ously low, the steel executives finally insisted on the president's intervention. But whatever they expected from this intervention, the
resulting agreement hardly pleased them. In fact, none of the corporations abided by its terms until the disputes were referred to the
NLB, with the result that a modified collective bargaining agreement was reached in many of the captive mines (Bernstein, 1971,
49–61).

Nor could the administration stay aloof from the battles of 1934
in Toledo, Minneapolis, and San Francisco, in which the business
community was stiffly opposed to worker demands, and to federal

proposals for settlement. Once involved, federal arbitrators, faced with unprecedented labor uprisings, did not side with the workers, but they did not side with employers either. That was enough to prove the undoing of the policy of business conciliation.

Although most businessmen had supported Hoover in 1932, at least some prominent leaders among them had endorsed Roosevelt, and others quickly joined when Roosevelt reopened the banks, cut government spending, and legalized beer within a month of taking office. As for the NIRA, the U. S. Chamber of Commerce itself had endorsed "the philosophy of a planned economy" before the election, and in 1933 its delegates gave Roosevelt a standing ovation. Meanwhile, at least partly thanks to the privileges granted industry under the NIRA codes, overall business conditions were improving. By the spring of 1934 the index of industrial production had picked up sharply, particularly in industries covered by the codes. Industry leaders regained their confidence and, as they did, became increasingly disgruntled with the turmoil set in motion in their own house by the New Deal labor policy. Just prior to the congressional elections of 1934 a group of major business leaders, including Alfred P. Sloan and William S. Knudsen of General Motors, Edward F. Hutton and Colby M. Chester of General Foods, J. Howard Pew of Sun Oil, Sewell L. Avery of Montgomery Ward, and the Du Ponts, joined with several political leaders who had been dethroned by the New Deal to form the American Liberty League, an organization dedicated to protecting property rights from the "radicalism" of the New Deal (Schlesinger, 1958, 486). Roosevelt's policy of conciliation notwithstanding, business had thrown down the gauntlet. But the election of 1934 was a New Deal sweep, bringing the Democratic margin to 45 in the Senate, and to 219 in the House—"the most overwhelming victory," the *New York Times* declared, "in the history of American politics."

The State Concedes to Labor Power

At this stage, implacable business opposition made the administration far more responsive to demands from other groups in its constituency. The New Deal brain-truster Raymond Moley wrote recently of Roosevelt:

> No man was less bound by ideology in approaching national problems. The strategy he adopted some time in 1935, devised with the

collaboration of Edward J. Flynn, was to gather into the Democratic Party many minorities, including the labor unions, through policies calculated to win the urban masses, while he held the farmers in line with cash benefits (559).

Roosevelt and his advisors had originally thought of labor concessions primarily in terms of unemployment relief and insurance, old age pensions, and wages and hours protections (Bernstein, 1971, 11). But rank-and-file agitation set new terms, and the terms would have to be met if labor was to be kept in line.

FEDERAL RESPONSE: THE WAGNER ACT

By 1935, with worker-employer battles mounting, it was clear that conciliation had failed. The administration had lost business support and, if worker demands went unappeased, it stood in danger of losing some labor support as well. In the spring of 1935 the NIRA and the president were being denounced by all sides. "Labor's public enemy Number One is Franklin D. Roosevelt," said Heywood Broun. The Supreme Court brought matters to a head on May 27, 1935, for it declared the NIRA unconstitutional, thus scuttling the New Deal's chief economic program. With even that protection gone, unemployment increased, wages dropped, and hours lengthened (Raybeck, 341). And the election of 1936 was on the horizon.

In the spring of 1934 Senator Robert Wagner had introduced a bill to establish a new labor relations board that, unlike its predecessors, would have enforcement machinery. The board would be authorized to hold employee elections, to prohibit employers from engaging in practices to coerce or restrain employees, and to require employers to negotiate with the designated representatives of a majority of the workers in any bargaining unit. The bill gave the board the power to issue cease and desist orders, with recourse to the circuit courts in cases of noncompliance.[49] Businessmen rose up

---

[49] The Railway Labor Act of 1926, as amended in 1934, is widely said to have established the precedents for the Wagner Act, but as Fleming points out, in several respects the Wagner Act went much further in supporting labor unions. It permitted the closed shop, which the Railway Labor Act had prohibited. It restrained coercion by employers, while the Railway Labor Act had restrained coercion from either side. And finally, the Wagner Act was passed over the fierce opposition of business, while the Railway Labor Act had been agreed upon by both labor and management (129).

in protest and Wagner found few supporters for his measure in Congress. The president also refused his support, opting instead for Public Resolution No. 44, which established the National Labor Relations Board. As Edelman says of Roosevelt:

> He invariably failed to support labor legislation actively until he was convinced it had adequate political support, and he sometimes sabotaged pro-labor policies already declared to be the law because of strong business pressure. . . . Always fairly sure the country would follow him on relief and recovery measures, he vacillated longest on long-range reform, for business and the middle class were most hostile here. Because he deliberately cultivated contacts with the whole gamut of group interests, he knew better than his predecessors what was politically expedient and what timing was indicated (182).

no question

A year later the timing was right, and labor agitation had helped make it so. When Wagner introduced a revised version of the bill that was to become the National Labor Relations Act, the measure found ready support. Since labor's right to organize had long been upheld in principle, proponents of the bill had little difficulty finding arguments, adding only that the bill was important as a means of achieving economic balance by preserving purchasing power, and as a bulwark against communism. With few exceptions, the business community continued to be vehement in its opposition, and the National Association of Manufacturers mobilized one of its largest campaigns to defeat the measure. *The Commercial and Financial Chronicle* called it "one of the most objectionable, as well as one of the most revolutionary, pieces of legislation ever presented to Congress" (Schlesinger, 1958, 404). The AFL remained aloof, as did the administration; Secretary of Labor Perkins, the only administration representative to testify, was ambivalent (Bernstein, 1971, 331). On May 2, 1935, the Senate Labor Committee reported unanimously in favor of the bill; the vote in the Senate was 63 to 12. Several weeks later, it passed the House by an overwhelming 132 to 42. Roosevelt, who until this time had kept silent, finally came out in favor of the bill and signed it on July 5, 1935.

But the fight was not over. Two weeks after the bill became law, the American Liberty League published a brief signed by fifty-eight lawyers declaring the Wagner Act unconstitutional. Industry then acted on the assumption that the law need not be obeyed and U. S. Steel, General Motors, and Goodyear Tire and Rubber rushed to the federal courts where they got injunctions that tied the hands of the new National Labor Relations Board; by June 30, 1936, the board was involved in eighty-three such suits (Bernstein, 1971, 646). Moreover, there was reason to think employers would be vindicated by the Supreme Court. During 1935 and 1936 the Court had nullified other major elements of the New Deal program, including the National Industrial Recovery Act. In 1936 the Court struck down the Guffey-Snyder Act, which laid down procedures for the coal industry very much like those of the Wagner Act. American industry had grounds for optimism.

INDUSTRY'S RESISTANCE IS OVERCOME

American workers, however, were also optimistic. The passage of the Wagner Act, at a time when working conditions were worsening after the temporary recovery of 1934, only reaffirmed for them the justice of their struggle and their sense that victories could be won. Congress had acted despite the threats and importuning of the leading industrialists of the nation. Moreover the defeat of many of those same industrialists in the election of 1934 was repeated in the election of 1936 when, despite the vigorous opposition of business interests, the New Deal won an overwhelming sweep. Workers probably understood that for the moment, at least, business had lost control of the state. Consequently, labor militancy surged in 1936 and 1937, especially in the mass production industries. The number of strikes continued to rise: 2,014 in 1935; 2,172 in 1936, and 4,740 in 1937. And more than half of the strikes were over the demand for union recognition under the terms laid out in the Wagner Act (Millis and Montgomery, 692, 701).

The first big strike after the Wagner Act occurred in Akron. The background for the strike was familiar. Akron was a one-industry town where employment had fallen by half after the stock market crash. By the spring of 1933 many of the rubber companies had shut down, Goodyear was on a two-day week, the main bank had failed, and the city was broke, laying off many of its own employees (Bernstein, 1971, 98–99). Then came section 7 (a), setting the rubber workers in motion. Federal locals were formed, and some forty to fifty thousand workers joined up, all of whom AFL leaders tried to parcel out among the international craft unions. At the end of 1934 the NLRB ordered elections in the Goodyear and Firestone plants, but the companies went to court and the issue was delayed indefinitely (Brecher, 179). The workers were pressing for a strike, but their union leaders signed a federally mediated agreement to await the outcome of the court action and Goodyear announced that the agreement made "no change in employee relations since the provisions are in complete accord with the policies under which Goodyear has always operated" (Brecher, 180). Discouraged by AFL and government maneuverings, men dropped out of the union.

But the workers' discontent did not dwindle, especially when in November 1935, and again in January 1936, Goodyear Tire and Rubber cut wages. Then, on February 10, the company laid off a large number of men without giving the usual notice. A few nights later, 137 workers, hardly any of them union members, shut off the power and sat down. Local Rubber Worker Union officials persuaded the sit-downers to leave, but 1,500 Goodyear workers met and voted to strike (Brecher, 183–184). The word went out, workers began to gather in the bitter cold, and by morning the eleven-mile perimeter of the Goodyear plant was circled by pickets. Few of the ten to fifteen thousand who struck were members of the union,[50] but the factory was at a standstill. Meanwhile, the picketers were digging in, building over 300 shanties for protection against the winter winds, from which they flew American flags, again named for the promise: "Camp Roosevelt," "Camp John L. Lewis," "Camp Senator Wagner."

Goodyear succeeded in getting a sweeping injunction against mass picketing from the common pleas court in Summit County, but the injunction was not enforced. When the sheriff threatened to open the plant with a force of 150 deputies, thousands of workers armed with clubs and sticks massed before the gates and the deputies withdrew. Later the rumor spread that a "Law and Order League" would attack the picket lines, but the rubber workers armed again, and the threat never materialized. Goodyear then turned to Governor Davey for troops, but a state election was approaching, popular sentiment in Akron was with the strikers, and the Akron Central Labor Union declared there would be a general strike if force was used. The governor agreed there was no justification for calling out the militia.

---

[50] Walsh reports 800 union members among the 14,000 Goodyear employees at the time of the strike (139).

At the end of February Assistant Secretary of Labor McGrady arrived on the scene to mediate. He recommended that the strikers return to work and submit the issues to arbitration. Some 4,000 workers met at the armory and jeered the proposal down, singing out "No, no, a thousand times no" (Bernstein, 1971, 595). In the fourth week of the strike Goodyear Tire and Rubber agreed to a settlement that granted reinstatement of the discharged employees, reduction of the work week, and recognition of union shop committees (Levinson, 143–146; Thomas Brooks, 181–182).[51]

The next outbreak was in the automobile industry, in the giant industrial empire of General Motors, controlled by the Du Ponts and J. P. Morgan.[52] GM had always stood firmly and successfully against unionism, partly by virtue of an elaborate program of "welfare capitalism" inaugurated during the upsurge of union activity following World War I. With the onset of the Great Depression, the welfare programs eroded, and after 1933 GM relied more on a vast spy network in its plants to discourage union activities. According to the La Follette Committee, GM was the best customer of the labor spy agencies, and its expenditure for espionage rose as unionization activities increased (Fine, 37), totaling at least a million dollars between January 1934 and June 1936 (Walsh, 109).

But if labor spies made the men fearful, they also made them angry, given the temper of the times. There were other grievances as well. Hourly wages in the auto industry were relatively high, but employment was extremely irregular, and workers suffered from severe economic insecurity. Between September 1933 and September 1934, for example, fully 40 percent of GM workers were employed less than twenty-nine weeks, and 60 percent earned less than $1,000. Workers were even more incensed over the speed-ups and model changeovers which exhausted them and which, they felt, meant the

---

[51] The agreement also specified that management would "meet with any or all employees individually or through their chosen representatives." This the Goodyear management did, again and again, without, however, agreeing to sign a collective bargaining contract until 1941 (Bernstein, 1971, 596–602). Some critics claim the rubber workers were prepared to hold out for a better settlement, but were discouraged from doing so by CIO leaders, and by Communist organizers in Akron as well (Buhle, 238).

[52] The far-flung GM network of sixty-nine automotive plants in thirty-five cities, including the Fisher Body Corporation, had at first been hard hit by the depression. Sales of cars and trucks in the United States dropped 74 percent between 1928 and 1932, and net corporation profits fell from $296 million to less than $8.5 million. Then, under the New Deal, the corporation recovered quickly. By 1936, sales of cars and trucks almost quadrupled, and the number of employees doubled (Fine, 20–25).

company was getting more profits for less work (Fine, 55–61). By 1933 spontaneous strikes began to spread in the industry. John Anderson, a rank-and-file leader of the time, gives an account of such a walkout:

> Briggs Manufacturing Company hired me as a metal finisher at 52 cents an hour, but they failed to pay me at that rate. The first week I got 45 cents an hour. The second week our rate was cut to 40 cents an hour, and the third week it was cut to 35 cents. These wage cuts were enough to provoke the men to strike. After being called to work on Sunday, they walked out at noon without telling the foreman. On Monday we went to work again, and before starting work we told the foreman: "We want to know what our wages are. We were hired at 52 cents an hour, and we're being paid 35 cents." The foreman said: "You see that line out there of men looking for jobs? If you fellows don't want to work, get your clothes and clear out. There are plenty of men who will take your jobs."
>
> This statement provoked the men into walking out as a body, not as individuals. They had no organization; they had no one to speak for them. There were several hundred of them milling around in the street wondering what to do. . . . I got on a car fender and suggested we demand the 52 cents an hour promised on our hiring slips. . . . I was blacklisted as a result of the strike . . . [but] I learned that as a result of the strike the wages of metal finishers had been raised to 60 cents an hour . . . (Lynd, 1969, 62–63).

After the passage of section 7 (a), auto workers had begun to join unions. Many of them had joined the AFL federal union (later to become the United Automobile Workers and to affiliate with the CIO).[53] But, under the constraining effects of AFL policies and government conciliation of the auto industry, total union membership had rapidly declined, to only 5 percent of the workers in the industry by early 1935. Still, unionized or not, with the passage of the Wagner Act, the landslide New Deal victory in the election of 1936, and the successes of the rubber workers in Akron, the auto workers' courage rose and ferment increased. By the fall and winter of 1936 each minor offense by management fell like whiplashes on aggrieved men chafing for action. There is the story, for example, of

---

[53] Some also joined independent unions: the Mechanics Educational Society of America, an independent union of auto tool and die makers organized by the Industrial Workers of the World; the Associated Automobile Workers of America; and the Automotive Industrial Workers Association, organized somewhat later by Richard Frankensteen.

an early sit-down in Flint that was triggered when a union man who protested a firing was led through the plant by a foreman, apparently to be discharged. As he walked the length of the belt-line, his face communicated the message, and every worker turned from the moving row of auto bodies until 700 men were idle. The company rehired the discharged man before work was resumed (Levinson, 175).[54] Brief walkouts and sit-downs at the Chrysler Corporation, at the Bendix plant in South Bend, and at the Midland Steel and the Kelsey-Hayes plants in Detroit ended with some degree of union recognition. In this mood, the struggle with General Motors was bound to come.

Although the fledgling United Automobile Workers, by now affiliated with the CIO, had assigned Wyndham Mortimer, a Communist rank-and-file leader from Cleveland, to begin an organizing campaign in Flint some months earlier, the GM strike actually began relatively spontaneously, erupting in different places at about the same time.[55] Several outbreaks at the Atlanta GM plant culminated in a strike on November 18, 1936, when the rumor spread that management intended to lay off several men for wearing union buttons. A few weeks later the workers at a GM Chevrolet plant in Kansas City walked out after the management had allegedly dismissed a man for violating a company rule against jumping over the line. On December 28 a small group of workers sat down on the line in the GM Fisher Body plant in Cleveland, and 7,000 people stopped working. Then, on December 30, about 50 workers sat down in the Fisher Body plant in Flint, presumably because of a management decision to transfer three inspectors who had refused to quit the union. That night the workers in a second and larger body plant in Flint also sat down on the line, and the Flint sit-down strike was on—at a time when the union could claim as members only a small minority of Flint workers.[56] The strike spread to other cities. Sit-

---

[54] See Kraus for a similar account of a sit-down in Flint in November 1936, just weeks before the big sit-down strike. Kraus was the Communist editor of the auto strike newspaper.

[55] When Walt Moore, a local Communist organizer in Flint, informed William Weinstone, head of the Michigan Communist Party, that the GM strike was imminent, Weinstone was shocked: "You haven't got Flint organized. What are you talking about?" Moore replied, "Well, Bill, we can't stop it. The sentiments are too great" (Keeran, 241–242).

[56] When Mortimer arrived in Flint the previous June, the Flint locals had only 122 members, and most of those were considered to be GM spies. Presumably more men and women signed up in the next few months before the GM strike, but just how many is unclear.

downers took over the GM Fleetwood and Cadillac plants in Detroit, and a lamp factory in Indiana; walkout strikes were called in St. Louis, Janesville, Norwood, Kansas City, and Toledo. By January 1, 1937, 112,000 of GM's production workers were idle.

Flint, the main battleground of the strike, was the center of the GM empire, and a GM town. The corporation controlled about 80 percent of the jobs. GM's upper crust was the town's upper crust and most of the political officials were former GM employees or stockholders. Accordingly, when company guards tried to bar the strike supporters from delivering food to the men inside the plant, they were quickly reinforced by Flint police and a battle ensued. The police used tear gas and guns, the strikers returned their fire with streams of water from GM fire hoses, and with automobile hinges, bottles, and rocks. About two dozen strikers and policemen were injured in what came to be known as the "Battle of the Running Bulls."

The disorder precipitated the intervention of the Governor of Michigan, Frank Murphy, who had been elected to office in the Roosevelt landslide of the previous November. He had received the endorsement of the entire Michigan labor movement, although he was also on close terms with auto industry executives, and was later revealed to have substantial GM holdings (Brecher, 200). Governor Murphy sent word to GM officials not to deny food or heat to the strikers in the interest of public health, and arrived on the scene with about 2,000 National Guardsmen who, however, were instructed not to take sides.[57] The governor then assumed the role of peacemaker, prevailing on the UAW leaders and General Motors officials to negotiate. But the negotiations proved futile, the workers evacuated three minor plants only to discover that GM had also agreed to negotiate with the Flint Alliance, a citizens' vigilante organization dominated by the corporation. By mid-January, Secretary of Labor Frances Perkins was importuning GM executives to meet with union representatives. The corporation was losing about $2 million a day in sales, but it nevertheless held fast, refusing to meet with the union until the plants were vacated. On January 27 GM announced that it intended to resume production, and went to court

---

[57] The governor also persuaded the Genesee County prosecutor not to use 300 John Doe warrants issued against strikers after the "Battle of the Running Bulls" and to release on bail Victor Reuther, Robert Travis, and Henry Kraus, all of whom were involved in the battle (Keeran, 264–265).

for an injunction against the sit-downers.[58] The strikers responded by occupying yet another plant in a dramatically covert maneuver, leading President Roosevelt to phone John L. Lewis with the message that he backed a plan calling for GM recognition of UAW for one month. Lewis is said to have replied, "My people tell me it's got to be six months," and the sit-down continued.

On February 2 the court acted. The order handed down by Judge Paul Gadola instructed the workers to leave the plants at three o'clock on February 3, and pressure was mounting on the governor to clear the plants by force. But worker pressure was mounting as well. On the evening of February 2 the strikers in one of the occupied plants sent a message to the governor. Their words virtually exulted in their sense of righteousness; the burden of violence was on the opposition:[59]

> We have carried on a stay-in strike for over a month in order to make General Motors Corporation obey the law and engage in collective bargaining. . . . Unarmed as we are, the introduction of militia, sheriffs, or police with murderous weapons will mean a blood bath of unarmed workers. . . . We have decided to stay in the plant. We have no illusions about the sacrifices which this decision will entail. We fully expect that if a violent effort is made to oust us, many of us will be killed, and we take this means of making it known to our wives, to our children, to the people of Michigan that if this result follows from the attempt to eject us, you are the one who must be held responsible for our deaths (Levinson, 164–165).

The spirit of the message from the sit-down strikers was the spirit of many workers outside the plants as well. On the morning of February 3, as the Guardsmen set up their machine guns and howitzers, the roads to Flint were jammed with thousands of trucks and automobiles—supporters of the strikers from surrounding cities who had come to join the picket lines. Rubber workers came from Akron; auto workers from Lansing, Toledo, and Pontiac; Walter Reuther brought several hundred men from his West Side local in Detroit; workers came from the Kelsey-Hayes plant in Detroit carrying a banner: "Kelsey-Hayes never forgets their friends." As the hour of the court order approached, a procession of perhaps 10,000 workers,

---

[58] Lee Pressman, a CIO lawyer, had scuttled an earlier injunction by revealing that the presiding judge owned substantial amounts of GM stock.

[59] The message was actually written by organizer Bob Travis and Lee Pressman, then approved by the sit-down strikers (Keeran, 272).

led by Women's Emergency Brigades carrying an American flag, circled the menaced plant. The marchers carried clubs and sticks, lengths of pipe, and clothes trees for the battle they expected. Thus the deadline passed.[60]

The crisis had reached the point where the White House was compelled to intervene in seriousness. At Roosevelt's request, and coaxed by the Secretary of Labor, corporation executives met with CIO and auto union leaders, and in the agreement that resulted, the union won a six-month period of what amounted to exclusive recognition in the seventeen plants closed by strikes.[61]

A similar sequence of events occurred in the Chrysler plants only a few short weeks after the GM strike was settled. (The overwhelming majority of Chrysler workers had voted in favor of an "employee representation" plan only two years earlier.) When discussions between Chrysler and UAW leaders bogged down, 60,000 workers struck, two-thirds of them by sitting down in Chrysler factories. The strikers held the plants for thirty days, defending their occupation with massive picketing. An attempt by the local sheriff to enforce a court order for evacuation of the plants was responded to by 30,000 to 50,000 massed strikers who encircled the plants. An agreement was finally signed with Chrysler early in April. Within a year, the UAW claimed 350,000 members (Walsh, 126–133).

Steel workers were also in motion. Wages in steel had fallen sharply from a weekly average of $32.60 in 1929, to $13.20 in 1932— for those lucky enough to work at all (Walsh, 60). The industry had dealt with worker demands during 1933–1934 by incorporating fully 90 percent of the 500,000 steel workers into "employee representation plans" or company unions (Robert Brooks, 79). Ironically, it was these company unions that became the first vehicles for collective action.[62] A steel worker tells the story:

---

[60] Both the sheriff and Judge Gadola explained that no action could be taken to enforce the injunction until GM sought a writ of attachment against the sit-downers. The writ commanding the sheriff to "attach the bodies" of all the sit-downers, as well as the picketers and the UAW officers, was secured two days later. The sheriff then requested the governor to authorize the National Guard to carry out the order but, by that time, GM was at the conference table and the governor demurred. In any case, the National Guard was apparently not inclined to hazard an assault upon the thousands inside and outside the plants (Fine, 292–294).

[61] Accounts of the General Motors strike can be found in Fine, 302–312; Keeran, 225–285; Thomas Brooks, 183–186; Levinson, 160–168; Prickett, 180–202.

[62] According to Matles and Higgins, company unions were also the vehicle for rank-and-file unionism at the General Electric plant in Schenectady (64), and at the Westinghouse plant in East Pittsburgh (78).

Well, we got interested in the union . . . because the steelmill people came into the mill around 1933 and handed us a piece of paper. We looked at it, and it was called "An Employee Representation Plan." . . . I looked at this paper as a young lad and said this thing could never work, because it said right at the outset that there would be five members from management to sit on a committee and five members from the union—the company union— to sit on the committee. I asked who settled the tie, and of course I found out the management did. . . . We tried to disband the company union, and we formed what we called the Associated Employees. This was just workers like myself attempting to do something by way of getting into a legitimate union. . . . One day we read in the newspapers that they were trying to do the same thing down in Pittsburgh (Lynd, 1969, 55–57).

Signs of restlessness within the company union structure became clear early in 1935 when employee representatives in the Pittsburgh and Chicago area plants began agitating for wage increases, an issue that was not considered to be within the jurisdiction of the employee representation plans, or even of the individual plant managers, who claimed that wages were a matter of overall corporation policy. As a result, company union representatives from different plants began to meet together to consider joint actions (Brooks, Robert, 85–89). In January 1936 thirteen out of twenty-five employee representatives in the Gary, Indiana, plant of Carnegie-Illinois Steel formed a union lodge. In Pittsburgh (where workers were especially angry about a 10 percent check-off being taken from their wages by Carnegie-Illinois as repayment for relief baskets) some twenty-five employee representatives met to set up a Pittsburgh central council to make district-wide demands on wages and hours issues through the company unions.

By the summer of 1936, rank-and-file unrest was bubbling up in spontaneous walkouts. In the mood of the time, any grievance could become a trigger, as in the incident Jessie Reese recounts at the Youngstown Sheet and Tube mills:

They fired our foreman, a nice fellow, and they brought over a slave driver from Gary. A white fellow told us he was an organizer for the Ku Klux Klan and said: "You all going to stand for that guy to come in here?" So I went down to the operators of the pickles and said: "Shut the pickles down." And they shut them down. I went over to see Long, the foreman, and I said: "Long, you lost your job . . . give me five minutes and we'll make them tell you where your job's at. . . ." I drove over to the hot strip where the white fellows were rolling hot steel, and I said: "Hey, fellows, just stop a minute rolling that steel. We're shutting down over there. We're fighting for ten cents an hour and our foreman back on the job." (It would look foolish fighting for your foreman and not for yourself.) And they said: "Oh, you got it organized?" And I said, "Yes, we shut it down. Look over there, we're down, we're not moving. . . ." So the white fellows said: "We'll follow you" (Lynd, 1969, 60–67).

On July 5, 1936, steel workers congregated in Homestead, Pennsylvania, to honor the Homestead martyrs and to hear a "Steel Workers Declaration of Independence," read by an erstwhile company union leader. Lieutenant Governor Kennedy of Pennsylvania, a former miner and officer of the UMW, told the crowd that steel was now open territory for union organizers and that they could count on government relief funds if there was a strike—a far cry from the treatment strikers received in Homestead during earlier struggles (Walsh, 49). Later that summer, Governor Earle told a Labor Day crowd of 200,000 assembled in Pittsburgh that never during his administration would the state troops be used to break a strike and "the skies returned the crowd's response" (Walsh, 171).

It was in this context that the CIO launched the Steel Workers Organizing Committee, putting 433 organizers into the field and suspending the customary dues and initiation fees to sign men up (Bernstein, 1971, 452–453). In November 1936, when the SWOC announced that 82,315 men had signed membership cards, U. S. Steel responded by announcing a 10 percent wage hike, and offering contracts to be signed only by the company unions. But many of the company union leaders had been drawn into the SWOC and refused to sign, while Secretary of Labor Perkins said that the leaders of the Employee Representation Plans "had no right to sign contracts." By March 1937 when SWOC had established 150 locals with 100,000 members (Raybeck, 351) and the company unions were wrecked, U. S. Steel signed with the union, without a strike.

There were probably several reasons for the easy victory. GM had capitulated only a few weeks earlier, after its production had ground to a complete halt,[63] and U. S. Steel must have been worried by

---

[63] Lynd quotes a letter written a few years later by Thomas W. Lamont (of the House of Morgan and U. S. Steel) to President Roosevelt explaining U. S. Steel's decision to negotiate. Apparently the board of U. S. Steel feared the enormous costs of a strike such as General Motors had just undergone. A strike, Lamont added, might also "prove

the losses a strike would cause at a time when the prospects of a war in Europe had created a booming demand for steel. Worker agitation in the steel mills was interfering with production just when U. S. Steel was negotiating vast contracts for armaments with the British, who were insisting on a guarantee of uninterrupted production. Unionism was a way to offer that guarantee, as Myron Taylor, head of U. S. Steel, had learned from the agreement signed in the captive mines in 1933 (Walsh, 73). It was also clear that U. S. Steel would get little political support in a showdown. Governor Earle of Pennsylvania, elected by a labor-liberal coalition, had promised the steel workers his backing. And on Capitol Hill, criticism of the steel industry for its espionage activities and its price fixing practices was growing. Finally, unlike the men who headed other steel companies, Myron Taylor was not a steel man, but had been installed by the financiers who dominated his board, and he appeared to have the flexibility and sophistication to respond to new conditions with new methods.[64] Unionization quickly followed in U. S. Steel's subsidiaries, and in some other independent steel companies. By May 1937 SWOC membership had reached 300,000 and over a hundred contracts had been signed (Raybeck, 351).

Little Steel—including the National Steel Corporation, Republic, Bethlehem, Inland Steel, and the Youngstown Sheet and Tube Corporation—did rot sign. In late May 1937 the SWOC called 70,000 men out on a strike, which was ultimately broken by the police and troops provided by hostile state and local governments. Local governments in Johnstown, Pennsylvania, in Canton and Youngstown, Ohio, and in Chicago cooperated openly with the steel corporations.[65] In Chicago police interfered with peaceful picketing from the beginning of the strike, and when strikers held a straggly Memorial Day march to protest an anti-picketing order and the arrest of pickets, the police shot them down, killing ten and wounding ninety (Taft

---

such a major crisis as to constitute almost a social revolution." The plan to avert the strike was not hard to contrive; simply "accredit the C.I.O. as a leading bargaining agency" (Lynd, 1974, 32).

[64] This kind of difference between industry men and Wall Street representatives in the handling of labor problems had been evident before in the steel industry. For example, financiers on the board of U. S. Steel had pushed through welfare programs early in the century, over the opposition of industry representatives.

[65] For a detailed account of the use of local police forces to break the Little Steel strike, and the techniques by which local government was made to serve corporation purposes, see Walsh, 75–95. In Youngstown, Ohio, for example, every organizer in the region was jailed at least once, and some five or six times (84).

and Ross, 358–359.)[66] In Ohio, Governor Martin L. Davey announced that troops would be used to open the mills, and the National Guard moved systematically across the state to break up picket lines and arrest local strike leaders. Altogether the Little Steel strike left 16 dead and 307 injured, according to Senator La Follette. The La Follette Committee reports summed up the record of the struggle at the Republic Steel Corporation plants:[67]

> . . . a mobilization of men, money and munitions occurred which has not been approached in the history of labor disputes in recent times. Although known to be incomplete, the committee has assembled data showing that a total of 7,000 men were directly employed as guards, patrolmen, deputy sheriffs, National Guardsmen, city police and company police on strike duty. Over $4,000,000 was expended directly attributable to the strike. A total of $141,000 worth of industrial munitions was assembled for use.

As in the Flint sit-downs, the workers looked to the president for help, but on June 30, 1937, the press quoted Roosevelt's response: "A plague on both your houses." In mid-July the strike was lost. It was the last of the depression battles, and spelled the end of an era. But while the Little Steel strike was lost in the mills, the movement of which it was a part produced the political concessions that were later to force union recognition by government tribunal.[68]

Throughout 1936 sit-down strikes and walkouts raced through industry and business. In 1936 there had been only 48 sit-down strikes; in 1937 there were about 500 such strikes lasting more than a day and involving about 400,000 workers. The peak came in March, when 170 sit-down strikes were in progress, affecting some 170,000 workers (Fine, 331). There must have been many more of shorter duration, for the sit-down was becoming the workers' ready weapon, as the song of the movement suggested:

> When they tie the can to a union man, sit down! Sit down!
> When they give him the sack, they'll take him back, sit down!
> Sit down!

---

[66] A newsreel of the event was suppressed by Paramount for fear of inciting riots throughout the country. The film was later secretly shown to the La Follette Committee and a blow-by-blow account of the film itself can be found in Hofstadter and Wallace, 179–184.

[67] Republic apparently was the largest purchaser of tear gas and sickening gas in the country, in addition to having acquired a veritable arsenal of munitions.

[68] By the autumn of 1941 the four main Little Steel companies recognized the union, although not without a militant strike at Bethlehem Steel.

When the speed up comes, just twiddle your thumbs, sit down! Sit
down!
When the boss won't talk, don't take a walk, sit down! Sit down!

The tactic was admirably suited to the unorganized struggle of the
mid–1930s. A small number of workers could sit down on the line
and stop production, without benefit of much advance planning or
advance commitment. With workers controlling the plant, employers
could not import strikebreakers. In cases like General Motors, where
many specialized factories depended on each other, a few sit-down
strikes could, and did, stop an entire corporation. Thus, relatively
small-scale and spontaneous actions could bring management to heel.
Most of the sit-down strikes ended with gains for the workers.[69]
Moreover, in the climate of the time, the sit-down, itself nonviolent,
did not usually precipitate police action.[70] And so the tactic spread,
from factory workers to salesgirls, to hospital workers, garbage col-
lectors, and watchmakers, to sailors, farmhands, opticians, and hotel
employees. An AFL business agent for the Hotel and Restaurant
Employees recalls:

> You'd be sitting in the office any March day of 1937, and the
> phone would ring and the voice at the other end would say,
> "My name is Mary Jones; I'm a soda clerk at Liggett's; we've thrown
> the manager out and we've got the keys. What do we do now?" And
> you'd hurry over to the company to negotiate and over there they'd
> say, "I think it's the height of irresponsibility to call a strike
> before you've even asked for a contract," and all you could answer
> was, "You're so right" (Thomas Brooks, 180).

By the fall of 1937, there were cases of operators in projection booths
of movie theaters who locked themselves in and stopped the shows
until their demands were met (Levinson, 173–175). Still more workers took part in walkout strikes. Before 1937 was over, nearly two
million workers had engaged in labor struggles in that year alone
(Millis and Montgomery, 692), more than half of them to secure
union recognition.

The strikes that spread through the country in 1936 and 1937
were victorious as economic struggles, but they were victorious only

---

[69] Fine reports that "substantial gains" were achieved in over 50 percent of the 1937
sit-downs, and compromises worked out in over 30 percent (332).
[70] Walsh estimates that only 25 out of some 1,000 sit-downs were defeated by police
(60).

because a century-long accommodation between government and economic elites had been broken. The workers' movement had exerted sufficient political force to protect the economic force of the strike. The rubber workers in Akron, the auto workers in Flint, the steel workers in Pennsylvania all had been able to overcome employer resistance only because governors dependent on the support of aroused workers were reluctant to send troops against strikers. And in Youngstown and Chicago, where state and local governments were hostile, the Little Steel strike was lost, the workers' economic power once more destroyed by government firepower.

Despite a new dive in the economy in 1937, the Department of Labor reported that wages of rubber workers increased by one-third over 1934, with the greatest increases in the lower wage brackets; the six-hour day was established in many rubber plants. The SWOC won wage increases in steel that led to an industry-wide minimum of five dollars a day, and the industry's wage bill increased by one-third over 1929. In the auto industry, workers won a seventy-five-cents-an-hour minimum and a forty-hour week. Maritime workers were earning a peak wage of $72.50 a month. Overall, in October 1937, Philip Murray estimated a billion dollars had been added in wages: $250 million in steel; $100 million in automobiles; about $60 million in textiles; $6 million in transport; and $12 million in electrical appliances.[71] Nearly a million workers had won a 35- or 36-hour week (Levinson, 260–277).

The political impact of rising worker agitation was also evident in the concessions wrung directly from government. Federal regulation of wages and hours had been an issue since the abortive NIRA codes, and had figured again in the 1936 election campaign. Late in 1937, after a new dive in the economy, Roosevelt began to push hard for a wages and hours bill (which the AFL continued to oppose). When the House Rules Committee, dominated by southern congressmen who had good reason to worry about the impact of minimum wage legislation in the South, prevented the measure from coming up for a vote in the regular session, Roosevelt called Congress back for a special session. Finally in January 1938 the Fair Labor Standards Act became law, affecting some 300,000 workers who were earning less than the twenty-five-cents-an-hour minimum, and some

---

[71] According to Arthur M. Ross, real hourly earnings between 1933 and 1945 in sixty-five industries show a direct relationship between the percent of unionization and wage increases. Cited in Bernstein (1971, 775).

1,300,000 workers whose official work week was over the forty-four-hour standard established by the law (Raybeck, 360). The new depression of 1937–1938 helped prompt several other measures to ease and appease labor, most importantly an increase in activity by the Public Works Administration, an expansion of the work relief rolls, the introduction of the federal public housing program, and a step-up of the due date for the first social security payments from 1942 to 1939.

But of all these measures, it was the Wagner Act and federal support of unionization that was most important in shaping the workers' political future. After business broke with Roosevelt in 1935 the president not only lent his support to the act, but appointed pro-labor members to the NLRB. Then in April 1937, several months before the debacle of the Little Steel strike, the Supreme Court handed down its decision upholding the Wagner Act in *National Labor Relations Board vs. Jones and Laughlin Steel Company*. With that decision, the protection of government for the right of labor to organize and to bargain collectively was reaffirmed.

From Disruption to Organization

The Wagner Act not only placed the ultimate authority of the state behind the right of workers to join unions and bargain collectively, it also established a series of mechanisms through which that authority was enforced. With the passage of the act, therefore, it was government as much as the unions that organized workers, a point to which we will return shortly. Moreover, as our account up to now should make evident, the unions could not take much credit for the uprisings that forced government to act to protect unionization either.

WHO MOBILIZED INSURGENCY?

In the minds of most people, worker struggles are usually linked with unionism; the right to join a union and to bargain collectively was often a central demand in worker uprisings long before the 1930s. But that does not mean that established unions played a central role in these uprisings. In fact some of the fiercest struggles in the nineteenth and early twentieth centuries occurred when the unions were weakest and sometimes despite the resistance of established union leadership.[72] But while existing unions could not often be credited with the great worker struggles of the pre-depression years, there were nevertheless organizers in these struggles. Some of these organizers were insurgents from the rank and file; others were radicals whose vision of an alternative future helped to account for their exemplary courage. Wherever these organizers came from, their vision helped goad workers into protest, and their courage gave workers heart and determination.

In the struggles of the 1930s, a similar pattern emerged. Many of the workers' battles were mounted to win union recognition. But neither the battles nor the victories were the result of existing union organization or union leadership. In fact the rising number of strikes after 1934 paralleled the decline in union membership as the AFL scuttled its own federal unions. Thus the battles in Toledo, Minneapolis, and San Francisco occurred either in the aftermath of failed unionization drives, or before unionization had taken hold. The textile strike of 1934 erupted among the rank and file after union leadership had settled with the industry, and later the United Textile Workers disclaimed any responsibility for the "flying squadrons" through which the strike had spread (Brecher, 169). The massive walkout of rubber workers at Goodyear in 1936 occurred when the United Rubber Workers had shrunk to a weak and small union; four days after the strike had begun, URW officials were still claim-

---

[72] For example, Brecher points out that the great railroad strikes of 1877 occurred during a low point in union organization; the membership of the national unions had fallen to about 50,000 from 300,000 in 1870 (9–10). Moreover, when the strikes broke out, the Trainsmen Union had nothing to do with them. In the strike wave of 1886 the Knights of Labor found itself a reluctant partner as workers walked out first, and joined the Knights later. Terrence Powderly, head of the Knights, complained that "the majority of the newcomers were not of the quality the Order had sought for in the past" and suspended the organizing of new assemblies of workers (Brecher, 38). At the start of the miners' strike of 1894, the United Mine Workers had no more than 20,000 members, but 150,000 men joined the walkout. And in the strike of the youthful American Railway Union against the Pullman company the same year, nearly half the 260,000 workers who joined the strike were not union members. Meanwhile, the older railway brotherhoods ignored the strike, and even encouraged strikebreaking, as they did again during the wildcat railway strike of 1919 (Brecher, 82; 89–92). Similarly, AFL support of the great steel strike of 1919 was reluctant, while the Amalgamated Association of Iron and Steel Workers actually ordered its men back to work during the strike.

ing it was not their affair (Brecher, 184). Later, when 15,000 men were on strike, the CIO sent organizers, funds, and negotiators. Bernstein writes that these experienced unionists guided the bargaining and restrained the "mountaineers' natural tendency to violence" (1971, 595). But it was the mountaineers' willingness to use violence in the face of violence that won the strike.

After the abortive experiences with the AFL during 1933 and 1934,[73] only a tiny percentage of auto workers had joined the newly named United Automobile Workers. When the sit-downs began in 1936,[74] the leaders of the new union were not quite in control of the wave of strikes that shook the industry. Homer Martin, the president of the UAW, was reportedly nonplussed when it became clear that the strike in the Atlanta GM plant was spreading and the union was faced with a GM strike. John L. Lewis, who had by this time broken with the AFL and established the Committee of Industrial Organizations, is said to have tried to head off the sit-downs, and CIO spokesman Charles Howard had told the 1936 UAW convention that the CIO was "not even considering the possibility of a strike in the auto industry, as we preach industrial peace" (Keeran, 126). According to J. Raymond Walsh, later research and education director for the CIO, "The CIO high command, preoccupied with the drive in steel, tried in vain to prevent the strike . . ." (112).[75] Once the sit-downs started, the CIO leaders came quickly after, rushing to catch up with and capture the spontaneous outbreaks of angry men and their local leaders. The vast ambition and keen instincts that had led Lewis to sense the opportunity for organizing industrial workers also led him to support the sit-downs once they had occurred, and to take over the negotiations with GM leaders.

---

[73] Brecher reports that in local auto strikes before the Flint outbreak, the AFL acted as strikebreaker, marching its men through the picket lines with police protection (187–188).

[74] The La Follette Committee reported that UAW membership in Flint was down from 26,000 in 1934 to 120 in 1936. Fine reports that in June 1935 the five Flint locals had 757 paid-up members, the GM Detroit locals 423 members, and the remaining GM locals in Michigan 65 members (41, 71).

[75] Fine does not think this is the whole truth. He points out that by August 1936 the CIO had three organizers in the auto industry, but agrees that prior to the GM sit-downs, the CIO did not make the kind of commitment that it was making in the steel industry (93). In fact, Adolph Germer, Lewis' representative in the UAW, thwarted the formation of a GM council among the unionists in an effort to forestall the GM confrontation (92–93).

In steel, where the CIO had intended to begin organizing, the workers were already prepared for action and often searched out Lewis and the SWOC:

I became president of the Associated Employees, and then we heard about a man named John Lewis who was very interested in trying to organize the unorganized. I wrote him a letter and said we had an independent union that would like to join up. He wrote back and told me if I held my short tail in he'd be down there in the near future and he'd send a man by the name of Philip Murray (Lynd, 1969, 57–58).

John Sargent, another steel organizer, recounts the situation at Inland Steel:

Without a contract; without any agreement with the company; without any regulations concerning hours of work, conditions of work, or wages, a tremendous surge took place. We talk of a rank-and-file movement: the beginning of union organization was the best type of rank-and-file movement you could think of. John L. Lewis sent in a few organizers, but there were no organizers at Youngstown Sheet and Tube. The union organizers were essentially workers in the mill who were so disgusted with their conditions and so ready for a change that they took the union into their own hands. . . . For example, as a result of the enthusiasm of the people in the mill, you had a series of strikes, wildcats, shut-downs, slow-downs, anything working people could think of to secure for themselves what they decided they had to have (Lynd, 1969, 74).

Len De Caux captures the temper of the movement:

The workers were waiting for CIO, pounding on its doors long before CIO was ready for them. I heard the pounding as soon as I started with CIO late in 1935—in delegations, on the phone, in the mail, in the news. It came from within the AFL, and from all the unorganized industries. . . . We heard from auto and rubber workers, seamen; from radio, electrical, shipyard, furniture, textile, steel, lumber workers; from gas, coke, glass and quarry workers; from sharecroppers, newspapermen. . . . All said "CIO, let's go!" (226).

Who, then, was mobilizing men and women in the plants and the shipyards and the shops to say "CIO, let's go"? In many industries rank-and-file organizers emerged, apparently thrust naturally into leadership by the sheer force of the workers' movement. In a number of industries, these rank-and-file leaders were also ideological radicals, socialists of one variety or another, whose militancy owed some of its fervor to their larger commitment to societal transformation, and to the moral and tangible support they received from likeminded radicals. In many strikes radicals who were not workers also joined in by providing a variety of supportive services to the strikers. Thus members of the old Industrial Workers of the World were active in some of the early auto strikes in 1933. In 1934, Musteites and Communists took the lead in encouraging strikers in Toledo to defy the courts. Trotskyists led the mobilization of striking teamsters in Minneapolis; and Communists and other radical rank-and-file longshoremen spurred the San Francisco dock strike, while a Communist-dominated Maritime Workers Industrial Union helped to spread the walkout.

Of all the radical groups, the Communists are generally agreed to have been the most influential,[76] and they were clearly an instigating force in the automobile and maritime industries, where small Communist nuclei served as key centers of agitation and mobilization. It may be useful, therefore, to pause to understand the role of the Communists, and how they came to play it.

The Communist Party entered the depression after a decade of isolation and decline.[77] At the beginning of the 1920s the party had established the Trade Union Educational League, dedicated to working within AFL unions to build industrial union organizations. During this period the Communists were virtually alone in their support of several desperation strikes in textiles and in mining. "Through the painful isolation of the twenties," writes Paul Buhle, "the Communists had tried first one formula, then another, in their attempts to reach the masses" (193). By the end of the decade the series of failures and a campaign of Communist expulsions by the AFL coincided with a change in Comintern policy, leading the party to adopt a new strategy of establishing independent (or "dual") unions. The Trade Union Educational League was reconstituted as the Trade Union Unity League in 1928, and some of the bitter early strikes of the depression were led by Communists affiliated with TUUL.

---

[76] This was even the assessment of Max Shachtman, himself a Trotskyist, who wrote that during the thirties, "It is no exaggeration to say that 95 percent of the people who became radicals in that time became Communists or moved within the orbit of [Communist] leadership . . . " (quoted in Keeran, 187).

[77] Party membership fell from about 16,000 in early 1925 to 9,500 at the end of the 1920s (Weinstein, 40).

As early as 1928 the scattering of Communists in the auto industry
—perhaps only two or three in a factory—began publishing shop
papers named the *Ford Worker, Packard Worker, Hudson Worker,*
and the *Fisher Body Worker* (Prickett, 110), and otherwise pressed
to build the Auto Workers Union, now affiliated with TUUL.

> It was a slow, difficult, unglamorous task. A meeting called after
> the wage cuts in the Briggs Waterloo plant drew only two workers.
> A week later, a second meeting was held with only four workers.
> They decided to organize first around a single grievance; the prac-
> tice of having men work two lathes. . . . The small nucleus of
> workers continued to meet and regularly distributed small leaflets
> which were passed hand-to-hand inside the plant (Prickett, 122).

The Communists worked with the mainly defensive auto strikes of
this period, but they did not lead them and, as one party leader said
at the time, they "did not really get a foothold in the factories."

The rise of worker defiance after the passage of the NIRA created
a new opportunity for the Communists. Workers were angry and
hopeful, eager for action, and rank-and-file Communists helped them
to act. As the unionization drive gained momentum during 1934
and 1935 the party, determined to work within the union movement,
abandoned dual unionism, softened its criticism of the AFL, and
Communists within the plants downplayed the party's political line
in favor of an emphasis on workplace grievances.[78] At this stage, the
Communists approached the issue of unionism as agitators from
below, trying to goad the workers on by exposing the compromises of
the New Deal[79] and of the AFL leadership, insisting that if workers
were to win concessions, they had to rely "on mass action and not
upon the promises of the NRA and high paid [union] officials"
(quoted in Keeran, 124). During this period, in other words, the

---

[78] Party leaders criticized Communists in Cleveland, for example, because they were "so
busy with the important details of union organization, that the Party is completely
forgotten as far as concrete work in the shop is concerned." And the party scored one of
the auto shop papers for ignoring political issues (Keeran, 162).

[79] Prickett quotes a speech by John Stachel, the party's trade union director, which
shows the party's awareness of the usefulness of New Deal rhetoric in stirring workers:
"Secondly, Roosevelt talks higher wages against sweatshops, and carries on investigations
against Morgan and Company, etc. As far as the workers are concerned, they have great
illusions, they believe in all that, and precisely because of their illusions, they become
indignant and are more ready to take up the struggle. Roosevelt says no sweatshops.
Good, we fight against them. Roosevelt says high wages. Very good, let's get high
wages. . . . The Recovery Bill and the Roosevelt program are a double-edged sword
which we can utilize for the shattering of the very illusions he is trying to create" (156).

Communists worked to build the movement, to stimulate anger and to encourage defiance. Because they worked to build the movement, the movement yielded the Communists some influence, at least while the defiant upsurge among the ranks continued. Keeran reports, for example, that before the GM strike a nucleus at the Cleveland Fisher Body shop had a dozen or so members, but then the nucleus grew to fifty (244). The persistence and determination of the Communists during the years of isolation and defeat before the depression were now being redeemed.

But the workers, and the Communists, were fighting for unionization, and it was the CIO that emerged the victor from the struggle. It was Lewis' genius to sense the unrest of the time and to move to capture and lead it, willingly sweeping in the Communist organizers whose discipline and fervor were helping to build his organization. John L. Lewis and the Congress of Industrial Organizations did not create the strike movement of industrial workers; it was the strike movement that created the CIO. In the longer run it did this mainly by forcing the federal government to protect unionization by law, and to enforce that protection administratively.

THE STATE ORGANIZES LABOR

To a large extent it was the National Labor Relations Board established under the Wagner Act that organized the member unions of the CIO. To an even greater extent it was the NLRB that kept the CIO unions organized in the face of the forces that had eroded union membership during earlier periods. The NLRB built and protected union membership in several ways. It effectively eliminated the use of such employer weapons as yellow dog contracts, labor spies, and even antiunion propaganda. It *required* employers to bargain collectively with the elected representatives of a majority of the workers. And it provided a government mechanism for conducting the actual elections.

During earlier periods union organization had depended on continual efforts by organizers to maintain the affiliation of workers. These efforts, difficult at best, were doomed when employers could easily replace workers. But the NLRB changed that, for it "put the coercive power of government to extort union recognition from their employers at the disposal of employees" (Greenstone, 47).[80] In 1938 the board in effect reversed the defeat in Little Steel, ordering the reinstatement of strikers, the elimination of company unions, and forbidding anti-union activities by the steel corporations (Bernstein, 1971, 727–728). Altogether in its first five years the NLRB handled nearly 30,000 cases, settling 2,161 strikes, and holding 5,954 elections and card checks in which two million workers voted (Bernstein, 1971, 652–653). By 1945 the board had handled 74,000 cases involving unfair labor practices and employee representation issues, and had held 24,000 elections to determine collective bargaining agents for six million workers (Raybeck, 345).

As a result union membership grew. By the end of 1937 the CIO could claim 32 affiliated national and international unions, including the giant mass production unions in steel, autos, coal, and rubber. In addition it had chartered 600 local industrial unions, and 80 state and city central councils. Membership had grown from less than a million in December 1936 to 3,700,000. Meanwhile, the AFL also prospered—sometimes because employers rushed to sign up with an AFL union in order to ward off the more militant CIO[81]—and membership in affiliated AFL unions rose to about equal that of the CIO.[82] Just as quickly, the organizational apparatus of the unions expanded;

---

[80] In an interesting argument, Mancur Olson reasons that no matter what the collective gains to be made by unionism, the affiliation of large numbers could not be maintained even under the most favorable circumstances, precisely because these gains were collective, and therefore could not be divided up as rewards for affiliation, or withheld as sanctions for nonaffiliation. Consequently, there was little incentive for the individual to maintain his contribution to the union. Government coercion, after 1937, overcame these rationalistic obstacles to unionism.

[81] The AFL clearly tried to take advantage of its more conservative image in its dealing with employers. Thus Arthur Wharton, head of the International Association of Machinists, sent a directive to IAM officers in the spring of 1937 that read in part: "The purpose of this is to direct all officers and all representatives to contact employers in your locality as a preliminary to organizing the shops and factories. We have not hesitated to tell the employers we have met that the best manner in which to deal with us is on the closed shop basis, because we are then in a position where we can require the members to observe the provisions of any agreement entered into, this with our well-known policy of living up to agreements gives the employer the benefits he is entitled to receive from contracts with our organization and it also places us in a position to prevent sit-downs, sporadic disturbances, slowdowns and other communistic CIO tactics of disruption and disorganization" (Quoted in Matles and Higgins, 48).

[82] Derber uses estimates of the increase of union penetration between 1930 and 1940 as follows: transportation, communication, and public utilities from 23 to 48 percent; mining, quarrying, and oil from 21 to 72 percent; and manufacturing as a whole from 9 to 34 percent (17). Overall, according to the U. S. Department of Labor, union membership as a percent of the nonagricultural labor force increased from 11 percent in 1933, to 27 percent in 1940 (U. S. Department of Labor, 1972).

by 1937 the CIO had established a network of forty-eight regional offices staffed by several hundred field representatives (Levinson, 275; Bernstein, 1971, 684).

The Consequences of Organization

The spirit generated by mass strikes had helped build the industrial unions. The disruptive political force exerted by mass strikes had compelled the federal government to establish a framework that would protect the unions over time. But once established, the unions in turn did not promote disruption, either in economic or in political spheres.

ORGANIZATION AND ECONOMIC POWER

To the contrary, the unions undertook from the outset to maintain internal discipline in the factories in exchange for recognition. This in fact was their trump card in bargaining with management at a time when spontaneous work stoppages were plaguing industry. Thus the principal GM negotiator at the end of the Flint sit-downs complained bitterly that there had been eighteen sit-downs in GM plants in the previous twenty days. The agreement that GM signed with the UAW obligated the union to ensure that there would be no work stoppages until an elaborate grievance procedure had been exhausted, and UAW officials had given their approval (Fine, 305, 325).[83]

---

[83] There were, nevertheless, a rash of work stoppages immediately after the agreement was signed. Walsh reports 200 stoppages by the end of June 1937 (134); Keeran reports that in the first two months following the GM settlement, General Motors workers engaged in 30 wildcat strikes, and in the two years between June 1937 and 1939, GM reported 270 work stoppages or slowdowns, Chrysler 109, Hudson over 50, and Packard 31 (292). Montgomery makes the point that, for the workers, "recognition of their unions tended to unleash shop floor struggles in the first instance, rather than to contain them" (73). But while the victory of union recognition no doubt gave the workers heart, the union itself disavowed the stoppages and, according to Walsh, promised to punish the union members responsible (134). In September 1937 Homer Martin, president of the auto workers' union, sent General Motors a "letter of responsibility" granting the company the right to fire any employee whom the company claimed to be guilty of provoking an unauthorized stoppage (Keeran, 302).

Out of context.

The CIO had never actually endorsed sit-downs, but with recognition it disavowed them. The Communists, by now well into their Popular Front phase and some of them into the union bureaucracy as well, endorsed the call for union discipline. Wyndham Mortimer issued a statement early in 1937 saying: "Sitdown strikes should be resorted to only when absolutely necessary" (Keeran, 294). And the *Flint Auto Worker,* edited by Communist Henry Kraus, editorialized that "the problem is not to foster strikes and labor trouble. The union can only grow on the basis of established procedure and collective bargaining" (Keeran, 294). Accordingly both the GM and the U. S. Steel contracts signed later in 1937 prohibited local strikes (DeCaux, xv).

Matles and Higgins offer a similar explanation of the United Electrical Workers' early successes in negotiating contracts with General Electric and Westinghouse. At General Electric:

> There was a tremendous restlessness among the workers in the company plants. Countless complaints piling up. Spontaneous stoppages more the rule than the exception. This was poor business for a company which had always operated on the principle that its "contented" work force meant steady production and a steady flow of profits. Swope and GE had to be aware that the old system of paternalism had broken down, and that something was needed to take its place if production and profits were to be maximized —especially in tight depression conditions (83).

At Westinghouse:

> [C]onstant stoppages, sitdowns, slowdowns, and piled-up grievances plagued production, as workers became steadily more militant and aggressive. So much so that the company began to get rumblings of dissatisfaction from various plant managers, who favored reaching agreements with the union if only to get on with the business of production. Westinghouse top officers had miscalculated. While Swope's GE agreement with the union had instituted orderly grievance procedure, the Westinghouse foremen and managers were up to their necks in snarls (122).

"It made sense" Bernstein points out, "to negotiate with responsible union officials like John L. Lewis, rather than with desperate local groups" (1971, 468).

If particular industrialists realized the advantages of unionism only under extreme duress, the federal government soon ensured the wide adoption of the union alternative with the passage of the Wagner Act. "We learn from experience," said William M. Leiserson, testifying in favor of the act, "that the only way we will ever have peace . . . is to say that . . . employees have the same right to associate themselves and act through a body that the investors . . . have" (Bernstein, 1971, 333). Taft and Ross sum up the whole of federal labor policy in just these terms:

> A fundamental purpose of the national labor policy, first enunciated by the Wagner Act and confirmed by its subsequent amendments in the Taft-Hartley and Landrum-Griffin Acts, was the substitution of orderly procedures for trials of combat. But in balancing the public interest in the peaceful settlement of industrial disputes with the freedom of labor and management to work out their problems in light of their needs and experience, the law did not outlaw the exercise of economic force. . . . However, this approval of the strike, the picket line, and the maintenance of hard bargaining lines by employers and unions was limited by the establishment of specified rules of conduct imposed on all parties (378–379).

And the unions kept their part of the bargain. Between contracts, the unions tried to curb work stoppages and maintain production. As time went on, the length of contracts and the duration of labor peace increased, and by 1950 the UAW signed a five-year no-strike contract with General Motors with no protection against the speedup. In 1956, George Meany, president of the now merged AFL-CIO, boasted to the National Association of Manufacturers:

> I never went on strike in my life, I never ordered anyone else to run a strike in my life, I never had anything to do with a picket line. . . . In the final analysis, there is not a great deal of difference between the things I stand for and the things that the National Association of Manufacturers stands for (quoted in Georgakas and Surkin, 39).

In 1973 the United Steelworkers of America moved even further in the direction of labor-management cooperation by signing an accord with ten major steel firms committing the union not to strike, submitting issues to binding arbitration instead (*New York Times*, June 5, 1973). When the agreement was signed, the Steelworkers had in any case not struck in fourteen years, and during that time they had fallen from the highest paid industrial workers to fourteenth on the list (Bogdanich, 172).[84] Other unions, including the Seafarers Union, followed suit, signing agreements to use third-party methods for resolving grievances in place of the strike.

Whether, by agreeing to refrain from leading work stoppages between contracts, the unions actually succeeded in reducing disruptions of production is not immediately self-evident.[85] Work stoppages occurred nevertheless. But the unions had undertaken the responsibility for trying to control the rank and file, standing as buffers between workers and management. In part, the unions did this by introducing some of the rituals of democratic representation into the work place, rituals which tended to delegitimize worker defiance when it did occur. In part, the union's role as regulator was implemented through elaborate grievance procedures which were substituted for direct action; these procedures tended to divert and dilute anger more effectively than they secured redress. Union disciplinary procedures also reflected this regulatory role, for the unions now either sanctioned company punishments against workers, or,

---

[84] During this fourteen-year period the steel companies simply built up inventories in anticipation of the end of each three-year contract, a practice in which the union collaborated, so that the no-strike accord was not really itself much of a change in the way the union performed (Bogdanich, 172).

[85] Radical historians have generally argued that the unions did in fact discipline the work force, and thus promoted industrial rationalization. They have also argued that the unions facilitated rationalization by collaborating with industry in capital intensification schemes. The latter argument seems to us weak, on both historical and logical grounds. The mechanization of the steel industry and the rationalization of production methods in steel was accomplished only after industrialists had succeeded in destroying the existing union of skilled workers, the Amalgamated Association of Iron, Tin and Steel Workers. The famous lockout by Carnegie at Homestead was the first battle in the planful campaign by the industry to destroy the union, and it was only after the union was decimated that mechanization took place (Stone). Moreover, it does not make sense to think that the absence of any unions at all, whether to resist or to collaborate, would have been an obstacle to capital intensification in the post–World War II period (when major unions such as the UAW, the UMW, and the ILA did in fact collaborate in such plans).

The first argument is, however, more central to our analysis, and it seems to us that the evidence is still inconclusive. There is not much question that the unions undertook the responsibility for maintaining uninterrupted production, but the strike waves of the 1940s and 1950s raise serious questions about their success at their appointed task. To clarify that issue, one would at a minimum need reasonably precise time-series data on man-days lost through strikes as a proportion of the work force, broken down by unionized and nonunionized sectors. The usual aggregate data on rising productivity rates in the manufacturing sector subsequent to unionization are not definitive. Unionization may well have accompanied rising productivity without playing an important role in making it possible.

beginning in World War II, undertook themselves to punish the leaders of local wildcats.[86]

What had happened, quite simply, was that the organizations born out of the workers' protests had become over time less and less dependent on workers, and more and more dependent on the regular relations established with management. This movement away from workers and towards management was, in part, a natural result of the tendency toward oligarchy in formal organizations. Thus Matles and Higgins write of the CIO leadership during the war years: "Industrial union leaders, rubbing shoulders in the giddy Washington scene with 'big government' and 'big industry' figures, were being transformed—although most of them hardly knew it—into 'labor statesmen' " (164).[87] In part, it was the result of the dependence of the unions for their own organizational stability on the well-being of the industry. Thus B. J. Widick writes:

> With rare exceptions, unions have joined with employers in seeking relief from taxes and government regulations, or in asking Congress to provide other assistance, be it tariffs, money or whatever. The railroad brotherhoods have urged Congress to lend railroads more funds; the communications workers union worries about the

---

[86] The UAW negotiated company security clauses with Chrysler and Ford as early as 1945 which explicitly gave plant management the right to discipline workers who engaged in unauthorized strikes (Lichtenstein, 67). C. Wright Mills reports a subsequent UAW proposal in 1946 in which the union would undertake prosecution (for a penalty or discharge) of "any employer or employees found guilty of instigating, fomenting, or giving leadership to an unauthorized stoppage of work." Shortly afterwards, a local of the Steelworkers signed a contract under which the union could be financially liable for the costs of strikes or work stoppages. For vivid contemporary accounts of the UAW as disciplinarian of rank-and-file insurgents, see also Gamson; Georgakas and Surkin; Ward; and Weir.

Michels had long before explained why the unions were useful in this role: "The masses are far more subject to their leaders than to their governments, and they bear from the former abuses of power which they would never tolerate from the latter . . . they do not perceive the tyranny of the leaders they have themselves chosen" (154).

[87] It is again worth remembering Michels' sober warnings: "For the great majority of men, idealism alone is an inadequate incentive for the fulfillment of duty. Enthusiasm is not an article which can be kept long in store. Men who will stake their bodies and their lives for a moment, or even for some months in succession, on behalf of a great idea often prove incapable of permanent work in the service of the same idea when the sacrifices demanded are comparatively trifling. . . . Consequently, even in the labour movement, it is necessary that the leaders should receive a prosaic reward in addition to the devotion of their comrades and the satisfaction of a good conscience" (126). It is perhaps needless to add that when many of these prosaic rewards are controlled by government and industry, so will the leaders of the labor movement be oriented to government and industry.

antitrust action against AT & T; the steelworkers join industry in demanding tariffs or quotas on steel imports; the auto workers union supports the Big Three's arguments for delaying emission-control deadlines; in the trucking industry Teamsters' lobbyists are working effectively at state and national levels to obtain an easing of load limitations, or to find fuel for its carriers; the clothing and textile unions seek to protect their employees from the competition of "cheap foreign goods" (170).

Finally, the orientation of the unions toward management was facilitated by the severing of union leadership from dependence on the rank and file, first through their reliance on the federal government for membership gains, and then through the dues check-off.[88] As a black auto worker wrote in 1970:

> The automatic dues check-off system has removed the union entirely from any dependence on its membership. The huge treasuries, originally conceived to stockpile ammunition for class warfare, have put the unions in the banking, real estate, and insurance business (quoted in Georgakas and Surkin, 45).

The logical outcome of the bargain the unions had struck is summed up by John Laslett, writing about an earlier period of American labor history:

> The notion of contract implies a recognition by the union of its responsibilities for the enforcement of the agreement, which sometimes placed even radical union leadership in the seemingly anomalous position of having to act against its own constituency, when the contract was violated by members of the rank and file. Thus, the price which the union had to pay for the benefits it received was to become part of the productive system itself . . . (297 ff).[89]

---

[88] During the Second World War years, the unions had become accustomed to winning membership gains without strikes. "After 1942, labor-board elections and decisions made strikes for union recognition unnecessary, maintenance-of-membership clauses ensured a steady flow of dues into union treasuries, and inexperienced union officials sat side by side with federal and corporate executives in manpower, labor-board and war-production hearings" (Schatz, 194).

[89] C. L. R. James makes the most condemning judgment of all: "The history of production since [the creation of the CIO] is the corruption of the bureaucracy and its transformation into an instrument of capitalist production, the restoration to the bourgeoisie of what it had lost in 1936, the right to control production standards. Without this mediating role of the bureaucracy, production in the United States would be violently and continuously disrupted until one class was undisputed master" (23).

Nor were those union leaders who were Communists immune from these influences, for as their organizational roles in the CIO developed, their politics became more ambiguous. Radical ideology was no defense against the imperatives created by organizational maintenance.[90]

ORGANIZATION AND ELECTORAL POWER

The unions not only limited the disruptive force of workers in the factories, they limited their disruptive impact in electoral politics as well. Before we go on to explain this point, however, we have to tell something of the efforts of the unions to become a significant force in electoral politics.

By the end of 1937 the labor unions had nearly eight million workers on their membership rolls, and membership continued to grow during the war years. If the organization of large numbers is what matters for power in electoral politics, then the labor unions ought to have been a substantial force from the outset and, as their membership grew, their influence ought to have grown. But this was not the case.

The organizational phase of the industrial workers' movement began just as the turbulent phase was cresting. While in 1936 the new CIO had not yet enrolled the millions of members it was soon to gain, it still began life with the not inconsiderable membership of the mine workers' and the garment workers' unions. And, from the beginning, the CIO tried to use its organizational apparatus and membership to exert influence in Washington through conventional electoral politics. Prodded by the rise of business opposition to the New Deal, and the sharp decline in business campaign contributions, the CIO launched a massive campaign to reelect the president in 1936. Labor's Non-Partisan League was established as the vehicle of union efforts, and the league's workers, operating very much like a party campaign organization—going on the radio, staging rallies,

---

[90] Prickett, an historian who is sympathetic to the Communists, nevertheless points out that as their organizational positions in the CIO consolidated, the political views of the Communists became obscure, and their ties with the Communist rank and file and with the party became tenuous (392).

passing out thousands of leaflets, and spending nearly a million dollars—began to contact voters in the industrial states of New York, Pennsylvania, Illinois, and Ohio (Schlesinger, 1960, 594; Greenstone, 49). In New York City, needle-trades union leaders resigned from the Socialist Party to join with Communists in creating the American Labor Party, making it easier for leftists who were reluctant to vote the Democratic ticket to back the New Deal. Roosevelt polled some 270,000 votes in New York on the ALP ticket. Later, the ALP also led the campaign for the reelection of Fiorello LaGuardia as mayor (Raybeck, 357; Schlesinger, 1960, 594). Meanwhile, the constituent unions of the CIO contributed $770,000 to Roosevelt's campaign chest, most of it from the mine workers' treasury. The magnitude of this contribution is suggested by the fact that during the previous thirty years the AFL executive had contributed only $95,000 to national political campaigns (Pelling, 166).

The election of 1936 was, of course, only the first step on the new course in pursuit of electoral influence. In 1938 the CIO lobby backed Roosevelt's Supreme Court reform, as well as an array of other New Deal legislative measures, and during the campaign the CIO distributed a bulletin called "How to Organize and Conduct a Local Political Campaign" (Greenstone, 49). Meanwhile Walter Reuther resigned from the Socialist Party to back Democrat Frank Murphy in the Michigan gubernatorial contest (Bernstein, 1971, 780). In 1940 John L. Lewis himself opposed Roosevelt,[91] but the CIO nevertheless gave FDR its overwhelming support: union delegates participated in the Democratic convention, and Roosevelt ran strongest in counties with high concentrations of CIO members.[92] In fact the CIO's commitment to Democratic Party politics had already become so firm that Lewis' split with Roosevelt earned him nothing but the enmity of union leadership, and he resigned as president of the CIO. In 1943 the CIO expanded its investment in

[91] According to De Caux, "Lewis was determined, if he died politically in the attempt, not to let Roosevelt take labor for granted," and he was furious with other CIO leaders "for sacrificing CIO bargaining power by offering FDR unconditional support" (357). Lewis' own decision in 1940 was to support the Republican candidate, Wendell Willkie, but under the circumstances it was a lost gesture.

[92] Bernstein reports an analysis of the results in sixty-three counties and fourteen cities which showed that the strength of the Roosevelt vote paralleled the concentration of CIO members (1971, 720). Schattschneider also reports polls taken at the time that showed CIO membership voted 79 and 78 percent Democratic in the 1940 and 1944 elections (49).

Democratic electoral politics[93] with the creation of the Political Action Committee (PAC), which developed a sophisticated and well-financed campaign organization, in some places capable of canvassing entire communities, from the precinct level up, operating in the primaries as well as the elections. Loyalty was the keynote: PAC discouraged its state units from challenging local Democratic parties in order to "weld together the unity of all forces who support the commander in chief behind a single progressive win-the-war candidate for each office" (quoted in Lichtenstein, 61).[94] PAC was widely credited with a crucial role in the Democratic victory of 1944, in which every CIO constituent union endorsed Roosevelt and the CIO spent some $1,328,000 (Pelling, 180). In 1948 the AFL followed the CIO lead by forming Labor's League for Political Education, which cooperated with PAC on campaign activities. With the merger of the AFL and the CIO in 1955 the Committee on Political Education (COPE) was established, and the investment of the unions in electoral politics and the Democratic Party continued to increase (Greenstone, 52–60).[95] In other words the unions had succeeded in following the prescribed American model for political influence; they had enlisted ever larger numbers of workers as members, and had combined the financial and voting resources of those members to exert influence through the channels of the electoral system. The question is, what did they get for their troubles?

---

[93] The CIO speeded up its campaign activity because of passage of the Smith-Connally Act which, among other antiunion provisions, prohibited union contributions to candidates in federal elections. To evade this restriction, the CIO engaged in "political education" well in advance of the elections (De Caux, 339–440).

[94] Lichtenstein goes on to say about the 1944 elections: "Where sentiment for an independent voice remained strong and threatened to disrupt an alliance with the Democrats, Hillman mobilized PAC forces to defeat it. In New York Hillman linked his once anti-Communist Amalgamated Clothing Workers with the Communist unions of the city to win control of the ALP from the Dubinsky social democrats and to make the state labor party an uncritical adjunct of the Democratic Party there. In Michigan, where a viable Democratic Party hardly existed, the PAC successfully fought efforts by some UAW radicals to put the state Political Action Committee on record as supporting only those Democratic candidates pledged to a guaranteed annual income and other well-publicized CIO bargaining demands" (61).

[95] However, the involvement of members in electoral politics clearly declined. Greenstone comments: "Two decades after World War II, a 'crisis' was most evident with regard to a decline in political interest among the rank and file and in the radicalism of union officials. By contrast, the commitment of organizational resources dramatically increased" (58).

In fact, from the outset, organized labor got very little. Lewis thought that his dramatic gestures of support in the 1936 election, including the huge contribution to campaign expenses, would win Roosevelt's support in the auto and steel struggles. During the Flint sit-downs, Lewis named the *quid pro quo* he expected:

> For six months the economic royalists represented by General Motors contributed their money and used their energy to drive this administration out of power. The administration asked labor for help and labor gave it. The same economic royalists now have their fangs in labor. The workers of this country expect the administration to help the workers in every legal way, and to support the workers in General Motors plants (quoted in Raybeck, 368).

Lewis' assessment was accurate; GM leaders were among Roosevelt's most vigorous opponents in the 1936 election. But his expectations were misplaced. When Roosevelt did finally intervene in the GM strike, it was reluctantly and cautiously. He intervened, not because he was politically beholden to union leadership, but because he was forced to do so by the escalating crisis in Flint. Again, in the Little Steel strike, when Roosevelt was reported to have called down "a plague on both your houses," Lewis claimed betrayal: "It ill behooves one who has supped at Labor's table and who has been sheltered in Labor's house to curse with equal fervor and fine impartiality both Labor and its adversaries when they become locked in deadly embrace" (quoted in Raybeck, 368).

But whatever lesson was to be learned was lost on CIO leaders (except perhaps for John L. Lewis himself). Although the investment of the unions in electoral politics increased, the ability of labor unions to protect the gains that had been won in the mid–1930s rapidly diminished. The strike wave had subsided by 1938, its momentum broken by the bitter defeat in Little Steel. Meanwhile business and government had begun a two-pronged assault on industrial unionism that was to culminate a decade later in the passage of the Taft-Hartley Act. One prong was the launching of a red-baiting campaign that severely weakened the unions internally by stimulating bitter factionalism and ultimately resulted in the purging of more militant Communist elements. The other prong was a campaign to limit the new protections won for unions under the Wagner Act.

The red purge in the CIO that is ordinarily located in the postwar McCarthy period actually began in 1938. It was merely interrupted by the war years, and then resumed vigorously in the late 1940s. The beginning of the campaign was signaled in 1938 by widely publicized hearings of the House Un-American Activities Committee under Chairman Martin Dies. John Frey testified and the *New York Times* headlined his message the next day: "Communists Rule the CIO, Frey of the AFL Testifies: He names 248 Reds" (Matles and Higgins, 104–105; Prickett, 374). Meanwhile the CIO was assaulted by unfavorable press and radio commentary depicting the unions as violent and communistic, or at the very least, "irresponsible" (De Caux, 291–292), while the National Association of Manufacturers financed the printing of two million copies of a pamphlet which depicted John L. Lewis holding a picket sign aloft that read, "Join the CIO and Build a Soviet America" (Matles and Higgins, 118).

By 1939 the signs were clear that the political tide had turned and measures to erode the concessions that labor had won began to be implemented. Under pressure from southern Democrats and Republicans in Congress, the NLRB was reconstituted to eliminate its pro-labor members;[96] the Supreme Court ruled that sit-downs were illegal; and state legislatures began to pass laws prohibiting some kinds of strikes and secondary boycotts, limiting picketing, outlawing the closed shop, requiring the registration of unions, limiting the amount of dues unions could charge, and providing stiff jail terms for violations of the new offenses. By 1947 almost all of the states had passed legislation imposing at least some of these limitations.

World War II did not interrupt the campaign to curb labor gains, but it greatly confused the issues by allowing government and industry to define questions of labor policy as questions of patriotism. In fact the policies of the Roosevelt Administration toward its staunch labor allies during the war years clearly revealed how much the influence of the rank and file had diminished. When war preparation began in earnest after the election of 1940, the demand for

---

[96] Harry Millis, a University of Chicago economist who had served on the pre-Wagner Act NLB, and who had been very much involved in the development of the Wagner Act, later wrote that by the mid-forties, the board was "leaning over backward to be fair to employers," and generally failing to enforce the protections of the Wagner Act (Millis and Brown).

labor suddenly soared. This was a boom such as American workers had not seen for a long time. Within a few months the number of unemployed dropped from 10 million to 4 million, and wages began to rise, from an average $29.88 a week in 1940 to $38.62 in December 1941 (Raybeck, 371). A new wave of strikes swept the country as the unions tried to enlist the new workers, and to take advantage of the rising demand for labor by pressing for higher wages.

But the Roosevelt Administration acted rapidly to suppress the strikes. When UAW workers at the Vultee aircraft plant in Los Angeles struck two weeks after the 1940 presidential election, the FBI and the attorney general branded the strike "Red" and government agents descended upon the strikers, who nevertheless won most of their demands (Green, 8–9; Keeran, 333).[97] Shortly afterwards UAW strikers shut down the Allis-Chalmers plant near Milwaukee; the local police and state militia were called out and Roosevelt threatened to seize the plant (Thomas Brooks, 195; Green, 9; Keeran, 334–336). When 20,000 CIO woodworkers went on strike in the northwest and decided not to return to work on terms dictated by the federal government, the press branded it a Communist strike (De Caux, 396–397). When 12,000 UAW workers struck North American Aviation in Los Angeles, Roosevelt ordered some 3,000 troops to take over the plant, and the strike was broken (Green, 10; De Caux, 398–399). In the fall of 1941 John L. Lewis, who had denounced Roosevelt bitterly for sending troops "to stab labor in the back," called a strike in the "captive" coal mines owned by the major steel companies. A federal mediation board ruled against the workers, but Lewis responded by calling out 250,000 other coal miners, and the strike was won.

After the attack on Pearl Harbor, Roosevelt dealt with the increased labor militancy by taking advantage of the upsurge of patriotic feeling to secure a no-strike pledge from the CIO and AFL. A War Labor Board was established to handle industrial disputes for the duration, and wages were to be set by the federal "little steel" formula in a program calling for "equality of sacrifice" of corporations, consumers, and workers. In fact, corporate profits zoomed,

---

[97] Communists were in fact important in this and other strikes in the prewar period. Moreover since this resurgence of Communist militancy was related to the Stalin-Hitler pact, and the party's branding of the European conflict as an imperialist war, there was some basis for the condemnation heaped upon them.

prices shot up, and wages lagged behind.[98] By 1943 worker restiveness was scarcely controllable, and the number of wildcats escalated rapidly.[99] But union leaders by and large kept their no-strike pledge, and the chairman of the War Labor Board called the policy an outstanding success. It was a success, for union officials were now themselves denouncing and containing the wildcats.[100]

Lewis and the miners bucked the trend. After rank-and-file walkouts early in 1943, Lewis demanded a two-dollar-a-day increase with no stretch-out or speed-up, and pay for time traveled underground. The mine owners refused to negotiate, the press screamed "traitor," Roosevelt threatened to use federal troops, but the miners nevertheless walked out. Reminded of the no-strike pledge, Lewis said it was not a strike, but that the miners would simply not trespass on company property if they had no contract. Roosevelt seized the mines, but the miners stayed out; he then demanded legislation that would permit the federal government to draft strikers, while Congress passed the Smith-Connally Act curbing strikes.[101] When the miners finally went back to work, they had won most of their demands. But what they had won, they had won by force of their belligerency in the mines, and not by their influence in the White House or in the halls of Congress. Of the 219 Democratic congressmen who had voted for Smith-Connally, 191 had been supported by PAC.

While efforts were made to muzzle strike power during the war, union leaders themselves were courted by government and industry, and the federal government continued to protect the ability of the unions to retain and enlarge their membership. This was not surprising, for the unions were performing a valuable service. A member of the War Labor Board commented on this issue: "By and large, the maintenance of a stable union membership and responsible union discipline makes for keeping faithfully the terms of the

---

[98] Real weekly wages increased during the war, but largely as a result of longer hours. Workers were also now bearing the burden of new war taxes, which extended the income tax to millions of low-wage workers who had previously been exempt.

[99] The number of wildcats increased steadily during 1943 and 1944. Preis reports that the number of man-days lost in strikes more than tripled in 1943 over 1942, and by 1944 there were, according to Brecher, more strikes than in any previous year in American history (223–226).

[100] Communists in the unions were among the most ardent supporters of the no-strike pledge, a policy dictated by the perilous situation of Soviet Russia during the war.

[101] Roosevelt vetoed the bill, Congress overrode the veto the same day. In gratitude for the veto, CIO leaders reaffirmed the no-strike pledge.

contract, and provides a stable basis for union-management cooperation for more efficient production" (quoted in Brooks, Thomas, 203).
As a result of the War Labor Board's "maintenance of membership"
policies, union membership grew.[102] By 1945, the CIO claimed 6
million members, the AFL claimed nearly 7 million. If ever there was
a time for labor to demonstrate the force of organized voting numbers
in electoral politics, a force no longer constrained by the imperatives
of war and the spirit of patriotism, now was the time. As it turned
out, the force of organized voting numbers could not even ward
off the Taft-Hartley Act.

With war contracts canceled and servicemen demobilized when
the war ended in the summer of 1945, unemployment rose, wages
declined as overtime was lost, and prices continued to rise, reducing
real take-home wages to levels below the prewar period. An unprecedented wave of strikes ensued, this time under official union
leadership. Virtually every major industry was shut down for some
period during 1946. President Truman responded by using his wartime powers—months after the end of the war—to seize oil refineries,
railroads, mines, and packinghouses. When railroad workers struck
anyway the president threatened to draft them and use the Army
to run the railroads;[103] when the miners struck, the government
secured an injunction, and the UMW was fined $3.5 million for its
defiance. "We used the weapons that we had at hand," Truman
said afterwards, "in order to fight a rebellion against the government . . ." (quoted in Brecher, 229). Truman had proposed legislation to draft strikers, but the Congress responded with its own
plan, the Taft-Hartley Bill, substantially modifying the Wagner Act
by specifying the rights of employers in industrial disputes and
restricting the rights of unions. Elaborate requirements were imposed
for the reporting of internal union procedures; non-communist
affidavits were required of union officers on penalty of losing the

---

[102] In 1942 in the wake of the no-strike pledge, some industrial unions began to lose
members and experience dues collection difficulties. The War Labor Board solved that
problem with its modified union shop policies (Lichtenstein, 53). With the exception
of the UMW (which had won the union shop in its 1941 strike) the board permitted
"maintenance of membership" clauses which provided a fifteen-day escape period during
which a new employee could quit the union.

[103] Sitkoff describes Truman's radio speech threatening to draft strikers and give the
Army authority to run the trains as "the most blistering antilabor speech by a President
since that of Grover Cleveland" (85).

services of the NLRB;[104] the closed shop was outlawed, as was the union shop, except where authorized by the majority of workers in a special ballot (and even this provision did not apply where states had enacted "right-to-work" laws); the check-off of union dues by employers was declared illegal except by written permission of the employee; and various forms of secondary boycotts were prohibited. Finally, certain strikes were to be delayed by a mandated sixty-day cooling-off period; strikes against the federal government were prohibited altogether; and the president was given special powers to intervene to halt strikes for eighty days which endangered the "national health or safety" (Pelling, 189–191). Truman, with the 1948 elections ahead, vetoed the act.[105] The Congress overrode the veto by a margin of 331 to 83 in the House, and 68 to 25 in the Senate, freeing Truman to use the legislation to curb strikes twelve times in the first year after its passage (Green, 34).[106] While Taft-Hartley was being debated in the Congress, the Cold War was being created in the White House, and with it the witch hunts and purges of leftists that further divided and weakened the CIO in the postwar years.

Taft-Hartley went far beyond the wartime actions of the federal government. It not only curbed the strike power, but it curbed the unions' capacity to organize as well. Union membership declined in the years immediately following the passage of the act, and thereafter recovered only slowly, reaching 18.9 million in 1968. But as a percentage of the total work force, union membership was lower in 1968

---

[104] Lewis once again tried to buck the trend of accommodation to government, proposing that if all unions refused to sign the non-communist affidavits, the provision would be ineffective. The AFL, with which the mine workers were again joined, turned his proposal down (De Caux, 478). Some of the CIO unions did resist signing, but only briefly (Matles and Higgins, 167–170).

[105] Many analysts agree that Truman's strategy in dealing with Taft-Hartley was calculated not to defeat the legislation but to gain a political advantage in the forthcoming election. Even his symbolic concession was probably necessary only because Henry Wallace was making a bid for labor support with his third-party candidacy. Truman's strategy was successful; organized labor supported him energetically. For example A. F. Whitney, head of the Brotherhood of Railway Trainmen, had threatened to spend his entire union treasury to defeat Truman after the president proposed to draft railway strikers. But the veto, Whitney announced, vindicated Truman, and support for Wallace was "out of the question" (Yarnell, 22–25). For similar accounts of the Truman strategy on Taft-Hartley, see Sitkoff, 92–97, and Hartmann, 86–91.

[106] Adlai Stevenson, in the presidential campaign of 1952, retreated even from the Truman posture of strong rhetorical opposition to Taft-Hartley. See Martin, 540, 643, 660, 691.

than in 1947. In the nineteen "right-to-work" states where compulsory open shop legislation is permitted by Taft-Hartley, union membership averages only half the proportion in the other states. These are restrictions that the unions bitterly opposed at the time, and that they have continued to oppose in the thirty years since the act was passed. But without success.

Our discussion has thus far emphasized the losses the unions sustained in the specific area of government labor policy. They fared no better in other areas of domestic policy that affected the conditions of working people: they did not succeed in expanding the gains wrested from government in the 1930s, and in some instances they did not even succeed in sustaining these gains. The list of labor's failures is long, but it self-evidently includes increasingly regressive federal income and corporate tax policies that help to erode whatever labor wins at the bargaining table; federal housing policies that have inflated the cost of workers' housing and profited the construction industry; federal minimum wage standards that have not been raised to keep pace with real wages; the poor record of federal performance in the area of industrial safety; and a social security system that bears more and more heavily on workers because of the extremely regressive formula by which it is financed.

This dismal overall record in electoral and legislative politics was accomplished by the largest issue-oriented voting bloc in the nation. In the decade between the Wagner Act that signified labor's political muscle, and the Taft-Hartley Act that signified its helplessness, the ranks of organized labor had increased until one-third of the population was union affiliated. During that decade the unions' organizational apparatus had also enlarged and become increasingly sophisticated and increasingly committed to electoral politics on all levels. But neither this vast bloc of voters nor the sophisticated machinery of their organization could muster power sufficient even to resist the erosion of the gains won earlier, in the days before the unions had organized.

Why? The answer is twofold. In part, it was that in the absence of a movement, the unions were not really capable of delivering the voting bloc they claimed to represent. The strike movement of the 1930s, by contrast, threatened to mobilize workers as voters in a way that overrode the usual multiple appeals of party, section, and ethnicity. While the labor vote had shifted to the Democratic column in the election of 1932, that vote was still insecure, and the industrial struggles waged by workers made it more insecure. The strike movement threatened electoral disruption. But once the movement subsided, it was the Democratic Party, not the unions, that gained the ability to command the allegiance of working-class voters and name the issues for which allegiance would be traded. In the absence of the extraordinary fervor provoked by a mass protest, the unions played at best a subsidiary role in disciplining the working-class vote.[107]

Moreover, there is substantial evidence that the unions really did not try to use the pressure their voting members represented to force mass concessions from electoral leaders. Union leaders became more dependent on the Democratic Party (for prominence, not concessions) than the party was on them. Acting accordingly, union leaders promoted partisan allegiance, and by doing so, blunted the electoral impact of worker discontent. The unions became the legitimate political voice of industrial workers, and that legitimate voice spoke out repeatedly against strikers, and in support of Democratic leaders.

Thus during the war years, worker discontent did not diminish. The war boom strike wave of 1941, and the wildcats of 1943, were each successively larger than the other, and larger than the strike wave of 1937. But discontented workers exerted little electoral force, and the less so because their own leaders supported the national government's policies. When the CIO woodworkers struck in 1941, Philip Murray, who had taken Lewis' place as head of the CIO, denounced the woodworkers' leadership, echoed press charges of communism, and demanded that the strike be called off (De Caux, 397). When the UAW workers struck North American Aviation the same year, UAW's Aviation Director Richard Frankensteen called the strike "communist-inspired" on national radio, and later addressed a meeting of strikers to order them back to work. It was after the workers booed Frankensteen and ignored his order that Roosevelt

---

[107] Writing in 1960 Schattschneider presents interesting data to show that the unions could at best swing 960,000 votes in a presidential election. He arrives at this conclusion by subtracting from the organized labor vote the percentage of workers who would probably have voted Democratic even if they did not belong to unions. Schattschneider concludes from this "that it is nearly impossible to translate pressure politics into party politics" (47–61).

Even with regard to the Taft-Hartley Act, the ability of the unions to influence their members was limited. Thus Wilson cites poll data from the 1952 election indicating that only 29 percent of union members favored repeal, 41 percent had no opinion on the matter, and the remainder actually favored retention of the act (1973, 338–339).

called out the troops (Green, 10), apparently with the approval of Sidney Hillman (Keeran, 340).[108] When Roosevelt seized the mines during the 1943 UMW strike to break the "little steel" formula, the executive board of the CIO repudiated Lewis and the UMW, and congratulated Roosevelt for his veto of the Smith-Connally Act despite the fact that the legislation reflected Roosevelt's own public proposals. In other words even when the unions failed to curb economic disruptions by workers, they succeeded in muting the electoral impact of those disruptions.

Conclusion

The circumstances which led to the uprisings of industrial workers, and gave them force, were rooted in the economic and social dislocations of the depression. Catastrophic unemployment and the sharp decline of wages made workers restive in the first place; the early moves by political elites to deal with the economic catastrophe, and with the electoral instability bred by catastrophe, only legitimized worker discontents, helping to escalate an industrial war. Still the federal government temporized, trying to appease both business and labor. But workers, seized by the spirit of the movement, refused to be appeased and, with industrial disorder increasing, the federal government's policy failed. The disgruntled business community deserted the Democratic Party, clearing the way for concessions to labor. Then, with the workers' movement still unabated, and with violence by employers escalating, reluctant political leaders finally chose sides and supported labor's demands. The disruptive tactics of the labor movement had left them no other choice. They could not ignore disruptions so threatening to economic recovery and to electoral stability, and they could not repress the strikers, for while a majority of the electorate did not support the strikers, a substantial proportion did,[109] and many others would have reacted unpredictably

---

[108] Wyndham Mortimer (who was suspended from the UAW for his role as an organizer of the North American strike) later said that he had told the UAW leadership that "if the strike was authorized, the Army would not come in" (cited in Keeran, 348).

[109] Mills reports that even during the Little Steel strike, which turned public opinion against the strikers, 44 percent of the lower class and 18 percent of the upper class supported the strikers (43).

to the serious bloodshed that repression would have necessitated. And so government conceded the strikers' main demand—the right to organize.

It is not likely that the worker agitations of the 1930s would have broken out under more stable economic conditions, and it is not likely that they would have had the force they did under more stable political conditions. In other words it required the widespread dislocations of a deep depression for the workers' movement to emerge, and to give it disruptive force in electoral spheres. Such times are rare and certainly not of anyone's deliberate making. Moreover disruptive political strategies, even during the infrequent periods when they are possible, are unpredictable and costly. The workers of the 1930s had no guidelines on which to rely and from which to gain assurance and protection, for their struggles defied the conventions of political influence and thereby also eschewed the protections afforded by these conventions. The workers paid heavily for their defiance, in thousands arrested, hundreds injured, and many killed. But then, they also won.

That industrial workers did in fact win in the 1930s, and that they won only through mass struggle, is underplayed in some radical interpretations. Such interpretations emphasize the advantages that unionization ultimately yielded management and seem therefore to imply that collective bargaining arrangements were yielded by an employers' conspiracy. It is clearly true that management came in time to find unions useful, perhaps because the unions helped to discipline workers and maintain production, and more certainly because they helped to depoliticize worker discontent when it did erupt. Moreover in some industries—such as electrical manufacturing—unionization promised to stabilize wages and thus reduce the uncertainty of corporate competition (Schatz, 188–189).[110] But for the most part, these were advantages that industrialists themselves recognized slowly at best and only under extreme duress. They granted union recognition after bitter resistance; they granted it

---

[110] Gerald P. Swope, head of General Electric, had as early as 1926 urged William Green of the AFL to form industrial unions. It would mean "the difference between an organization with which we could work on a business-like basis and one that would be a source of endless difficulties" (Radosh). Bernstein makes a similar assessment of the motives of oil mogul Harry Sinclair in signing an agreement with the oil workers in May 1934 (1971, 115). In some industries, particularly the garment trades, the unions also played a large role in regulating a fragmented industry made up of many small enterprises.

only in the face of mass strikes and government coercion. In effect, industrialists learned to use unions after the workers had fought for and won them. Industrial unionization was not a management strategy but a workers' victory.

And the victory was worth winning. Clearly, the straightforward concessions in higher pay and shorter hours and in government social welfare measures offered up at the height of the turmoil of the 1930s were worth winning. The more ambiguous concession was the right to organize itself. But, on balance, unionization must also be considered a gain for industrial workers simply because they have been better off with it than they were without it; they are better off in the 1970s than they were in the 1920s. They are better off because unions still lead strikes; they still use some disruptive leverage, and because they do, most workers in the mass production industries have held their own in economic spheres. Wages have kept pace with rising productivity and profits.[111] Moreover, through unionization, workers gained a measure of job security. In particular, workers are now protected against reprisals in union-led strikes.

On the other hand, unionization also ritualizes and encapsulates the strike power, thus limiting its disruptive impact on production, and limiting the political reverberations of economic disruptions as well. And the unions themselves have never exerted direct influence in electoral spheres comparable to the electoral influence of the workers' movement of the 1930s.

Industrial workers are by any measure the exemplary case of mass-based permanent organization. No other stratum of the lower class has comparable opportunities for organization on so large a scale. The main reason is that no other group possesses comparable disruptive power. Labor won from elites the resources necessary to sustain a mass organization precisely because the enormous disruptive power of the strike had to be contained. Having been ceded the right to organize—including especially the legal sanction to coerce workers into union affiliation—labor could solve its organizational maintenance problem; through coerced affiliation, a mass base has been

---

[111] Thus Leonard Silk estimated that in 1969 the average annual income of blue-collar workers was substantially above the national median income (11). However, these data also make clear that other workers who were not located in mass production industries and were not unionized did not do nearly so well and, as consumers, bore the inflationary burden of rising profits and rising wages in the mass production industries.

successfully sustained. But what other group in the lower class has the disruptive power to enable it to win equivalent resources for organizational maintenance?

Industrial workers are also the exemplary case by which to test beliefs about the effectiveness of mass-based organization in electoral spheres. Through organization, labor ostensibly commanded vast resources for political influence: millions of organized voters and multi-million-dollar treasuries from dues. Still, these resources yielded them little in the electoral process. What, then, of the potential for electoral influence of the more typical lower-class organization, usually with a few hundred or a few thousand members at best, and usually on the verge of bankruptcy?

As for the labor experience itself, the political moral seems to us clear, although it is quite different from the moral that organizers are wont to draw. It can be stated simply: the unorganized disruptions of industrial workers in the 1930s produced some political gains, but the organized electoral activities of the unions could not sustain them. New gains await a new protest movement—a new outbreak of mass defiance capable of spurning the rules and authorities of the workplace and of politics, and capable of spurning the rules and authorities of the union system as well.

References

Ash, Roberta. *Social Movements in America*. Chicago: Markham Publishing Co., 1972.

Aronowitz, Stanley. *The Shaping of American Working Class Consciousness*. New York: McGraw-Hill Book Co., 1973.

Bendix, Reinhard. *Nation Building and Citizenship*. New York: John Wiley and Sons, 1964.

Bernstein, Irving. *The New Deal Collective Bargaining Policy*. Berkeley: University of California Press, 1950.

———. *The Lean Years: A History of the American Worker, 1920–1933*. Baltimore: Penguin Books, 1970.

———. *Turbulent Years: A History of the American Worker, 1933–1941*. Boston: Houghton Mifflin Co., 1971.

Bird, Caroline. *The Invisible Scar*. New York: David McKay Co., 1966.

Bogdanich, George. "Steel: No–Strike and Other Deals." *The Nation*, September 7, 1974.

Boyer, Richard O., and Morais, Herbert M. *Labor's Untold Story*. New York: United Electrical, Radio and Machine Workers of America, 1955.

Brecher, Jeremy. *Strike!* Greenwich, Connecticut: Fawcett Publications, 1974.

Brooks, Robert R. R. *As Steel Goes*. New Haven: Yale University Press, 1940.

Brooks, Thomas R. *Toil and Trouble: A History of American Labor*. New York: Delacorte Press, 1971.

Buhle, Paul Merlyn. "Marxism in the United States, 1900–1940." Unpublished Ph.D. dissertation, University of Wisconsin, Madison, 1975.

Chandler, Lester V. *America's Greatest Depression, 1929–1939*. New York: Harper and Row, 1970.

Davis, Mike. "The Stop Watch and the Wooden Shoe." *Radical America* 9 (January–February 1975).

Derber, Milton. "Growth and Expansion." In *Labor and the New Deal*, edited by Milton Derber and Edwin Young. Madison: University of Wisconsin Press, 1957.

Edelman, Murray. "New Deal Sensitivity to Labor Interests." In *Labor and the New Deal*, edited by Milton Derber and Edwin Young. Madison: University of Wisconsin Press, 1957.

Fine, Sidney. *Sit-down: The General Motors Strike of 1936–1937*. Ann Arbor: University of Michigan Press, 1969.

Fink, Leon. "Class Conflict in the Gilded Age: The Figure and the Phantom." *Radical History Review* 3 (Fall–Winter 1975).

Fleming, R. W. "The Significance of the Wagner Act." In *Labor and the New Deal*, edited by Milton Derber and Edwin Young. Madison: University of Wisconsin Press, 1957.

Gamson, William A. *The Strategy of Social Protest*. Homewood, Illinois: Dorsey Press, 1975.

Georgakas, Dan, and Surkin, Marvin. *Detroit—I Do Mind Dying: A Study in Urban Revolution*. New York: St. Martin's Press, 1974.

Gordon, David M.; Edwards, Richard C.; and Reich, Michael. "Labor Market Segmentation in American Capitalism." Unpublished paper presented at the Conference on Labor Market Segmentation, Harvard University, March 16–17, 1973.

Green, James. "Fighting on Two Fronts: Working-Class Militancy in the 1940s." *Radical America* 9 (July–October 1975).

Greenstone, J. David. *Labor in American Politics.* New York: Vintage Books, 1969.

Gutman, Herbert G. *Work, Culture and Society in Industrializing America.* New York: Alfred A. Knopf, 1976.

Hartmann, Susman M. *Truman and the 80th Congress.* Columbia: University of Missouri Press, 1971.

Hofstadter, Richard, and Wallace, Michael, eds. *American Violence: A Documentary History.* New York: Vintage Books, 1971.

James, C. L. R. "Excerpts from *State Capitalism and World Revolution (1949)*." *Radical America* 4 (May 1970).

Josephson, Mathew. *The Robber Barons.* New York: Harcourt, Brace and Co., 1934.

Karsh, Bernard, and Garman, Phillip L. "Impact of the Political Left." In *Labor and the New Deal*, edited by Milton Derber and Edwin Young. Madison: University of Wisconsin Press, 1957.

Keeran, Roger Roy. "Communists and Auto Workers: The Struggle for a Union, 1919–1941." Unpublished Ph.D. dissertation, University of Wisconsin, 1974.

Kraus, Henry. "The General Motors Sit-down: Skirmishes." In *American Labor Radicalism: Testimonies and Interpretations*, edited by Staughton Lynd. New York: John Wiley and Sons, 1973.

Laslett, John H. M. *Labor and the Left: A Study of Socialist and Radical Influences in the American Labor Movement, 1881–1924.* New York: Basic Books, 1970.

Lens, Sidney. *Radicalism in America.* New York: Thomas Y. Crowell, 1966.

Lescohier, Don D., and Brandeis, Elizabeth. *History of Labor in the United States, 1896–1932* (in the 4-volume series *The History of Labor in the United States*, compiled by John R. Commons and his associates). New York: Macmillan Co., 1935.

Levinson, Edward. *Labor on the March.* New York: Harper, 1938.

Lichtenstein, Nelson. "Defending the No-Strike Pledge: CIO Politics during World War II." *Radical America* 9 (July–October, 1975).

Lorwin, Lewis. *The American Federation of Labor.* Washington, D.C.: The Brookings Institution, 1933.

Lynd, Staughton, ed. "Personal Histories of the Early CIO." *Radical America* 5 (May–June 1969).

———. "The United Front in America: A Note." *Radical America* 8 (July–August 1974).

Martin, John Bartlow. *Adlai Stevenson of Illinois.* Garden City: Doubleday and Co., 1976.

Matles, James J., and Higgins, James J. *Them and Us: Struggles of a Rank-and-File Union.* Englewood Cliffs, N.J.: Prentice-Hall, 1974.

Michels, Robert. *Political Parties: A Sociological Study of the Oligarchical Tendencies of Modern Democracy.* Glencoe: The Free Press, 1949.

Millis, Harry A., and Brown, E. C. *From the Wagner Act to Taft-Hartley.* Chicago: The University of Chicago Press, 1950.

————, and Montgomery, Royal E. *Organized Labor* (Vol. 2 of *The Economics of Labor*). New York: McGraw-Hill Book Co., 1945.

Mills, C. Wright. *New Men of Power.* 1948. Reprint. Fairfield, N.J.: Augustus M. Kelley, Publishers, 1969.

Moley, Raymond. "Comment." *Political Science Quarterly* 87 (December 1972).

Montgomery, David. "Spontaneity and Organization: Some Comments." *Radical America* 7 (November–December 1973).

Nadworny, Milton J. *Scientific Management and the Unions 1900–1932.* Cambridge: Harvard University Press, 1955.

Nyden, Paul J. "Miners for Democracy: Struggle in the Coal Fields." Unpublished Ph. D. dissertation, Columbia University, 1974.

Olson, Mancur Jr. *The Logic of Collective Action: Public Goods and the Theory of Groups.* New York: Schocken Books, 1969.

Pelling, Henry. *American Labor.* Chicago: The University of Chicago Press, 1962.

Perlman, Selig. *A Theory of the Labor Movement.* New York: Macmillan Co., 1928.

Preis, Art. *Labor's Giant Step: 20 Years of the CIO.* New York: Pioneer Publishers, 1964.

Prickett, James Robert. "Communists and the Communist Issue in the American Labor Movement, 1920–1950." Unpublished Ph. D. dissertation, University of California, Los Angeles, 1975.

Radosh, Ronald. "The Corporate Ideology of American Labor Leaders from Gompers to Hillman." *Studies on the Left,* November–December 1966.

Raybeck, Joseph G. *A History of American Labor.* New York: The Free Press, 1966.

Rees, Goronwy. *The Great Slump: Capitalism in Crisis, 1929–1933.* New York: Harper and Row, 1970.

Reich, Michael. "The Evolution of the United States Labor Force." In *The Capitalist System*, edited by Richard C. Edwards, Michael Reich, and Thomas J. Weisskopf. Englewood Cliffs, New Jersey: Prentice-Hall, 1972.

Rogin, Michael. "Nonpartisanship and the Group Interest." In *Power and Community*, edited by Philip Green and Sanford Levinson. New York: Vintage Books, 1970.

Rudé, George. *The Crowd in History*. New York: John Wiley and Sons, 1964.

Schatz, Ronald. "The End of Corporate Liberalism: Class Struggle in the Electrical Manufacturing Industry, 1933–1950." *Radical America* 9 (July–October 1975).

Schattschneider, E. E. *The Semisovereign People: A Realist's View of Democracy in America*. New York: Holt, Rinehart and Winston, 1960.

Schlesinger, Arthur M. Jr. *The Age of Roosevelt*, Vol. 1: *The Crisis of the Old Order, 1919–1933*. Boston: Houghton Mifflin Co., 1957.

————. *The Age of Roosevelt*, Vol. 3: *The Politics of Upheaval, 1935–1936*. Boston: Houghton Mifflin Co., 1960.

Silk, Leonard. "Is There a Lower-Middle Class Problem?" In *Blue Collar Workers: A Symposium on Middle America*, edited by Sar A. Levitan. New York: McGraw-Hill Book Co., 1971.

Sitkoff, Harvard. "Years of the Locust: Interpretations of Truman's Presidency since 1965." In *The Truman Period as a Research Field,* edited by Richard S. Kirkendall. Columbia: University of Missouri Press, 1974.

Stone, Katherine. "The Origins of Job Structures in the Steel Industry." Unpublished paper presented at the Conference on Labor Market Stratification, Harvard University, March 16–17, 1973.

Taft, Philip, and Ross, Philip. "American Labor Violence: Its Causes, Character, and Outcome." In *The History of Violence in America: A Report to the National Commission on the Causes and Prevention of Violence,* edited by Hugh Davis Graham and Ted Robert Gurr. New York: Praeger Publishers, 1969.

U. S. Bureau of the Census. *Statistical Abstract of the United States, 1940*. Washington, D.C.: U.S. Government Printing Office, 1941.

U. S. Department of Labor. *Handbook of Labor Statistics, 1972*. Washington, D.C.: U.S. Government Printing Office, 1973.

Walsh, J. Raymond. *CIO: Industrial Unionism in Action*. New York: W. W. Norton and Co., 1937.

Ward, Matthew. "UAW." In *American Labor Radicalism: Testimonies and Interpretations*, edited by Staughton Lynd. New York: John Wiley and Sons, 1973.

Wecter, Dixon. *The Age of the Great Depression.* New York: Macmillan Co., 1948.

Weinstein, James. *Ambiguous Legacy: The Left in American Politics.* New York: New Viewpoints (A Division of Franklin Watts, Inc.) , 1975.

Weir, Stanley. "Rank-and-File Labor Rebellions Break into the Open: The End of an Era." In *American Labor Radicalism: Testimonies and Interpretations,* edited by Staughton Lynd. New York: John Wiley and Sons, 1973.

Widick, B. J. "Labor 1975: The Triumph of Business Unionism." *The Nation,* September 6, 1975.

Wilson, James Q. *Political Organizations.* New York: Basic Books, 1973.

Yarnell, Allen. *Democrats and Progressives: The 1948 Presidential Election as a Test of Postwar Liberalism.* Berkeley: University of California Press, 1974.

CHAPTER
4

The Civil Rights
Movement

World War II brought the Great Depression to a rapid end. Booming war production was followed by rapid economic expansion in the postwar years which, together with Keynesian macroeconomic policies, produced a degree of stability and prosperity in the lives of many American workers. These improved economic conditions, coupled with the growth of industrial unionism, moderated unrest among the industrial working class. The next great struggles occurred among blacks, many of whom were outside, or at the very bottom of, the industrial working class.

The black struggle was waged for two main goals. One was to secure formal political rights in the South, especially the right to the franchise; the other was to secure economic advances. In retrospect it is clear that the main victory was the extension of political rights to southern blacks (together with a larger degree of black political representation in the northern cities).

Beginning in the 1940s the federal courts reversed historic doctrines and began to undercut the legality of southern caste arrangements, a trend that culminated in the 1954 Supreme Court decision which declared racially separate schools unconstitutional because they were inherently unequal. Then, between 1957 and 1965, four civil rights bills were enacted which, taken together, finally granted a broad range of democratic political rights to blacks, and provided the mechanisms to enforce those rights. As a consequence, public accommodations were desegregated, blacks began to serve on the southern juries which had for so long provided immunity to southern

Very good here

whites employing terror against blacks, and the franchise was finally granted. From a historical perspective, a long leap forward had been made.

In the South the deepest meaning of the winning of democratic political rights is that the historical primacy of terror as a means of social control has been substantially diminished.[1] The reduction of terror in the everyday life of a people is always in itself an important gain. Myrdal has emphasized that "threats, whippings, and even serious forms of violence have been customary caste sanctions utilized to maintain a strict discipline over Negro labor" (229). But now, with the winning of formal political rights, the reliance on terror— on police violence, on the lynch mob, on arbitrary imprisonment— has greatly diminished as the method of controlling blacks. Why this historic transformation came about, and the role of the civil rights movement in producing it, is the subject of this chapter.

By contrast, economic gains were limited. Many blacks entered the middle class, taking advantage of the liberal employment policies of both public and private institutions which the turbulence of the period produced. For most poor blacks, however, occupational conditions did not much improve. For many of them the main gain was the winning of liberalized welfare practices to insure their survival despite widespread unemployment and underemployment. That gain, and the movement which won it, will be discussed in the next chapter.

In the largest sense, political modernization in the South followed from economic modernization. Throughout the twentieth century industrialization had been advancing in the states of the Outer South and in some cities of the Deep South.[2] Meanwhile, in the rural areas of the Deep South, mechanization and new agricultural technologies swept over the traditional plantation system, especially in the post-World War II period. These economic transformations rendered the semifeudal political order that prevailed in much of the South

---

unquestionably

[1] Among some on the left, there is a tendency to ignore this gain. Robert L. Allen, a spokesman on the black left, typifies this attitude when he remarks: "In its heyday the integrationist civil rights movement cast an aura which encompassed nearly the whole of the black population, but the black bourgeoisie was the primary beneficiary of that movement" (26). This statement is clearly true for the economic gains made during the civil rights era: the existing and the new black middle classes were the chief beneficiaries. But this said, we believe that the diminution of terroristic methods of social control was a major gain for the mass of southern black poor.

[2] Louisiana, Georgia, Mississippi, Alabama, and South Carolina.

obsolete, the vestige of a labor-intensive plantation system that was passing into history.

The economic changes that made traditional patterns of political domination archaic also generated the force to bring new political arrangements into being. Changing economic circumstances, and the demographic and social ramifications that soon followed, created mounting unrest among masses of blacks, eventually culminating in a black struggle against the southern caste system. By the mid–1960s national political leaders finally responded to the rising tide of black protest and imposed modernizing political reforms on the South. That they could do so was a measure both of the underlying economic transformation which had occurred, and of the force of black insurgency.

In the analysis which follows, we have focused on the relationship between economic change, mass unrest, and the national electoral system. If political reforms throughout the South were made possible by change in the southern economy, and if economic change, by producing mass unrest, also made those reforms imperative, it was the electoral system that registered and mediated the pressures and which yielded the reforms. Political rights were finally conceded to southern blacks by a national Democratic Party whose leaders had for decades consistently refused to interfere with caste arrangements in the South. Then, in a series of actions culminating in the mid–1960s, Democratic presidents and a Congress dominated by Democratic majorities forced political reforms on the southern wing of their party.

It is our view that the civil rights movement was a vital force in this process because of the impact of its disruptive tactics on the electoral system. By defying caste domination, and by thus provoking southern whites to employ terroristic methods that were losing legitimacy, the civil rights movement succeeded in exacerbating electoral instabilities which had already been set in motion by economic modernization in the South. The national Democratic Party bore the brunt of these electoral conflicts and weakening party allegiances. The party's electoral majority had been eroding in the postwar years as polarization between southern whites on the one hand, and blacks and northern white liberals on the other, worsened. Consequently when the black assault against the caste system took form in the 1950s, polarizing northern and southern sentiments all the more, the leaders of the national Democratic Party maneuvered to reduce their electoral losses by imposing political reforms on the South. By this time there was no other way that the profound conflicts dividing the northern and southern wings of the party could be lessened. Nor, except by enfranchising blacks and incorporating them in the southern wing of the party, could Democratic strength in the South be regained.[3] We turn, then, to an amplification of these points.

Blacks in the Southern Political Economy

No group in American society has been as subjected to the extremes of economic exploitation as blacks. Each change in their relationship to the economic system has mainly represented a shift from one form of extreme economic subjugation to another: from slaves to cash tenants and sharecroppers; from cash tenants and sharecroppers to the lowest stratum in an emerging southern rural free labor system; and, finally, to the status of an urban proletariat characterized by low wages and high unemployment. In effect, the black poor progressed from slave labor to cheap labor to (for many) no labor at all.

In one period of American history after another, conflict has broken out among white dominants for control over the changing forms of economic exploitation of blacks; from the debate among the framers of the Constitution as to whether blacks were men or property; to the "free soil" conflict which brought on the Civil War; to the inconclusive Hayes-Tilden election and the Compromise of 1877, which restored southern white hegemony and the Democratic Party in the South; to the "massive resistance" movement led by southern elites against the national government in the post–World War II era.

In each period ascendant elites employed the powers of the national

---

[3] As this book went to press, we came across a monograph by C. L. R. James and his colleagues, first published in 1958 and then reissued in 1974, containing a passage which anticipated the electoral aspects of the analysis to be developed in this chapter. Though brief, the remarks were prescient, and we wish to acknowledge them: "The Negroes in the North and West, by their ceaseless agitation and their votes, are now a wedge jammed in between the Northern Democrats and the Southern. At any moment this wedge can split the party into two and thereby compel the total reorganization of American politics. They have cracked the alliance between the right wing of the Republicans and the Southern wing of the Democratic Party. By patient strategy and immense labor, they have taken the lead in the movement which resulted in the declaration of the Supreme Court that racial segregation is illegal. Now the people of Montgomery, by organizing a bus boycott which for a year was maintained at a level of over 99 percent, have struck a resounding blow at racial discrimination all over the United States and written a new chapter of world-wide significance in the history of struggle against irrational prejudices" (150).

and local governments to enforce the subjugation of blacks. The entire apparatus of government—its legislatures, its judiciaries, its executive branches—has been mobilized to perpetuate caste arrangements in the South and segregation and discrimination in the North. Legislatures enacted laws to deprive blacks of political rights and refused to prevent private institutions from depriving blacks of economic and social rights; the courts wove a net of opinions which legitimized the actions of other branches of government and of private institutions; and the executive levels of government employed their powers, especially police powers, to enforce the interests of private elites in exploiting the black labor force.

The particular arrangements by which government buttressed the economic subjugation of blacks during the last hundred years had their origins in the post-Reconstruction period. The gains of the Civil War and of Reconstruction had, in principle, been considerable. Blacks were freed from slavery by the Emancipation Proclamation, and the Fourteenth Amendment was enacted in 1868 to provide due process and equal protection of the law. Two years later the Fifteenth Amendment guaranteed all citizens the right to vote regardless of race or other characteristics. In 1875 the Civil Rights Bill was enacted to provide "equal enjoyment" of public accommodations and other facilities. But, by the turn of the century, most gains had been lost, and all would be by the end of the first decade of the twentieth century.

"Racism grew up as an American ideology," Arnold Rose has said, "partly in response to the need to maintain a reliable and permanent work force in the difficult job of growing cotton . . ." (xviii). That economic imperative was not lessened with the emancipation of the slaves. The southern economy was in a shambles; the restoration of the plantation system depended on once again securing a reliable and permanent work force, and one that could be made to work on terms not much different than those which had prevailed during slavery. Although legal slavery was no longer possible, a roughly equivalent status of economic serfdom was. During the last third of the nineteenth century and the first decade of the twentieth, southern elites, with the acquiescence of their northern counterparts, forged the system of political domination required to return blacks to servitude. Moreover, the resolution of the black's economic role vitally affected the place of the poor white in the southern economy.

For all practical purposes the withdrawal of federal troops in 1877 freed the South to restore caste relations between blacks and whites.

This transformation was achieved at the state and local level through mob and police violence, through legislative measures, and through court rulings—all tacitly or explicitly condoned in the North and by the federal government.

The hallmark of white violence against blacks has been the lynch mob. Mob violence was among the most fundamental means by which the black was restored to servitude in the post-Reconstruction era, for "the evidence of race conflict and violence, brutality and exploitation in this period is overwhelming. It was, after all, in the eighties and early nineties that lynching attained the most staggering proportions ever reached in the history of that crime" (Woodward, 1974, 43). (During the next seventy years the NAACP would record nearly 5,000 known cases of lynching.) The mobs, of course, were composed mainly of poor whites, leading Cox to conclude that "poor whites themselves may be thought of as the primary instrument of the ruling class in subjugating the Negroes" (536).[4] It was also the case that the police agents of the South achieved national renown for their tactics of terror against blacks. Sometimes they led lynch mobs. More commonly they simply made it known that they would not interfere with mob actions led by others. (And the Congress refused to make lynching a federal crime until after World War II.)

As the nineteenth century came to a close, legislation was widely enacted to isolate and stigmatize blacks, thus legitimizing their economic exploitation.[5] Segregated arrangements soon pervaded every

---

[4] Myrdal, who tends to underplay the role of class relations in understanding the American "dilemma," nevertheless reaches a similar conclusion regarding the role played by poor whites in maintaining black subjugation: "Plantation owners and employers, who use Negro labor as cheaper and more docile, have at times been observed to tolerate, or cooperate in, the periodic aggression of poor whites against Negroes. It is a plausible thesis that they do so in the interest of upholding the caste system which is so effective in keeping the Negro docile" (598).

[5] In the political chaos created by the war and Reconstruction, the possession of the franchise by blacks at first posed an obstacle to the restoration of white domination. But as the political parties—Republican, Populists, and Democrats—struggled to build political support, each came to view the political rights of blacks as a serious impediment to their success. Republicans, burdened by their identification with both northern and black interests, simply adopted a "lily-white" strategy. The radical agrarians in the various state populist parties at first stressed the similarity of interests between poor whites and poor blacks and tried to build coalitions with blacks; but that alliance could not survive southern racism and the Populists subsequently repudiated blacks in an effort to hold the support of poor whites. In any case, the planter-backed Democrats soon overwhelmed the Populists by casting blacks in the role of the common enemy and by this strategy generated broad popular support for the political hegemony of the white planter, banker, and merchant class over both poor blacks and whites in the South.

aspect of southern life, from schools to cemeteries. These legislative enactments were approved by the Supreme Court, which found in 1883 that the Civil Rights Bill of 1875 was unconstitutional; and in 1896, in an opinion that was to affirm the validity of segregation for more than half a century, the Court established the legal fiction that racial segregation was not in violation of the Fourteenth Amendment provided the facilities afforded blacks were equal. Finally, the vote was gradually denied to blacks by a variety of measures, including literacy and property tests, poll taxes, and "grandfather clauses" (which allowed persons to vote only if their ancestors had voted), and these actions were spurred by the Supreme Court which found in 1898 that a plan advanced by Mississippi to disenfranchise blacks was not unconstitutional.

By the end of the first decade of the twentieth century the movement to restore caste arrangements had succeeded. It was a movement which, by then, found support in virtually all walks of southern life; from the disillusioned agrarian radicals to the most conservative leaders of the planter class. Most important of all, it found favor among the mass of poor whites who were led by their various leaders to endorse measures to disenfranchise blacks—such as poll taxes and literacy tests—which disenfranchised many of them as well. That this could be so is owed to the great success with which the southern ruling class played upon economic competition among blacks and whites, for "the Southern 'aristocracy' . . . could not endure without the hatred which it perpetuates among the white and black masses, and it [has been] by no means unmindful of that fact" (Cox, 577). Poor whites paid dearly for that hatred, for many of them not only lost certain political rights, but they permitted themselves to be relegated to a condition of economic servitude not much different than that to which they condemned blacks. Thus Perlo points out:

> While the planters lost much from the Civil War, they had certain compensations. . . . The new system of exploitation, involving "free" labor, could and was extended to the poor whites as well. As agriculture in the South became more concentrated, hundreds of thousands of small white farmers lost their land. Many became city workers. But many others became wage laborers or sharecroppers on the plantations. They became subject to the same type of extreme exploitation as the Negro farm population (71).

If the Compromise of 1877 marked the beginning of northern tolerance for southern practices, that tolerance was not shaken by the renewed subjugation of blacks as the nineteenth century drew to a close. In part this was because northern capitalism had entered a new imperialist phase, and racism as an ideology became more important in the North as well:

> . . . in the year 1898, the United States plunged into imperialistic adventures overseas under the leadership of the Republican Party. These adventures in the Pacific and the Caribbean suddenly brought under the jurisdiction of the United States some eight million people of the colored races. . . . As America shouldered the White Man's Burden, she took up at the same time many southern attitudes on the subject of race. . . . At the dawn of the new century the wave of Southern racism came in as a swell upon a mounting tide of national sentiment and was very much a part of that sentiment (Woodward, 1974, 72–74).

Landless, illiterate, and without recourse in the law or the political process, blacks were effectively returned to servitude as the twentieth century dawned. All of this was made possible by national acquiescence in the full range of mechanisms which made up the southern caste system. The federal government would not intervene to prevent the harsh exploitation of black labor, nor to alter the social and political structures by which that exploitation was achieved. The result was the consolidation in the South of a ruling class which could easily control the whole of southern life and which faced little opposition until the post–World War II years. "The one party South . . . and the low political participation of even the white people favor a de facto oligarchic regime," Myrdal points out. "The oligarchy consists of the big landowners, the industrialists, the bankers, and the merchants. Northern corporate business with big investments in the region has been sharing in the political control by this oligarchy" (453).

Given the totalitarian system which prevailed in the South until World War II, no defiant movement could either emerge or succeed in winning concessions. Economic interests could fire and evict and withhold credit at will; white mobs could lynch and burn at will; police agents could beat, maim, and kill at will; political leaders could call up the militia at will; the courts could imprison at will. All of the coercive measures available to public and private elites were employed in their most untrammeled and undisguised form to compel acquiescence by blacks to their station. As Lomax put it, the "Negro world was an enclave of terror" (40). Nor were the occasions frequent when force needed to be applied. Defiance was largely precluded by the socializing structures of southern society—its educational system, its religious institutions, its media, and a culture in which symbols of white supremacy were the hallmark. All were organized to inculcate the belief among blacks that their lot in life was the only rightful one or, at least, the only possible one. The structure of coercion and of socialization was so formidable that defiance simply could not be contemplated.

Even had black insurgency developed on any scale, it would have resulted in bloody repression as long as the national government accommodated to these sectional arrangements. The alliance of the national government and southern state and local governments was an overwhelming force. It would require some fundamental change, some large transformation, to disrupt this collusion. That transforming force was economic modernization in the South, a force that gradually altered national politics and, by doing so, helped give rise to an insurgent black movement.

Economic Modernization in the South

Even as caste arrangements were being consolidated in the South at the beginning of the twentieth century, large-scale economic forces were at work that would, in time, disrupt those arrangements. The most important effect of these economic forces, for our analysis, was the dramatic shift in the character of black participation in the labor force, together with mass migration out of the South. As to the first: "During slavery, practically all Negroes were engaged in southern agriculture or were household servants. This was still true of 87 percent in 1900 and 80 percent in 1910. But in 1960 less than 10 percent were in agriculture and 15 percent in domestic services" (Ross, 31). Regarding migration, more than 90 percent of blacks lived in the South at the beginning of the twentieth century; by 1960 about half lived in the North. In the course of slightly more than a half century the occupational position of blacks was transformed, and great numbers were redistributed from the agricultural South to the industrial North.

In the broadest terms, these shifts were caused by industrial expansion in the North during the first part of the twentieth century, by the decline in agricultural markets after World War I, together with federal agricultural policies originating in the 1930s, which took great masses of land out of production, and by the rapid pace of agricultural and industrial modernization in the South during and after World War II. Northern industrial expansion began to draw many blacks out of agriculture and out of the South in the early part of the century. "After the turn of the century," Ross points out, "American industrialism came into full flower. From an annual average of $13 billion in the last decade of the nineteenth century, the gross national product increased . . . to $40 billion in the 1909–1918 period. Total employment rose from an average of 27 million in 1889–1898 to 39 million in 1908–1918" (11). With the outbreak of war in Europe, the waves of immigration which had provided the labor supply for industrial expansion were sharply diminished, causing northern industry to look to the South for a source of labor. With these changes the first massive migration of blacks out of the South began; between 1910 and 1920 about half a million blacks moved to northern and western states.[6]

The post–World War I years brought a sharp reduction in the need for agricultural products, both because of curtailed wartime exports and curtailed immigration; the result was the beginning of a long period of intense hardship for agricultural workers. This trend reached catastrophic proportions in the Great Depression. The collapse of agricultural markets, together with New Deal policies which attempted to deal with agricultural surpluses by reducing production, forced millions off the land throughout the United States. In the South, where the vast majority of blacks were still located, "Cotton land in cultivation declined from 43 million acres in 1929 to 23 million acres in 1939. Negroes in every status—landowners, cash tenants, share tenants, sharecroppers, and laborers—were displaced in large numbers . . ." (Ross, 14). Under the circumstances, migration was the only choice for many. By 1940 almost one-quarter (23 per-cent) of blacks had come to live outside the South.

World War II reversed the decline in agriculture, but it also provided the impetus for a large-scale modernizing trend:[7]

---

[6] Population Reference Bureau, 72.

[7] There were many reasons for the slow progress of mechanization in southern agriculture prior to World War II. Among the most important has been the abundance of cheap labor, which enabled the South to compete despite mechanization in other agricultural regions. But "under the stimulus of high incomes and a shortage of manpower" during World War II, mechanization began to sweep the South (Hoover and Ratchford, 110).

The boom of World War II and subsequent war preparations gave southern landlordism a new lease on life by raising the price of cotton and increasing the profit from the exploitation of share-croppers and wage labor. At the same time this boom accelerated the technical development of southern agriculture. As large-scale purely capitalist farming grew at an unprecedented pace for the South . . . the anachronism of semi-slave, hand and mule labor on the sharecropper units became more acute (Perlo, 113).

The modernization of southern agriculture also stimulated increasing concentration of land ownership. Although the amount of southern acreage in farm production declined only slightly between 1940 and 1960, the number of farms dropped by nearly half, and the average farm size increased from 123 acres to 217 acres.[8] Taken together, mechanization, new agricultural technologies, federal policies which removed land from production, and the enlargement of land holdings dramatically altered the labor requirements of southern agriculture.

The traditional tenant labor force of the South thus found itself increasingly obsolete, forced to search elsewhere for the means to subsist. White surplus farm labor found employment in the developing southern textiles mills and related industries. But blacks continued to be excluded from such employment. This pattern of segregated employment served the southern (and the northern) employing classes well. The availability of a huge black labor surplus could be used as a threat to impede demands by whites for higher wages and for unionization. By excluding blacks the manufacturing class made "the underpaid white worker satisfied with his 'superior' status" and "threatens implicitly to bring in the Negro in case of 'difficulties' with the white workers" (Perlo, 99). Low wages and docile workers, in turn, helped to spur industrial expansion all the more, for the cheap labor pools available in the South led northern capital to make increasingly heavy investments in that region.

The relative exclusion of blacks from southern industry had a further consequence of great importance for the analysis being developed in this chapter—it gave many blacks little choice but to migrate northward. To be sure, a good many blacks migrated to southern cities, with the result that by 1960 only about 40 percent of the blacks who remained in the South still lived in rural areas.

[8] Bureau of the Census, 1976, 460–461.

But their experience in the southern cities was one of intense economic hardship: they occupied the very bottom rung of the urban proletariat, finding employment mainly available in those forms of work that were considered "unsuitable" for whites (e.g., domestic service, and other unskilled service jobs). Consequently their economic circumstances both in agriculture and in the southern cities created an inexorable pressure upon blacks to migrate northward, producing the greatest exodus of southern black agricultural workers in the nation's history: "During the decade of 1940–50 over 1.5 million Negroes left the South and 1.5 million left during the next decade. . . . On the other hand, the net outmigration of whites from the South was only 0.1 percent in the 1940s and 1.7 percent during the 1950s" (Henderson, 83).[9] With this trend growing, the proportion of blacks living outside of the South rose from 23 percent to almost 50 percent between 1940 and the mid-sixties. For all practical purposes, then, the South succeeded in redistributing a substantial part of its surplus labor to other regions of the country.

Taking all of these changes together, the results are striking: "In 1910, 75 percent of the nation's blacks lived in rural areas and nine-tenths lived in the South. [By the mid-sixties] three quarters were in cities and half resided outside of the southern states" (Foner, 325). In the course of a few decades a depressed southern rural peasantry had been transformed into a depressed urban proletariat.

With a massive agricultural and industrial transformation underway, a system of political domination based on terror and disenfranchisement was no longer essential to the southern ruling class in order to insure their labor needs on terms favorable to them. In other words economic modernization had made the South susceptible to political modernization. In the large-scale mechanized agriculture that was developing in the rural South, market incentives were slowly substituted for the older system of serf labor. A wage labor supply— one that was somewhat more skilled (especially in the use of machinery)—was coming to be required. This transition to wage labor was

---

[9] Just how great an upheaval this was for blacks is suggested by the Department of Agriculture which estimated "that 42 percent of the Negro farm people of 1940 who were still living in 1950 had left the farm during the 1940's" (Population Reference Bureau, 73). In the 1950s, the largest migration occurred in the post-Korean period: "Between 1954–59, the number of Negro-operated farms declined by 35 percent—a measure of how greatly cuts in acreage allotments on cotton and tobacco and how the use of machinery had curtailed the need for the tenant farmer in only five years" (Population Reference Bureau, 73).

greatly facilitated by the huge labor surpluses which were continually thrown up by the process of agricultural modernization itself. The constant threat of unemployment was a powerful inducement for rural workers to accept wage work on terms dictated by the planter class.

In the industrializing areas of the South a new capitalist class was emerging, especially during and following World War II. In large part it was tied to northern corporate power, for a considerable segment of southern industrial enterprise was initiated and controlled by northern capital. This new urban-based industrial class relied mainly on market mechanisms to insure its labor needs. To be sure, the inferior status of blacks continued to be a useful mechanism to insure maximum profits. But the deliberate exacerbation of racial competition for jobs was a strategy long used by employers to control labor both in the North and in the South, and was far from being equivalent to a system of caste. As a social system to allocate and control labor, in short, southern caste arrangements were becoming obsolete.

It was also the case that the southern white, whatever his class, had less reason in the post–World War II years to fear the extension of political rights to blacks, including the granting of the franchise. An extensive depopulation of the black belt South was well under way as a result of the large northward movement of blacks. Whatever electoral threat blacks might once have represented, migration greatly lessened it.

As economic modernization overtook the South, other changes were taking place in the North which also weakened opposition to the extension of formal rights to blacks. As we noted in an earlier section the imperialistic adventures launched by northern capitalism at the beginning of the twentieth century were in part justified by a racist ideology which borrowed much from the South. But with the rise of communism the United States was thrown into intense competition for world domination, a circumstance that demanded an ideology of "democracy" and "freedom." By the post–World War II period and the outbreak of the "cold war," this ideology reached full flower in international relations. Increasingly the circumstances prevailing in the South constituted a national embarrassment and support for these arrangements by dominant economic elites weakened. Imperialistic requirements which had in one era helped return blacks to servitude thus helped in another era to release them from servitude.

The stakes of northern capitalism in domestic racism also weakened after World War II. Early in the century, as black numbers in the northern industrial centers grew, employers had relentlessly pitted blacks against whites, exacerbating racial tensions in order to weaken working-class solidarity. One measure of the success of this strategy was the outbreak of white mob violence against blacks in the post–World War I period, for "some twenty-five race riots were touched off in American cities during the last six months of 1919," as an upsurge of unemployment followed the slowing of war production and the demobilizing of the armed forces. "Mobs took over cities for days at a time, flogging, burning, shooting, and torturing at will. . . . During the first year following the war more than seventy Negroes were lynched, several of them veterans still in uniform" (Woodward, 1974, 114). Blacks were slowly forced out of many of the industries where they had obtained wartime employment, and they were excluded from unions as well. To survive, they were pressed all the more to cooperate with nonunion employers against white workers. The problem was so extreme that the National Urban League found it necessary in 1919 to enact policies broad enough "to permit the autonomous local Leagues to proceed as they deemed best—to endorse and work with unions, to refer Negroes as strikebreakers, or to remain neutral" in the struggle between the employing and working classes (Meier, 1967, 175).

By the World War II period, however, northern capitalism had largely acceded to the unionization of the industrial working class, and to that extent the exploitation of racial cleavages had begun to lose its former utility. This change, together with the growing requirement for a liberal racial ideology with which to meet the threat of Communism in international affairs, eroded support for the southern social system among economic dominants in the North. As the nation approached mid-century, then, the leaders of northern capitalism and their counterparts in the South no longer had great cause to resist modernizing political trends in the southern region. Arnold Rose surely overstated the point when he remarked that caste arrangements had become "an expression merely of a traditional psychology," but the remark nevertheless contained much truth (xxvi).

Economic Modernization and Electoral Instability

Economic change, by weakening the stakes of agricultural and industrial leaders in the maintenance of caste arrangements, also freed national political leaders to act against those arrangements. By the fourth and fifth decades of the twentieth century, the perpetuation of caste arrangements was being reduced to a question of public opinion. In the absence of significant opposition from economic dominants, the question was whether shifts in the alignments of broad electoral groupings would create the necessary pressures to compel national leaders to act. The Democratic Party was the main arena in which this drama of gradually intensifying electoral conflict and realignment was played out.

Since the post-Reconstruction period, the one-party South has constituted the regional foundation of the national Democratic Party. Periodic efforts by the Republican Party to revive its political fortunes by mounting a "southern strategy"—either to forge a coalition between southern whites and blacks, or simply to garner conservative white voters—have foundered on the shoals of a virulent racism inculcated by the Democratic political leaders of the South and by the economic elites whom they served. The poor whites of the South, whatever their populist inclinations, continued in the twentieth century to be deeply moved by racial fears and by the slight advantages in economic position and social status which caste arrangements afforded them. Consequently poor whites continued to align themselves with the ruling class of the South, submerging their own class interests in a political alliance against blacks.

The realignment of the Democratic Party in 1932 did not change the politics of the South, for a national coalition was formed that joined together the industrial working class in the North and the one-party agrarian South. But two sources of strain were in the making even as that alliance was formed.

For one, northern urban blacks joined that coalition in 1936. With that shift, the "American dilemma" became a Democratic dilemma, as it had been a Republican dilemma for more than half a century. Just as the race question had plagued the party of Lincoln (it especially plagued Republican presidential contenders who had to deal with a delegation of northern and southern blacks at nominating conventions), now it was to plague the party of the New Deal and ultimately to divide it along regional lines.

But that division would be several decades in the making. In the meanwhile blacks got little, as a racial group, for their participation in Democratic politics: a few leavings of municipal patronage from the local parties, a few symbolic gestures from Democratic presidents. In 1936 the Democratic Party removed the rule that required a two-thirds majority for nominations and thereby also removed the South's veto power over presidential candidates. In the early 1940s a Roosevelt-oriented Supreme Court declared the white primary unconstitutional, and Roosevelt established the Fair Employment Practices Commission (in response to the threat that blacks, led by A. Phillip Randolph, would mount a march on Washington). Even such minor concessions, however, marked the beginning of a new posture by national Democratic leaders toward the black cause, and engendered intense antagonism among southern leaders, thus creating a deep strain between the northern and southern wings of the party.

The social and economic policies of the New Deal generated a second source of regional strain. New Deal programs to spur recovery and to solidify popular support provoked open conflict with the traditional elites of the South, whose power was based on the plantation economy. This "banker-merchant-farmer-lawyer-doctor-governing class" considered the New Deal a threat to its pervasive control over the structure of southern rural and smalltown life:

> For these people, the New Deal jeopardized a power that rested on the control of property, labor, credit and local government. Relief projects reduced dependency [on employers]; labor standards raised wages; farm programs upset landlord-tenant relationships; government credit bypassed bankers; new federal programs skirted county commissioners and sometimes even state agencies (Tindall, 31).

Southern economic interests did not, of course, eschew the New Deal programs that were of direct benefit to them; they opposed only those programs whose impact would weaken their power. Thus, for example, New Deal agricultural policies paid plantation owners generously to take land out of production, and the owners were glad for the subsidies. But, at the same moment, they opposed the giving of federal emergency relief to the superfluous work force resulting from the reduction of agricultural activity:

> The share tenant's situation is the impossible one of being forced by the inadequacies of the present system, on the one hand, to seek relief as the only means of keeping alive; and, on the other

hand, of having this relief opposed by the landlord because it may spoil him as a tenant, if and when he can be used again. There are other fears back of the landlord's attitude; the fear that the tenant will be removed from the influence of the landowner and learn that he is not entirely dependent on him; and the fear that the relief will raise the standard of living to the extent that bargaining on the old basis will be difficult. It can readily be seen that from the point of view of the landlord government relief is demoralizing (Johnson, Embree, and Alexander, 52).

In response to these two basic sources of strain, independent electors appeared on the ballots of several southern states in 1936. Although it was another decade before the movement toward independent or unpledged electors gathered momentum, the election of 1936 was a harbinger of the deep strains in Democratic presidential politics that would soon split the party.

But whatever their antagonism toward New Deal programs, southern leaders were in no position to bolt the party, for they had little hope of carrying the southern rank and file with them. Roosevelt's policies for economic recovery and social reform resonated with a long tradition of economic populism among the southern white masses, and thus solidified his electoral strength throughout the South. However, the tensions originating in the New Deal period led southern congressional delegates to coalesce with the Republicans; in exchange for opposition by southern Democrats to many progressive economic and social welfare measures put forward by the Democratic leadership (measures which, in any case, conservative southerners were quite prepared to oppose for their own reasons), the Republicans in turn withheld support from civil rights proposals which were so repugnant to the South.

To cope with this strain in the party, Roosevelt chose to avoid head-on clashes with the South over the race issue (by refusing support to anti-lynching legislation, for example). Instead he argued that blacks could best progress by being loyal to the New Deal, thus benefitting from the array of social and economic legislation sponsored by the New Deal. There can be no doubt that blacks did benefit from many of these programs (although they were badly hurt by some, especially federal agricultural policies). But as an excluded and exploited racial group, they got virtually nothing. In effect, the civil rights issue was submerged in order to maintain greater party unity.

By 1940 blacks began leaving the South in great numbers. Year by year the impact of this demographic revolution on the northern electoral system was immense, for blacks were concentrating in the northern cities of the most populous, industrialized states. In other words they were concentrated in the electoral strongholds of the Democratic Party. And as their voting numbers swelled, leaders in the northern wing of the party began to acknowledge that concessions to blacks would have to be made.

The race issue emerged in the election of 1948. It probably would not have emerged so early as a presidential campaign issue were it not for the formation of the Progressive Party led by Henry Wallace: Wallace directed his appeals to northern liberals and to blacks. Clark Clifford, Truman's chief campaign strategist, was worried about the president's strength among blacks, and not just because of Wallace. The Republicans were also making symbolic appeals to the black voter. Thus Clifford warned Truman that

> the Republicans were doing everything they could to win back this electorate. He predicted that the Republicans would "offer an FEPC, an anti-poll tax bill, and an anti-lynching bill" in the next Congressional session. To counter, the president had to push for whatever action he felt necessary "to protect the rights of minority groups." Although the South might not like this action, it was the "lesser of two evils" (Yarnell, 44).[10]

At the same time, Clifford advised Truman that "as always, the South can be considered safely Democratic. And in formulating national policy, it can be safely ignored" (Cochran, 1973, 230).

Accordingly Truman gave the appearance of championing civil rights. "Although he went much further than any previous President . . . he failed to match rhetoric with concrete efforts . . ." (Hartmann, 150–151). Thus Truman called for a broad range of civil rights measures in an address to Congress on January 7, and on February 2, he delivered a special civil rights message to Congress which outlined a ten-point program, including outlawing the poll tax, establishing a permanent FEPC, and making lynching a federal crime. But having promised to issue executive orders abolishing segrega-

---

[10] There is considerable dispute among analysts of the election of 1948 over the question of whether Truman's rhetorical position on civil rights during the campaign was owed to the Wallace threat, or to the threat that the Republicans would capture votes among blacks. Among those who make a strong case that Wallace was the primary force are Bernstein, Berman, and Vaughan. By contrast, Yarnell reaches the conclusion that the Republicans were the much greater threat (see especially 35, 44, and 69). For the purposes of our analysis, this dispute is not crucial. What is crucial is that the civil rights question was gradually emerging as an electoral issue.

*Northern Negro electorate as primal
cause of 1948 Dem. C.R. plank
— through Northern urban bosses.*

199   — *The Civil Rights Movement*

tion in the armed forces and discrimination in federal employment
—actions which were within his immediate power—he did neither
(not, at least, until after the unanticipated and turbulent events of
the nominating convention in the summer).

The nominating convention scuttled Truman's essentially rhetorical civil rights strategy. Liberal leaders intent on securing a strong
civil rights plank despite Truman's opposition were joined by influential northern machine leaders who believed Truman would lose
the election. They "were less concerned with Southern diehards
bolting than with solidifying the Negro vote behind their local and
state candidates. Henry Wallace was making a powerful appeal to
this constituency in major cities. Any spectacular demonstration of
the Democrats as resolute defenders of Negro interests that would
head off the Wallace threat was to be welcomed" (Cochran, 1973,
230). Consequently a strong civil rights plank was pushed through
on the floor of the convention, leading Alabama and Mississippi to
walk out. The Dixiecrat forces, drawing upon dissident elements
throughout the South, convened two days later in Birmingham to
form a States' Rights Party with Senator J. Strom Thurmond of
South Carolina as its presidential nominee. With these events
Truman was pushed all the more to the left on the race question,
and he immediately issued the executive orders he had promised
months earlier. "Thus a border-state politician intent on pursuing
an ambiguous racial policy had the torch of civil rights unexpectedly
thrust into his hands" (Cochran, 1973, 231). In the ensuing election,
Truman won (with the aid of the black vote) despite the loss of
four Deep South states—Louisiana, South Carolina, Alabama, and
Mississippi—to the States' Rights Party.

The militancy of southern leaders in 1948 reflected the continuing,
though rapidly diminishing, political and economic stakes in the
exploitation of blacks, especially in the Deep South. Moreover the
hoisting of the States' Rights banner afforded southern leaders an
opportunity to mobilize opposition to the offensive social and economic policies of the New Deal and the Fair Deal. Lubell refers to
this as "a double insurgency: an economic revolt aimed at checking
government spending and the power of labor unions, and a racial
reaction designed to counter the influence of Negro voting in the
North" (1966, 186).[11]

*modern
'Black
Code'
— had
the same
(unintended)
effect.*

---

[11] On this point see also Sindler, 1962, 141.

Thus it cannot be said that the cause of securing civil rights legislation was immediately advanced by these events. Southern defections in the election of 1948 foreshadowed the possible dissolution of that regional base, and so concessions to the South—namely, maintaining the racial status quo—became the order of the day, as Stevenson's posture in campaigning for the Democratic nomination in 1952 revealed. In one speech prior to the convention Stevenson declared that "I reject as contemptible the reckless assertions that the South is a prison in which half the people are prisoners and the other half are wardens" (Cochran, 1969, 222). During the nominating convention he expressed great concern that the fight over civil rights "might drive the South out of the party—the party needed unity" (Martin, 1976, 589). With his acquiescence, the delegation from Illinois voted to seat the Dixiecrat delegations without a "loyalty pledge," a position which antagonized many northern advocates of civil rights. By reason of his personal convictions and his concern that the South had to be kept within the framework of the Democratic Party, Stevenson emerged as a compromise candidate, defeating Kefauver and Harriman after several ballots. He then named Senator John Sparkman of Alabama as his running mate.

Throughout the campaign Stevenson continued to appease the South, and gave relatively little attention to the black vote in the northern cities (Cochran, 1969, 221–222). "He repeatedly indicated concern about losing the South" (Martin, 1976, 597), and time and again he asserted that the responsibility for dealing with the race problem properly resided with the states:

> He fell back on an old proposal that the federal FEPC relinquish jurisdiction to states that had FEPC's of their own. What about the filibuster? "I suppose the President might properly be concerned with the rules of the Senate. . . . I should certainly want to study it. . . . I am told that it has disadvantages as well as advantages. There are other considerations involved in unlimited and free debate that must not be overlooked in our anxiety to advance in one field alone" (Martin, 1976, 611).[12]

---

[12] As a matter of principle, Stevenson spoke strongly in favor of civil rights: "In the South he talked of the necessity of civil rights for Negroes, if anything more emphatically than he had in Harlem" (Muller, 101). But the point is that he steadfastly resisted suggestions that he advocate federal actions designed to impose these principles upon the South.

As it happens, this policy of conciliation did not stem the tide of defections in the subsequent election because an entirely different force was also at work. To be sure, the Dixiecrat states, where race was the preeminent issue, returned to the Democratic ranks, although South Carolina and Louisiana did so by very slim majorities. But in the Outer South the Republicans made big gains; Virginia, Florida, Tennessee, and Texas delivered their electoral votes to Eisenhower. Republican strength in the Outer South was especially noticeable among the growing white middle classes in the cities, while Democratic strength tended to be concentrated among whites in the declining small towns and rural areas of the Deep South (Lubell, 1956, 179 ff.).

The election of 1952 thus revealed the political effects of a second form of economic change that was sweeping the South: industrial modernization. This modernizing trend was casting up a new white middle class in the cities and suburbs (especially in the states of the Outer South) whose political sympathies inclined toward the Republican Party. These changes in the class structure became apparent in the election of 1952, which "marked a turning point in Republican fortunes, the beginnings of a southern Republicanism that would contest elections, first at the presidential level, then at the state and local levels, evolving gradually into a credible opposition party everywhere except the inner core of the Deep South—and even there sporadically" (Tindall, 49).

In other words, the rupture between the northern and southern wings of the Democratic party which occurred in 1948 was no transient phenomenon. Both agricultural and industrial modernization were contributing to a deep and widening fissure. Each of these economic forces was eroding the Democratic Party's base in the South in a different way. Indeed some political analysts even reached the conclusion at the time that the Democratic Party might not survive. Lubell was one:

> The most heavily Democratic districts in the North . . . are becoming those which are poorest economically and which have the largest Negro populations—two characteristics which tend to pull the representatives of these districts back to the old appeals of the New Deal. If this trend continues, as seems likely, the Congressmen from these districts will find themselves in sharpening conflict with the Southern districts, both with the anti-Negro sentiments, so strong in the rural South, and the economic conservatism of the rising middle-class elements in the Southern cities. . . . The underlying

tensions between these two wings of "sure" Democratic seats are sufficiently intense so that the cracking apart of the Democratic party must be rated a possibility (1956, 215–216).

In this prediction, of course, Lubell was wrong. His mistake was partly in failing to take account of the large stakes the dominant leadership of the South, its congressional delegation, had in the Democratic party. From the start of party splintering in 1948 the southern congressional delegation kept its distance from third-party adventurism. "Continued agitation for an independent political movement came primarily from the Citizens' Councils and aging Dixiecrat forces" at the state and local level (Bartley, 290). As a result of its .longevity in Congress the southern delegation enjoyed tremendous power in national affairs; it had a large claim on federal patronage, and had a decisive impact on the allocation of billions of dollars in defense funds for the construction of military, space, and industrial complexes, many of which came to be located in the South. Nor were shifts in party identification free of risks to electoral incumbency itself. The mystique of the Democratic Party still held sway below the Mason-Dixon line despite the racial tensions of the times. Consequently southern congressional leaders confined themselves to encouraging presidential Republicanism, unpledged electors, and other stratagems to threaten the national Democratic Party, but they did not bolt. In effect they defined the limits of the southern white resistance movement and thereby weakened it. But within these limits they helped the North-South fissure grow.

Because of this fissure, blacks did not benefit much at this stage from their growing voting numbers in the North. Black loyalty to the Democratic Party was not in doubt; in fact it had been intensifying. Referring to the trends in black voting with migration to the North, Lubell observed that "as their numbers have increased so has their Democratic party loyalty. . . . Truman got a heavier proportion of the Negro vote than did Roosevelt, while Stevenson [in the election of 1952] did even better among the Negroes than Truman" (1956, 214). The firm allegiance of black voters thus encouraged Democratic strategists to decide that it was defections among southern voters which constituted the main problem of the party. For this reason the civil rights issue continued to be sacrificed to the goal of regional unity. It was the South, in short, that initially benefitted from electoral instability. But that was to change, for if the South was becoming antagonized and restive over the race issue, so too were blacks.

Economic Modernization and the Rise
of Black Defiance

As economic modernization thrust blacks out of one socioeconomic system and into another, their capacity to resist caste controls was substantially enlarged. Controls which were so readily enforced in a rural society characterized by dispersion and face-to-face interaction could not be well enforced in the urban community where ghettoization produced concentration and separation. Consequently, "behind the walls of segregated isolation, Negroes were better able to build resistance to subordination" (Rose, xviii).

The historical process of building "resistance to subordination" was initiated in the North where there was no tradition of caste controls and no socially sanctioned tradition of terror against blacks. Since industrialists had encouraged migration to cope with labor shortages and to combat labor insurgency, they entered into a certain kind of alliance with blacks that provided a measure of protection. Political leaders were also restrained from the more extreme forms of racist demagoguery by incipient black electoral influence. The northern urban environment was harsh, to be sure, but it did not preclude protest.

Protest emerged simultaneously with mass migration. Freed from feudal controls, blacks began to protest the oppression they had always known. Moreover, segregation in the northern ghettos provided a degree of security and concentrated numbers provided a sense of strength. Thus with the first large migratory wave in the World War I period, Marcus Garvey was able to draw a million northern blacks into his Universal Negro Improvement Association by appeals that converted "the Negro-American's stigmatized identity into the source of his personal worthiness" (Michael Lewis, 158).[13] He succeeded in attracting this huge constituency because a people just recently released from a station of enforced inferiority needed to

---

[13] Black protest was sometimes directed against white society and was sometimes a reaction away from it, for "American Negro history is basically a history of the conflict between integrationist and nationalist forces in politics, economics, and culture, no matter what leaders are involved and what slogans are used" (Cruse, 564). We pass over this important distinction, which is useful for other purposes; but for the purpose of understanding the evolution of black protest, each movement—whatever its specific direction—nurtured the capacity for collective action.

have their sense of worth affirmed. At the same time and in many of the same ghettos "Negroes showed a new disposition to fight and defend themselves" against the white mobs that terrorized blacks in several dozen American cities as the war ended (Woodward, 1974, 114). Cast in the role of scabs, blacks repeatedly fought white workers for the right to work. During the depression they confronted the police in eviction actions and joined in the struggles of the unemployed against the relief system. In the great uprisings that led to the Congress of Industrial Organizations, they united with white workers in strikes against those mass production industries where they had gotten an occupational foothold. They combined during World War II to challenge Roosevelt's wartime government with a mass "March on Washington Movement" to protest discrimination in war industry and segregation in the armed forces. In the southern military camps and surrounding communities they engaged in armed combat against whites who attacked them. In other words, once they were free to do so, blacks acted "beyond the limits of institutionalized politics" to protest their condition (Michael Lewis, 151).

Concentration and separation also generated a black economic base, despite the poverty of most of the black urban wage workers who contributed to that base. One significant result was the gradual emergence of a black occupational sector which was relatively invulnerable to white power, a sector consisting of clergymen, small entrepreneurs, professionals, and labor leaders. In an earlier period, and particularly in southern rural society, very few—if any—blacks were located in these occupations, and those few were usually dependent on whites. The emergence of an independent leadership sector was accompanied by institutional expansion and diversification, and by greater institutional independence of the white community. This development, too, was made possible by the economic base which resulted from concentration and segregation. Churches acquired mass memberships, fraternal and other communal associations proliferated, small businesses could be sustained, segregated union locals were formed, and a black press could be nourished. These institutions provided the vehicles to forge solidarity, to define common goals, and to mobilize collective action.

In the evolving history of black protest these developing occupational and institutional resources were of crucial importance. The March on Washington Movement instigated by A. Philip Randolph, president of the Brotherhood of Sleeping Car Porters, is an outstanding example. Head of a segregated international union, Randolph could act with considerable immunity from white sanctions and his union afforded financial resources and organizing talent. Acting as couriers and organizers in the northeastern and midwestern cities where they stopped over, his trainmen instigated rallies and marches to pressure Roosevelt into issuing an executive order establishing a Fair Employment Practices Commission (FEPC) to insure blacks access to wartime defense employment. The black press, too, was of critical importance, for it almost uniformly supported Randolph and continually featured the movement's activities. With this mobilization under way, greater solidarity across class lines was forged:

> [Middle-class black leaders] were unable to withstand the militant mood of the frustrated group they sought to lead. However reluctantly, the organizing of masses of Negroes [by Randolph] to engage in a national direct-action demonstration came to be widely agreed upon as a necessary action. It was viewed as a last resort, a dramatic gesture to force the white majority to take notice of the dire distress of its Negro brothers (Garfinkel, 42).

In these ways economic modernization, coupled with separation and concentration, both freed blacks from feudal constraints and enabled them to construct the occupational and institutional foundation from which to mount resistance to white oppression.

Urbanization had another important effect: blacks at the bottom of the urban social order were not only loosened from racial controls, they were loosened from social controls more generally. Social disorganization usually accompanies rapid agricultural modernization and the result of southern modernization was no different. The fundamental cause was unemployment and underemployment. In the rural South people may have lived close to the margin of subsistence, but they were nevertheless enmeshed in an economic system; they were also deeply enmeshed in a semifeudal system of social relations. But with modernization, unemployment spread, driving people into the cities where unemployment and underemployment became a more or less chronic condition for many.[14]

---

[14] When blacks were located in agriculture, their unemployment rates were lower than white rates. With migration, this relationship was reversed. "By the late 1940s the black unemployment rate was about 60 percent higher than the white rate and since 1954 it has been double the white rate, which itself has risen " (Killingsworth, 50). Moreover there is substantial reason to think that a good deal of black unemployment is "hidden" —undetected because of biases in official reporting procedures. Some authorities believe that blacks generally suffered a rate of unemployment three times that of whites in the

In turn, persistent unemployment shredded the social fabric. The impact could be sensed in the gradually rising proportion of families headed by females, for men without work were unable to form and sustain families. As for the men themselves, unemployment deprived them of the meaning of work and removed them from the discipline of work. In this way agricultural modernization created a depressed and deregulated class and thus a potentially volatile class from those ranks civil disorder could erupt. One form that disorder took was rioting: a major riot broke out in Harlem as early as 1935 and again during World War II.

As the numbers of blacks in the cities grew, their protests began to produce concessions from political leaders. Each concession, however rhetorical, conferred legitimacy on the goals of the struggle and gave reason for hope that the goals could be reached, with the result that protest was stimulated all the more. The concessions were yielded by northern political leaders, especially in the Democratic Party and in the federal judiciary. The Great Depression probably marked the beginnings of this new posture by political leaders. Although Roosevelt did all that he could to avoid the civil rights issue directly for fear of antagonizing the South, he gave blacks "a sense of national recognition. He did so more in terms of their interests in economic and social injustice than of their title to equal rights. Yet he threw open the gates of hope" (Schlesinger, 935). But the number of blacks in the North was mounting and protest was intensifying. By World War II racial concessions had to be made. Despite his uneasiness over how an FEPC would affect defense industries in the South, and the possibility of alienating the southern congressional delegation, Roosevelt was confronted by the prospect of a march on Washington that would cause considerable national and international embarrassment to a country identified with the struggle for "freedom abroad." With the scheduled march only days away, he conceded and signed an executive order establishing an FEPC on June 25, 1941.

In the presidential campaign of 1948 the issue of granting blacks basic rights emerged directly and forcefully, thrusting the issue of race to the very center of national politics. With both Truman and

[handwritten marginalia: no — Blacks themselves opened their gates. Schlesinger wrong (again)]

years following the Korean War (Killingsworth, 62; Ross, 22 and 26). With white rates regularly reaching 6 percent during that recessionary period, it could well have been the case that true black unemployment rates were running as high as 20 percent. In the central city ghettos the rates were even higher. Additional data on black unemployment will be presented in chapter five.

Wallace aligned against segregation and discrimination and with southern leaders aligned to defend the caste system, the rhetoric of race became more inflamed than during any period since the Civil War.

Other segments of the national political leadership stratum also responded in this period. This was nowhere better exemplified than in the opinions of the U. S. Supreme Court. After 1940 the Court upheld the rights of blacks to eat in unsegregated dining cars on interstate carriers, to register and vote in southern white primaries, and to enroll in publicly supported institutions of higher education. This assault on racism through the courts had been many years in the making by the NAACP, and in a growing climate of black protest the courts granted concessions. By the early 1950s:

> The legal Defense Fund of the National Association for the Advancement of Colored People had developed a nearly completed brief against the principle of separate but equal, plus a staff of lawyers with the skill and acumen to plead their case. In the Sipuel, Sweatt and McLaurin cases during the first five years after the end of the war, they had persuaded the Supreme Court to narrow the definition of equality, so that there remained only the bare principle that segregation was constitutional only if there were real equality. Now the NAACP was ready to attack that principle (Killian, 39).

The culmination of this judicial repudiation of southern racism came in 1954 with the striking down of the "separate but equal" doctrine in public education. It was a sweeping victory, one that was destined to unleash the forces of reaction throughout the South, giving rise to campaigns of massive resistance against federal power by the political leaders of the southern states. But it had equally large consequences in the black community; the highest court in the land had been compelled to yield the struggle against racism a new and large measure of legitimacy.[15]

---

[15] The National Association for the Advancement of Colored People and the National Urban League were developed before World War I by black intellectuals and professionals, liberal whites, and corporate leaders. Their emergence represented a form of institutional and leadership development in the black community, although "neither organization has ever had anything approaching a mass constituency among the Negroes themselves. In spite of their significant contributions to the Negro's welfare . . . neither organization has ever fired the loyalties of the rank and file. Court tests, behind-the-scenes negotiations, and educational efforts are not the kinds of activities which evoke passionate commitments from those who live their lives outside of the middle-class context. For the Negro masses, these organizations have represented a

The concessions forced from northern leaders by northern blacks reverberated in the southern ghettos. By mid-century, southern ghettos were also swollen with the displaced agricultural poor. Protest had become possible; victories had become possible. Except for freedom from caste relations, all of the structural developments essential to a protest movement that were present in the northern ghettos were also to be found in the southern ghettos: the economic base formed by a wage laboring class; the consequent occupational and institutional expansion and diversification; the volatile underclass produced by unemployment and underemployment. Concentrated, separated, more independent of white domination than ever before, and with more cause for hope than ever before, southern urban blacks burst forth in protest.[16]

The most dramatic early protest occurred in Montgomery, Alabama.[17] On Thursday, December 1, 1955, Rosa Parks, a seamstress

---

somewhat vague benevolence bestowed from beyond the boundaries of their personal world" (Michael Lewis, 156). The legal talent represented by the NAACP was a resource in the black struggle, although the role of legal talent as a factor in winning court victories against segregation tends to be exaggerated. Such factors as modernization, migration, concentration, the rise of protest, and the cold war struggle against Communism had the decisive impact on political opinion, including judicial opinion.

[16] In contrast to the factors we stress to explain the rise of black insurgency, other analysts point to the frustration generated by "rising expectations," which in turn were generated by rising incomes. In the period under study the data to confirm a theory of rising expectations are abundant. In fact, evidence is available to confirm several variants of the theory as well.

Referring just to overall economic improvement, blacks made their greatest advance between 1939 and 1951, when the income of male black wage and salary workers rose from 37 percent to 62 percent of the income of male white wage and salary workers. There is also support for the notion that rapid economic improvement, followed by an abrupt downturn, is at the root of unrest. Between the apex of black prosperity in 1951 and the early 1960s, male black wage and salary income as a percentage of male white wage and salary income fell from 62 to about 53. Finally, there can be no doubt that a rising class of blacks experienced extreme status inconsistency, for despite their improved income which gave them a claim to middle-class status, caste and racial degradation still afflicted them. Of the several variations of the rising expectations theory, we would incline most, in explaining the postwar black movement, towards the discontents originating in status inconsistency. However, we think the variables we employ in the text have much greater explanatory power. For the studies from which these generalizations about income changes are taken, see Ross; Killingsworth; and Henderson.

[17] As John Walton has recently pointed out, Floyd Hunter's work on Atlanta based on research conducted as early as 1950 noted the changing mood of blacks. Hunter judged that blacks were becoming increasingly demanding and that "traditional methods of suppression and coercion are failing" (149). Hunter attributed this change to the emergence of a black leadership stratum that had become somewhat more economically secure. For several of many descriptions of the Montgomery bus boycott, see King, 1958; Reddick; Lewis, 1964; and Lewis, 1970.

in a local department store, refused to sit in the section of a bus restricted to blacks and was arrested under local segregation ordinances. She was the fifth person arrested that year for violating segregated seating arrangements on the Montgomery buses. Indignation over segregation had been mounting, with the bus company a particular target of anger. Not only were blacks subjected to the indignities of segregated seating but armed drivers were notoriously abusive and had killed several blacks. There had been some talk of a boycott and even some concrete planning by the Women's Political Council, an organization of middle-class black women (formed when the local League of Women Voters refused to admit blacks) who had been influenced by the example of a successful boycott staged in Baton Rouge a year earlier. Various meetings to discuss grievances had been held with the bus company managers, but to no avail.

As word of the arrest spread, a remarkably instantaneous mobilization of the black leadership took place, spurred by the heads of the Women's Political Council and by E. D. Nixon, a well-known activist who was both an influential member of the Brotherhood of Sleeping Car Porters and a resident of Montgomery. The black ministerial alliance joined in and preparations advanced rapidly. By midafternoon on Friday 40,000 leaflets calling for a boycott the following Monday morning were being distributed througout the black community of 50,000 persons. Much of the distribution was done by the drivers for a black taxi company who also agreed to transport passengers for the price of the bus fare. A newspaper reporter who was sympathetic to the black cause managed to place a boycott story on the front page of the Sunday edition of a local white newspaper and black ministers throughout the community exhorted people from the pulpits to join the boycott.

On Monday morning, only four days after the triggering arrest, the boycott was nearly 100 percent effective. In the afternoon Martin Luther King, a newcomer to the community and thus a figure still not marred by factional identifications, was elected to head a permanent boycott committee, the Montgomery Improvement Association (MIA). That night 4,000 blacks—8 percent of Montgomery's black population—assembled in a local church to wonder at and to celebrate what they had done.

The struggle in Montgomery had begun. In the year before it ended, all of the elements in the upheaval that dominated the South for the next ten years were revealed. The bus company and local city officials were adamant in refusing to make concessions, and so the black community dug in for a long fight. A car pool, with forty-eight dispatch points and forty-two collection points, was organized and it operated with remarkable efficiency throughout the year. City officials and white citizen groups, for their part, mounted a campaign of harassment. Riders waiting at the car pool dispatching and collection points were arrested for vagrancy, for hitchhiking, and on other grounds; car insurance was cancelled; leaders of the movement lived with constant telephoned threats of assassination.

The dynamiting of King's home in late January nearly set off a race riot. When King was also arrested for speeding, he was refused bail until hundreds gathered before the jail. City officials tried to prevent MIA from establishing an office to coordinate the affairs of the boycott. Using the excuse of local building and fire ordinances of one kind or another, they forced MIA to move its offices repeatedly until a haven was finally found in a building built and owned by a local union of black brick layers.

Moderate elements in Montgomery were effectively silenced during these events. Even the downtown merchants who were hard hit by the boycott brought only half-hearted pressure for a settlement, for they were immobilized by the openly displayed anger of the white community. When the White Citizens' Council invited Senator Eastland to speak in Montgomery in mid-February, some 12,000 people assembled to hear him. And local business leaders had been warned that white boycotts would follow any gestures of conciliation toward the black movement.

If positions in Montgomery were thus frozen, the opinions of others beyond Montgomery were not. The Montgomery struggle attracted attention throughout the country and the world. Money poured in from the NAACP, from the United Automobile Workers (which had a substantial black membership), and from thousands of individuals, especially in the North. National opinion was all the more aroused when the leaders of the movement were indicted in late February for conspiring to interfere with business. The trial itself attracted worldwide press attention, providing dozens of black witnesses with an opportunity to denounce the southern caste system before an international audience. The leaders were found guilty in Alabama, of course, but the verdict brought with it invitations for speaking engagements in many northern cities and thus the opportunity to garner northern support.

The struggle wore on until, in November, a local court enjoined the car pool. Had that action been taken much earlier, it might have broken the boycott (the boycott leaders believed they could not defy the courts without tainting their claims to moral justification in the eyes of the nation). But midway through the trial, with MIA leaders awaiting the inevitable negative decision, word was received that the U.S. Supreme Court had declared Alabama's state and local bus segregation laws unconstitutional.

The reprisals in the wake of victory were staggering: four churches and several homes were dynamited; several shootings occurred; and there were many beatings. The atmosphere of violence so alarmed businessmen whose economic losses were by then considerable that they finally brought effective pressure to bear on the city administration with the result that seven whites were arrested for terrorist acts and violence began to subside. The black movement of the post-World War II period had staged its first major battle and won its first major victory.

The Mobilization of White Defiance

a fundamental error -- one only a very innocent observer of Southern society could make.

The white extremism and violence so characteristic of the South historically and so evident during the course of both the Montgomery boycott and other protests of the period hardly needed encouragement from elites. But it was provided in any case, for as the caste system came under assault, traditional southern white leaders rose up in outrage. Respected and influential figures denounced the courts, the federal government, and civil rights organizers for unwarranted infringements upon states' rights. They did more than denounce: Senator Harry Flood Byrd of Virginia called for a program of "massive resistance" by state and local governments to nullify the power of the courts. The most dramatic symbol of this elite movement was the "Declaration of Constitutional Principles"—the so-called "Southern Manifesto"—which was sponsored by Senator J. Strom Thurmond of South Carolina. When it was issued in 1956 it bore the signature of 82 Representatives and 19 Senators or 101 of the 128 national legislators from states in the former Confederacy. The statement called the Brown decision a "clear abuse of judicial powers" that was being exploited by "outside agitators." The Supreme Court, it was said, "undertook to exercise their naked judicial power and substituted their personal political and social ideas for the established law of the land." And the document ended with a pledge to "use all lawful means to bring about a reversal of this decision which is contrary to the Constitution." These and other pronouncements by white southern leaders (Governor Herman Talmadge of Georgia proclaimed that the Supreme Court's decision was "national suicide") had considerable impact; virtually every state in the former Confederacy, for example, enacted legislation to prevent or hamper enforcement of the Brown decision, including closing and padlocking the public schools.

The legitimacy which southern leaders thus conferred on defiance of the federal courts encouraged the emergence of a movement of massive resistance among whites. New South-wide segregationist organizations mushroomed (some estimates put the number as high as fifty), their membership drawn mainly from the small towns and rural areas of the black belt. Most of them were eventually swept into the better-organized and financed White Citizens' Council movement which, at its height in 1956, could claim 250,000 members. But these

> organized segregationists exercised an influence far more pervading than membership rolls implied. Their ranks included the . . . cadres of massive resistance. Effective leadership and organization . . . [enabled] . . . Council spokesmen to usurp the voice of the white community. An uneasy but workable alliance with powerful political figures gave its leaders influence at the highest policy levels (Bartley, 84).[18]

At the local level, Citizens' Councils turned out massive amounts of propaganda in support of segregation, denounced and intimidated whites who spoke up in support of court compliance, and instigated systematic retaliation against black activists. The boycott in Montgomery had been followed by a similarly successful campaign in Tallahassee in June 1956, and boycotts against white businesses were spreading to other parts of the South. In response, Citizens' Councils organized or supported the use of economic sanctions against blacks. Blacks as well as civil rights sympathizers were evicted from tenant farm shacks, were fired from jobs, were denied loans, and had their

---

18 In *Deep South Says Never*, John Barlow Martin also vividly portrays the ideology and activities of the White Citizen's Councils.

mortgages foreclosed. With black boycotts spreading and economic reprisals against blacks worsening, it could be fairly said that economic warfare was being waged in the South in the latter half of the 1950s.

In the presidential campaign of 1956 national political leaders attempted to play down the divisive race issue, particularly avoiding the inflammatory Brown decision. The Republican platform said that the party "accepts the [Brown] decision"; the Democrats said that the decision had generated "consequences of vast importance."[19] During the campaign Eisenhower declared, "I don't believe you can change the hearts of men with laws or decisions," and Stevenson, in response to the question of whether he would employ federal troops to enforce the orders of the courts, replied "I think that would be a great mistake. That is exactly what brought on the Civil War. It can't be done by troops, or bayonets. We must proceed gradually, not upsetting habits or traditions that are older than the Republic" (Anthony Lewis, 1964, 108). In other words, the civil rights stance of the Democrats in 1956 was designed to regain the insurgent South.

Although both parties avoided the school desegregation issue, the Republicans saw opportunities in the difficulties being experienced by the Democratic Party over the race question. There was the possibility of playing upon this issue to make further gains among whites in the South,[20] or of making equally important gains among blacks in the ghettos of the North. In some measure Republican strategists were uncertain of the proper course:

> Like the Democrats, the Republicans were torn between conflicting strategies. Some GOP leaders looked longingly toward the Negro vote in the northern states and recommended a vigorous civil rights policy. Other party strategists, watching the disintegrating position of the national Democratic party in the South, visualized further

---

[19] As Muller has said, the Democratic platform "wobbled on civil rights. While pledging continued efforts to eradicate all discrimination the key plank added: 'We reject all proposals for the use of force to interfere with orderly determination of these matters by the courts'" (177). During the campaign Stevenson continued to reiterate his general support for civil rights, but also continued to resist advocating specific remedies, such as the use of federal force to compel compliance with court orders.

[20] For more than two decades the South was the only region of the country where Republicans had been making gains. In the election of 1932 they polled 18 percent of the vote in the eleven southern states; by 1948, they polled 27 percent. (In 1956, they would poll half of the southern vote.) See Lubell (1966, 226).

Republican gains among white voters below the Potomac and coun-
seled a cautious approach to the problems of desegregation (Anthony
Lewis, 1964, 62).

However, the Republicans finally cast their lot with the potential
for gain among northern blacks, for the congressional Republicans
were all from northern states where blacks were concentrating. Under
the urging of Herbert Brownell, the attorney general, and of other
party leaders, Eisenhower sent a civil rights bill to Congress in 1956
and Republicans pushed for it, prodded as they were by a president
"who was demanding party support for a civil rights bill that con-
ceivably could revolutionize Negro politics and bring the Negro
vote back to the party of Lincoln" (Evans and Novak, 126).[21] For
northern Democrats the Republican action presented a major dilemma, especially in an election year. Many felt it was essential to
take decisive action on civil rights; others feared the impact of such
action on southern support. In the end Lyndon B. Johnson, the
Senate Majority Leader, conspired with other southern congressmen
to kill the bill, and the Congress adjourned.

The election of 1956 indicated that the Democratic strategy of
avoiding civil rights issues was not succeeding. The basis of the
North-South Democratic coalition was inexorably weakening. On the
one side, southern defections continued. When the returns were in
Stevenson fared slightly worse than he had in the election of 1952.
Four states in the Outer South—Florida, Virginia, Tennessee, and
Texas—remained in the Republican column, a reflection in part of
the two-party system developing as a result of industrial modernization. And in the Deep South, Louisiana defected. The Democrats,
despite a policy of conciliation on the race question, thus suffered
a net loss of one additional southern state over the election of 1952
and analysts began to speculate that the two-party system in the
south might be reviving.

On the other side, the election of 1956 revealed that black allegiance
to the Democratic Party was also weakening. "Partisan as well as
non-political spokesmen for the race had warned [in advance of the
election] that resurgence of racial bigotry in the South endangered
the old alliance. Polls indicated that the Democrats could not count

---

[21] Eisenhower had been deeply upset by the *Brown* decision; he told aides that he
thought "the decision was wrong." But he did appear to believe that "every American
citizen was entitled to the right to vote" (Alexander, 118, 194).

on the overwhelming majorities from Negro districts which had been returned consistently during the past 20 years" (Moon, 1957, 219). When the ballots were counted, a Gallup poll reported that "of all the major groups in the nation's population, the one that shifted most to the Eisenhower-Nixon ticket . . . was the Negro voter." Stevenson had won about 80 percent of the black vote in 1952, but he won only about 60 percent in 1956. The upward trend of black support for the Democratic Party initiated in the election of 1936 was broken.

Analysts of the election of 1956 uniformly attribute the falloff in the Democratic black vote to Stevenson's efforts to maintain party unity at the expense of the civil rights issue. Matthews and Protho state: "The significant shift to Eisenhower in 1956 was caused by the belief that neither Stevenson nor the Democratic party was sound, from the Negro viewpoint, on the race issue" (391–392). Considerable support for this view derives from the regional pattern of defections: "Significantly, the closer the Negro lived to the resurgent terror, the sharper was his defection from the dominant party" (Moon, 1957, 226). In many southern precincts the dropoff in black Democratic votes was startling. For example, "In 1952 the Illinois governor carried Atlanta Negro precincts better than 2 to 1. Four years later he received less than 15 percent of the vote in these same precincts" (Moon, 1957, 221).[22]

Although the sharpest black defections occurred in the South, many northern black voters signaled their disapproval of the Democratic Party in another way:

> There was a sharp decline in balloting in many Negro districts throughout the country, but particularly in Northern industrial centers from which, in previous years, the Democrats had received huge majorities. This, despite an increased Negro population in most of these cities. . . .
>
> In Philadelphia, 27,000 fewer votes were cast than in 1952 for a loss of 14.7 percent. Voting in the Negro wards of Kansas City, Mo., was off a fifth for a decline of 5,900 in the number of ballots cast. The percentage loss was even higher in Boston where the vote was down 28.5. The Negro vote declined 19 percent in Atlantic City;

---

[22] Lubell (1966) also describes these extreme reversals among black voters in a number of southern cities. For a detailed examination of black voting patterns in northern cities which shows that "the peak of Negro allegiance to the Democratic Party . . . was reached in 1952," see Glantz.

15.6 in Toledo; 15.4 in Pittsburgh; 12 in Chicago; 9.3 in Brooklyn; 9.1 in Youngstown, Ohio; 6.4 in Cleveland; and 5.9 in Harlem (Moon, 1957, 228).

In addition to black discontent over the civil rights question, defections and low turnout may also have reflected the fact that the northern urban Democratic Party apparatus was doing little to assure black allegiance. Blacks were not being quickly absorbed into the political organizations in the northern cities. Northern urban political organizations, which drew their main support from working-class and middle-class white groups, were hardly prepared to yield much to their enlarging black constituency. In part this was because racial antagonism among whites in the cities was intensifying as black numbers grew. In part it was because Democratic control of many large cities was assured and did not depend on black votes, so that few urban Democratic leaders felt compelled to mount voter registration campaigns in the ghettos, or to draw blacks into party councils, or to encourage and reward their political participation with patronage.[23] And so, as the numbers of northern blacks swelled, the reins which urban politicians held over the otherwise steadfastly Democratic ghettos fell slack.

Black voting defections in 1956 were a cause for alarm, however, among national Democratic political leaders. By the mid-fifties, migration had brought a great many blacks into the North; moreover, some 90 percent of them settled in the central cities of the ten most populous industrial states, and thus in states of crucial importance in presidential contests. In a number of these cities blacks had come to be the largest "ethnic" bloc. From the perspective of potential electoral influence in presidential contests, blacks were strategically concentrated. Moreover as southern defections developed in the elections of 1948 and 1952, the Democratic Party became all the more dependent on the northern vote.

Despite the growing importance of the black vote, Democratic

---

[23] Just how little blacks benefited from municipal politics, despite their enlarging numbers in many cities, is revealed by a study conducted in the 1960s in Chicago, where blacks had been a substantial bloc for years: "What we found was that in 1965 some 20 percent of the people in Cook County were Negro, and 28 percent of the people in Chicago were Negro. . . . Out of a total of 1,088 policy-making positions in government Negroes held just 58" (Baron, 28–29). For an exhaustive historical study of racist patterns in the distribution of municipal patronage in Chicago and New York, see Katznelson.

leaders had continued to resist granting civil rights concessions. "The northern Democratic leaders recognized that historic injustices had to end," Schlesinger suggests, "but they thought that steady and rational progress step by step over a period of years would suffice to satisfy the victims of injustice and contain their incipient revolution" (926). More likely, Democratic leaders simply did not want to further endanger electoral allegiances in the South. Nor, until 1956, did they have to take that risk, for blacks had remained steadfastly loyal. But once the black vote, like the southern white vote, also became unstable, the Democratic strategy of proceeding cautiously in order not to antagonize the South could no longer succeed. It was not, contrary to what other analysts have said, the rise of a substantial black electoral bloc in the northern states that finally set the stage for civil rights concessions; it was the rise of black defections.

One of these concessions was to come in the year immediately following the election of 1956, when Congress enacted the first Civil Rights Act since 1875. Electoral instability played a significant role in the formation of the coalition in Congress which brought about passage of the bill. For the Democrats, there was little choice but to champion the measure; perhaps the party could afford southern de-defections, or black defections, but it could not afford both. For the Republicans, black defections confirmed the potential of their modest civil rights appeals prior to the election. Consequently the Republicans again seized the initiative and resubmitted the previously rejected civil rights bill. In doing so, they broke ranks again with southern Democrats. The cleaving of this alliance, which had previously thwarted all efforts to secure civil rights legislation, was a direct consequence of voting defections among northern blacks.

With a civil rights bill once again before Congress, Johnson quickly seized control, and it was he who engineered the necessary compromises to forestall a southern filibuster. Johnson's evolution on the civil rights question was itself a reflection of the impact of electoral dissensus on the Democratic Party, for until the mid-fifties Johnson had consistently refused to support civil rights legislation:

> Ever since 1937, when he first entered the House, Johnson had voted *no* on civil rights 100 percent of the time; *no* on an anti-lynching bill in 1940; *no* on a Democratic leadership amendment in 1940 eliminating segregation in the armed services; *no* on anti-poll-tax bills in 1942, 1943, 1945; *no* in 1946 on an anti-discrimination amendment offered by Representative Adam Clayton Powell of

Harlem to the federal school-lunch program; *yes* in 1949 on an anti-Negro amendment proposed by Mississippi's Senator James Eastland to the perennial District of Columbia home rule bill. The list was long, the record unbroken (Evans and Novak, 121).

For Johnson the rise of the civil rights issue, and of Republican efforts to profit from it, posed an excruciating dilemma. Although his power in the Senate was based on the southern bloc, he had strong presidential ambitions. To achieve that ambition he had to decide whether he was "a Westerner and *national* Democrat," or "a Southerner and *regional* Democrat" (Evans and Novak, 122). By 1956 Johnson's decision was no longer seriously in doubt; he did not, for example, sign the "Southern Manifesto." To continue a course of opposition to civil rights was to foreclose a larger career in national Democratic politics.

The evolution of Johnson as the mock champion of civil rights began after the splintering of his hopes in 1956 [in which he lost a bid for the Vice-Presidential nomination owing largely to northern opposition]. He got the message: victory lay in the cities, victory lay within the union blocs, the black blocs, the immigrant blocs, the big city bosses, with the independent voters, and if possible with farm blocs, though that was the last to worry about. Johnson saw that he who gets the South gets naught. . . . LBJ saw that he had to get the magnolia blossom out of his lapel, and he coolly set about it. He would pass a civil rights act. If necessary, he would pass two . . . (Sherrill, 193).

The chief problem confronting Johnson was the prospect of a southern filibuster—it would have to be forestalled. The bill contained provisions (and an amendment) which angered the South; on the other hand, Republicans and northern Democrats were prepared to press for Senate rule changes that would weaken the power of the filibuster if the South obstructed passage of the bill. With each camp fearful of the other's power, Johnson was able to gain support for a compromise bill that was essentially symbolic and it passed (without a filibuster) by an overwhelming margin (72 to 18, with Lyndon Johnson and four other southerners in the majority).

In other words the Democratic Party had once again weathered the deep division within its ranks. But there was this difference: it had done so *only* by enacting a civil rights measure, however weak its provisions may have been. The Civil Rights Act of 1957 was significant for that reason, for it presaged the end of an older strategy of coping with regional divisions by avoiding the civil rights issue. The growing size and instability of the black vote had forced the beginning of a new mode of adaptation to those divisions, an adaptation in which concessions would be made to blacks. Henceforth the struggle would be over the substance of those concessions.

Even as the Civil Rights Act of 1957 was being debated and enacted, the massive resistance strategy of southern whites intensified, for it was clearly the intent of "the dominant political leadership in the deep South . . . [to] . . . force all hesitant communities into irreconcilable opposition to the Supreme Court" (Lubell, 1956, 196). Considering the outright defiance of the federal courts which this entailed, a major crisis was inevitable. Little Rock, Arkansas, was one of those hesitant communities, and it became a major locus of the looming crisis.

Governor Faubus, a moderate on race, gradually lost control over the white populace in Arkansas as the ideology of massive resistance swept the South. Faced with overwhelming evidence that white violence would be provoked if the Little Rock school board implemented its court-ordered desegregation plans, Faubus appealed to Eisenhower for federal support.[24] When that appeal failed, he ordered out the Arkansas National Guard on September 2, 1957, to prevent desegregation. The beleaguered school board turned to the federal courts for instructions and was promptly ordered to persist in carrying out the desegregation plan. Nine black students then braved violent white mobs to enter Central High School, but were turned back by Guardsmen. School officials again appealed to the federal courts for a temporary suspension of desegregation plans, but were refused. The court also ordered the U. S. Justice Department to file for an injunction against Governor Faubus and top officials in the National Guard, and on September 20, hearings were held on that petition. That same day the court ordered Governor Faubus and the National Guard to desist from obstructing desegregation, and the

---

[24] Eisenhower's clear displeasure with the *Brown* decision, and his repeated statements that the race problem was a problem to be solved in the states and "in men's hearts" must have encouraged southerners to believe that resistance could succeed, even outright defiance of the courts. As late as July 1957, as the crisis in Little Rock took form, Eisenhower told a press conference that "I can't imagine any set of circumstances that would ever induce me to send federal troops into an area to enforce the orders of a federal court." As Dunbar has remarked, "To calculate . . . the violence done to the public peace by the President's six-year-long policy of neutrality would be neither easy nor unfair" (20).

governor promptly withdrew the Guardsmen. Little Rock officials were horrified by the prospect of mob violence which would surely follow and appealed for federal marshals, but Eisenhower again refused to intervene. Finally, as mob violence worsened during the next few days, Eisenhower had to federalize the Arkansas National Guard and send in paratroops to restore order.

The Little Rock episode went far toward polarizing racial sentiments across the country. At the time both camps in the civil rights struggle probably drew comfort from it. For blacks and their allies federal intervention could be defined as a triumph of federal power over sectional racism. On the other hand white southern leaders could not fail to recognize the deep reluctance of the federal executive branch to be drawn into the controversy, except under the most extreme conditions, thus suggesting that other methods of circumventing the courts might well continue to succeed.

There were many forms such resistance could take. In 1958 for example, a concerted attack on the Supreme Court "reached its height . . . when the House of Representatives passed five bills designed to curb the Court's authority. These measures failed to receive Senate approval, but the anti-Court coalition evidenced substantial strength in the upper chamber" (Bartley, 291). The militancy of southern resistance to desegregation, the passage of anti-integration laws in one state after another (including closing the public schools), and the anti-Court movement within Congress combined "to bring the Supreme Court under the heaviest attack it had experienced since [the court-packing episode] in 1937" (Bartley, 291). One result was that the Court moderated its views: while continuing to affirm the general principle of equal protection of the laws as stated in *Brown*, it upheld the concept of discretionary pupil placement, and thus granted southern school officials the means to engage in tokenistic modes of school desegregation. Massive resistance, in short, still had momentum.

Nevertheless, mounting regional tensions, together with the tentative and fumbling efforts by the Republicans to exploit them, were beginning to produce some gains for blacks. A modest gain was made in 1960 with the passage of a second civil rights act:

> Johnson realized from the start of the 86th Congress that the massive Democratic majorities elected in 1958 would demand another civil rights bill to close loopholes in Negro voting protection. Consequently, he hoped to pass a minimal bill as quickly as possible in 1959, again avoiding a Southern filibuster, and well in advance

of the 1960 election. On January 20, 1959, Lyndon Johnson introduced his first civil rights bill. A four-part measure, it featured the racial conciliation service he had considered in 1957 but discarded. The reaction was uniformly unfavorable, from civil rights advocates and segregationists alike. A much broader civil rights bill sponsored by President Eisenhower became the framework for debate (Evans and Novak, 220).

Eisenhower's bill was debated in early 1960. There was no way Johnson could persuade the southern delegation to accept the bill, and no way he could persuade the Senate liberals to modify it. The result was a filibuster that dragged on for months, and could not be beaten. Finally, "to appease the triumphant Southerners, Johnson and Eisenhower's Attorney General, William P. Rogers, agreed to delete the bill's two toughest sections (aimed at the desegregation of schools and jobs)," and that assured the bill's passage (Evans and Novak, 221). What remained of the original bill were criminal penalties for bombings, bomb threats, and mob action designed to obstruct court orders, especially school desegregation orders, and an ineffective provision for court-appointed voting referees. Every Republican Senator voted affirmatively, and Eisenhower signed the bill on May 6.

The Resurgence of Black and White Defiance

Just as the Democrats were to regain the presidency in 1960, defiance by blacks erupted again, and on an increasingly massive scale. It was no longer mainly the white leaders of the South who provoked confrontations with the federal government; in this period, civil rights activists began to embrace a "strategy of using civil disobedience to force local governments into conflict with federal authority" (Killian, 63). In reaction white violence worsened, spurred by southern leaders, especially governors, and acted out by police agents and white mobs.

On February 1, 1960, four students from the Negro Agricultural and Technical College in Greensboro, North Carolina, entered a variety store and were refused service at the lunch counter where they sat in violation of caste rules. Fueled by "the discrepancy between the promise of desegregation and the reality of tokenism" (Killian, 59), the sit-in movement swept like a brush fire from one locale to another. By the second and third weeks of February similar actions were occurring throughout the state, organized by students from Duke University and North Carolina College. Despite arrests and violence Fisk University students in Tennessee quickly took up the tactic, as did students from universities located in Atlanta. Within those first few weeks, "sit-ins spread to fifteen cities in five southern states" (Zinn, 6).[25]

The spread of the movement to Atlanta was of special significance, for after a series of organizational meetings following the Montgomery boycott, King formed the Southern Christian Leadership Conference (SCLC) and located its offices in Atlanta, where he also took a new pastorate. Quick to see the significance of the student-initiated sit-in movement, SCLC officials offered moral and financial support (despite the opposition, it should be noted, of officials in several established national civil rights organizations). In April, with SCLC aid, student delegates from dozens of universities assembled at Shaw University in Raleigh, North Carolina, to form the Student Nonviolent Coordinating Committee (SNCC).

The students who composed SNCC were animated by a belief in the efficacy of civil disobedience. Zinn described them as having "tremendous respect for the potency of the demonstration, an eagerness to move out of the political maze of normal parliamentary procedure and to confront policy-makers directly with a power beyond orthodox politics—the power of people in the streets and on the picket line" (13). And Clark said that "SNCC seems restless with long-term negotiation and the methods of persuasion of the Urban League, and it assumes that the legislative and litigation approach of the NAACP" had exhausted its possibilities (259).

Through the summer and fall of 1960 militant SNCC activities mushroomed. No one could say what precisely was happening, or who was involved. There was no organization to monitor protest activities,[26] one participant said, "because the students were too busy protesting. . . . No one really needed 'organization' because we then had a movement" (Zinn, 36). Following the earlier organizing meeting several hundred delegates assembled in Atlanta in October,

---

[25] Graphic descriptions of the sit-ins and related direct action campaigns are available in a number of sources. For example, Patrick discusses the actions in Winston-Salem; Proudfoot discusses Knoxville; Walker discusses Atlanta; and Killian and Smith discuss Tallahassee. See also the Southern Regional Council (1961).

[26] Except, of course, for the FBI.

ostensibly to bring some semblance of structure to the movement which they had created. Even then, little by way of structure resulted. SNCC "was not . . . a membership organization. This left the adhesion of individuals to the group fluid and functional, based simply on who was carrying on activity. . . . The twig was bent, and the tree grew that way" (Zinn, 37–38). In this same vein Clark remarked: "Instead of a single leader, SNCC has many 'leaders' " (259–260). (Among these many leaders, Bob Moses, Jim Forman, Stokely Carmichael, and John Lewis were perhaps the best known.)

*Stokely
was
there
in
1960.*

Indeed none of the direct-action organizations in this struggle were either much organized or much oriented toward building formal membership. CORE also typified this point. Although its money-contributing membership rose from a few thousand in 1959 to 80,000 in 1964, the active members never exceeded 3,000–5,000, distributed among over one hundred chapters (Rich, 124; Meier and Rudwick, 227). The point is that "direct action . . . requires only small numbers of persons, but these must be so highly motivated and involved that they are willing to risk the great hardships involved in direct action. . . . Southern CORE typified this generalization" (Bell, 90). In short, the direct-action organizations which developed during the civil rights struggle were cadre organizations.[27]

The cadres—whether in SNCC or CORE or SCLC—at first engaged in exemplary actions. Thus "the essence of SNCC leadership appears to be this willingness to assume personal risks, to expose oneself to imprisonment and brutality. Its members play the important role of commando raiders on the more dangerous and exposed fronts of the racial struggle" (Clark, 260). Often in groups of just two or three or a half dozen, the cadres were the most active demonstrators. "The first sit-in students who actually served their full jail terms in the 1960 sit-ins," for example, "were members of Tallahassee

---

[27] These cadres had their origins in the new southern urban black working class being produced by economic modernization. "If one were to generalize roughly about the SNCC staff in the Deep South, one would say they are Negro, they come from the South, their families are poor and of the working class, but they have been to college" (Zinn, 10). Bell's analysis of a southern CORE chapter yielded a similar conclusion: "Clearly then, these CORE members stemmed from the 'upper lower' class within the Negro community's system of social stratification. Their parents were members of the unskilled but steady and respectable working class. The CORE members themselves were upwardly mobile . . . being college students" (89). See Ladd (218–223) and Meier (1970) for additional confirming data. For a discussion of the way in which these activist cadres spurred the more traditional leadership into action, see Walker.

*very similar to the Alliance
structure in the 1890's.*

CORE. The first of the Freedom Riders to serve their full jail terms rather than appeal were members of New Orleans CORE'" (Rich, 116). SNCC participants called this tactic "Jail-no-bail":

> When ten students were arrested in Rock Hill, South Carolina, in February 1961, the SNCC steering committee, meeting in Atlanta, made its boldest organization decision up to that date. Four people, it was agreed, would go to Rock Hill to sit in, would be arrested, and would refuse bail, as the first ten students had done, in order to dramatize the injustice to the nation. . . . "Jail-no-bail" spread. In Atlanta, in February, 1961, eighty students from the Negro colleges went to jail and refused to come out (Zinn, 38–39).

Such exemplary actions, in turn, inspired a mass mobilization. "All over, the number of people on [CORE] picket lines sky-rocketed," but only a few were CORE members (Meier and Rudwick, 227). And although SCLC had sixty-five chapters throughout the South, its formal structure was "amorphous and symbolic" so that the large numbers of people drawn to its demonstrations were not members (Clark, 255–256). This mobilization took place mainly through segregated institutions where people were already "organized": the black colleges, churches, and ghetto neighborhoods. In the 1960–1961 period, the activists from SNCC, CORE, and SCLC were extremely successful in arousing black college students throughout the South. Twenty-five percent of the black students in the predominantly black colleges in the eleven states of the South participated in the sit-in movement during the first year, according to Matthews and Prothro. And they did so despite constant retaliation. Of these active students, "One out of every 6 . . . was arrested; one of every 20 was thrown in jail. About 1 in every 10 reported having been pushed, jostled, or spat upon; the same proportion was either clubbed, beaten, gassed, or burned; another 8 percent were run out of town. Only 11 percent of the protestors reported that nothing untoward had happened to them" (412–415). The cadres also mobilized large numbers of poor and middle-class blacks throughout the South for civil disobedience. As a result, "Over 50,000 people—most were Negroes, some were white—participated in one demonstration or another in a hundred cities, and over 3,600 demonstrators spent time in jail" in the first year following the lunch counter sit-ins (Zinn, 16).

PRESIDENTIAL EFFORTS TO COPE
WITH ELECTORAL INSTABILITY

The arrests, the mob violence, and the police brutality that were
provoked by these protest activities rapidly created major dilemmas
for national political leaders. For example, on October 25—a few
days before the presidential election of 1960—King was arrested
and convicted for violating a twelve-months' term of parole which
had been meted out for an earlier and minor infraction of the traffic
codes. The parole violation consisted of joining students in a sit-in
and the sentence was four months at hard labor in the Reidsville
State Prison, a penal camp in rural Georgia. Overnight the White
House was deluged with telegrams and letters from governors, congressmen, citizens, and foreign dignitaries, all of whom feared for
King's safety at the hands of rural southern penal officials.

President Eisenhower and candidate Nixon weighed the potential
electoral gains and losses of intervening, deciding against taking
action. Kennedy decided otherwise and it was that decision which
has since been credited by some observers with having turned the
election to him (Schlesinger, 930). His call to King's wife, together
with a call by Robert Kennedy to the judge who had committed
King to prison, caused little short of delirium in black communities
throughout the nation. Within days of King's prompt release from
prison two million copies of a brochure condemning Republican
inaction and exalting Kennedy's action were being circulated in
the ghettos.

On the whole, however, the Democratic presidential campaign
was marked by ambivalence on the race issue. Nothing in Kennedy's
career suggested that he held strong feelings about the race question:

> Since Negro rights played so important and dramatic a part in his
> Presidency, historians will always be interested in Kennedy's earlier
> stand on civil rights. Until the Presidential campaign of 1960, Ken-
> nedy was not an aggressive fighter for the Negro. During his quest
> for the vice-presidential nomination in 1956, he wooed the Southern
> delegations and stressed his moderation. After 1956, he sought to
> keep alive the South's benevolent feeling for him, and his speeches
> in that region, sprinkled with unflattering references to carpetbag-
> gers like Mississippi Governor Alcorn and praise for L. Q. C. Lamar
> and other Bourbon "redeemers," had a faint ring of Claude
> Bowers' *Tragic Era*. In 1957, during the fight in the Senate over

the Civil Rights Bill, Kennedy lined up for the O'Mahoney amendment to give trials to those held in criminal contempt of court.
Civil rights militants regarded this as emasculating, since those accused of impeding Negro voting would find more leniency in
Southern juries than in federal judges (Carleton, 279).[28]

At the nominating convention a major confrontation with southern
extremists was carefully prevented, for "the Kennedy forces avoided
antagonizing southerners with any action beyond a strong civil
rights plank" (Tindall, 42).[29] The Republican campaign was marked
by a similar ambivalence. Nixon, despite a plank endorsing civil
rights in strong language, campaigned vigorously among whites in
the South, probably counting on southern defections in response to
the Catholic issue, but also appealing covertly to the segregationist
vote.[30] In this muddy situation Florida, Tennessee, and Virginia defected to the Republicans, and Alabama and Mississippi voted for
unpledged electors. As for the black vote, it moved back to the Democratic Party; Kennedy received 68 percent, up about eight points
from the election of 1956.

Moreover, it must be said that the black vote moved back in
just the right places. Landslide majorities in some of the nation's
largest ghettos helped Kennedy carry key states by razor-thin majorities:

> It had been Kennedy's strength in the great Northern cities to which
> Southern Negroes had migrated that produced hairline victories for
> the Democrats in the eight states experts consider crucial to success
> in any close election—New York, Illinois, Pennsylvania, Michigan,
> Maryland, Missouri, Minnesota, and New Jersey. All but one—
> Missouri—went to Eisenhower in 1956. All eight went for Kennedy

---

[28] On the other hand, Kennedy appeared to understand that a transformation was
occurring in the Democratic Party. In the late 1950s, responding to a question as to how
he would manage North-South divisions in the party were he to become president,
Kennedy made this comment: "My judgment is that with the industrialization of the
South you are going to find greater uniformity in the Democratic party than you had in
the past" (Burns, 276).

[29] For a discussion of the intraparty struggles which afflicted the Democratic Party
throughout this period, see Sindler (1962).

[30] "As a smart politician, [Nixon] could make fatal errors. The plainest example in the
campaign was his stand—or failure to take a stand—on the issue of civil rights. Having
fought hard for a strong plank in his party's platform, which might win the Negro vote
in the North, he proceeded to talk out of the other side of his mouth in the South,
hoping to win its vote too. . . . In his shocked inability to understand why his protégé
lost to Kennedy, Eisenhower might have thought a bit about the obvious reasons why
[Nixon] lost both the South and the Negro vote in the North" (Muller, 258).

in 1960, on the strength of the big-city vote. The Republican National Committee, using Philadelphia as a laboratory, made a precinct-by-precinct study of why this happened. The study revealed, among other things, that their candidate won only 18 percent of the Negro vote, leaving 82 percent for Kennedy (Fuller, 113).

If any group had reason to expect presidential action on its behalf, it was blacks following the election of 1960. Without the huge black majorities in the key industrial centers of the nation, Kennedy could not have been elected.[31] Still, "Almost two years were to pass before Kennedy telephoned again" (David Lewis, 1970, 130). He had won office, but narrowly, and white southern defections had been no small cause of his near defeat. A policy of conciliation toward the South still appeared to be the expedient course of action.

Moreover, Kennedy (like earlier Democratic presidents) was concerned that a confrontation with Congress over civil rights would cost him support on other domestic legislation. "The reason was arithmetic. . . . To solidify the conservative coalition—by presenting an issue on which Southerners had traditionally sought Republican support in exchange for Southern opposition to other measures—would doom his whole program" (Sorensen, 475–476; see also Schlesinger, 93). Instead of legislative action, therefore, the president opted for a strategy of executive action:

> Kennedy's task was to accomplish so much by Executive action that the demand for immediate legislation could be kept under control. Power to enforce existing civil-rights law lay in the Department of Justice. And the hand that would wield it was the Attorney General's. A Kennedy in that position could convey not only the color of Presidential authority but the personal moral force of the President as well. . . . If Kennedy's Attorney General won the confidence of those chiefly concerned with civil rights and maintained a strong impression of forward motion in this field, the President could stall on supporting new civil-rights legislation until after Congress had

---

[31] Thus Theodore F. White writes that Kennedy "felt that he must campaign personally for the big Northeastern industrial states. . . . These grand calculations worked. Of the nine big states . . . Kennedy carried seven. . . . The most precise response of result to strategy lay, however, in the Negro vote. . . . In analyzing the Negro vote, almost all dissections agree that seven out of ten Negroes voted for Kennedy for President. . . . It is difficult to see how Illinois, New Jersey, Michigan, South Carolina, or Delaware (with 74 electoral votes) could have been won had the Republican-Democratic split of the Negro wards and precincts remained as it was, unchanged from the Eisenhower charm of 1956" (1961, 384–386). See also Schlesinger, 930.

approved his social and economic program—and that required Southern votes (Fuller, 112, 116).[32]

The Justice Department thus became the chief instrument of civil rights action by the administration. Civil rights litigation was given higher priority within the department and more litigation was undertaken than had previously been the case, especially in school desegregation and on voting rights. At the same time, however, Kennedy appointed southerners to the federal bench who caused great dismay among blacks. James Farmer reflected the sentiments of activists:

> To be sure, the Justice Department was more active in initiating voter registration suits in the South than it had been under Eisenhower, but, presumably with the concurrence of the Justice Department, Kennedy had appointed three known racists to the federal bench: William Harold Cox of Mississippi (who described two hundred voter applicants as a "bunch of niggers . . . chimpanzees who ought to be in the movies rather than being registered to vote"); J. Robert Elliott of Georgia ("I don't want those pinks, radicals, and black voters to outvote those who are trying to preserve our segregation laws and traditions"); and E. Gordon West of Louisiana (who called the 1954 school desegregation decision "one of the truly regrettable decisions of all time"). Racist federal judges are perhaps the greatest obstacle to federally enforced equal rights in the South today (40).

In the field of employment Kennedy issued an executive order against discrimination in federal employment, and hired more blacks than any previous administration, including the appointment of a number of blacks to top positions in the administration. He also instructed all departments to systematically upgrade blacks. Consequently, "The number of Negroes holding jobs in the middle grades of the civil service increased 36.6 percent from June 1961 to June 1963; in the top grades, 88.2 percent" (Schlesinger, 933). The president also strengthened federal efforts to reduce private discrimination in employment through the President's Committee on Equal Employment Opportunity, headed by Vice-President Lyndon B. Johnson, although no federal contracts with private employers were canceled as a result of this committee's efforts.

---

[32] Fuller describes the strategy of executive action in some detail. So too do Schlesinger; Sorensen; Fleming; Navasky's account is the fullest and the most useful.

DEFIANCE SPREADS

But the Kennedy Administration's activity on the civil rights front was both too much for southern leaders and far too little for civil rights activists. Consequently both camps escalated tactics of defiance, one seeking to weaken efforts by the federal government to enforce the law, the other to strengthen the federal role in enforcing the law. The most dramatic tactics in this period were the "freedom rides" organized by civil rights activists, and the confrontations over the desegregation of institutions of higher education precipitated by several southern governors.

One of the most conspicuous symbols of southern caste arrangements was the segregation of bus and train terminals—from waiting areas, to eating facilities, to restrooms. Since these public areas were under the jurisdiction of a federal agency—the Interstate Commerce Commission (ICC)—they were a logical arena in which to force confrontations over the segregation issue. In the spring of 1961 the Congress of Racial Equality, under the leadership of its new executive director, James Farmer,[33] decided to send "freedom riders" into the South.[34] The freedom rides (which were subsequently joined in by SCLC, SNCC, and the Nashville Student Movement) brought on some of the worst mob violence of the era. There were in all about a dozen different freedom rides involving about one thousand persons (Lomax, 144; Schlesinger, 936). With each outbreak of arrests and mob violence, the federal government was faced with the decision whether to intervene, for it was clear that the civil rights activists would not desist. James Farmer expressed the spirit of the freedom rides when he declared that "Jails are not a new experience for the Riders, but the Freedom Riders were definitely a new experience for Mississippi jails" (Zinn, 57). In fact many of the participants in the various freedom rides were already familiar with the jails of the South; they were veterans of the sit-ins and "jail-no-bail" protests.

---

[33] Farmer had been the prime mover in the formation of CORE in 1942, while Race Relations Secretary for the Fellowship of Reconciliation.

[34] CORE had organized two freedom rides through the Upper South in 1947, both of which are described in *Freedom Ride* by James Peck. In this as in other ways CORE anticipated the direct action tactics of the southern phase of the civil rights movement. It had employed sit-ins and other tactics to force desegregation for two decades before the sit-ins and freedom rides of the early 1960s.

The southern jails had become the crucible in which the cadres of civil disobedience were being formed.

The Kennedy Administration was continually drawn into the conflict created by the clashing forces throughout the South. Its actions, in turn, added fuel to the fire, for when the federal government supported the goals of the movement—either symbolically or through various executive actions—the participants in the movement gained encouragement, however frustrated they may have also felt with delays and compromises in the federal government's responses. For example, when the president was asked about the freedom rides during a press conference, he replied: "The Attorney General has made it clear that we believe that everyone who travels, for whatever reason they travel (sic), should enjoy the full constitutional protection given to them by the law and the Constitution" (Schlesinger, 936). Moreover the attorney general intervened to protect the freedom riders in Montgomery, for the events there were too violent to be ignored:

> The violence became so intense and open that Attorney General Robert Kennedy sent 400 U.S. marshals to Montgomery to maintain order. On the evening of May 21, Dr. King held a mass meeting in Montgomery's First Baptist Church. As the mass meeting proceeded, a mob of white segregationists gathered outside the church. Standing between the 1,000 Negroes in the church and the mob was a squad of U.S. marshals and a few Montgomery city policemen. Someone in the mob shouted, "We want to integrate, too. Let us at them." Then a barrage of bottles and bricks was rained on the church. The marshals countered with tear gas. A battle raged for most of the night.

> Inside the church the Negroes linked arms and sang the marching song of the civil rights movement, "We Shall Overcome."

> We are not afraid . . . We are not afraid . . . We are not afraid today . . . Oh, deep in my heart, I do believe . . . We shall overcome someday (Bleiweiss, 84–85).

Within a matter of months the federal courts and the ICC ordered the desegregation of all terminal facilities for both interstate and intrastate passengers.

PRESIDENTIAL EFFORTS TO CHANNEL
THE BLACK MOVEMENT

In the wake of the student sit-ins and the freedom rides, the Kennedy Administration attempted to divert the civil rights forces from tactics of confrontation to the building of a black electoral presence in the South. The Kennedy Administration's posture on these matters is not difficult to understand. Tactics of confrontation, together with the police and mob violence which they provoked, were polarizing national sentiments. The excesses of southern police violence and of white mob violence generated one excruciating political dilemma after another for the Kennedy Administration as to whether it should intervene to protect civil rights demonstrators and uphold the law. Each intervention, or the lack of it, angered one or the other major constituency in the civil rights struggle, thus worsening the electoral lesion in the Democratic Party.

Consequently the Kennedy Administration moved to reduce the level of conflict by attempting to divert civil rights activists away from confrontations over desegregation of schools, waiting rooms, rest rooms, parks, and pools which so inflamed white southerners. They suggested instead that activists concentrate on voter registration for the reason, Schlesinger says, that "Negro voting did not incite social and sexual anxieties; and white southerners could not argue against suffrage for their Negro fellow citizens with quite the same moral fervor they applied to the mingling of the races in the schools. Concentration on the right to vote, in short, seemed the best available means of carrying the mind of the white South" (935). (It was a view that failed, inexplicably, to take into account the deep vested interest of the existing stratum of white southern political leaders in the disenfranchisement of the black; nor did it take into account the stakes—declining but still important—of the black belt plantation leaders in the subordination of blacks.)

At the same time, the extension of the franchise to blacks—as both Sorensen and Schlesinger make plain—was gradually coming to be seen by the Kennedy Administration as a way of regaining Democratic strength in the South. The southern blacks represented a huge untapped pool of potential Democratic voters; their numbers could offset southern white defections. It was a strategy that called for giving more emphasis to voting rights. Thus when

the ban on poll taxes in Federal elections, which had been sought
for twenty years . . . finally passed both houses, [it] was pushed by
the President and Democratic National Committee in the state
legislatures, and became the Twenty-fourth Amendment to the
Constitution. The number of Negroes and less affluent whites enabled to vote by that measure alone, the President believed, could
make a difference in his 1964 re-election race in Texas and Virginia
(Sorensen, 475).

By the same token, when the president reviewed his attorney general's report on two years of voting progress, he wrote, "Keep pushing the cases" (Sorensen, 479). Schlesinger thought he saw in these
events a parallel with the early years of the New Deal: "A generation ago Roosevelt had absorbed the energy and hope of the labor
revolution into the New Deal. [Likewise] Kennedy moved to in-
corporate the Negro revolution into the Democratic coalition and
thereby help it serve the future of American freedom" (977). The
question of helping to serve the future of American freedom aside,
there is little doubt that incorporating southern blacks into the New
Deal coalition would help to serve the future of the Democratic
Party.

Consistent with this political strategy, the Kennedy Administration
argued in its dealings with civil rights groups that the franchise
was "the open-sesame of all other rights" (Navasky, 169; see also
Sorensen, 478; Schlesinger, 935). Accordingly the proper role of
the federal government was to litigate to enfranchise blacks, and
the proper role of the civil rights movement was to register blacks
to vote. In these dealings, however, the Kennedy Administration
did more than try to persuade civil rights leaders of the wisdom
of this approach. It also mobilized financial inducements in what
Schlesinger calls "a behind-the-scenes effort" of such urgency as
to be "reminiscent of the campaign to save the Bay of Pigs prisoners" (935). In June 1961 "representatives of SNCC, SCLC, the National Student Association, and CORE met with the Attorney General" at his invitation. "Kennedy asserted that in his opinion voter
registration projects would be far more constructive activity than
freedom rides or other demonstrations. He assured the conferees
that necessary funds would be available through private foundations,
and that Justice Department personnel, including FBI teams, would

provide all possible aid and cooperation" (Meier and Rudwick, 1973, 173; Zinn, 58).[35]

Within the civil rights movement these presidential channeling efforts caused both considerable dismay and considerable enthusiasm. "While many activists in CORE, SNCC and SCLC were suspicious of Kennedy's proposal, seeing it as a calculated attempt to divert them from direct action, others had already concluded that direct action was no panacea, and that voter registration would provide a necessary basis for further progress" (Meier and Rudwick, 1974, 172). Others, like King, felt that both approaches were essential: "We would agree with the importance of voting rights, but would patiently seek to explain that Negroes did not want to neglect all other rights while one was selected for concentrated attention" (1963, 20).

This issue nearly split SNCC apart. One faction, which stressed the importance of direct action, was convinced that the Kennedy Administration's interest in voter registration was a disguised effort "to cool the militancy of the student movement," while the other faction was convinced that voter registration was the key to toppling the caste system in the South (Zinn, 59). A split was finally averted by insulating each program strategy in a separate division of the organization; one faction continued to pursue confrontation tactics (directed particularly at segregated public accommodations) and the other faction undertook voter registration drives. With all of the civil rights organizations responding in some measure to the lure of the ballot and with federal assurances of both funding and protection, a voter registration drive was inevitable. By early spring 1962

> the Voter Education Project finally got underway. . . . Designed to last two and a half years, it cost $870,000, nearly all of which

---

[35] Meier and Rudwick also express the opinion that there was a direct relationship between these channeling efforts and the planning by the Kennedy Administration for the election of 1964: "Kennedy Administration officials had been impressed by the results of voter registration drives that they had encouraged in several northern black communities prior to the 1960 election; they perceived possibilities for creating an enlarged bloc of black voters in the South who would support Kennedy in 1964. It was in this milieu of heightened interest in voter registration, combined with the sense of crisis produced by the Freedom Rides that the idea of a foundation-financed voter-registration campaign developed" (172–173). Matthews and Prothro make the same point: "As more southern Negroes vote in the future, they can be expected to swell the Democratic ranks . . . a fact that has not escaped the attention of the Kennedy and Johnson administrations' civil rights strategists" (391–392).

came from the Taconic and Field Foundations and the Stern Family
Fund. With less than 25 percent of the southern blacks registered
at VEP's start, the drive was expected to achieve substantial change
in time for the 1964 presidential election (Meier and Rudwick, 175).

Although the Kennedy Administration succeeded in turning many
in SNCC and in other civil rights organizations toward voter registration, it did not, as it turned out, succeed in diverting them from the
tactics of confrontation. No matter how orthodox their beliefs about
the electoral system, the cadres who went out to register the black
poor were nevertheless animated by the élan of the sit-ins and freedom rides, by the tactics of confrontation. Moreover, given their
objective of building power through the ballot, it was natural enough
that they would choose counties in the heart of the black belt where
potential black electoral majorities existed. But for just that reason
they confronted the most embittered and threatened local political
leaders, backed by police agencies whose capacity for unrestrained
terror was unique in the nation. Moreover, these leaders brought
every available form of economic pressure to bear on the black
poor to prevent voter registration, including firings, evictions, and
cutting off federal food supplies:

> As the stream of voting applicants in Greenwood [Mississippi] in-
> creased (though in SNCC's first six months there, only five Negroes
> were actually declared by the registrar to have passed the test), the
> economic screws were tightened on the Negro community. Winters
> were always lean in the farming towns of Mississippi, and people
> depended on surplus food supplied by the Government to keep
> them going. In October, 1962, the Board of Supervisors of Leflore
> County stopped distributing surplus food, cutting off 22,000 people
> —mostly Negro—who depended on it (Zinn, 86).

Voter registration activists thus entered some southern rural counties
where, at the close of a year's work, they could count innumerable
arrests and beatings, and even some killings, but they could count
no registered black voters.

Confronted with this miscalculation the administration reneged on
its promises of federal protection for the voter rights activists. The
administration hoped to gain votes in the South, to be sure, but not
at the price of worsening the southern white rebellion (especially
in Congress) against the national Democratic Party. Given this choice

the civil rights activists were sacrificed. Despite extensive documentation of voter rights violations and extensive documentation of violence inflicted upon civil rights activists, the Kennedy Administration failed time and again to intervene.

To justify its continuing political concern with conciliating the South, the Kennedy Administration argued that the federal government lacked the authority to act against southern governors, law enforcement officials, and other political leaders (Navasky, 221). In the end even the Kennedy Administration's strategy of litigation foundered, for federal judges in the South (and not least of all Kennedy's own appointees) were often among the most intransigent:

> The demonstrable damage these judges inflicted was threefold. First, they cruelly postponed justice—thus further delaying the enforcement of Constitutional rights already one hundred years overdue. Second, they dealt a severe blow to the civil rights movement, which became increasingly frustrated, fragmentized and radicalized as a direct result of the open injustice exhibited by the official, federal justice-dispensing instrument. . . . Third, through deceit, delay and direct, extralegal challenges to federal authority, they undermined the Justice Department's fundamental strategy of litigate-rather-than-legislate (Navasky, 247–248).

[margin, handwritten: no — not at this time; movement grew in both experience + solidarity.]

As a result the white massive resistance movement in the South continued to be given wide latitude to fend off the civil rights challenge.

As it turned out the civil rights movement had also miscalculated. Voter registration activities were widely dispersed and many were conducted in relatively isolated rural areas by activists working in twos and threes. The resulting confrontations were many, but on a small scale, and usually unpublicized. They could thus be ignored by the White House. In this unexpected way the channeling efforts of the Kennedy Administration had succeeded.

It remained, then, for the civil rights movement to continue to provoke mass civil disorder, for it was only when mass civil disorder erupted in its most extreme forms (and sometimes not even then) that the federal government did what it claimed it did not have the authority to do. "We put on pressure and create a crisis," James Farmer said, "and then they react." One important crisis occurred in Albany, Georgia, although it, too, failed to provoke federal intervention.

[margin, handwritten: I'm skeptical: the movement was learning - preparing itself for Freedom Summer.]

DEFIANCE ESCALATES

The precipitating incident in Albany was an order issued by the Interstate Commerce Commission. Responding to the turbulence caused by the freedom rides, Robert Kennedy petitioned the ICC to ban segregated terminal facilities in interstate travel. The ICC issued the necessary order on September 22, 1961, to become effective on November 1. But many southern communities ignored the order or desegregated interstate passenger facilities and left intrastate facilities segregated as before. The same month that the ICC order was to become effective SNCC organizers in Albany, who had developed wide-ranging connections in the black community, boarded a bus in Atlanta bound for Albany where they intended to test the ban on desegregated terminal facilities and test the readiness of the black community for direct action.[36] The anticipated arrests did in fact occur. Several additional tests followed, with the Department of Justice being notified in each case. But there was no response from Washington. On December 10, SNCC members again traveled by train toward Albany and hundreds of blacks gathered to meet them. Eight out of nine riders were quickly arrested and that was enough to galvanize the community. Over the next few days mass marches were staged by hundreds of blacks to protest the arrests of the preceding weeks. "By December 15, nearly five hundred people were in jail" (David Lewis, 1970, 146).

When negotiations with city officials failed, the leaders of the Albany Movement (a confederation of black organizations which had formed as part of the civil rights upheaval) called upon SCLC for help. Two days later mass marches, led by King, began again and were met by large contingents of police. Upwards of one thousand demonstrators were subsequently arrested and jailed, including King, who refused bond. He then appealed for clergymen throughout the country to come and join in a vigil while he remained jailed over the Christmas period. Through what was apparently a misunderstanding, however, King accepted release a few days later, only to learn that the concessions from local political and business leaders

---

[36] Accounts of the events in Albany during 1961–1962 are available in some detail. See, for example, Zinn; Watters; Anthony Lewis (1964), and David Lewis (1970).

which he thought had been won had not in fact been granted. Despite the bitterness of this defeat and the embarrassment in the national press which the incident created, the struggle in Albany continued through the spring and summer of 1962. The campaign included all forms of direct action, from boycotts to sit-ins to marches and mass demonstrations. During one week in August 1962, 1,000 demonstrators were imprisoned. Many were injured by the police; still others suffered economic reprisals of various kinds. But it was all to no avail, at least in the sense that mass demonstrations and mass arrests yielded no concessions from city officials. "Negroes won nothing in Albany. . . . It was not until the Civil Rights Bill of 1964 that even token integration came to Albany, Georgia" (Bleiweiss, 86).

but usually out of sight of camera and the public.

Two explanations of that failure have been advanced. On the one hand, "There is universal agreement among the Movement leaders that they were mistaken in simultaneously attacking all the manifestations of segregation in the city instead of concentrating on one or two—employment, bus segregation, an integrated police force, or free access to places of entertainment" (David Lewis 1970, 169). On the other hand, some observers and participants felt that the campaign had been haphazardly managed owing in part to internecine factional strife. King himself seemed to agree with both of these explanations, for he said at the close of the campaign that the movement had "jumped too far, too soon, and with improper preparation" (Bleiweiss, 86).

But whatever the reasons that the Albany Movement won nothing from the local white leadership, there is another vantage point from which that experience was an extraordinary success. Victories or not, Albany had shown that large masses of southern blacks could be mobilized for marches and demonstrations; Albany "represented a permanent turn from the lunch counter and the bus terminal to the streets, from hit-and-run attacks by students and professional civil rights activists to populist rebellion by lower-class Negroes . . . [and thus became] . . . the prototype for demonstrations that later rocked Birmingham and dozens of other cities throughout the nation" (Zinn, 123).

yes, this is the real point,

y(e)

The tactics also differed significantly from those employed in Montgomery and in similar boycotts elsewhere in the South in the late 1950s. Boycotts required of people that they avoid transportation facilities, or avoid various white businesses. There were surely inconveniences and some hardships as a result; moreover, people also had to be prepared for retaliatory measures—such as threats to jobs —which such boycotts provoked. But they did not generally have to be prepared to suffer the brutality inflicted by the police and the possibility of injury or even death. Albany proved that the movement could arouse masses of blacks to confront the police and to fill the jails of the South and that was its chief significance, or so it seems to us.

The campaign in Albany also demonstrated that southern whites were far more recalcitrant than most had imagined and that white moderates—if they existed at all—had been effectively muzzled by the rising tide of extremist sentiment and coercion. White extremism continued unabated.

When sufficiently provoked by that extremism, the Kennedy Administration did intervene. In this period some of the most celebrated actions taken by the Kennedy Administration were in the field of higher education and they were taken because of the same kind of mob violence which had forced Eisenhower's hand in Little Rock. Thus in September 1962, when Governor Ross Barnett refused to allow James Meredith to enroll at the University of Mississippi, in defiance of the Supreme Court decision, Kennedy sent in federal marshals and federalized the Mississippi National Guard, largely to maintain order:

> In the battle-scarred history of the Negro revolution since the 1954 Supreme Court decision, Oxford was a nightmare. For two horrible days—Sunday, September 30 and Monday, October 1, 1962—the battle raged, with upward of 2,500 frenzied whites repeatedly charging the Federal marshals, the federalized Mississippi National Guard and the Regular Army troops who protected the seething campus. . . . The campus trembled now to exploding tear-gas bombs and the screams of the whites: "Give us the Nigger!" In the holocaust two men, a French journalist and a local Oxford resident, fell dead and at least 375 were injured. But in the end, defiant Governor Ross Barnett yielded and James Meredith entered the university (Brink and Harris, 1964, 40).

Similar action was taken by the Kennedy Administration when Governor Wallace, "standing in the schoolhouse door," made the flamboyant gesture of refusing to desegregate the University of Alabama. (It was Wallace who declared, "I draw the line in the dust and toss the gauntlet before the feet of tyranny, and I say segregation now,

segregation tomorrow, segregation forever!") Such a flagrant challenge to federal authority by a southern governor was not intended
to be ignored, and it was not.

The Winning of Political Rights

In the years 1963 through 1965 the balance of electoral considerations shifted decisively to favor the granting of black rights in the
South. In this period, as in no other, the civil rights movement proved
its capacity to incite large numbers of southern blacks to join the
struggle and their actions, in turn, aroused favorable public opinion
throughout the country.

The main elements in the changing political balance were these.
First, the civil rights movement was contributing to the rising tide
of anger in the ghettos, and that was an acute problem for the Kennedy Administration. With a presidential election less than two years
away the potential instability of the black vote was a cause for   *yes*
concern. Indeed the potential instability of the ghettos themselves
had become a cause for concern. Kennedy officials were fearful that
"the nonviolent resistance strategy . . . was not deeply rooted in
Negro traditions and there were signs that it might give way to
a more violent strategy uncontrolled by responsible leaders" (Sorensen, 495).

The events in the South also provoked broad support for civil
rights demands among northern whites. Despite worsening conflict
between blacks and working-class whites in the northern cities, the
most insistent black demand was for political rights in the South and
that was no threat to the northern white working class. The huge
white middle class which had developed in the affluent post–World
War II years gave its support more readily, for this class was largely
insulated from blacks as a result of suburbanization and of its
privileged occupational position.

At the same time, resistance in much of the South was collapsing.
This was especially the case in the states of the Outer South. In addition to all of the forces which had weakened economic stakes in the
caste system, the perpetuation of these arrangements was beginning
to exact certain costs. Many southern communities, for example,
wanted to attract northern industry, but northern industry shied away

from locations in which white intransigence and racial turmoil were intense. Northern executives explained that their employees did not want to relocate in communities where the schools might be closed, or where continued civil disorder was likely. This message was not lost on many white communities. Consequently business leaders brought pressure on local political leaders to make concessions that would either prevent disorder or restore order.

> In Charlotte, as in Memphis and Dallas and Atlanta, and a dozen other communities throughout the South, the powerful white leaders recognized that the revolution on their streets was full of danger. They were afraid of losing money. They were afraid that Northern industry would not want to set up its regional offices in their towns. They could add up on paper the money they might lose from convention business. They may have had moments of sober reflection on the moral issues at stake, but their actions didn't show it. In the end, those among them who were fairly intelligent, and those who were not under pressures from tyrannical governors or legislatures, and those who had not been made afraid of vigilante groups, decided to seek settlements that would produce peace in the city and money in their pockets (Powledge, 117).

This division among southern leaders—particularly between those of the inner and outer states of the South—went far toward weakening the capacity of the South to ward off threats to its traditional social structure.

The Deep South, in short, had become isolated from significant sources of support. Being isolated, it had become vulnerable. But still its political leaders could not give way to racial change without risking office. In a few years a new and more moderate leadership stratum would emerge; meanwhile the older leadership persisted in a futile strategy of resistance. This resistance was met with a mass black mobilization: the civil rights forces drew increasing numbers to demonstrations and inspired greater militancy and courage in the demonstrations.

THE MASS BLACK MOBILIZATION

Following the defeat in Albany, SCLC leaders turned to Birmingham. In the campaign that followed blacks confronted the police and were arrested by the hundreds. However improved the coordination and focus of the Birmingham campaign may or may not have been compared to the campaign in Albany, it was the confrontation between the people and the police that was its distinguishing feature and the source of its influence on the national government.

From the perspective of SCLC leaders Birmingham was an ideal locale to draw the battle lines with the Kennedy Administration, for Birmingham was easily among the least racially advanced of major southern cities. The Commissioner of Public Safety, Eugene "Bull" Connor, had established himself as a bulwark of the southern racist creed. The city administration had responded to the civil rights challenge by such actions as closing public parks and the city had experienced a virtual epidemic of bombings of black churches, an omen of the violence that would surely follow if Birmingham were made into a civil rights battlefield. For just these reasons the SCLC leadership believed that a campaign in Birmingham would provoke and expose southern racism and extremism as no other campaign had.

The planning for Project "C" (confrontation) was extensive, much more so than in any previous campaign, with hundreds of volunteer cadres schooling masses of people in the philosophy and tactics of nonviolent offensives.[37] Targets for sit-ins, demonstrations, and selective boycotts were picked from among the city's businesses. Influential people in the North were briefed, particularly those in a position to provide funds for bail.

Lunch counter sit-ins, selective boycotts, and other small-scale demonstrations began on Tuesday, April 2, 1963. The police, anticipating an injunction, made peaceful arrests. By Friday thirty-five had been jailed. On Saturday forty-five more were arrested during a silent march on City Hall. The expected injunction was issued on Wednesday, April 10, and fifty volunteers were designated to demonstrate on Friday in defiance of it. All were arrested, including King, who was placed in solitary confinement. SCLC leaders decided "that one historic phone call deserved another," and so on Sunday Coretta King telephoned the president (David Lewis, 1970, 186). The call was returned that evening by the attorney general who gave assurances that her husband was safe. By Monday bail money began to arrive and the White House was deluged with mail and telegrams

---

[37] The campaign in Birmingham has been described in such accounts as David Lewis (1970) and Zinn. The reactions of the federal government are described in Sorensen, Schlesinger, and Navasky.

Decisive role of Bevel underplayed in all these accounts -- and by Walker, too.

protesting the events in Birmingham. From prison, King issued his now famous "Letter from a Birmingham Jail" addressed especially to southern clergymen who had attacked him, SCLC, and the direct action tactics of the movement. It was a document that provided moral and theological justification for nonviolent protest against unjust laws and practices and it went far toward galvanizing church-men and others in the North.

On Thursday, May 2, the battle worsened as "959 of some 6,000 children . . . ranging in age from six to sixteen, were arrested as they marched, singing, wave upon wave from Sixteenth Street Baptist Church into town. . . . More would have been taken away if the police had not run out of wagons" (David Lewis, 1970, 192). The next day police restraint, such as it was, broke. As 1,000 demonstrators were preparing to march, the police sealed off the exits of the church where they were assembling, with the result that only half got out, there to meet unleashed police dogs, flailing nightsticks, and jet-streams from high-pressure water hoses. Only a handful reached the intended target, City Hall. With television cameras everywhere, the hoped-for crisis was finally in the making.

On Saturday, Assistant Attorney General Burke Marshall arrived in Birmingham to restore calm, but both sides were unmovable. Marches continued for several days and were marked by police violence; younger blacks abandoned song and prayer to throw rocks and bottles. More than 2,000 people had been imprisoned; the jails, both regular facilities and improvised ones, were filled. Still, several thousand people were ready to resume the marches.

Officials in the Kennedy Administration, trying desperately to avoid open intervention with all of its attendant political ramifications, unsuccessfully maneuvered behind the scenes to persuade and coerce civil rights activists and Birmingham's political leaders to settle. They brought pressure directly to bear on local officials, and they buttressed it indirectly by inducing northern leaders in business, industry, religion, philanthropy, law, and other institutional areas to telephone their southern counterparts in Birmingham to urge them to intervene.

The demonstrations on Monday, May 6, were again marked by police violence, and when marches resumed on Tuesday morning, high-pressure water hoses broke legs and caved in rib cages. By afternoon, while masses of demonstrators were scattered throughout the business district praying and singing before the deserted stores, younger participants began to throw rocks and bottles. The black community was exhausting its capacity for nonviolent discipline. As rioting spread, business leaders called for a truce to which SCLC agreed.

Outraged by these flanking maneuvers, Commissioner Connor called for and received 500 state troopers from Governor Wallace, and then arrested King. SCLC ordered immediate demonstrations, knowing that law enforcement officials were awaiting them. Little but unparalleled carnage could result. To avert it the attorney general called local officials to declare that the federal government had reached the limits of its tolerance, and to threaten decisive action if a settlement was not made. On May 10 an agreement was reached that provided for the desegregation of lunch counters, rest rooms, and drinking fountains, for less racist hiring and promotion practices in local businesses, and for the immediate release of 3,000 imprisoned demonstrators.

And then the bombings began: first King's brother's house, followed by a motel where SCLC was headquartered. Although no deaths resulted, the black community seethed into tumult, leading to mob rioting on May 11. For five hours "the Negroes boiled into the streets, wielding knives, overturning cars, hurling rocks and bricks at anyone who moved, even other Negroes. One wounded Negro moaned: 'They were insane'" (Brink and Harris, 1964, 44).

Unable to temporize any longer, the president ordered in federal troops and brought Governor Wallace into line by threatening to federalize the Alabama National Guard. In public statements he praised the courage and restraint of the movement and gave assurance that the federal government would stand behind the terms of the agreement negotiated with Birmingham's white officials. (A few days later the Birmingham Board of Education expelled 1,100 students for their role in the demonstrations, although the federal courts later reinstated them.) With these events, protests burst forth across the country: "During the week of May 18, the Department of Justice noted forty-three major and minor demonstrations, ten of them in northern cities" (Franklin, 631).

THE FEDERAL GOVERNMENT ACTS

The final victory of the Birmingham campaign came on June 11 when President Kennedy, in a televised address to the nation, announced that he was requesting the Congress to enact as expeditiously as possible a comprehensive civil rights bill. In February he had submitted a relatively weak bill and had done little to secure its passage. As James Farmer aptly said, "It is clear that . . . the President intended to drop civil rights legislation from the agenda of urgent business in order to safeguard other parts of his legislative program. But he had not reckoned on Birmingham" (40–41). By June, however, Kennedy admitted to civil rights leaders privately "that the demonstrations in the streets had brought results, they had made the executive branch act faster and were now forcing Congress to entertain legislation which a few weeks before would have had no chance" (Schlesinger, 970). Mass protest had forced federal action. It was a point the attorney general also conceded: "The Administration's Civil Rights Bill . . . is designed to alleviate some of the principal causes of the serious and unsettling racial unrest now prevailing in many of the states" (Navasky, 205).

In his nationally televised address, the president referred to the "rising tide of discontent that threatens the public safety" and said, "It cannot be met by repressive police action. . . . It cannot be quieted by token moves or talk. It is time to act in the Congress. . . ." According to the results of a *Newsweek* poll, "Almost nothing that had happened to the Negroes in the last ten years heartened them quite so much as the President's speech. . . . Finally and irrevocably the leader of their country had told the nation that their cause was right and just and should be fulfilled" (Brink and Harris, 1974, 46).

Just hours after Kennedy spoke to the nation, Medgar Evers, secretary of the Mississippi NAACP, was shot in his driveway. His funeral in Jackson on June 15 turned into a riot. The *New York Times* reported:

> After the last of the four-block-long line of marchers had reached the funeral home . . . the younger Negroes apparently decided to make an attempt to demonstrate in the white business district. . . . Four motorcycle patrolmen let them through one intersection, but [they were met] with twenty officers as they approached the main thoroughfare. . . . [Now numbering approximately one thousand, they chanted] "We want the killer! We want the killer! We want equality! We want Freedom!"
> Officers using police dogs moved in. . . . One demonstrator after another was grabbed and hustled into waiting patrol wagons. . . . They began throwing rocks, bottles and other missiles at the police.

. . . The crowd screamed. . . . The growling and barking of the
police dogs, the crash of the bottles on the pavement and the cursing
of the policemen added to the uproar. . . .

[When it was over] the mood of the Negroes was still one of
bitterness and anger. "The only way to stop evil here is to have
a revolution," muttered a young man in a doorway. "Somebody
have to die" (Anthony Lewis, 1964, 227–228).

Throughout the country, demonstrations multiplied: "In a three-
month period during the summer of 1963, the U. S. Justice Department counted 1,412 separate demonstrations. The newspaper pic-
tures showing the limp bodies of Negroes being carried to police
wagons became a great tapestry of the times. Over the land echoed
the Negro hymn, 'We Shall Overcome' " (Brink and Harris, 1964, 46).

Despite Kennedy's announcement that he would press Congress for
a greatly strengthened civil rights program, there was every reason
to believe it would be filibustered into oblivion. Prodded by the
restless mood of the black community, civil rights leaders had already
decided that a demonstration of national support for civil rights
legislation was both possible and necessary. Earlier, in November
1962, A. Philip Randolph had proposed a March on Washington for
Jobs and Freedom. Many in the northern civil rights community at
first greeted the proposal with something less than enthusiasm; the
National Urban League simply opposed it. In part black leaders
were stalemated by chronic competition for leadership; some were
also edgy about demonstrations, fearing that their access to high government officials and private elites would be impaired. By the late
spring of 1963, however, their mood had changed in response to
the changing mood in the black community together with the victory in Birmingham and evidence that the Kennedy Administration was finally prepared to act more decisively in the field of civil
rights. A planning conference was set for early July and support
came from many quarters. The president, of course, opposed the
march, fearing the repercussions in Congress if the march turned
violent or if the turnout was disappointing. On the other hand,
"Negroes had discovered that demonstrations had accomplished what
other measures had not" (Franklin, 630). The heads of some major
unions pledged support and the leaders of some of the largest
northern religious denominations made commitments to what was
to be the largest demonstration in the history of the movement and
the largest demonstration of any kind staged in Washington up to
that time. When August 23 dawned, the streets of Washington rapidly

filled; by afternoon more than 250,000 had assembled to demand the passage of civil rights legislation as well as economic measures to ease the poverty of blacks.

On September 15, just three weeks following the march, a church in Birmingham was bombed, killing four little girls. It was an act of southern terror that resounded throughout the world and was denounced by the president the following day on national television. Just two months later, Kennedy was assassinated.

Lyndon Johnson had little choice but to commit his administration to the cause of civil rights. On November 27, 1963, he told Congress: "We have talked long enough in this country about equal rights. It is time now to write the next chapter—and to write it in the book of law." The main problem was to secure the votes for cloture in the Senate, for a filibuster (which lasted eighty-three days) immobilized Congress. Northern Republicans again made the difference. The Senate Minority Leader, Everett Dirksen of Illinois, rose on the Senate floor to proclaim: "This is an idea whose time has come. It will not be stayed. It will not be denied." As in 1957 and in 1960, northern Republicans responded to the masses of aroused blacks and whites in the North. When cloture was finally invoked and the bill came to a vote, 27 of 31 Republican Senators voted affirmatively and the president signed the Civil Rights Act of 1964 on July 2.

In the fall Lyndon Johnson won a landslide victory over Goldwater in an election that revealed how completely isolated the Deep South had become. Johnson received 61 percent of the popular vote. Aside from Arizona his losses were limited to the five states of the Deep South where the most stubborn and virulent resistance to black voting rights persisted. In the northern urban ghettos, black Democratic majorities ran as high as 95 percent. "Behind the statistics was a revolution in American politics. The first Southern President since the Civil War captured 90 percent of the Negro vote and lost the Deep South by large margins" (Evans and Novak, 481). In the eleven states of the Old Confederacy, where the number of black registered voters had increased from 1.4 million in 1962 to 2.2 million in 1964, the black vote was beginning to play a role in Democratic fortunes: "Of the six southern states carried by the Democratic Party, four (Arkansas, Florida, Tennessee and Virginia) clearly would have gone Republican had it not been for the Negro vote. Only in President Johnson's home state of Texas among the eleven states

[handwritten top margin: No — majority of whites voted Republican. Demo. got in because both the Black + the Chicano vote went heavily Democratic. "White" in this sentence should be changed.]

247   *The Civil Rights Movement*

of the South did the Democratic Party clearly receive the majority of white votes."[38] There was, in short, no longer any reason to suffer the intransigence of the Deep South.

The Civil Rights Act of 1964 ostensibly guaranteed blacks the right to vote and ostensibly signified the federal government's resolve to enforce that right. Even before the act was passed, however, there was skepticism among civil rights groups that voting officials in the South would comply with the law and that in the absence of compliance the federal government would intervene forcefully. CORE and SNCC's voter registration drives had already provided substantial basis for that skepticism. Moreover, the Mississippi Freedom Democratic Party which was formed in late 1963 to challenge the regular Mississippi Democratic organization had met with no success; during the spring of 1964 blacks were barred from the primaries, denied access to regular party caucuses, and otherwise prevented from participating in regular party functions.[39] Consequently, direct action campaigns were planned in the spring to force the voting rights issue despite the imminent passage of the civil rights act.

Under an umbrella organization called the Council of Confederated Organizations (which had been operating voter negotiation campaigns) SNCC, CORE, and the Mississippi branch of the NAACP prepared hundreds of northern white students to help mobilize blacks for marches on the offices of voting registrars where local law enforcement officials could be expected to press them back. Even before most of the students reached the field, three disappeared, to be found murdered and buried beneath an earthen dam two months later.[40] The bodies of two murdered blacks were also found floating in the Mississippi River. Between June and October twenty-four black churches were bombed in Mississippi alone.

---

[38] Southern Regional Council, Press Release, November 15, 1964.

[39] And when the delegates from this party mounted a challenge to the seating of the regular Mississippi delegates at the Democratic convention in the summer, they were rebuffed by national party leaders for the obvious reason that national party leaders did not want to encourage black splinter parties in the South. The Democratic state parties in the South had to be reorganized and strengthened; incorporating blacks into those parties was the key to achieving that objective because blacks could be expected to be loyal to the national party. *[handwritten margin: this is NOT the reason. The MFDP was not a splinter — it was Demo.]*

[40] The slain young people were Michael Schwerner and Andrew Goodman, both whites from New York, and James Chaney, a black from Meridian, Mississippi. These highly publicized deaths, as well as earlier ones, helped greatly to build pressure for the civil rights acts of 1964 and 1965.

Simultaneously with the killings and bombings in the South, the northern ghettos erupted in rioting. Rioting broke out in Cambridge, Maryland, in June, just before the signing of the Civil Rights Act of 1964. In mid-July riots erupted in Harlem and Bedford-Stuyvesant; then as the summer wore on the rioting spread to Rochester, Jersey City, Paterson, Elizabeth, a suburb of Chicago, and Philadelphia. It was the beginning of a series of riot-torn summers unlike any period in the nation's history. The black masses joined the protest in the only way they could, given their institutional circumstances. As King aptly said, "A riot is the language of the unheard" (Killian, 109). In some part, rioting was probably precipitated by civil rights demonstrations in the North, for activists had also brought the struggle to the northern cities.[41]

The southern voter registration drive thus gave continued evidence of southern intransigence, even while black protest was spreading to the northern ghettos. Consequently, a solution which had been considered and rejected by presidents and Congresses for a decade —the use of federal voting registrars—seemed the only means by which the right to vote could be ensured. But the solution required new legislation. To generate the necessary pressure on the president and the Congress, civil rights leaders decided to stage new demonstrations on the order of Albany and Birmingham.

The target chosen was Selma, Alabama, where SNCC voter registration activities had already provoked white violence, much of it by the police under the command of Sheriff James Clark. The campaign began in early January, 1965, with a succession of marches to the courthouse. As the weeks passed the numbers joining the demonstrations increased and so did the numbers jailed. On February 1, King led a demonstration which resulted in more than 700 arrests; on February 2 some 550 more demonstrators were imprisoned:

---

[41] Franklin describes a number of these demonstrations: "There were about as many demonstrations in the North and West as in the South. The emphasis was on increased job opportunities and an end to *de facto* segregation in housing and education. In New York and Philadelphia demonstrators sought to block tax-supported construction of schools in all-negro neighborhoods. They staged sit-ins in the offices of Mayor Robert Wagner of New York City and Governor Nelson Rockefeller of New York. In Boston, Chicago, New York, and Englewood, New Jersey, they sat-in at schools or staged school strikes to protest racial imbalances. In Los Angeles and San Francisco crowds of more than 20,000 held rallies to protest the slaying of Medgar Evers and of William Moore, a Baltimore postal employee who was shot from ambush while making a one-man freedom march to Mississippi" (631).

"[T]he great majority, as the day before, were school children. Defiantly, they sang 'Ain't Gonna Let Jim Clark Turn Me Around' " (David Lewis, 1970, 268). During the first four days of February more than 3,000 demonstrators were arrested. "Jim Clark is another Bull Connor," an SCLC staff member said. "We should put him on the staff" (Bleiweiss, 125). On February 4 a federal court banned literacy tests and other technical devices by which voter applicants were rejected, thus adding one more declaration of legitimacy for the voting rights cause. But securing compliance by southern voter registrars was another matter.

On February 9 King met with Vice-President Humphrey and Attorney General-designate Nicholas Katzenbach in Washington, D.C., and "was given firm assurance that a strong voting act would be sent to Congress 'in the near future' " (David Lewis, 1970, 269). The demonstrations in Selma continued. Congressmen and other dignitaries came to see at firsthand the denial of voting rights; some joined in demonstrations. In a neighboring county 400 blacks marched on February 18 to protest the jailing of a civil rights activist, and one of them—a boy named Jimmie Lee Jackson—was shot in the stomach. He died a week later, whereupon King called for a massive march from Selma to Montgomery.

Governor Wallace issued a statement prohibiting the march; the attorney general of the United States pleaded with the leaders of SCLC to cancel it. On Sunday, March 7, 500 marchers set out for Montgomery. At the Pettus Bridge on the outskirts of Selma, they confronted "a blue line of Alabama's troopers":

> First there was gas, then the posse on horseback galloped into the swarm of fleeing blacks with cattle prods and clubs flailing maniacally. The marchers were driven back across the bridge and into their houses and those of friends who dared to open their doors to shelter them. . . . At one point, a number of blacks retaliated, hurling rocks and bricks at the police, even forcing Clark and his men momentarily to retreat. But the combat was unequal. While the white spectators whooped approval of the rout and gave the piercing rebel yell, Sheriff Clark bellowed, "Get those God damn niggers!" Protected by masks, the police and troopers hurled tear-gas cannisters into the panic-stricken mob. . . . [A] high school student recalls that "the gas was so thick that you could almost reach up and grab it. . . ." A Southern newspaperman saw Clark repeatedly charging the demonstrators who had retreated to the church, even

though he was bloodied by a rock. With their anger rising, and feeling more secure in this section of town, many of the marchers were becoming belligerent, seizing whatever objects could be made to serve as weapons (David Lewis, 1970, 274–275).

A groundswell of northern support followed these events, probably larger than in any earlier period. Demonstrations were organized in one city after another. Northern dignitaries—and if not they, then their wives and sons and daughters—converged on Selma by the hundreds. Their names read like a *Who's Who in the North*. With intensive negotiations being pursued by members of the national administration, the Alabama governor's office, the federal court, the police officials and political leaders of Selma, and the civil rights forces, a compromise was apparently reached that would allow the marchers to proceed once again to the bridge, whereupon they were to turn back. Just who had been a party to the arrangement is to this day unclear and there are conflicting accounts. In any event, many in the throng of 1,500 on Tuesday, March 9, believed they were going straight through to Montgomery and King apparently did nothing to dispel that belief. At the bridge, beyond which the police were massed, he called for the march to continue, only seconds later to reverse himself, much to the dismay and anger of younger activists, especially in SNCC and CORE. That same night, three white northern clergymen were attacked on a Selma street by a white gang; one, Reverend James Reeb, died of his injuries on Thursday.

With the country in an uproar, Wallace asked for a meeting with the president. On Saturday, March 13, he assured the president that the state of Alabama could manage the disorder without the intervention of federal troops. For the moment Johnson accepted those assurances. On Monday, appearing before an extraordinary evening session of Congress, Johnson called for the passage of a voting rights act:

> Their cause must be our cause too. Because it is not just Negroes but really it is all of us who must overcome the crippling legacy of bigotry and injustice. And we shall overcome.

The president's speech was interrupted by several standing ovations and more than thirty intervals of applause, an unmistakable sign that congressional approval of a voting rights act would quickly result. On Thursday, March 18, Governor Wallace tried to shift the onus of dealing with the conflict to the White House by wiring that he could not protect the Selma marchers and requesting "sufficiently adequate federal civil authorities":

> That was all Johnson needed. He set the stage with a statement deploring the need for federal intervention. "It is not a welcome duty for the federal government to ever assume a state government's own responsibility for assuring the protection of citizens in the exercise of their constitutional rights," said Johnson. He immediately federalized the Alabama National Guard and 1,862 guardsmen, as well as regular soldiers and federal marshals were ordered to guard the route of march from Selma to Montgomery. Johnson was delighted that Wallace's blunder had enabled him to intervene, thereby satisfying civil rights protestors, and at the same time placed the responsibility squarely on Wallace, the champion of the bitter-end segregationists (Evans and Novak, 495).

On March 21, the march began. Some 8,000 people, their ranks sprinkled with the powerful and prestigious, walked singing to the Pettus Bridge, where a smaller band continued on to Montgomery. "It was a miniature March on Washington" (David Lewis, 1970, 290). When the marchers reached the outskirts of Montgomery five days later, they were joined by 30,000 sympathizers in a triumphal march to George Wallace's capitol building. That night Viola Liuzzo, a housewife from Detroit who had participated in the march, was shot to death by members of the Ku Klux Klan as she drove back to Selma.

Beginning in April, as Congress deliberated on the president's call for a voting rights act, intensified voter registration drives were staged in some 120 counties from Virginia to Louisiana where few blacks had been permitted to register. Considerable violence followed, dramatizing the need for the pending legislative remedy. Congress acted with extraordinary dispatch: the bill that had been introduced on March 17 was signed into law by the president on August 6. Every Republican Senator except J. Strom Thurmond of South Carolina voted affirmatively. Its main provision authorized the attorney general to place federal voting registrars in counties where it was determined that blacks were being denied the vote, the criteria being that a state or county "maintained a test or device as a prerequisite to registration or voting as of November 1, 1964, *and* had a total voting age population of which less than 50 percent were registered or actually voted in the 1964 Presidential election." The states covered by this act included Alabama, Alaska, Georgia, Louisiana, Mississippi, South Carolina, Virginia, and approximately twenty-six counties in North Carolina.

With this legislation, national Democratic leaders finally dismantled the feudal apparatus of the post-Reconstruction era. By the time they acted, there were specific political advantages in doing so. Not only did civil rights concessions cement existing black voters to the Democratic Party, but the provisions extending the franchise to five million potential black voters in the South (over two million had been registered by the election of 1964) created a substantial bloc whose allegiance to the Democratic Party could also be counted on. That bloc, in turn, would help to offset permanent defections among the more racially intransigent southern whites in the Deep South, and to offset the trend toward Republicanism in the industrializing states of the Outer South as well. The basis was thus laid for rebuilding southern Democratic majorities by combining white moderates, many poor whites who would vote their economic interests over their prejudices, and newly enfranchised blacks. By finally endorsing and pressing hard for civil rights measures, in other words, national Democratic leaders promoted the means to heal the fissures in their party. That they were free to do so is a measure of the diminished importance which caste arrangements had come to have, first in the national economy, and then in the southern economy.

The civil rights movement was not, then, the fundamental cause of this political transformation; the fundamental cause was economic change, and the political forces set in motion by economic change. Still, it took a long, arduous, and courageous struggle to force the political transformation which economic conditions had made ready.

From Disruption to Organization

With this transformation under way, the coalition of groups composing the southern civil rights movement began to fragment. In most accounts of the period the fragmenting is attributed to divisions within the movement, especially to the growing frustration and militancy of the younger members in SNCC and CORE. A precipitating incident that is widely pointed to occurred on June 6, 1966, when James Meredith, while staging a one-man march through the Deep South, was wounded by a sniper on a road just inside the Mississippi state line. A small number of leading civil rights leaders then converged on the spot to complete the march, during which the younger militants (especially from SNCC) denounced nonviolence and racial cooperation and raised their fists for "Black Power." For them, there had been one bullet too many and one federal betrayal too many.

Divisiveness is endemic in movements and it always has a weakening effect. But as an explanation of the demise of the black movement, we find it less than satisfactory. The disintegration of the movement was inevitable given the integrative impact of the very concessions won. If anything, the "black power" ideology aided in that transformation by providing a justification for the leadership stratum (and a growing black middle class more generally) to move aggressively to take advantage of these new opportunities. Despite the initial identification of the concept with nationalistic "extremism" and political "radicalism," it came quickly to have a much more moderate and conventional meaning for most movement participants, as expressed by Carmichael and Hamilton: "The concept of black power rests on a fundamental premise: *Before a group can enter the open society, it must first close ranks* . . . solidarity is necessary before a group can operate effectively from a bargaining position of strength in a pluralistic society" (44; their emphasis). Defined this way the concept was especially suited to the ideological needs of a black leadership stratum seeking to exploit the new possibilities for electoral and bureaucratic influence.

Of the various concessions granted the movement none had a greater integrative effect than the right to vote, for activists were rapidly channeled into traditional electoral politics. The extension of the franchise and the guarantees of federal enforcement of the right to vote held out the promise that blacks could finally make substantial progress toward full equality through regular electoral processes. As a result protest lost legitimacy, undermined by the force of American electoral beliefs and traditions. The turn from protest was also promoted by northern liberals who defined the intelligent use of the vote as the true salvation of blacks and who (acting through private foundations, religious institutions, and the Democratic Party) provided the funds to further voter registration and related electoral efforts. Furthermore, for the leadership stratum, the incentives of public office were compelling, leading them to turn away from protest, and even to denounce it. An incident associated with the rise of the "black power" controversy illustrates the point. After civil rights leaders had converged on Mississippi to complete the "Meredith March," Charles Evers, director of the Mississippi NAACP, strongly objected that he did not "see how walking up and down a hot highway helps; I'm for walking house to house and fence to fence to get Negroes registered" (David Lewis, 1970, 321). The march leaders agreed and the marchers emphasized voter registration in various towns along the way. Subsequently Evers was elected mayor of Fayette, Mississippi.

The point is that even as the controversy over "black power" broke out, resistance in the South to political modernization had finally collapsed. On July 6, 1967—just two years after the signing of the Voting Rights Act—the Department of Justice reported that more than 50 percent of all eligible black voters were registered in the five states of the Deep South. By every measure the process of electoral change in the South accelerated even as factionalism in the black movement worsened. In 1964 three southern states—Tennessee, Georgia, and North Carolina—numbered blacks among their national Democratic convention delegates; in 1968 every southern state did so. With blacks voting in enlarging numbers, southern Democratic governors of moderate persuasion on the race question began to be elected; Republican governors tended to be similarly moderate. Upwards of 900 blacks had been elected to office in the South by 1972. And with some 3.5 million blacks registered throughout the South by the election of 1976, the black vote turned out to be the decisive factor in the election of Jimmy Carter to the presidency, for Carter won in the South (he could not have won without the South) despite the fact that Ford took 55 percent of the southern white vote. The reorganization of the southern wing of the Democratic Party had succeeded. In virtually no time at all the movement had been incorporated into the electoral system, its leaders running for office throughout the South and its constituencies enjoined to devote their energies to making these bids for office a success in the name of "black power."

The socioeconomic programs of the Kennedy-Johnson years also helped to absorb and divert the civil rights movement. More will be said about these programs in the next chapter. For now it need simply be noted that the Kennedy Administration attempted to ward off pressures for civil rights legislation by stressing the need for socioeconomic legislation to deal with the poverty of blacks. The "Great Society" programs were the result, notably the antipoverty program, and large numbers of civil rights activists took the new federally financed jobs that became available, presumably as a way of wielding black power. In their account of CORE's demise, for example, Meier and Rudwick take particular pains to show how the antipoverty program diverted activists from direct action and undermined the fragile cohesion of existing CORE chapters:

> Leaders who accepted the well-paying positions with CAP programs found it difficult to maintain active connections with their local affiliates, and since they were generally the most experienced chapter members, the loss was substantial. . . . People on [CORE's National Action Commmittee] even began to complain that the anti-poverty program "has been used to buy off militant civil rights leaders." Equally important, CORE's efforts with the CAP projects absorbed considerable energy, thus deflecting activity away from specifically CORE projects. . . . On both counts the War on Poverty proved to be a significant contributing factor in the decline of chapter activity (363–364).

The antipoverty program was only one of a number of "Great Society" programs in which blacks came to play a role. The Elementary and Secondary Education Act was another, as was the "Model Cities" program. Each helped to integrate the leadership stratum of the black movement (and each also provided the services and benefits which helped to quiet the black masses).

The movement was not absorbed by the electoral system and related governmental institutions alone. Many other institutions in the society also began to admit blacks: business and industry responded to mass unrest by hiring blacks; institutions of higher education, themselves rocked by the struggles of the period, revised their admissions policies to admit more minority group members, some of whom had been in the front ranks of the civil rights struggle. Having gained entry to these institutions, blacks frequently formed "caucuses" or developed other intra-institutional subgroups in order to exert "black power." In short, the society overtook the movement, depleting its strength by incorporating its cadres and by organizing blacks for bureaucratic and electoral politics.

Electoral Organization and Economic Advance

The weakening of caste arrangements in the South has brought with it some important gains. Chief among these is the reduction of terror as the principle means of social control. On this count, if on no other, the successful struggle for political modernization in the South represents a large victory for the mass of blacks. (On May 4, 1966, for example, more than 80 percent of Alabama's registered blacks voted in the Democratic primary, with the result that sheriffs James Clark (Selma) and Al Lingo (Birmingham) failed to secure renomination.)

But many blacks in the South continue to suffer economic exploitation and the manifold forms of social oppression which make them vulnerable to exploitation. The crucial question is whether the winning of formal political rights will now enable blacks to progress economically. It was a question put by John Lewis, chairman of SNCC, as he addressed the tens of thousands assembled at the March on Washington in 1963: "What is in [Kennedy's civil rights bill] that will protect the homeless and starving people of this nation? What is there in this bill to insure the equality of a maid who earns $5.00 per week in the home of a family whose income is $100,000 a year?" Put another way, the question is whether the exercise of the franchise and the now virtually exclusive emphasis upon electoral strategies by southern black leaders will produce a meaningful improvement in the conditions of life of the southern black poor. We think not.

The election of a modest number of southern black officials will clearly not create the political power necessary to secure national full employment policies; nor to secure substantial changes in the hiring and wage and promotion practices of private industry; nor the huge subsidies required to house the southern urban minority poor decently; nor any measures, such as land reform coupled with federal subsidies, that might enable some of the rural black (and white) poor to remain in independent farming in an era of agribusiness; nor reform of the welfare system to insure an adequate minimum income for all who cannot or should not work; nor any one of a dozen other policies and programs that might improve the living conditions of the black poor.

Others have made the same point. At the very moment that the Voting Rights Act was being enacted, for example, Sindler wrote: "The ability and willingness of whites to use the political process to resist and confine Negro political influence will make of the latter something less than the critical lever for racial advance it is assumed to be" (1965, 53). The conclusion, in short, is hardly a radical one. Even James Q. Wilson has written that

Negro political activity must be judged as a strategy of limited objectives. Where Negroes can and do vote, they have it in their power to end the indifference or hostility of their elected representatives, but these representatives do not have it in their power to alter fundamentally the lot of the Negro: the vote . . . can force . . . the removal from office of race-baiters and avowed segregationists. [But] *it can only marginally affect the income, housing, occupation, or life chances of Negro electorates* (456; our emphasis).

Aside from a general affirmation of the traditional American belief in the efficacy of electoral politics, the proponents of a black electoral strategy employ the argument that blacks can now successfully engage in "swing vote" politics because of their concentration in key northern states together with their growing vote in the South. That, it seems to us, is a potential for power much more apparent than real. The success of swing vote politics simultaneously requires not only an extraordinary unity, but an extraordinary independence. The elections since 1936 (with the exception of the election of 1956 and to a lesser extent that of 1960) amply demonstrate that black unity is more than possible. The trend in loyalty to the Democratic Party has risen steadily since the New Deal period, and is, if anything, stronger today than at any time in the past three decades. In the elections of 1968 and 1972, for example, blacks voted Democratic 87 and 86 percent, respectively. And in the election of 1976 some 6.6 million black voters delivered 94 percent of their votes to the Democrats.

These data on black unity do not suggest the possibility for electoral independence; they clearly suggest the reverse. If there was some weakening of black allegiance to the Democratic Party in the elections of 1956 and 1960, the concessions of the civil rights era have more than shored up those loyalties. By any measure blacks are now the most steadfast bloc in the Democratic coalition. How black political leaders might regularly induce these voters to shift allegiance from one election to another is, therefore, far from clear.

Nor is it clear that most minority political leaders would want to foster shifting black allegiances, even were they able to do so. Black leaders are not themselves independent; many owe their positions less to the resources offered by the black community than to those provided by white party officials. Moreover, the positions of most black political leaders depend on the Democratic Party and its continued ability to command a majority of the electorate. To the extent that a deregulated black vote might jeopardize the ability of the Democratic Party to maintain power, to that same extent would many black officials find their hold on public office jeopardized.

None of this is to say that the black vote may not at some future time become volatile. But should that occur, we suspect that the cause will not be the exhortations of minority political leaders, but new social and economic changes and the eruption of a new period of mass defiance.

References

Allen, Robert L. *Black Awakening in Capitalist America*. New York: Anchor Books, 1970.

Alexander, Charles C. *Holding the Line: The Eisenhower Era, 1952–1961*. Bloomington: Indiana University Press, 1975.

Baron, Harold (with Harriet Stulman, Richard Rothstein, and Rennard Davis). "Black Powerlessness in Chicago." *Trans-Action*, November 1968.

Bartley, Numan V. *The Rise of Massive Resistance*. Baton Rouge: Louisiana State University Press, 1969.

Bell, Inge Powell. *CORE and the Strategy of Non-Violence*. New York: Random House, 1968.

Berman, William. *The Politics of Civil Rights in the Truman Administration*. Columbus: Ohio State University Press, 1970.

Bernstein, Barton J. "The Ambiguous Legacy: The Truman Administration and Civil Rights." In *Politics and Policies of the Truman Administration*, edited by Barton J. Bernstein. Chicago: Quadrangle Books, 1970.

Bleiweiss, Robert M., ed. (with Harris, Jacqueline L., and Marfuggi, Joseph R.). *Marching to Freedom: The Life of Martin Luther King Jr.* New York: The New American Library, 1969.

Brink, William, and Harris, Louis. *The Negro Revolution in America*. New York: Simon and Schuster, 1964.

———. *Black and White*. New York: Simon and Schuster, 1966.

Burns, James MacGregor. *John Kennedy*. New York: Harcourt, Brace and Co., 1959.

Carmichael, Stokely and Hamilton, Charles V. *Black Power: The Politics of Liberation in America*. New York: Random House, 1967.

Carleton, William G. "Kennedy in History: An Early Appraisal." *The Antioch Review* 24 (1964).

Clark, Kenneth B. "The Civil Rights Movement: Momentum and Organization." *Daedalus* 95 (Winter 1966).

Cloward, Richard A., and **Piven**, Frances Fox. *The Politics of Turmoil: Essays on Poverty, Race, and the Urban Crisis.* New York: Pantheon Books, 1974.

Cochran, Bert. *Adlai Stevenson: Patrician Among Politicians.* New York: Funk & Wagnalls, 1969.

————. *Harry Truman and the Crisis Presidency.* New York: Funk & Wagnalls, 1973.

Cox, Oliver Cromwell. *Caste, Class, and Race.* New York: Monthly Review Press, 1959.

Cruse, Harold. *The Crisis of the Negro Intellectual.* New York: William Morrow and Co., 1967.

Dunbar, Leslie. *A Republic of Equals.* Ann Arbor: The University of Michigan Press, 1966.

Evans, Rowland, and Novak, Robert. *Lyndon B. Johnson: The Exercise of Power.* New York: The New American Library, 1966.

Farmer, James. *Freedom—When?* New York: Random House, 1965.

Fleming, Harold C. "The Federal Executive and Civil Rights: 1961–1965." *Daedalus* 94 (Fall 1965).

Foner, Eric, ed. *America's Black Past.* New York: Harper and Row, 1970.

Franklin, John Hope. *From Slavery To Freedom.* New York: Vintage Books, 1969.

Fuller, Helen. *Year of Trial.* New York: Harcourt, Brace and World, 1962.

Garfinkel, Herbert. *When Negroes March.* New York: Atheneum Publishers, 1969.

Glantz, Oscar. "The Negro Voter in Northern Industrial Cities." *Western Political Quarterly* 13 (December 1960).

Hartmann, Susman M. *Truman and the 80th Congress.* Columbia: University of Missouri Press, 1971.

Henderson, Vivian W. "Regions, Race, and Jobs." In *Employment, Race, and Poverty,* edited by Arthur M. Ross and Herbert Hill. New York: Harcourt, Brace and World, 1967.

Hoover, Calvin, and Ratchford, B. U. *Economic Resources and Policies of the South.* New York: Macmillan Co., 1951.

Hunter, Floyd. *Community Power Structure: A Study of Decision Makers.* Chapel Hill: University of North Carolina Press, 1953.

Ions, Edmund S. *The Politics of John F. Kennedy.* New York: Barnes & Noble, 1967.

James, C. L. R.; Lee, Grace C.; and Chaulieu, Pierre. *Facing Reality.* Detroit: Bewick Editions, 1974.

Johnson, Charles S.; Embree, Edwin R.; and Alexander, Will W. *The Collapse of Cotton Tenancy.* Chapel Hill: University of North Carolina Press, 1935.

Katznelson, Ira. *Black Men, White Cities.* New York: Oxford University Press, 1973.

Killian, Lewis M., and Smith, Charles U. "Negro Protest Leaders in a Southern Community." *Social Forces* 38 (March 1960).

Killian, Lewis M. *The Impossible Revolution?* New York: Random House, 1968.

Killingsworth, Charles C. "Negroes in a Changing Labor Market." In *Employment, Race, and Poverty,* edited by Arthur M. Ross and Herbert Hill. New York: Harcourt, Brace and World, 1967.

King, Martin Luther, Jr. *Stride Toward Freedom.* New York: Harper and Row, 1958.

————. *Why We Can't Wait.* New York: The New American Library, 1963.

————. *Where Do We Go From Here: Chaos or Community?* New York: Harper and Row, 1967.

Ladd, Everett Carl Jr. *Negro Political Leadership in the South.* Ithaca, N.Y.: Cornell University Press, 1966.

Lewis, Anthony and *The New York Times. Portrait of a Decade.* New York: Random House, 1964.

Lewis, David L. *King: A Critical Biography.* New York: Praeger Publishers, 1970.

Lewis, Michael. "The Negro Protest in Urban America." In *Protest, Reform, and Revolt,* edited by Joseph R. Gusfield. New York: John Wiley and Sons, 1971.

Lomax, Louis E. *The Negro Revolt.* New York: Harper and Row, 1962.

Lubell, Samuel. *Revolt of the Moderates.* New York: Harper and Row, 1956.

————. *White & Black* 2nd ed., rev. New York: Harper Colophon Books, 1966.

Maclachan, John M. "Recent Population Trends in the Southeast." *Social Forces* 35 (1956).

Martin, John B. *Deep South Says Never.* New York: Ballantine Books, 1957.

————. *Adlai Stevenson of Illinois.* Garden City: Doubleday and Co., 1976.

Marx, Gary T. *Protest and Prejudice*. New York: Harper Torchbook Edition, 1969.

Matthews, Donald R., and Protho, James W. *Negroes and the New Southern Politics*. New York: Harcourt, Brace and World, 1966.

McCord, William. *Mississippi: The Long, Hot Summer*. New York: W. W. Norton and Co., 1965.

Meier, August. "On the Role of Martin Luther King." *New Politics* 4 (Winter 1965).

————. "Civil Rights Strategies for Negro Employment." in *Employment, Race, and Poverty*, edited by Arthur M. Ross and Herbert Hill. New York: Harcourt, Brace and World, 1967.

————. "Who Are the 'True Believers'?—A Tentative Typology of the Motivations of Civil Rights Activitists." In *Protest, Reform, and Revolt*, edited by Joseph R. Gusfield. New York: John Wiley and Sons, 1970.

Meier, August, and Rudwick, Elliott. *CORE: A Study in the Civil Rights Movement, 1942–1968*. Urbana: The University of Illinois Press, 1975.

Moon, Henry Lee. *Balance of Power: The Negro Vote*. Garden City: Doubleday and Co., 1948.

————. "The Negro Vote in the Presidential Election of 1956." *The Journal of Negro Education* 26 (Summer 1957).

Muller, Herbert J. *Adlai Stevenson: A Study in Values*. New York: Harper & Row, 1967.

Myrdal, Gunnar. *An American Dilemma: The Negro Problem and Modern Democracy*. New York: Harper and Brothers, 1944.

Navasky, Victor S. *Kennedy Justice*. New York: Atheneum Publishers, 1971.

Patrick, Clarence H. *Lunch Counter Desegregations in Winston-Salem, North Carolina*. Atlanta: Southern Regional Council, 1960.

Peck, James. *Freedom Ride*. New York: Simon and Schuster, 1962.

Perlo, Victor. *The Negro in Southern Agriculture*. New York: International Publishers, 1953.

Piven, Frances Fox, and Cloward, Richard A. *Regulating the Poor: The Functions of Public Welfare*. New York: Pantheon Books, 1971.

Population Reference Bureau. "The American Farmer." *Population Bulletin* 19 (May 1963).

Powledge, Fred. *Black Power, White Resistance*. Cleveland: The World Publishing Co., 1967.

Proudfoot, Merrill. *Diary of a Sit-in*. Chapel Hill: University of North Carolina Press, 1962.

Reddick, L. D. *Crusader Without Violence.* New York: Harper and Row, 1959.

Rich, Marvin. "The Congress of Racial Equality and Its Strategy." *The Annals of the American Academy of Political and Social Science* 357 (January 1965).

Rose, Arnold. *The Negro in America.* New York: Harper Torchbook Edition, 1964.

Ross, Arthur M. "The Negro in the American Economy." In *Employ-ment, Race, and Poverty,* edited by Arthur M. Ross and Herbert Hill. New York: Harcourt, Brace and World, 1967.

Schlesinger, Arthur M., Jr. *A Thousand Days.* Boston: Houghton Mifflin Co., 1965.

Sherrill, Robert. *The Accidental President.* New York: Grossman Publishers, 1967.

Sindler, Allen P. "The Unsolid South." In *The Uses of Power,* edited by A. Westin. New York, Harcourt, Brace and World, 1962.

————. "Protest Against the Political Status of the Negro." *The Annals of the American Academy of Political and Social Sciences* 357 (January 1965).

Sorensen, Theodore C. *Kennedy.* New York: Harper and Row, 1965.

Southern Regional Council. *The Student Protest Movement: A Recapitulation.* Atlanta: Southern Regional Council, September 29, 1961, Special Report.

Tindall, George Brown. *The Disruption of the Solid South.* Athens: The University of Georgia Press, 1972.

U. S. Bureau of the Census. *Statistical Abstract of the United States.* Washington, D. C.: U. S. Department of Commerce, 1975.

U. S. Bureau of the Census. *Historical Statistics of the United States.* Washington, D. C.: U. S. Department of Commerce, 1976.

U. S. National Advisory Commission on Civil Disorders. *Report of the Advisory Commission on Civil Disorders.* New York: Bantam Books, 1968.

Vaughan, Philip H. "President Truman's Committee on Civil Rights: The Urban Implications." *Missouri Historical Review* 66 (April 1972).

Walker, Jack L. "The Functions of Disunity: Negro Leadership in a Southern City." *Journal of Negro Education* 32 (Summer 1963).

Walton, John. "Community Power and the Retreat from Politics: Full Circle after Twenty Years." *Social Problems* 23 (February 1976).

Watters, Pat. *Down to Now: Recollections of the Civil Rights Movement.* New York: Vintage Books, 1976.

White, Theodore H. *The Making of the President, 1960.* New York: Atheneum Publishers, 1961.

————. *The Making of the President, 1972*. New York: Bantam Books, 1973.

Wilson, James Q. "The Negro in American Politics: The Present." In *The American Negro Reference Book*. Englewood Cliffs, New Jersey: Prentice-Hall, 1966.

Woodward, C. Vann. *Origins of the New South*. Baton Rouge: Louisiana State University Press, 1951.

————. *The Strange Career of Jim Crow*. 3rd rev. ed. New York: Oxford University Press, 1974.

Yarnell, Allen. *Democrats and Progressives: The 1948 Presidential Election as a Test of Postward Liberalism*. Berkeley: The University of California Press, 1974.

Zinn, Howard. *SNCC: The New Abolitionists*. Boston: Beacon Press, 1964.

CHAPTER

5

The Welfare Rights
Movement

In appraisals of the postwar black movement, much is made of the fact that the main economic beneficiaries were members of the middle class (or those who were prepared by education to enter that class). But in fact the black poor also made economic gains, although not through the occupational system. One major expression of the postwar black movement was the rise in demands for relief, especially after 1960 and particularly in the large urban centers of the North. A great many of the southern black poor who were driven from agriculture in the 1940s and 1950s did not find jobs in the northern cities; extreme hardship rapidly became pervasive. But that hardship was subsequently eased by the outpouring of relief benefits which the turbulence of the sixties produced. The turbulence of the sixties also enabled many more poor whites to obtain benefits, so that the American lower class as a whole gained from black protest in this period.

The magnitude of the gain can be measured by the numbers of additional families aided and by the additional billions of dollars distributed through the relief system. In 1960 there were only 745,000 families on the Aid to Families with Dependent Children (AFDC) rolls and they received payments amounting to less than $1 billion; in 1972 the rolls reached 3 million families and the payments reached $6 billion.

Accounts of the civil rights era are curiously myopic on this point;

the matter is not even mentioned. Except for the rioting that swept from one city to another, one would have to conclude from these accounts that the urban black poor were inert. This oddity is all the greater given the tendency of many analysts to define the riots as a form of rebellion; by similar reasoning, the great rise in relief insurgency can be understood as a rebellion by the poor against circumstances that deprived them of both jobs and income. Moreover, the relief movement was in a sense the most authentic expression of the black movement in the postwar period. The many hundreds of thousands who participated were drawn from the very bottom of the black community. They were neither integrationist nor nationalistic; they were neither led nor organized. This movement welled up out of the bowels of the northern ghettos so densely packed with the victims of agricultural displacement and urban unemployment. It was, in short, a struggle by the black masses for the sheer right of survival.

As this broad-based relief movement burst forth in the early 1960s, some black people (and a few whites) banded together in an organization dedicated to attacking the relief system. Just as unemployed groups sprang up during the Great Depression and eventually formed the Workers' Alliance of America, so in the middle 1960s welfare rights groups began to appear and then joined together in the National Welfare Rights Organization (NWRO). In this chapter our purpose is to examine the extent to which NWRO contributed to the relief movement—to the huge rise in demands for relief and the explosion of the relief rolls that followed.

NWRO is of interest for another reason as well. It was formed at a time when the southern civil rights movement had all but ended and when many activists were turning northward, drawn by the increasing turbulence of the black urban masses. This turbulence, together with the concentrations of black voters in the north, encouraged the belief that political power could be developed through mass organization. The disruptive protests which had characterized the southern movement, in short, were quickly superseded by an emphasis on the need for "community organization" in the northern ghettos. NWRO was one expression of that change, for its leaders and organizers—while animated by the spirit of protest—were nevertheless more deeply committed to the goal of building mass-based permanent organizations among the urban poor. There were other such efforts in the same period, but none gained the national scope of NWRO.[1] An analysis of the experience of NWRO thus affords some basis for appraising the viability of this political strategy.

Virtually nothing has been written about NWRO. During its brief life it received relatively little support from civil rights groups and it has since received little attention from historians or social scientists.[2] The analysis in this chapter is therefore based almost entirely on our own observations, for we were intimately involved in the affairs of NWRO: we participated in discussions of strategy, in fund-raising efforts, and in demonstrations.[3] We were strong advocates of a particular political strategy—one stressing disruptive protest rather than community organization—which was a continual source of dispute among NWRO's leadership, as will become evident later in this chapter. To what extent our involvement and partisanship may have distorted the analysis which follows is for the reader to judge.

The Rise of a Relief Movement

Aid to Families with Dependent Children was created under the Social Security Act of 1935.[4] By 1940 all states had enacted the necessary enabling legislation and people were beginning to be admitted to the rolls. But the main thing to be understood about this widely hailed reform is that few of the poor benefited from it; welfare statutes and practices were designed to enforce work norms and to insure the availability of low-paid laborers by restricting aid.

---

[1] Meier and Rudwick's account of CORE's activities in the northern cities contains a good deal of documentation on this shifting emphasis to community organization in the mid-sixties. It also portrays the rather dismal failure of CORE's efforts in employing this strategy.

[2] There are a few doctoral dissertations and other essays by students. Steiner is the only senior social scientist to have written about NWRO (see his chapter eight).

[3] The reader should know that we were close to George A. Wiley, its executive director, who died in an accident in the summer of 1973. He was a marvelously talented leader, and a good friend. We feel his loss deeply.

[4] There were three categories of public assistance: Old Age Assistance, Aid to the Blind, and Aid to Dependent Children (later changed to Aid to Families with Dependent Children). AFDC was the main category of aid to poor families, and it was this category which showed the great rise in the 1960s. These programs were supervised by and partially financed by the federal government, but the states and localities administered them. A fourth category, Aid to Permanently and Totally Disabled, was added in 1950.

All able-bodied adults without children, as well as all two-parent families, were simply disqualified by federal law; state and county statutes and practices disqualified many more of the remaining poor. Cost was also a factor in keeping the rolls down. The federal government paid part of relief costs; states and localities paid the remainder. Local officials thus had a strong incentive to make relief difficult to obtain.

In the 1960s and early 1970s the relief rolls greatly expanded,[5] especially in northern states and localities. The force underlying this expansion was the rise of a relief movement.

UNDERMINING THE LEGITIMACY OF POVERTY

As we noted in chapter 4, economic distress worsened among large segments of the poor after World War II. Unemployment became pervasive in agriculture, especially in the South, and urban unemployment was also high. Unemployment declined briefly during the Korean War but then rose abruptly. Blacks were especially hard hit. Official nonwhite unemployment stood at 4.5 percent in the last year of the war, rose to 13 percent in the recession of 1958, and remained above 10 percent until the escalation of the war in Vietnam. In the northern urban ghettos, unemployment reached depression levels. "For example, 41 percent of the Negro men in one census tract in Detroit, wholly populated by Negroes, were jobless in 1960; in certain census tracts in Chicago, Los Angeles, and Baltimore—where 90 percent or more of the inhabitants were Negro—the rates ranged from 24 percent to 36 percent."[6]

But hardship did not lead poor people to apply for public aid in large numbers. The ethic of self-reliance and the denigration of the pauper are powerful controlling forces. Moreover government did

---

5 All figures in this section, and elsewhere in this chapter, pertaining to the relief expansion of the 1960s are taken from the Source Tables contained in the Appendix of Piven and Cloward (1971). Data on applications and approvals are contained in Source Table 5; data on the number of AFDC families are contained in Source Table 1. The relief rises for the largest cities in the nation are contained in Source Table 2. The figures include AFDC-UP cases and are for the contiguous United States only.

6 U. S. Department of Labor, 1964, 48.

not respond to economic distress: of those few families who did apply for aid, roughly half were simply turned away. The result was a negligible rise in the relief rolls—from 635,000 families in 1950 to 745,000 in 1960, an increase of only 110,000 families (or 17 percent) during a decade in which millions of the displaced agricultural poor migrated to the cities. These people simply endured their hardships.

But that was shortly to change. One factor was the emergence of poverty as a national political issue. The recessions of the late 1950s figured prominently in the presidential campaign of 1960. Kennedy repeatedly called for "an economic drive against poverty" (Schlesinger, 1006), and when the ballots were counted, an embittered Nixon attributed his defeat in no small part to Eisenhower's economic policies, which had failed to prevent recessions, particularly in the year of the presidential campaign itself.[7] Within a few days after he assumed office, Kennedy forwarded legislation to the Congress proposing "to add a temporary thirteen-week supplement to unemployment benefits . . . to extend aid to the children of unemployed workers . . . to redevelop distressed areas . . . to increase Social Security payments and encourage earlier retirement . . . [and] . . . to raise the minimum wage and broaden its coverage . . ." (Sorensen, 397).

Although Kennedy's concern with economic problems was mainly a response to his broad working-class constituency, it was to some degree a response to his black constituency. From the moment he took office, he needed to defend himself against civil rights critics who believed he was reneging on his pledges to send a civil rights bill to the Congress:

> When civil rights leaders . . . reproached [Kennedy] in 1961 for not seeking legislation, he told them that an increased minimum

---

[7] It was the fourth serious recession since the close of World War II. Each had been followed by a higher plateau of long-term unemployment—the Department of Labor called it a "squeeze-out": "The major increase in this squeeze-out from the labor force among nonwhites seems to have occurred after 1958, a year of recession from which there has been only imperfect recovery in many respects. Unemployment among non-whites had in fact risen sharply during each of the postwar recessions, and since 1954 had failed to recover to the same extent as white unemployment rates during each subsequent business pick-up. The familiar pattern of 'first to be fired, last to be rehired' appears to have become 'first to be fired, and possibly never to be rehired' " (1964, 82). When Kennedy assumed office, the last of these recessions had left the nation with an official unemployment rate of 7 percent—6 percent among whites and 12.5 percent among nonwhites.

wage, federal aid to education and other social and economic measures were also civil rights bills (Schlesinger, 976).[8]

At the start, then, the Kennedy Administration's emphasis on poverty
was a way to evade civil rights demands while maintaining black
support.

But the civil rights struggle intensified, and as it did blacks became
more indignant over their condition—not only as an oppressed
racial minority in a white society but as poor people in an affluent
one. The civil rights victories being won in the South would, after
all, be of greatest immediate benefit to southern blacks and particularly to southern blacks who were already in, or were prepared to
enter, the middle class. By the early 1960s dozens of rural counties
in which blacks were finally winning the right to vote or to take
any seat they wished on a bus no longer contained many blacks to
do either. Agricultural unemployment together with punitive southern relief practices which kept displaced agricultural workers off
the rolls had compelled the migration that inexorably diminished the
ranks of the rural black poor. In the cities, unemployment, underemployment, low wages, and relief restrictions created new hardships. A civil rights revolution was occurring but poor urban blacks
had little to show for it.

By 1962 and 1963 many civil rights activists had begun to shift
their emphasis to economic problems. They organized boycotts,
picket lines, and demonstrations to attack discrimination in access
to jobs; rent strikes were organized to protest substandard housing
conditions and rent gouging; urban renewal sites were overrun with
protestors. Economic issues thus emerged as a major focus of discontent, and the March on Washington for Jobs and Freedom in
August 1963 gave national prominence to this discontent.

---

[8] As is his wont in interpreting the actions of presidents, Schlesinger attributes only
statesmanlike motives to Kennedy. Unemployment did not worry Kennedy "politically
because he was sure the unemployed would never turn to the Republicans to create
jobs for them. But it worried him socially. Unemployment was especially acute among
Negroes, already so alienated from American society, and among young people, and it
thereby placed a growing strain on the social fabric" (1006). But, of course, the "strain
on the social fabric" was a political problem, whether one refers to the organized
protests over unemployment and discrimination or to the reactions of other groups to
the growing crime rates and other manifestations of social disorder resulting from the
lack of integration of blacks in the occupational system. Moreover, it was a rapidly
intensifying political problem, for with the outbreak of ghetto riots in 1964, the
reverberations of this "strain on the social fabric" alienated many whites and helped
return the Republicans to power in 1968.

Even as the March on Washington was being planned, officials in the national government launched a new wave of rhetoric about economic injustice together with pronouncements regarding the importance of creating new programs to deal with poverty. The process of planning began in a cabinet meeting in June, just following the civil rights crisis in Birmingham and just before the March on Washington:

> Kennedy devoted a large part of . . . [this meeting] . . . to a discussion of the problem of Negro unemployment, and he initiated a series of staff studies on that subject. Throughout the summer of 1963, professionals in the relevant executive agencies—the Council of Economic Advisors, the Bureau of the Budget, the Department of Labor and HEW . . . were at work producing what was shortly to become a flood of staff papers. In November President Kennedy advised . . . [his aides] . . . that he intended to make an attack on poverty a key legislative objective in 1964 . . . (Donovan, 23).

If Kennedy had launched a wave of rhetoric about poverty, Johnson swelled it to the proportions of a tidal wave following the assassination. In his State of the Union Address on January 8, 1964, he began by calling for an "unconditional war on poverty in America. [We] shall not rest until that war is won." Later in January the president proposed to the Congress the Economic Opportunities Bill of 1964 (the antipoverty program),[9] and throughout the spring of 1964 he campaigned vigorously for the antipoverty program among various interest groups: among labor leaders, business leaders, religious leaders, civil rights leaders. In speeches and press releases Johnson mobilized public opinion to support the program. The result was that "public awareness of poverty in the United States, virtually non-existent a year earlier, [became] pervasive. But most important, Johnson had made the War on Poverty part of the national consensus" (Evans and Novak, 431). The Congress acted with extraordinary dispatch, and the president signed the bill in August, just before the presidential election.

---

[9] The bill was based on a report from the Task Force on Manpower Conservation, a cabinet-level committee which had been appointed by President Kennedy on September 30 (just weeks after the March on Washington).

ANTIPOVERTY SERVICES

What the antipoverty program actually did was to greatly expand
an array of service programs initiated on a smaller scale during
the Kennedy years. One of these Kennedy programs was the Juvenile
Delinquency and Youth Offenses Control Act (1961) under which
"community action programs" had been established in twenty cities.
In addition the Manpower Development and Training Act had
been legislated in 1962, followed by the Community Mental Health
Centers Act (1963). Later in the decade the Demonstration Cities
and Metropolitan Development Act became law (1966).

For a time these programs did not so much moderate unrest as
provide the vehicles through which the black ghettos mobilized to
demand government services.[10] They activated a new leadership
structure in the ghettos and they also activated masses of black poor.
This occurred because some funds from these programs were permitted to flow directly into ghetto neighborhoods—a form of direct
federal patronage to minority groups. And ghetto groups were encouraged by federal policymakers to use these funds to create organizations and to press their own interests, especially in the arena of
municipal services and politics.

The role of the new service programs in stimulating applications
for public assistance after 1965 was very large. As thousands of social
workers and community aides who were hired by community action
agencies across the country came into contact with the poor, they
were compelled to begin to learn the welfare regulations and to learn
how to fight to obtain aid for their new clients. To have done anything else would have been to make themselves irrelevant to those
who were presumably their constituents. Quite simply, the poor
needed money; the lack of money underlay most of the problems
which families brought to antipoverty personnel in storefront centers and other community action agencies across the nation.

In short order antipoverty lawyers also became active in these
efforts. Thus, when community action workers could not succeed
in establishing a family's eligibility for assistance, attorneys instituted

---

[10] For an extended discussion of the Kennedy and Johnson Administrations' economic
and service strategy for coping with black unrest, see chapter nine of Piven and Cloward
(1971); see also the various articles by Piven in part four of Cloward and Piven (1974).

test cases and won stunning victories in state courts and then in the federal courts, including the Supreme Court. Man-in-the-house rules, residence laws, employable mother rules, and a host of other statutes, policies, and regulations which kept people off the rolls were eventually struck down.[11] The consequence of these court rulings was to make whole new categories of people eligible so that many who would previously have been turned away had to be granted assistance. Furthermore, as antipoverty staff began to discover that thousands of potentially eligible families populated the slums and ghettos, "welfare rights" handbooks were prepared and distributed by the tens of thousands, with the result that many more people were informed about the possibility of assistance. After 1965, in short, the poor were informed of their "right" to welfare, encouraged to apply for it, and helped to obtain it. A multifaceted campaign against welfare restrictiveness had formed with the federal government as its chief source of both resources and legitimacy.[12]

THE IMPACT OF RIOTS

The mass rioting throughout the nation between 1964 and 1968 had a substantial impact on the new service programs. There were twenty-one major riots and civil disorders in 1966 and eighty-three major disturbances in 1967. July of 1967, for example, was a month of riots. In Milwaukee four persons died; in Detroit forty-three died. Disturbances occurred across the entire nation: in Cambridge, Maryland; in Lansing, Kalamazoo, Saginaw, and Grand Rapids, Michigan; in Philadelphia; Providence; Phoenix; Portland; Wichita; South Bend; Memphis, Tennessee; Wilmington, Delaware; San Francisco, San Bernardino, Long Beach, Fresno, and Marin City, California; Rochester, Mt. Vernon, Poughkeepsie, Peekskill, and Nyack, New

---

[11] The most prominent attorney involved in this nationwide litigation thrust was Edward Sparer, who began welfare litigation as an attorney for Mobilization for Youth, an antipoverty program. He continued this work as director of the Center on Social Welfare Policy and Law and as chief counsel for the National Welfare Rights Organization.

[12] Chapter ten of Piven and Cloward (1971) contains a detailed description of the role of the Great Society programs, especially the antipoverty program, in promoting the welfare explosion of the 1960s.

York; in Hartford, Connecticut; in Englewood, Paterson, Elizabeth, New Brunswick, Jersey City, Palmyra, and Passaic, New Jersey. As the month of July ended a Civil Disturbance Task Force was established in the Pentagon, and the president established a "Riot Commission." Just seven months later (February 1968), the commission called for "a massive and sustained commitment to action" to end poverty and racial discrimination. Only days before, in the State of the Union Message, the president had announced legislative proposals for programs to train and hire the hardcore unemployed and to rebuild the cities.

Given these momentous forces of mass protest and government conciliation, the service personnel in the programs of the Great Society had little choice but to turn more militant if they were to satisfy their constituents. Thus they no longer negotiated wih their counterparts in local agencies (the school systems, the urban renewal authorities, the welfare departments); they demanded responses favorable to their clients. They no longer held back on law suits that might be especially offensive to local political leaders and agency administrators; they sued and often won. And they no longer shied away from organizing the poor to protest the policies and practices of local agencies; they led them. This was one cause of the relief explosion of the 1960s.

A RELIEF MOVEMENT EMERGES

With a rising curve of antipoverty rhetoric, of funding for new antipoverty services, and of ghetto rioting, applications for relief formed a similarly rising curve. Many of the poor had apparently come to believe that a society which denied them jobs and adequate wages did at least owe them a survival income. It was a period that began to resemble the Great Depression, for in both periods masses of people concluded that "the system" was responsible for their economic plight, not they themselves, and so they turned in growing numbers to the relief offices.

In 1960, 588,000 families applied for AFDC benefits. In 1963, the year that political leaders first placed poverty on the national agenda, 788,000 families applied—an increase of one-third. In 1966, the first year antipoverty programs were in full swing across the country, the number reached 903,000—up by more than half over 1960. In 1968, the year that rioting finally reached a crescendo, applications had doubled over 1960 to 1,088,000—and they exceeded one million in each year thereafter.[13] A relief movement involving millions of participants had unmistakably emerged.

GOVERNMENT RESPONSES TO THE RELIEF MOVEMENT

The rising curve of applications was matched by the curve of approvals. As more families applied, proportionately still more families were granted assistance. In 1960, 55 percent of applicants got relief. The figure reached 57 percent in 1963, 64 percent in 1966, and 70 percent in 1968. Approval levels in many northern cities were even higher; it is only slightly exaggerated to say that virtually any low-income family who walked into a welfare center toward the end of the 1960s received aid.

The liberalized practices of the relief system were also the result of a complex of forces. State and local welfare officials were influenced by the national rhetoric on poverty and injustice, and they were surely harassed by the staff of the new federal service programs into making more liberal decisions. Moreover, relief officials (and the political leaders to whom they reported) were frightened of rioting. Some of these riots, in fact, were directly related to welfare demonstrations or were provoked by welfare injustices. The riot in the summer of 1966 in Cleveland's Hough area was precipitated by the demeaning treatment by the police of a welfare recipient who was trying to collect money to forestall the final indignity of a pauper's funeral for another recipient who had just died (Stein, 3–4). In the spring of 1967 welfare rights groups in Boston staged a sit-in at the welfare department. When the police beat the demonstrators, they screamed from the windows to the streets below, triggering three days of rioting—the first in that especially violent summer.[14] Gen-

---

[13] No data are available which directly relate rioting and rises in the AFDC rolls. However one study is available on the impact of rioting on the General Assistance rolls. Thus Betz says: "Data on 23 riot cities are compared to 20 nonriot cities of similar size. . . . Analysis revealed riot cities had larger budgetary increases in welfare the year following their riot" (345).

[14] For a discussion of the origins and political consequences of this riot, see Fiske, 21–22.

erally speaking, public officials in the northern cities moved gingerly in those years: the police were schooled to avoid provocative incidents, urban renewal authorities were not so quick to bulldoze slum and ghetto neighborhoods, and welfare officials handed out relief more freely.

The mood of applicants in welfare waiting rooms had changed. They were no longer as humble, as self-effacing, as pleading; they were more indignant, angrier, more demanding. As a consequence, welfare officials—especially the intake workers who are the gatekeepers of the system—employed their discretion more permissively. Traditional procedures for investigating eligibility broke down: home visits were no longer made with any frequency, requirements that forms be sent to various agencies to determine whether the family might have collateral income or eligibility for other forms of assistance (veteran's pensions, etc.) tended to be neglected. For all practical purposes, welfare operating procedures collapsed; regulations were simply ignored in order to process the hundreds of thousands of families who jammed the welfare waiting rooms.

Welfare agencies also became less harsh in dealing with those who obtained assistance. Termination rates began to drop, especially terminations for "failure to comply with departmental regulations" —a catch-all category that included anything from refusal to help locate a "responsible" father to failing to appear for an interview.

As a result of these changes the relief rolls rose precipitously. In 1960, 745,000 families received assistance; in 1968, the number reached 1.5 million. Then, between 1968 and 1972, the rolls surged to 3 million families—an increase of 300 percent over 1960. Money payments, less than $1 billion in 1960, reached $6 billion in 1972. Unacknowledged and unled, a relief movement had emerged, and it was achieving income gains for the participants.

A Proposal to Mobilize an
Institutional Disruption

In 1965 we had completed research showing that for every family on the AFDC rolls, at least one other was eligible but unaided. A huge pool of families with incomes below prevailing welfare grant schedules had built up in the cities as a result of migration and unemployment. If hundreds of thousands of families could be induced to demand relief, we thought that two gains might result. First, if large numbers of people succeeded in getting on the rolls, much of the worst of America's poverty would be eliminated. Second, for reasons we will explain, we thought it likely that a huge increase in the relief rolls would set off fiscal and political crises in the cities, the reverberations of which might lead national political leaders to federalize the relief system and establish a national minimum income standard. It was a strategy designed to obtain immediate economic aid for the poor, coupled with the possibility of obtaining a longer-term national income standard.

These ideas were spelled out in a mimeographed paper entitled "A Strategy to End Poverty,"[15] which we circulated among organizers and activists in late 1965. With turmoil spreading in the cities, with the prohibition against going on relief already being defied on a large scale by the poor, and with the resources of the antipoverty program available to be drawn upon, we argued that activists of all kinds should join in a massive drive to mobilize the unaided poor to disrupt the relief system all the more by demanding relief.

One person who was responsive to the idea of organizing in the welfare arena was George A. Wiley, whom we knew from CORE. He was at the time on the verge of resigning as CORE's associate national director, mainly in opposition to the rising surge of black nationalist sentiment that was engulfing that organization in early 1966. George had been mulling over the possibility of undertaking a broad, multi-issue organizing effort among the northern urban poor, but had not settled on a definite plan. Our proposal, together with the fact that a few "welfare rights" groups had already formed (mainly under the auspices of local antipoverty programs, and mainly in New York City), suggested a way to begin.[16]

At that particular moment, civil rights activists, and especially northern activists, were shifting away from caste problems to economic problems. This, together with the rising insurgency among urban blacks signified by rioting, suggested that a powerful move-

---

[15] This article was published in *The Nation* magazine on May 2, 1966; reprinted in Cloward and Piven (1974). Unless otherwise indicated, all quotations in this section are taken from this article.

[16] When George subsequently formed the National Welfare Rights Organization, he attracted a number of CORE veterans to welfare rights organizing, among them Bruce Thomas.

ment directed toward economic gains could be developed. The responsiveness of national political leaders in this period also suggested that victories could be won, that change was possible. But it was not clear how activists could, as a practical day-to-day matter of organizing, mount an attack on poverty by attacking its main cause—underemployment and unemployment. What our plan proposed instead was a way of attacking the lack of income resulting from unemployment; it was appealing to some organizers for that reason.

For George, the first question was whether welfare was a promising area in which to mount an initial organizing effort, as contrasted with housing or education or health. To consider that question he convened a series of small meetings with us and a few friends from the civil rights movement. These meetings took place during the spring of 1966 in New York City. Much of the discussion was about the workings of the welfare system itself and about the estimates we had made of the many hundreds of thousands of families with incomes below scheduled welfare eligibility levels in various northern cities. We had also gathered data showing that few of the families already on the rolls were receiving all of the benefits to which they were entitled.

At first, there was some skepticism about our assertions regarding the existence of a huge pool of eligible but unaided families. When George tried to obtain confirmation of these assertions by consulting prominent social welfare professionals, some of them advised him that our data were not valid and that we were engaged in a campaign of propaganda against the welfare system. (Some even said the data were faked.) Nor were there supporting data from other studies. Dominant cultural definitions of the deleterious consequences of relief-giving were so strong that it was simply not a question that researchers had asked. To resolve his uncertainties, George asked a close associate, Edwin Day, to replicate our studies. Day's subsequent conclusion was that we had erred in being much too conservative in our estimates of the size of the pool of eligible but unaided families. A consensus was thus reached that campaigns to drive up the rolls and to create a welfare crisis were worth trying. George made this clear in a public debate in the late spring of 1966:

> Well, I'd have to say that the appearance of the strategy by Cloward and Piven has represented a shot in the arm to a lot of the civil-rights activists around the country. A lot of us who have come out of the civil-rights movement have been concerned that there

develop a significant movement in the northern ghettos, and a lot of people who have been trying to work in the ghettos in major urban areas have been really quite frustrated about finding significant handles for bringing about some substantial change in the living conditions of people there.

This idea of releasing the potential for major economic pressure through trying to encourage people to gain their rights in the welfare system is one that has had immediate response and has been enormously attractive to activists working in urban areas. I may say that a lot of us have been hampered in our thinking about the potential here by our own middle-class backgrounds—and I think most activists basically come out of middle-class backgrounds—and were oriented toward people having to work, and that we have to get as many people as possible off the welfare rolls. And I think the idea that for millions—particularly people who can't work, people who are senior citizens or female heads of household—just encouraging them to assert their rights is a very attractive thing. I think that this strategy is going to catch on and be very important in the time ahead. In the history of the civil-rights movement the thing that attracted me is the fact that the substantial changes that have taken place such as the Civil Rights Act of '64 and Voting Rights Act of '65 particularly have come about as the result of major drives in one or more cities where substantial confrontations have taken place which have plunged the nation into significant crises. And I think that a crisis strategy has been the only one that has really produced major success in the civil-rights field (from "Strategy of Crisis: A Dialogue," reprinted in Cloward and Piven, 1974).

CONFLICTING THEORIES OF POLITICAL INFLUENCE

Despite this initial enthusiasm, there were some differences over strategy that emerged during these discussions, and they all led back directly or indirectly to the general question of how the poor could exert political influence. In "A Strategy to End Poverty," we had argued a perspective that ran counter to the conventional wisdom regarding the nature of the American political system; and our views about organizing also ran counter to traditional organizing doctrines. Three specific areas of disagreement emerged.

First, we argued against the traditional organizing notion that poor people can become an effective political force by coming together in mass-based organizations. We did not think the political system would be responsive to such organizations, even if large numbers of the poor could be involved on a continuing basis. We had been studying earlier efforts—the Workers' Alliance of America, the southern civil rights movement, the northern rent strikes in the early 1960s. Organizational pressure did not seem to yield much but disruptive protests sometimes did.

We thought the welfare system was particularly vulnerable to disruption by the poor because of the large concentrations of potentially eligible families in the northern industrial states produced by migration and urban unemployment. These states and their localities were also the most exposed to ghetto discontent. At the same time, because of the method by which welfare was financed (states with high grant levels—mainly northern states—received proportionately less federal reimbursement than states with low grant levels), these same states were the most susceptible to fiscal distress if demands for welfare mounted. Finally, the northern industrial states were crucial to the fortunes of the national Democratic Party and so disturbances in these states could have large political ramifications at the federal level:

> A series of welfare drives in large cities would, we believe, impel action on a new federal program to distribute income. . . . Widespread campaigns to register the eligible poor for welfare aid . . . would produce bureaucratic disruption in welfare agencies and fiscal disruption in local and state governments. These disruptions would generate severe political strains, and deepen existing divisions among elements in the big-city Democratic coalition: the remaining white middle class, the white working-class ethnic groups and the growing minority poor. To avoid a further weakening of that historic coalition, a national Democratic administration would be constrained to advance a federal solution to poverty that would override local revenue dilemmas. By the internal disruption of local bureaucratic practices, by the furor over public welfare policies, and by the collapse of current financing arrangements, powerful forces can be generated for major economic reforms at the national level.

In order to maximize the disruptive potential of such drives, we thought that whatever organizing resources could be obtained should be concentrated on developing enrollment campaigns in a small number of big cities in states of critical national electoral importance (e.g., New York, Michigan, Illinois, Ohio, California, Pennsylvania, etc.), thus improving the chances of creating a political crisis of sufficient importance to warrant intervention by national political leaders.

As for the poor themselves, there was every reason to believe that they would join in such a mobilization, for the statistics on rising welfare application rates demonstrated that they already were, separately but in concert, fulfilling the outlines of a disruptive strategy. All that remained, we argued, was for organizers to enlarge and sustain the disruptive behavior in which masses of the poor were unmistakably beginning to engage.

But organizers in the 1960s took a different view. They had inspected the American political landscape and observed that other groups were well represented by organizations that asserted their special interests. Homeowners formed associations to resist government actions which might lower property values, workers joined unions to advance labor legislation, and industrialists joined associations that pressed for favorable treatment of corporations by a host of government agencies. While homeowner associations were hardly as powerful as the American Petroleum Institute, that seemed less important at the time than the fact that other groups were organized and the poor were not. Accordingly it was argued that if the poor organized they too could advance their interests.

Of course, everyone recognized that organizations of the poor lacked the substantial resources possessed by other organizations which could be brought to bear on the political process—the control of wealth, of key economic activities, of the media, and the like. Still, the organizers said, this lack of resources could be compensated for by the sheer numbers which the poor represented. If large numbers could be organized, political influence would result. It was this perspective which tended to prevail in these early discussions.

GOVERNMENT RESPONSES TO A WELFARE CRISIS

A second and related area of disagreement had to do with the problem of controlling government responses to a welfare crisis. There were two points of difference. One concerned the possibility that government might respond with repressive measures. Everyone foresaw that rising welfare costs would arouse large sectors of the public to demand that mayors, county officials, and governors slash the rolls and cut grant levels. For our part, we did not think most public officials would accede to such demands while the ghettos remained in turmoil. Markedly repressive welfare measures would entail the risk that rioting might worsen. Blacks had also become a modest electoral force in the northern cities; deep slashes in either the rolls or grant levels could be expected to engender considerable antagonism among those voters.

But mainly we argued that even if the welfare rolls were cut, poor people as a group would not be worse off than they had been before the rolls expanded, when large numbers of families had been denied relief in any case. If many now succeeded in getting on the rolls only to be cut off again, they would at least have made a temporary gain.

For their part, organizers in these early discussions agreed that impulses toward repression would probably be tempered and that a temporary gain was better than no gain at all. But they also felt they had an obligation to protect the poor against *any* possibility of repression. The way to do this, as they saw it, was to create an organized body of welfare recipients who could bring pressure directly to bear on public officials, thus counteracting the pressures of groups who would call for restrictive welfare policies.

Organizers also thought that a large-scale poor people's organization would be required to win a national minimum income from the Congress. This brings us to the second point in our disagreement over the question of how government would respond. We maintained that the way to bring pressure on government was through the disruption of the welfare system itself and through the electoral crisis that would probably follow. We thought that the role of crisis as a political resource for the poor had not been understood, either by political analysts or by organizers. What we meant by a political crisis was electoral dissensus—the extreme polarization of major electoral constituencies. When acute conflicts of this kind occur, political leaders try to promulgate policies that will moderate the polarization, in order to maintain voting majorities.

Since we all agreed that extreme repression was not a likely response, what then would mayors and governors do in order to manage the political divisions created by welfare disruptions? We thought they would try to deal with their problem by calling upon the federal government with increasing insistence to take over the welfare program, thus solving their fiscal and political problems. In other words, we said, a disruption in welfare could be expected to activate lobbying by other and far more powerful groups for a goal which the poor could not possibly hope to achieve were they simply to lobby themselves. (This is not very different from what did in fact happen; by the late 1960s political leaders in the major northern states became articulate spokesmen for federal action in the welfare area.[17])

With what new policies would national Democratic leaders respond? There was no certain way of knowing, but there was some basis for speculation. Already faced with deepening cleavages among large blocs in the urban strongholds of the party—cleavages that would be rapidly worsened by a welfare crisis—Democratic leaders might be prompted to press for a national minimum income program to relieve urban conflicts (and to slow the migration that was fueling those conflicts):

> Deep tensions have developed among groups comprising the political coalitions of the large cities—the historic stronghold of the Democratic Party. As a consequence, urban politicians no longer turn in the vote to national Democratic candidates with unfailing regularity. The marked defections revealed in the elections of the 1950's and which continued until the Johnson landslide of 1964 are a matter of great concern to the national party. Precisely because of this concern, a strategy to exacerbate still further the strains in the urban coalition [by driving up the welfare rolls] can be expected to evoke a response from national leaders. If this strategy for crisis would intensify group cleavages, a federal income solution would not further exacerbate them.

But this perspective was deeply troubling to organizers. We were saying that the poor can create crises but cannot control the response to them. They can only hope that the balance of political forces provoked in response to a disruption will favor concessions rather than repression. To organizers, this amounted to asking the poor to "create a crisis and pray." It seemed speculative and very risky. Consequently they felt that the strategy had to be modified to assure greater control by the poor over the outcome of a welfare crisis. The way to develop that control was by building a national mass-based organization. Then, as political leaders weighed alternative ways of dealing with the crisis, they would have to contend with a powerful pressure group that had its own remedies to put forward.

---

[17] In this regard the parallel with the Great Depression is striking. As we noted in chapter three, the United States Conference of Mayors formed in the 1930s for the express purpose of lobbying for federal fiscal aid to relieve localities of burgeoning welfare costs.

We could only agree that our proposal entailed risks. But we also thought there were no gains for the poor without risks. In this connection, the one case we invoked in support of a disruptive strategy—the civil rights movement—actually served to weaken our argument. Some of the people in these early discussions had been involved in the southern phase of the civil rights movement and were disenchanted with mass-mobilization and mass-confrontation tactics. They believed that these tactics—mass defiance of caste rules, followed by arrests and police violence—were wrong because they had failed to build black organizations in local southern communities. When an SCLC campaign ended, for example, and SCLC moved on to another city to mobilize further confrontations, the local people were left unorganized and vulnerable to retaliation by whites. The influence this criticism of the civil rights movement had upon the thinking of those who subsequently became welfare rights organizers has been noted by Whitaker:

> Wishing to avoid what they perceived as the most debilitating mistakes of the civil rights movement—failure to create a strong, organized constituency and failure to develop internal sources of funds—the [NWRO] promoters concentrated their first three years' efforts upon the creation of a national organizational structure and the recruitment of membership (120–121).

It could not be denied that from a conventional political perspective SCLC's strategy was manipulative. SCLC did not build local organizations to obtain local victories; it clearly attempted to create a series of disruptions to which the federal government would have to respond. And that strategy succeeded. We did not think that local organizations of the southern black poor (even if they could have been developed on a mass scale) would have ever gained the political influence necessary to secure a Civil Rights Act of 1964 or a Voting Rights Act of 1965, and they probably would not have won significant local victories, either. It had taken a major political crisis—the literal fragmenting of the regional foundation of the national Democratic Party—to finally force those legislative concessions to southern blacks. Similarly, we argued that while building a network of welfare rights groups might result in some victories in contests with local welfare administrators, these local groups could not possibly build the political pressure from which a national income standard for all of the poor might result. Any hope for such a large outcome depended on mobilizing a major political crisis;

it depended on producing a divisive welfare explosion that would threaten to fragment the Democratic coalition in the big northern cities. Our views, however, were not persuasive.

MOBILIZING VERSUS ORGANIZING

Finally, we maintained that political influence by the poor is mobilized, not organized. A disruptive strategy does not require that people affiliate with an organization and participate regularly. Rather, it requires that masses of people be mobilized to engage in disruptive action. To mobilize for a welfare disruption, families would be encouraged to demand relief. Just by engaging in that defiant act, they could contribute to a fiscal and political crisis. On the other hand, if they were asked to contribute to an organization on a continuing basis, we did not think most would, for organizers had no continuing incentives to offer.

To mobilize a crisis, we thought it would be necessary to develop a national network of cadre organizations rather than a national federation of welfare recipient groups. *This organization of organizers*—composed of students, churchmen, civil rights activists, antipoverty workers, and militant AFDC recipients—would in turn seek to energize a broad, loosely coordinated movement of variegated groups to arouse hundreds of thousands of poor people to demand aid. Rather than build organizational membership rolls, the purpose would be to build the welfare rolls. The main tactics should include large-scale "welfare rights" information campaigns; the enlisting of influential people in the slums and ghettos, especially clergymen, to exhort potential welfare recipients to seek the aid that was rightfully theirs; and the mobilization of marches and demonstrations to build indignation and militancy among the poor.

Our emphasis on mass mobilization with cadre organizations as the vehicle struck organizers as exceedingly manipulative. Their perspective on organizing was imbued with values which they considered democratic. The poor had a right to run their own organizations, and to determine their own policies and strategies. Given this perspective, organizers defined two roles appropriate for themselves as outsiders in a poor people's organization. First, they should act as staff, subordinating themselves to policymaking bodies composed exclusively of the poor. As staff, they would contribute their technical skills to the work of the organization. They would, for example, provide information on the technical aspects of various issues with which the organization was dealing—in this case, the extremely complex rules and regulations of the welfare system. They would also run training programs in methods for dealing with the welfare bureaucracy—how to negotiate with welfare officials, or how to organize demonstrations. Second, they would cultivate those with leadership potential, tutoring them in techniques of leadership in the expectation that the role of the organizer would wither away. This is the model that NWRO and most of the local WROs subsequently came to espouse. (The subordination of organizers went so far that at national conventions they were barred from attending meetings where the elected recipient leaders from the various states convened to establish overall policy for the organization.)

THE PROBLEM OF INCENTIVES

Our approach, then, conflicted at several points with the perspective of organizers. They were more sanguine than we about the capacity of the poor to exert influence through the regular channels of the political system, for they felt that the poor could be influential if they were brought together in a mass-based national organization. Furthermore they felt that a mobilizing strategy, as distinct from an organizing strategy, would give the poor insufficient control over resolution of the crisis that a welfare movement might succeed in creating. Finally, they were antagonistic to the idea of building "organizations of organizers" on the ground that it was a manipulative approach to the poor.

But they were left with a problem of substantial importance. How could the poor be induced to affiliate and to participate on a continuing basis in a welfare rights organization? What incentives could be offered? Despite all of the differences in perspective which we have noted, the paper we had been circulating held enormous interest for the participants in these early discussions and subsequently for organizers throughout the country who became involved in the welfare rights movement, because it appeared to provide an answer to that question. The answer was in one of the two types of data we had presented on benefit deprivation. Our main interest was in the estimates we had reached that only half of the eligible poor were on the rolls. But we had also shown that most of those already on the rolls did not receive all of the benefits to which they were entitled under existing regulations. Regarding this second point, we said:

> Public assistance recipients in New York [and in many other states] are also entitled to receive "nonrecurring" grants for clothing, household equipment and furniture—including washing machines, refrigerators, beds and bedding, tables and chairs. It hardly needs to be noted that most impoverished families have grossly inadequate clothing and household furnishings . . . [but] almost nothing is spent on special grants in New York. In October 1965, a typical month, the Department of Welfare spent only $2.50 per recipient for heavy clothing and $1.30 for household furnishings. . . . Considering the real needs of families, the successful demand for full entitlements could multiply these expenditures tenfold or more— and that would involve the disbursement of many millions of dollars indeed.

Here, organizers thought, were the concrete incentives that might be employed to induce poor people to form groups and to affiliate in a national organization. If welfare departments, under the pressure of militant tactics by groups of recipients, could be forced to yield these "special grants" to large numbers of people, then the problem of how to attract the poor to a national organization appeared to have been solved.

This conclusion, it must be said, received clear support from events which were already occurring. As stated previously, a modest number of welfare groups had begun to form in the mid-1960s, mainly under the sponsorship of antipoverty programs. These groups consisted of existing recipients. What seemed to be making group formation possible was the availability of special grants, for protests at welfare departments were succeeding in producing cash grants for the protesters. Moreover, the amounts of money received sometimes ran as high as $1,000 per family; some families had been on the rolls for a number of years without ever having received special grants so that it took relatively large sums to bring them "up to standard." The success of these special grant protests was decisive in

Ponder this

settling the question of the strategy which the movement would follow. It was a strategy that could produce groups and groups would be the foundation of a national organization.

George Wiley also had the immediate and practical problem of dealing with the few welfare recipient groups that had already developed. If he were to lead a movement, he felt that he had to negotiate the right to lead existing groups. That pragmatic problem also helped to determine the course which welfare agitation would follow, for these groups were made up of existing recipients who were focused on special grants.

As it thus turned out, the strategy which NWRO, once formed, would pursue was dictated by the belief of organizers in the political efficacy of organizations of the poor. These beliefs were buttressed by evidence that a few recipient groups were already forming for the purpose of obtaining special grants, and by the promise that additional groups could be similarly organized. And if these groups were brought together in a "national union of welfare recipients," George and others felt that the resulting poor people's organization would be able to wield sufficient influence to compel a national income concession from Congress.

The decision was thus made to undertake the formation of a national organization, with benefit campaigns for existing recipients as the inducement to organization building. It was a fateful decision. Benefit campaigns for existing recipients became NWRO's exclusive strategy. As events would soon show, however, a strategy of organizing existing recipients into a national network based on inducements such as special grants could not be sustained. For a few years, campaigns to obtain special grants spread like brush fires across the country; hundreds of groups did form and many hundreds of millions of dollars in benefits were obtained from local welfare departments. But just as suddenly the groups diminished—first in size, then in number—until none were left. Why this happened is clear enough. For one thing, once people received a special grant, many saw no further purpose in affiliating with the organization; moreover a number of state legislatures eventually abolished special grant programs, thus undermining the organizing strategy by shutting off the flow of incentives. In other words, the central dilemma of mass-based, permanent organizing theory—how to sustain continuing participation in the absence of continuing inducements to participation—had not been solved. It was not a new dilemma.

But this would all become clear only later. At the time our differences did not seem so large. While George and others were oriented toward developing a national union of welfare recipients, George did not reject the "crisis strategy": mobilizing drives to double and treble the rolls could be mounted, he argued, once an organizational base of existing recipients had been created.

We agreed that drives among existing recipients to insure that they received all of the benefits to which they were entitled were worth undertaking. In fact, even as these discussions were taking place, we were already involved in organizing such drives in New York City. While other organizers envisaged these benefit campaigns as a way of inducing people to form groups, we were focusing on the hundreds of millions of dollars that could be extracted from the welfare system, thus contributing to a welfare crisis. But whatever the motive, all of us could agree on that particular tactic as a starting point. Most important of all, our discussions were animated by a belief that agitation among the poor around welfare issues had great potential for success, so that differences in strategy seemed less important than the imperative of action itself. In a word, the omens were good; everyone was eager to begin.

And so we took the first steps toward creating a national organization. As George was so fond of saying, "First you make a plan, and then you make it happen."

A Poor People's Organization Is Formed

The plan, briefly, consisted of three steps: to raise money for several staff members and an office in Washington, D.C.; to announce that a "National Welfare Rights Organization" was being formed; and to initiate the process of building the local, state, and national structure of that organization.

All things considered, these steps were taken with remarkable ease and rapidity. On May 23, 1966, George and a staff of four opened an office in Washington, D.C., called the Poverty/Rights Action Center. Some fifteen months later, in August 1967, a founding convention was held, and NWRO was officially formed, with George as its chief executive. In point of fact, however, NWRO existed almost from the day George announced its formation, in

June 1966; the months between then and the founding convention in August 1967 were filled with a variety of activities oriented toward constructing and financing an intricate national structure.

THE FORMATION OF THE NATIONAL WELFARE RIGHTS ORGANIZATION

Of the problems entailed in the formation of NWRO, the most difficult was developing support and resources. To raise money for staff and a national office required that the idea of a "welfare rights organization" gain some degree of legitimacy among potential funding sources and among prominent people who could influence funding sources.

At first, George attempted to interest the Citizens' Crusade Against Poverty (CCAP) in becoming the sponsor. Initiated by Walter Reuther of the United Automobile Workers, CCAP brought together northern leaders—mainly unionists and officials in northern religious denominations—to counteract conservative groups who were seeking to limit the range and forcefulness of federal programs to ameliorate poverty. When George resigned as associate national director of CORE in February 1966, he took a job with CCAP. His first assignment was to build a coalition in support of minimum wage legislation in Congress. During the next few months, as he established contact with a variety of groups across the country, it became evident to him that groups were emerging in the northern ghettos and focusing on such issues as health care, education, the control of antipoverty programs, and, of course, the public welfare system. Since it appeared to him that these grassroots groups were dispersed, uncoordinated, and without an effective means of communicating with one another, he proposed that the CCAP sponsor and fund the formation of a national agency devoted to performing these functions, with a special emphasis on welfare rights organizing. When this proposal was turned down, George made the decision to establish an independent office to perform the same functions, with welfare rights as its initial focus.[18]

---

[18] A detailed and accurate account of these events in the spring of 1966 can be found in Martin (1972, 75–85).

By late May there was about $15,000 in hand. We had obtained $5,000 from a small family foundation; George had received $5,000 from a wealthy contributor to the civil rights movement whom he had known from his CORE days, and he used his own savings of $5,000. With those funds, George and Edwin Day moved with their families to Washington and opened the P/RAC, making this announcement to the press:

> Many activists have left major organizations and are scattered in a myriad of local programs across the country. The tenuous lines of communications which once connected them have been disrupted. We see ourselves as trying to service and help them develop a movement of the poor (Bailis, 15).

At the outset, George still intended P/RAC to act as the national coordinating agency for a wide range of poor people's organizations seeking to influence federal departments and Congress. The stated objectives were these:

1. To develop nationwide support for major anti-poverty and civil rights measures (e.g., to press for "maximum feasible participation" of the poor in the anti-poverty program, and to generate support for a guaranteed annual income).
2. To develop nationwide support for significant local anti-poverty and civil rights movements.
3. To provide surveillance and pressures on federal agencies handling programs designed to help the poor (e.g., to monitor activities and policies of the OEO, the Department of Agriculture, the Department of Labor, HUD, HEW, etc.).
4. To provide advice and assistance to local groups coming to Washington to lobby for support of their programs before federal agencies (Jackson and Johnson, 57).

However broadly its objectives may have been defined, P/RAC soon focused on welfare rights, partly because of our series of discussions, but much more importantly because welfare client groups were springing up by the summer of 1966 and thus George was prompted to move to weld them into a national body.

The first major opportunity to advance the formation of a national welfare rights organization was provided by groups in Ohio who had joined together in the Ohio Committee for Adequate Welfare. In February 1966 organizers from Ohio decided they would stage a 155-mile "Walk for Adequate Welfare" from Cleveland to the steps of the state capitol in Columbus, hoping thereby to generate support for higher welfare payment levels in Ohio. George and a few others worked feverishly in the weeks before the march to spread word of it among welfare groups around the country and to stimulate these groups to hold supporting demonstrations. A meeting was called in Chicago on May 21 of organizers known to be working with welfare recipients, most of them from Detroit, Ann Arbor, Columbus, Cleveland, Syracuse, and especially New York City (where a city-wide organization of WROs had already formed). The results were encouraging and George announced to the press that demonstrations would occur across the country on June 30, the final day of the walk.

On June 20 Reverend Paul Younger and Edith Doering, paid by the Cleveland Council of Churches to organize around welfare issues, led about forty welfare recipients and sympathizers out of Cleveland on the first lap of the 155-mile march to Columbus, there to present complaints about public welfare to Governor Rhodes. As the marchers passed through cities and towns on the route, local recipients, ministers, social workers, and other sympathetic citizens, sometimes hundreds of them, fell in line for a short distance. On the morning of June 30, when they finally reached Columbus, the forty marchers were joined by busloads of recipients from all over Ohio, and some 2,000 protesters led by George paraded down Broad Street to the capitol to argue the case against Ohio's welfare system.

Simultaneous demonstrations occurred elsewhere. In New York 2,000 picketers, most of them recipients, marched in the hot sun while their children played in City Hall Park. And in fifteen other cities, including Baltimore, Washington, Los Angeles, Boston, Louisville, Chicago, Trenton, and San Francisco, some 2,500 people in groups of 25 to 250 demonstrated against "the welfare."

The demonstrations received encouraging coverage in the press, including a statement issued by George announcing "the birth of a movement." Shortly afterwards George called for a national meeting of organizers and recipient leaders to lay the basis for a national organization of welfare rights groups. The meeting convened in Chicago on August 6 and 7; some one hundred people attended, both recipients and organizers. The recipients were from groups that had already formed, ranging from the Mothers for Adequate Welfare in Boston to the Mothers of Watts; from Chicago's Welfare Union of the West Side Organization composed of unemployed black men, to the Committee to Save the Unemployed Fathers of eastern Kentucky. The organizers were members of Students for a Democratic Society, church people, and, most prominently, VISTA and other antipoverty program workers. The conferees voted to establish a National Coordinating Committee of Welfare Rights Groups composed of one welfare recipient from each of the eleven states where welfare organizing had already led to the establishment of groups. This body was mandated to determine policy for the organization, to make recommendations for the further development of a national structure, and to promote and coordinate a series of nationwide welfare campaigns in the fall of 1966. These campaigns were intended to

> . . . feature demands for the right [of welfare groups] to represent recipients before welfare administrations and at hearings; the right to organize and bargain collectively on behalf of recipients, and . . . demand benefits now being illegally denied recipients. The drive will include tactics such as pickets, sit-ins, school boycotts, and the pressing of demands for hearings and court actions. Violations of the law practiced by welfare administrations in denying benefits to recipients, invading the privacy of recipients, and failing to grant fair hearings will be exposed in the campaign (Jackson and Johnson, 59).

From the perspective of national organization building, this meeting was a huge success. George's leadership was acknowledged; his proposal for a national coordinating body composed of recipient leaders was widely and enthusiastically accepted by the representatives of disparate groups of recipients and organizers; and local organizations agreed to join in nationally sponsored campaigns. A national poor people's organization was clearly in the making.

This meeting, like others to follow in the first three years, was characterized by spirit, militancy, anger, and hope, which bordered on pandemonium. The chairpersons of the various sessions could not hold to the agendas or maintain parliamentary order. People just rose up from their seats—organizers and recipients alike—and lined up at the microphones, as many as twenty or thirty at a time. One after another they condemned "the welfare" for its abuses: for grant levels so low that nothing was left after the rent was paid, for capricious and punitive rejections and terminations, for invasions of homes, for insults to dignity. The early meetings were like rallies, full of indignation and full of joy that the occasion had finally come for the people to rise up against the source of their indignation.

New groups formed rapidly, mainly in the densely packed ghettos of the midwestern and northeastern cities. The civil rights struggle in the North provided a context that encouraged group formation, as this personal account reveals:[19]

> When I first came on welfare, I was ashamed, because society has taught us to be ashamed . . . you are taught it from childhood. We were taught that welfare was begging, charity . . . so I hid it. I heard about the Milwaukee Welfare Rights Organization through a cousin of mine. She kept trying to get me to go to these meetings with her and I said, "No, I'd never go to anything like that. . . ." In the meantime, Milwaukee was having civil rights marches . . . and my kids were growing up . . . so they told me that they were going on the marches for civil rights. Well, I was afraid of those kinds of things . . . but when the kids decided that they were going . . . I had to go with them. . . . I noticed that when we went on the marches, we were the ones being fired upon with rocks and bricks and sticks, but it was as if we were doing the provoking when they put it on the news. So I started reading the black papers. I started reading things in a different light. . . . Then I joined this [welfare rights] organization . . . (Milwaukee Welfare Rights Organization, 25–26).

NWRO stimulated this development all the more by producing and distributing thousands of brochures entitled "Build Organization!" The workers in antipoverty programs were especially responsive to the call to organize. Perhaps three-quarters of all welfare rights organizers were antipoverty workers, many of them VISTAs.

As client insurgency spread, further steps were taken to consolidate a national structure. In December 1966 the National Coordinating Committee met in Chicago and designated P/RAC as the headquarters of the National Welfare Rights Organization, thus further buttressing George's claim to leadership of the mushrooming welfare rights phenomenon. In addition a conference was called for the following February in Washington, D.C. More than 350 recipients and organizers were attracted to this meeting, representing some 200 WROs in seventy cities and twenty-six states. A national legislative program was developed to be presented to HEW and to Con-

---

[19] This account of the process by which civil rights demonstrations helped influence an AFDC mother to become a NWRO participant actually refers to a slightly later period in the 1960s. The slight time difference is irrelevant, for if accounts were available from an earlier period, they would also reveal the important role of the civil rights struggle in the formation of NWRO.

gress. Workshops on a variety of subjects were held: "How to Form a Group"; "Staging a Demonstration"; "Raising Money"; "Techniques of Lobbying"; and the like. Plans were laid for a nationwide series of "special needs" campaigns (i.e., campaigns to obtain grants of money for clothing and household furnishings) to be conducted throughout the country during the spring, and to culminate in simultaneous local demonstrations once again on June 30.

Special grant campaigns followed throughout the spring and millions of dollars were obtained by recipients. As planned, simultaneous demonstrations once again occurred on June 30 and it fairly could be said that a national organization had come into being. Tim Sampson, who subsequently became NWRO's associate director, assumed the major role in promoting these nationwide organizing campaigns.

Meanwhile the National Coordinating Committee had reconvened in April to adopt the membership and delegate rules that would lay the basis for a formal national structure. (Any group, it was decided, of at least twenty-five recipients that forwarded annual dues of $1 per person to the national office was entitled to elect a delegate to future national conventions.)[20] The official founding convention took place in August 1967 in Washington, D.C. It is a measure of the extent to which local groups already conformed to the membership, dues-paying, and delegate-designating rules laid down by the National Coordinating Committee that 178 delegates and alternates representing approximately seventy-five WROs in forty-five cities and twenty-one states attended to adopt a constitution, elect national officers, and endorse a set of goals, all to form the National Welfare Rights Organization—the first national relief organization since the Great Depression. Many other welfare rights groups existed and some of them sent representatives to the conference as well. But they had yet to conform with national rules (electing officers, paying dues, etc.) and thus were barred from official participation. In time most would conform and affiliate.

Briefly, the overall structure consisted of a National Convention which was to convene every two years; it was to establish broad policy and elect nine officers who would compose an Executive Committee.

---

[20] For every 25 to 49 members, one delegate and one alternate; for 50 to 99 members, three delegates and three alternates; for each additional 100 members, one additional delegate and alternate.

During the off years, a National Conference would be held to formulate policy. Between meetings of these bodies, the National Coordinating Committee, which consisted of one delegate and one alternate from each state affiliated with NWRO, together with the members of the Executive Committee, would meet to establish policy. Generally speaking, the Executive Committee was to meet about eight times annually and the National Coordinating Committee about four times. NWRO rules required that all groups in each state convene to create a roughly parallel state structure and to vote for a state delegate and alternate to the National Coordinating Committee. In large cities such as New York similar coordinating and delegate bodies were also created. In a very short time, in other words, NWRO had developed a nationwide, statewide, and sometimes citywide system of structures.

As the membership data in the accompanying table reveal, however, this intricate national structure was created before a national mass base had emerged. In 1967, when the details of the structure were being completed, NWRO had 5,000 dues-paying families. In 1969 when the membership base reached its peak, about 22,000 persons paid dues:

> The states with the largest membership were, in descending order, New York, California, Pennsylvania, Michigan, Virginia, Massachusetts, Ohio, New Jersey, and Illinois. When broken down by cities, New York City had by far the largest membership; there were more members in Brooklyn than in any other city in the country. Boston groups had the second largest total membership, while Detroit, Los Angeles, and Chicago completed the list of the five top cities (Bailis, 11).

But, distribution of members aside, the point is that NWRO's dues-paying membership never exceeded the level of 22,000 reached in 1969; thereafter the membership rolls declined rapidly.

NWRO's inability to enlarge its base, or to sustain the modest base it had succeeded in developing, was first and most dramatically revealed in New York. In 1967, 51 percent of NWRO's membership was located in New York; when the national membership doubled in the next year, the proportion of the total membership contributed by New York dropped to 17 percent, which meant that the absolute number of members dropped as well. By the spring of 1969 the New York organization had collapsed. That was an ominous sign, to say the least. What it revealed is that NWRO's organizing strategy could not overcome problems of organizational maintenance. More-over precisely the same problems of maintenance beset the Massa-chusetts organization shortly after the New York organization de-clined; by 1970 the Massachusetts organization had also collapsed. Since New York City and Boston were by far the most important urban strongholds of the movement and since their organizing strategy was being emulated throughout the country, we turn to the question of why these organizations did not survive (and why dozens of other WROs which adopted a similar strategy also eventually failed).

Approximate Membership of National Welfare Rights Organization (Number of Family Heads Paying Dues)

PLACE	1967	1968	1969[21]
U.S.	5,000	10,000	22,500
N.Y. City	2,550	5,870	4,030
Brooklyn	1,350	3,370	2,440
Queens	100	380	330
Manhattan	1,070	1,400	500
Bronx	30	720	760

The Problem of Maintaining a Mass Membership

Our analysis of NWRO's demise has been undertaken in four parts. In the present section, the problem of maintaining a mass member-ship is considered. Then we examine, in turn, the problems created by the elaborate internal leadership structure on which the organiza-tion came to rely; the problems resulting from external leadership incentives; and, finally, the problems flowing from the ebbing of mass unrest in American society toward the late 1960s. Together

---

21 An internal NWRO document prepared to calculate delegate strength for the con-vention in 1969 revealed that there were 523 local groups throughout the United States, of which 376 had the required twenty-five dues-paying members (Jackson and Johnson, 116). Whitaker also confirms these figures (180).

these problems eventually destroyed the organization. In the interim before that happened, however, the organization was slowly transformed: political beliefs became more conventional, militancy diminished, and the membership base dwindled.

BUILDING ORGANIZATION BY SOLVING INDIVIDUAL GRIEVANCES

Welfare rights organizing throughout the country relied primarily on solving the grievances of existing recipients as an organizing technique. This approach usually worked to build groups, for grievances were legion. Families were often capriciously denied access to benefits, or failed to receive checks, or received less than they were entitled to, or were arbitrarily terminated, or were abused and demeaned by welfare workers. The promise that such grievances could be solved brought recipients together.

Grievances were dealt with in a variety of ways. In the beginning organizers often performed the grievance work, thereby demonstrating that the complexities of welfare regulations could be mastered and that welfare personnel could be made to give in.[22] Gradually some welfare recipients were schooled in the regulations and in techniques of representing other recipients. Some groups placed tables in welfare waiting rooms or on the streets outside with signs announcing the offer of assistance to people who were experiencing difficulty in the centers. Some of the more structured groups established "grievance committees" to which families with problems were referred.

The most effective tactic was to stage group actions on grievances. A group of recipients descended on the welfare center to hold a demonstration, demanding that all grievances be settled before the group left, with the threat that a sit-in would follow if the demand were not met. These actions generally succeeded, for with the ghettos of the cities seething, welfare officials feared confrontations. Organizers and recipients understood this vulnerability and capital-

---

[22] An interesting discussion on the role of organizers in demonstrating that welfare personnel could be made to yield is contained in the accounts of welfare rights in Mississippi (Kurzman).

ized on it. If welfare officials tried to cope with demonstrators by
saying that some of the grievances would be dealt with immediately
but that others would have to wait, the demonstrators often refused
to leave. They sensed the importance of standing together and they
were alert to the dangers of being dealt with one by one in back
offices removed from the tumult of the waiting rooms. Organizers
and leaders usually tried to reinforce this intuition by reaching
agreements in advance that no one would leave until everyone's
problems had been solved; during the demonstration, group pressure
reinforced that agreement. This principle heightened solidarity,[23]
helping to engender the feeling that the welfare of each depended
upon the welfare of all. It encouraged people to act altruistically, to
act at the expense of their immediate self-interest. And, of course,
this emphasis on the group acting together heightened the feeling
that group struggle was effective. These general observations are
corroborated by studies in various locales, as in the following example from Massachusetts:

> When Massachusetts WRO grievance workers came across cases in
> which the prospects of success were particularly dim, they invited
> the member to accompany them to the next demonstration at her
> welfare office. In the heat of welfare office confrontations, many
> members proved to be more willing to help their fellow members
> than one would have guessed. . . . In part, they may have realized
> that they too might be involved in a similar situation in the future
> and would like others to pitch in and help them. But for the most
> part, the decision to stay and fight for others after one's own
> demands were met appeared to represent a feeling of "community"
> emerging in demonstrations. In the heat of the confrontation situa-
> tion, a high proportion of recipients appeared to derive satisfaction
> from declaring their solidarity with others involved in heated strug-
> gle with "the common enemy" and from seeing caseworkers back-
> ing down regardless of whether they personally gained tangible
> benefits or not (Bailis, 64).

The objective of these activities for most organizers and recipient
leaders, as well as for the national staff, was to expand membership
affiliation. In effect this meant insisting that recipients join a group,

---

[23] It also produced outraged responses from welfare directors, often in the form of
press releases or internal memoranda to welfare staff members declaring that "our
clients" are being "coerced" or "used" or "manipulated" or "exploited."

the democracy worked
too well? Too much empowerment?

299   *The Welfare Rights Movement*

pay dues, and accept a membership card before their grievances
would be attended to. The reasoning was that by conditioning assistance on affiliation, stable group membership would result. For the
most part organizers and local leaders followed this dictum:

> People who come in to the city-wide offices and want help are
> first asked to join DMWRO (Detroit Metropolitan Welfare Rights
> Organization). They join up on a group basis according to where
> they live. They are required to pay two dollars on the spot and
> their name is forwarded to the local group which is located in
> their area. One dollar goes to the local group for NWRO dues
> and the other dollar goes to DMWRO. They are also told when
> the next meeting is scheduled and where it is to be held. Then we
> see what we can do about their welfare problem if they have one
> (Martin, 158).

However, WROs did not become permanent. Nor is there any
evidence that groups which strictly followed the procedure of conditioning help on affiliation, as against those which did not, lasted
any longer; most lasted a year or two at best, whatever the organizing techniques. There are a number of reasons why this turned out
to be the case.

First, most families who benefitted from a grievance action then
dropped out of the group simply because they no longer needed
assistance. To be sure, recipients returned from time to time as
new grievances arose, but most did not participate in any continuous way in the life of the organization. "The basic problem with
grievance work was that a settled grievance, like other fulfilled
needs, left no further incentive to contribute to the group" (Bailis,
65). Moreover, as the welfare rights organizations created a body of
recipients who were experienced in dealing with the welfare system,
many of these individuals found that they no longer required the
aid of the group in solving their individual problems or those of
their friends and neighbors. They simply acted on their own, a
circumstance that continually depleted the ranks of organized groups.

Second, grievance work required an enormous investment of time
and staff or recipient effort:

> A recipient called the office (in Chicago) and said her caseworker
> had cut her welfare off. I called the caseworker and told her what
> she did was illegal and asked if she had heard of the December 1969
> law that recipients could not be cut off without notification. This
> was the Golliday decision. The caseworker said she would talk to her

supervisor. I went by the recipient's house and we went to the welfare office to file an appeal and talk to the caseworker. The caseworker was sorry but she couldn't do anything. She said she cut the aid because the woman's rent receipts had different signatures. The next day I got a VISTA lawyer to tell the caseworker about the new law. The caseworker still didn't do anything and the lawyer told her he would go to court. Then the caseworker asked him to talk to the district office supervisor. The lawyer did and the supervisor released the woman's check (Martin, 156).

Such work was also extremely tedious. There were satisfactions, to be sure, especially those deriving from the sense that one has rendered a service to another human being, and there were recipients who gained deep gratification from the effort. But on the whole the recipients who enjoyed this work were not numerous, and as the months and years dragged by it became increasingly difficult to sustain grievance activities except by continually training new cadres to replace those who wearied and dropped out.

Grievance activities were perhaps less tedious when the entire group was involved. But this method literally absorbed the whole of the group's energies and resources. However useful this strategy may have been in maintaining solidarity and in securing favorable responses from the welfare system, it nevertheless severely limited the scale of grievance work and thus the success of organizing itself. Consequently groups showed little expansion of membership once a level of fifty to one hundred had been reached.

It might also be noted that grievance work was a natural avenue to positions of leadership, for serving others provided a way of building a constituency. But once the grievance worker had succeeded in being elected to office, she usually came to be preoccupied with the responsibilities and satisfactions of that office. And since the leadership of these groups tended to be stable, new grievance workers could not similarly entertain the hope of winning office through service to others. This circumstance made the drudgery of grievance work all the less attractive.

Finally, one consequence of the grievance strategy was the gradual evolution of formal arrangements with welfare departments for the solving of these problems. Just how this came about will be taken up in a subsequent section. It is sufficient to say here that once such arrangements developed, groups needed to rely less and less upon collective action in order to secure responses from the welfare system. The consequence was to subdue militancy, to create recipient leaders who had a large investment in the maintenance of their privileged relationship to the welfare system, and to diminish efforts to organize new members.

In summary, individual grievance strategies produced a rapid proliferation of WROs across the country in the period between 1966 and 1970. But these groups rarely exceeded one hundred members. Moreover the membership of these core groups showed high turnover. Thus individual grievance work failed to build a mass membership.

BUILDING ORGANIZATION BY SOLVING
COLLECTIVE GRIEVANCES

If individual grievance work did not appear to have the potential for building a mass membership, action on collective grievances did appear to, at least for a while. These actions were based on the regulations of some welfare departments which provided special grants, in addition to regular food and rent grants, for clothing and household furnishings as needed. Few people knew about these provisions, even fewer applied for them, and still fewer received them. Since these were forms of assistance for which large numbers of recipients were ostensibly eligible, they presented the possibility that collective actions could be mounted to solve hundreds and perhaps thousands of grievances at one time, thus bringing large numbers of families into local WROs with a minimum of organizing investment.

Experiments with this form of collective grievance action were first conducted in 1965 by a few organizers affiliated with Mobilization for Youth on New York's Lower East Side.[24] They were extremely successful: when confronted with fifty or one hundred recipients demanding special grants, the district welfare offices in New York City conceded and checks were issued. By the spring of 1967 the tactic had spread to most of the antipoverty agencies in the city and to some settlement houses and churches as well. Literally

---

[24] See Rabagliati and Birnbaum, and Birnbaum and Gilman, for a description of Mobilization for Youth's campaigns.

thousands of people joined in special grant demonstrations. As these actions multiplied, a central office was created to stimulate the growth of more demonstrations throughout the city and the New York City-wide Coordinating Committee of Welfare Groups was formed.[25]

For organizers the main purpose of these campaigns was to build a permanent organization of welfare recipients. Thus the campaigns were intended to "enable local groups to establish their organizational validity among their constituents, and to establish their role as the representative of individual clients at the local welfare center . . ." (Birnbaum and Gilman,1). This way of thinking partly reflected a concern with controlling the outcome of a welfare crisis. As one organizer put it, "Without 'client power,' when the system is bankrupt, we are still dependent on those in power to establish a new system" (quoted in Sardell, 47).

The special grant campaigns and the formation of the City-wide organization generated enormous excitement among activists and AFDC recipients. Weekly meetings called by City-wide were attended by larger and larger numbers of recipients, antipoverty organizers, and antipoverty attorneys. At these sessions the spirit of a movement began to develop; training sessions in the details of conducting special grant campaigns were conducted, and plans for demonstrations—either simultaneously in dozens of district offices or jointly at the central welfare offices—were agreed upon. In addition tens of thousands of kits of special grant campaign literature were distributed—the main piece being a mimeographed checklist of the items of clothing and household furnishings people were supposed to have (according to welfare regulations). These checklists were distributed by local organizers, people filled them out and returned them, and they were then bundled up and presented to district welfare office directors in the course of countless demonstrations.

As new individuals or groups heard about the campaigns and made inquiries of City-wide, they were generally advised to proceed in the same way:

> City-wide strategists developed a formula for local groups to use in their organizing efforts. Groups' members were to leaflet outside welfare centers and to talk to clients about welfare entitlements. Recipients would be encouraged to join local groups and to attend

---

[25] See Jackson and Johnson, and Sardell. In these sources the City-wide special grant campaigns are described in detail.

meetings where "welfare rights" and special grants would be discussed. Special grant forms would be filled out and the group would
return to the welfare center with the forms and hold demonstrations for immediate action on the grants (Sardell, 55).

Recipients were also encouraged in this period to file a "fair hearing"
request form with their special grant form. This put the welfare
department on notice that if the special grant request were denied,
justification for that decision would have to be made at a hearing
held before a state official. In 1964 there had been fourteen fair hearings throughout the entire state; sixteen in 1965 and twenty in 1966.
However, under the impact of City-wide's fair hearing strategy in
1967, 4,233 fair hearing forms were filed:

> In 1967 there was a virtual explosion in fair hearings requests. This
> explosion resulted primarily from the activities of the organized
> client movement. Almost all new requests were from New York
> City. . . . This increase in requests led to the appointment of four
> additional hearings officers and, in December 1967, the opening
> of the New York City Office of Fair Hearings. Clients were repre-
> sented at the hearings by lawyers, volunteer law students, and some
> trained lay advocates. . . . Over 3,000 hearings were scheduled
> between September and January. However, 90 percent of these
> hearings never occurred. Oftentimes, local centers contacted clients
> before the dates scheduled for their fair hearings and granted their
> requests for special grants. In one-half of the cases in which hearings
> were actually held, clients received substantially all of their requests,
> while most of the remaining clients received at least partial grants
> (Jackson and Johnson, 114).

By the late fall of 1967 this organizing formula had produced a
mass movement among welfare recipients in New York's ghettos
and barrios.

The militancy in this period was high. AFDC mothers (often
with their children in tow) staged hundreds of sit-ins and confrontations at the district welfare offices in Brooklyn, Manhattan, Queens,
and the Bronx. These local demonstrations ranged from 25 to 500
persons. When demonstrations at the central welfare offices were
called, from 500 to 2,000 appeared. Social workers, welfare workers,
and other sympathizers sometimes joined in. Sit-ins, which often
accompanied the demonstrations, sometimes lasted for several days.
Scores of arrests occurred, although generally city officials were loath
to arrest recipients in those turbulent times; instead, they issued
checks. By the spring and summer of 1968, when the special grant

campaigns reached their zenith, the welfare department had found it necessary to establish a "war room" in its central offices filled with telephones and staff members whose job it was to keep abreast of the constant demonstrations taking place in the city's several dozen district offices.

George was so impressed with the organization-building potential of these campaigns that the national organization began to push this strategy across the country. In the spring of 1967 the national office prepared special kits of colorfully printed materials to be used by local groups ("DEFEND YOUR FAMILY!"; "MORE MONEY NOW!"), and worked vigorously to promote campaigns. Soon there were national campaigns in the late summer for school clothing, in the fall for winter clothing, in the spring for Easter clothing or school graduation clothing. Household furnishing campaigns also proliferated, spurred in part because so few recipients had adequate bedding and other items.

However, Massachusetts was the only state, other than New York, where genuinely large-scale campaigns resulted.[26] Millions of dollars resulted from the campaigns in Massachusetts beginning in the summer of 1968. "Welfare Department figures indicated in the Boston area alone, $250,000 was disbursed in July, $600,000 in August, and $3,000,000 in September" (Fiske, 37, 96). When the Massachusetts commissioner of welfare was called before a legislative committee in mid-August to justify this enlarging outflow of welfare monies, he replied: "If anyone had been at Roxbury Crossing in June 1967, when a riot occurred, he would have noticed some of the same elements here at the welfare office on July 30, 1968" (quoted in Fiske, 34). Still, there was considerable difficulty getting checks issued. One welfare center issued checks and then voided them; another placed police blockades before its doors, allowing only ten recipients to enter at a time; other offices simply shut down in response to client turbulence. The militancy of the demonstrations also intensified:

> Thus . . . when fifty recipients returned to Roxbury Crossing Center (in November) twelve telephones were ripped out, eight offices were "ransacked," social workers were "verbally abused," and one was shoved against the wall. The nonprofessional union members

---

26 The most detailed descriptions of the special grant campaigns in Massachusetts are contained in Fiske and in Bailis.

were instructed to walk-out under police escort; forty social workers left immediately for the State Welfare Headquarters to protest their harassment; and the police escorted the director out of the center at 12:30 p.m. Thus another office closed early for the day (Fiske, 56).

The demonstrations throughout Massachusetts were the most consistently militant of any in the country. One demonstration in Springfield led to a riot. Fiske again quotes an organizer:

> When the director announced that people would be arrested if they didn't leave the Center, the protesting recipients asked the students to go outside. Once outside, there were no bullhorns and no one directing the masses. When the paddy wagon arrived, the protestors outside thought the recipients inside were being arrested and, consequently, started rocking the paddy wagon. The police started shoving people inside and then drove through the crowds at a dangerous speed. The crowd became enraged and started throwing rocks and bottles at the wagon (89).

At that moment, the Springfield riot began, and Bill Pastreich, MWRO's chief organizer, was arrested for the twelfth time, with bail set at $3,000.

THE ABOLITION OF SPECIAL GRANTS

As special grants campaigns mushroomed throughout the country, local and state governments began to respond by instituting "flat grant" systems. It was an inevitable development. By this simple device the rising costs of special grant disbursements were curbed and the welfare rights organizations were severely crippled. New York State was first to institute this "reform," for a vast reservoir of potential claimants still existed to be tapped, posing what the *New York Times* editorially called a "threat to [New York City's] treasury." To keep the lid on welfare costs welfare officials in New York City began to redesign the special grant system, proposing to "reform" it by substituting an "automatic grant" of $100 per year payable in quarterly installments of $25 to each recipient.

In June the State Board of Social Welfare approved the plan, allowing it to go into effect on September 1. The reasons were candidly given when Hugh R. Jones, chairman of the State Board of Social Welfare, announced that the automatic grant reform would both "stabilize outgoing expenditures" and "very seriously handicap" the welfare recipients' organization. Throughout the summer and fall discussions were held among City-wide WRO leaders and advisors to develop a strategy to counter these developments. Three options were considered at one time or another. One was to continue to mount militant demonstrations in the local centers to keep the welfare system in chaos and to threaten the possibility of wider chaos in the ghettos if the plan were implemented. This strategy was attempted, but half-heartedly. A second option—one which we proposed—was to mount a "spend-the-rent" campaign. By spending their rent welfare recipients could circumvent the income reduction represented by the automatic grant; what the city and state saved, the clients would more than recoup. In the heat of the moment this option was approved, but the recipient leadership did nothing to implement it. For a few weeks the threat of a rent strike campaign served certain rhetorical purposes.

Instead, the recipient leadership opted for a lobbying campaign in Albany, the state capital. In large part this decision evolved because of promises of support by various middle-class groups in the city: some church confederations, several upper-middle-class women's civic groups, women's peace groups, a confederation of settlement houses, and the like. Throughout the fall of 1968 City-wide mobilized for the lobbying campaign which culminated in a "bus caravan" to Albany where political leaders generally avoided meeting with recipient delegations. The lobbying campaign was put together at great expense of time and money and totally consumed the resources of the City-wide organization. The response by the legislature was to cut grant levels about 10 percent.

The last major protest demonstration occurred on April 15, 1969. About 5,000 persons, most of them welfare workers, antipoverty staff, students, and other sympathizers, assembled in Central Park for a rally and then marched down Fifth Avenue. On 42nd Street between Fifth and Madison Avenues, the demonstrators sat down, clogging traffic for several hours, and Hulbert James, New York's chief welfare rights organizer, was pulled down from a lamp post from which he was addressing the crowd and charged with inciting to riot. That demonstration was the end of the resistance campaign in New York. By then local WROs were already weakened and the relief centers had been largely abandoned. The course of events was no different in Massachusetts:

The relationship between the institution of the flat grant and welfare rights organizing was treated fairly candidly in Massachusetts. The MWRO activities received considerable coverage in the newspapers and on radio and television. . . . Many people in Massachusetts apparently associated welfare rights demonstrations with rising welfare costs and assumed the former caused the latter, all of which served to make welfare an increasingly controversial public issue. A number of state legislators gained publicity by investigating alleged welfare fraud and by introducing bills to cut welfare costs. The governor made his ability to resist welfare demonstrators and his institution of the flat grant a major issue in his re-election campaign in 1970. Three of his radio advertisements mentioned welfare demonstrators and one of them was entirely devoted to an explanation of the flat grant (Bailis, 142).

As in New York, the Massachusetts welfare rights group joined together with sympathetic liberal groups in the Massachusetts Welfare Coalition. This coalition was composed mainly of religious and social welfare groups and lacked sufficient influence to block the flat grant decision. The welfare rights organization in Massachusetts soon fell into disarray. Other states also instituted flat grants in this period; it was a simple and successful way to simultaneously undermine organizing among the poor and curb welfare costs.

MOBILIZING VERSUS ORGANIZING

There was one major difference in the approach to building welfare rights groups in New York and Massachusetts, a difference about which much was made by organizers throughout the country in this period. In New York, little stress was placed on creating dues-paying groups (except in Brooklyn under the leadership of organizer Rhoda Linton); the opposite was the case in Massachusetts. George strongly favored the latter procedure. The issue first arose in 1967 after NWRO was officially formed and a program of nationwide special grant campaigns had been announced. George's view was that welfare recipients should not be afforded access to special grant information, forms, and assistance unless they first joined a group and paid dues. A number of us in New York opposed this requirement, believing that the impact on the welfare system would be much greater if information about the availability of the special grants was disseminated as widely as possible through antipoverty agencies, settlement houses, churches, and civil rights groups. In New York, our view prevailed, and the subsequent campaigns were much looser affairs than occurred in most other places.

In Massachusetts, however, a different model of organizing developed. It became known widely in welfare rights circles as the "Boston Model," and it was just as widely emulated throughout the country. Strict emphasis was placed on formal group affiliation as a prerequisite to receiving any form of assistance. Sometimes, for example, special grant applications were not distributed to recipients until they were actually on the welfare premises as part of a demonstration. It was assumed that stable, enduring groups evolved from this approach. However, the detailed inquiry by Bailis of events in Massachusetts reveals that stable groups did not in fact develop. Often they did not survive from one special grant campaign to another:

> The Boston Model organizing drives almost invariably produced successful first meetings and first confrontations. But few of the local groups created in those drives were able to maintain their momentum—or their membership—for very long. Despite a spectacular birth and a vigorous youth consisting of well-attended meetings and militant demonstrations, the typical MWRO affiliate soon moved into a period of doldrums, marked by a lingering death. The life cycle was a relatively short one. . . . For most of its history, the MWRO was able to disguise its inability to maintain local group strength by concentrating its efforts upon repeated Boston Model organizing drives and thus constantly created new groups to replace those that were falling by the wayside. These new groups helped to maintain the MWRO membership rolls, to provide the bulk of the participants in statewide demonstrations, and to keep the welfare rights movement in the headlines (55).

Moreover, Bailis asserts that "most MWRO affiliates were moribund long before the institution of the flat grant" in Massachusetts (60).

The "Boston Model" required a much greater investment of organizing resources than was true of the "mobilizing model" followed in New York. MWRO successfully attracted a large number of students to perform organizing tasks; it also had a VISTA training contract, and the VISTAs were trained in welfare organizing. In New York, there were relatively fewer organizers. But no matter: WROs did not persist in either state, and that is the main point.

The Consequences of Internal
Leadership Structures

The collapse of welfare rights organizing in New York and Massachusetts was deeply troubling, both because some of the nation's most liberal political leaders held office in those states, and because the organized recipient bases in both states were NWRO's largest. If a strategy of building a mass membership by extracting special grants from the welfare system failed under these conditions, what then of the fate that awaited organizing efforts in places with more conservative political leaders and fewer recipients?[27] The groups that remained were widely scattered throughout the United States; few contained as many as fifty members. In fact by 1970 these groups had also begun to falter. One reason was the development of an elaborate organizational structure, and the constraining influence of this structure on NWRO's leadership.

The development of an organizational structure had immediate consequences for welfare rights groups. The ease and rapidity with which the organization came into being validated the belief in mass-based organization doctrine, in the potential for political influence through organization. Although most WROs had only a small dues-paying membership—ranging from twenty-five to seventy-five members—there were upwards of 500 groups throughout the country toward the late 1960s, each of which was permitted to send at least one delegate and alternate to national conferences and conventions. Consequently, these national meetings were populated by hundreds of recipient delegates and alternates, and by equally large numbers of organizers, all of which conveyed the impression that the welfare rights struggle was being conducted by grassroots forces of massive proportions. (Welfare rights demonstrations throughout the country also received a fair amount of press coverage and this, too, helped buttress convictions regarding the viability of traditional organizing doctrine.) Thus it was generally thought that the welfare rights

---

[27] The success of the campaigns in New York and Massachusetts was not duplicated in most other places. In Detroit demonstrations for school clothing grants led political officials to shut down the welfare department temporarily. In Chicago the geographical boundaries of the district offices were changed to isolate and confine the area where welfare rights agitation was greatest, thus making it easier to cope with demonstrations (Martin, 126, 161–163).

struggle was burgeoning, was vital, was making gains, despite the demise of mass benefit campaigns. But the truth is that the development of a complex organizational structure at the neighborhood, city, state, and national levels was an inhibiting force from the outset. In particular, it inhibited the expansion of membership.

The elaboration of organization meant the elaboration of leadership positions on the neighborhood, city, and state levels. Once groups had formed and affiliated with NWRO and leaders had been duly elected, these leadership positions became a source of intense preoccupation and competition. Considering the hard and dreary lives which most welfare recipients had previously led, the rewards of prestige and organizational influence which accrued to those who could win and hold office were enormous. An equally enormous investment in the politics of leadership naturally followed. These circumstances constrained the expansion of membership, for the leaders came to have an investment in membership stasis.

Recipient leaders at all levels of the organization had to be periodically reelected; new members represented a threat. Struggles for leadership succession might ensue; existing leaders might be toppled. Once a group had formed and developed an acknowledged leadership stratum, therefore, the leaders tended to focus on cultivating and strengthening their ties within the group. City and state representatives were similarly preoccupied; they concentrated on cultivating and strengthening their ties with local leaders in their city or state. Consequently leaders resisted new membership organizing ventures, as this example reveals:

> The Massachusetts Welfare Rights staff pressed for a provision in the state-wide organization's by-laws that voting strength for each local group at the annual conventions would be proportional to the number of dues-paying members it had in the hope that this would give all recipient leaders seeking higher office an incentive to build their membership. Unfortunately, once that higher office had been attained, and until just before the next convention, there was little reason for most recipient leaders to pay much attention to maintaining or expanding their groups. Some lay leaders opposed staff efforts to revitalize their groups partly because of their fear that the new membership faction might hold potential challengers to the incumbent's chairmanship. At times, leaders of a dwindling group agreed to new organizing drives but stipulated that no new local elections be held. In such cases, stalemates oc-

curred; the MWRO staff refused to help recruit new members under these conditions.

Opposition to staff plans for major new organizing drives in those sections of Boston's black ghetto that had not yet been organized was opposed by the predominantly black MWRO leadership who, in part, feared the creation of new centers of power in the organization. In one case, such a drive took place only because the MWRO Executive Board members felt sure that those who would be elected leaders of the new group would respect their seniority. In another, the worst fears of the Executive Board were realized when the chairman of a newer black group in Roxbury challenged and defeated the incumbent MWRO statewide chairman at the 1970 MWRO convention (Bailis, 72–73).

Problems of leadership maintenance were also the chief cause of resistance among WROs to organizing recipients from other relief categories—such as the aged and working poor. In 1968 we had published an article entitled "Workers and Welfare" in which we estimated that hundreds of thousands of working poor families were eligible for relief supplements from "general assistance" programs in the welfare systems of the northern states. In some of these states, such as New York, a large family with a minimum wage income could obtain a wage supplement that would have doubled its income. We thus advocated campaigns to swell the general assistance rolls.[28] In conversations with both George and other leaders, however, it became clear that there was no longer any interest in producing a welfare disruption. The earlier idea that a welfare recipients' organization would also become the vehicle for mobilizing drives to recruit potential recipients to the relief rolls was all but forgotten. Instead exclusive priority was placed on building the existing organization, for by this time George and others were convinced that a mass-based national union of welfare recipients was in fact coming into being. He thus chose "to play down disruptive tactics, at least for the time being, and [to put] a first emphasis on building up a dues-paying organization . . . (Steiner, 290).[29]

---

[28] This article is reprinted in Cloward and Piven, 1974.

[29] NWRO's top leadership frequently complained that the main reason they did not mount enrollment campaigns is that no one knew how to do it. Echoing this criticism, Steiner says: "The real difficulty is that Cloward and Piven do not explain how to get all the eligible poor people on the rolls . . . they leave unanswered the crucial question: how to find, motivate and sustain these people while they are getting on

But George was excited about the possibility of organizing among people in other relief categories, such as the working-poor and aged recipients. He was beginning to believe that NWRO's membership base was too narrow, that an organization consisting exclusively of AFDC recipients would inevitably fail to attract substantial support from groups with influence and money and other resources. And it would inevitably be hampered in its efforts to exert political influence by the stigma associated with AFDC mothers. The broader base he envisioned would not only consist of other categories of relief recipients, but of the unemployed as well. He also wanted to expand from the focus on welfare issues to include agitation around other governmental programs that affected the poor (such as publicly assisted health programs). Moreover, George had developed a network of contacts and goodwill which led him to think that many groups (for example, existing organizations of the aged, of tenants, and of the unemployed) could be brought together in a single national structure under his general direction. It was a vision of mass-based, multi-constituency, multi-issue, permanent organization writ large. But that is not our point. The point is that he wanted NWRO's recipient leadership and central office staff to endorse the concept of incorporating new groups.

Largely at his urging, therefore, the recipient delegates at NWRO's convention in 1969 voted to extend formal membership eligibility to all people with incomes below NWRO's adequate income standard, which was then $5,500 for a four person family; previously, only AFDC recipients had been eligible for membership. George was elated: "The big thing is . . . that membership is going to be based on income from now on. Any family that gets less than $5,500 a year can join. I think these people will join. We want to reach all poor people; we've got to grow . . ." (Martin, 129). This theme was reiterated in his opening address one year later at the convention in Pittsburgh:

> Our political strength hasn't really been felt yet. We've been organizing, building, and demonstrating for an adequate income for

---

the rolls" (297). On the contrary, "these people" did not have to be "found" or "motivated"; they were flooding the welfare centers with millions of applications, and many were being turned away. To have located and aided them in fighting through the eligibility process, one had only to go to the welfare centers across the nation. But Steiner also says (without recognizing the contradiction) that NWRO's leadership had little time for the welfare centers because they were preoccupied with "bureaucrats, scholars, and lobbyists in all-day conferences to plan welfare changes . . ." (285).

all Americans, whether they're on welfare or not, and we're serving notice that we expect to escalate that strategy. We're going to have even more people in our movement, and we're going to attack more of the real problems in this country, like the lack of adequate health care. We have got to get it together on health rights and medical care and with the people who don't make an adequate income but don't get welfare either, and with the aged, and with the disabled—all those people who don't know their rights yet (Martin, 130).

While it is true that the national recipient leadership and much of the organizing staff acquiesced to the changes in constitution and rhetoric, it was also true that they had no incentive to act on them. It took little organizational acumen to anticipate that a diversified constituency would lead ineluctably to struggles for leadership. Persons from other relief categories, for example, differed by age or by sex from AFDC recipients, and they were oriented to different problems involving different relief programs. Had they been brought into the organization, they would surely have pressed for the nomination of leaders with characteristics similar to their own, and with interests similar to their own. Organizing drives among these categories would have enlarged and diversified the membership base, to be sure, but the very existence of an elaborate formal leadership structure precluded that possibility. Consequently, resistance to the implementation of proposals for new organizing drives was mounted at all levels of the organization, a circumstance which George took note of during an interview in 1970:

> We are trying to branch out beyond ADC mothers but we've had little success so far. . . . The ADC mothers, naturally enough, are interested in ADC issues and they control the organization right now. They are not going to make a real effort to go out and organize the working poor. It's not in their immediate self-interest, though it is in their long-run interest. All people, poor people included, do not willingly give up power that they have worked for and still have. Especially for poor people, when it is probably the only power they have and it isn't much (Martin, 32).

One approach to this dilemma was to have staff organizers begin developing new groups without the cooperation of NWRO's recipient leadership, and then to precipitate power confrontations. George spoke of this possibility in the same interview:

> Issues develop around a constituency. Welfare issues developed around a welfare constituency. We'll have to organize people like

the aged and the working poor and bring them in so they will be making demands on the organization just like the ADC mothers are doing now. We really have to subsidize this ourselves. The staff will have to organize groups like the working poor without much help from the mothers, and then bring the organized groups into NWRO to challenge the mothers. Through a challenge like this, some kind of accommodation will be worked out (Martin, 132).

At the time, however, George took no such drastic action, and restricted his efforts to cultivating relationships with other organizations. Then in 1972 he attempted to capitalize on these relationships by calling for a "Children's March for Survival." This event was designed to bring together a broad coalition of child-oriented groups to lobby in Washington, as his appeal for support of the impending march revealed:

Children suffer from poverty, and because of poverty, from hunger. Children suffer from racism. Children suffer from war, from an exploited environment, from poor schools, and from poor health. We will gather to condemn policies and programs of the Nixon Administration and the Congress which perpetuate these conditions and in many ways worsen them.

We condemn:
— the veto of the Child Care Bill
— cuts and restrictions in child feeding programs
— delays in health, housing, and education programs
— and most of all—the proposal of the so-called
    Family Assistance Plan instead of real welfare reform

We call today for a Children's March for Survival to focus national attention on the problems of children and to begin an action plan to save our nation's children.

The march occurred on March 25; about 40,000 people gathered at the Washington Monument. The composition of the march reflected the internal struggle taking place in NWRO. About 80 percent of the participants were children from the Washington, D.C., schools. They had been encouraged to attend by militant black Washington school board officials who had gained office on the crest of black unrest in the late 1960s. Another 10 percent were children bussed into Washington by workers from child-care centers in surrounding states. Another 10 percent were middle-class sympathizers from groups involved in children's rights, hunger, and peace issues. It is doubtful that welfare recipients comprised one percent of the crowd. The recipient leadership, in other words, did not view this demonstration as their own; nor did many organizers, with the result that little support was received from those WROs that were still functioning at the local level.

In the end George backed away from the effort to expand the membership base by diversifying it, concluding that the fight could not be won without destroying NWRO itself in a factional struggle. Instead he resigned from NWRO in December 1972 and announced that he and Bert DeLeeuw (a longtime aide) were going to undertake the formation of a multi-constituency organization to be called the Movement for Economic Justice. His resignation was a direct outgrowth of this conflict with NWRO's established leadership.[30]

As a matter of fact, the concept of membership itself had by the 1970s lost much of its meaning. In organizing doctrine, membership means something more than merely formal affiliation through the payment of dues. It also means active participation in the life of the organization—in demonstrations, for example. Mass participation is ostensibly the functional equivalent of the political resources (such as wealth) which interest groups elsewhere in the social structure possess. As organizers sometimes put it, poor people have numbers. Membership, in short, means regular participation by masses of people.

But NWRO's history reveals that membership eventually came to mean little more than formal affiliation through the payment of dues, and in the end there was not much emphasis placed even on the maintenance of the dues system. What mattered was winning and holding office. An illustration will make the point. In the summer of 1970, a recipient leader in New York City, who was then an officer of the national organization, undertook a "school clothing campaign." It was, from every perspective, a sad affair. The New York City-wide Coordinating Committee of Welfare Rights Groups had for some time been nothing more than a shell, consisting mainly of an executive committee composed of a few recipient leaders from the various boroughs who were still hanging on to their positions although most of the members of the groups which had originally yielded them these positions were gone. This group met irregularly, and its meetings consisted mainly of bickering over the distribution of such funds as the organization was still able to raise.

---

[30] When George died some eight months later, DeLeeuw assumed the executiveship of the Movement for Economic Justice.

In the fall of 1970 word was passed through what little welfare rights infrastructure remained in New York City that it would be possible for poor people to obtain a grant of money for school clothing from funds available to the Board of Education under the federal Elementary and Secondary Education Act of 1965. Some 14,000 people signed forms requesting a grant, having been required in advance to sign a NWRO dues card and to pay the annual fee of $1.00. Little effort was then made to integrate these thousands of people into the few welfare rights groups that remained, or to organize them into new groups. However 14,000 dues cards resulted from the campaign, and permitted this particular recipient leader to win still higher national office at the NWRO convention in the summer of 1971, since the fractional weight of ballots cast by NCC members in electing national officers was determined by the number of dues-paying members in their respective states. This was one example of the extent to which the goal of a mass membership had been subordinated to leadership strivings. In these different ways, then, the proliferation of organizational leadership positions constrained the expansion of organizational membership. Simply put, organization prevented organizing.

The Consequences of External Leadership Incentives

By the late 1960s, it was clear that NWRO was in grave difficulty. Mass-benefit campaigns were faltering; the leadership was also inhibiting the expansion of membership. Consequently the national staff was virtually paralyzed; it simply did not know what to do in order to resuscitate its constituency. The only plan available was to expand to new groups, such as the working poor and the aged, but we have already described the intense resistance by established leaders to this course of action. For all practical purposes, NWRO was becalmed.[31]

---

[31] Some mention should be made of the effort by NWRO and its local affiliates to sustain membership by promoting other issues: Attempts were made to obtain credit card agreements with Sears & Roebuck and Montgomery Ward, and with local department stores in a number of cities. Day care issues, education, health care, housing, surplus foods, school lunches, and the like were also promoted. It was hoped that by developing a broader multi-issue program NWRO's flagging membership base could be revived. These efforts never caught on, however.

Nevertheless NWRO's organizational apparatus expanded in the period between 1969 and 1972. The national budget rose, the national staff grew, and NWRO's national reputation enlarged. That this could be so was a consequence of a swelling tide of support from outside sources. Within a year or two after NWRO formed in 1967, various groups—churchmen, public officials, social welfare organizations, unions, civil rights groups, foundations, media representatives—began either to initiate relationships with NWRO or to respond to overtures for relationships. In this way organizational resources were obtained—public legitimation, money, the appearance of influence.

But this enlarging flow of resources did not lead to enlarged organizing; it undermined organizing. As NWRO gradually became enmeshed in a web of relationships with governmental officials and private groups, it was transformed from a protest organization to a negotiating and lobbying organization. This transformation was total; it occurred at the national level and among local groups everywhere. In the end it produced a leadership deeply involved in negotiating and lobbying, but on behalf of a constituency that was organized in name only.

THE SOURCES AND FORMS OF SUPPORT

The success with which NWRO developed relationships with a variety of groups was due mainly to two forces. The more important was the larger black movement and the responsiveness being shown it. NWRO could easily capitalize on this. It was a national organization and large numbers of representatives from local groups attended national conventions, so that NWRO could present itself as the representative of the welfare poor. Moreover, the vast majority of NWRO's membership was black; this, too, helped to identify NWRO as an expression of the larger black movement and enabled NWRO's leadership to seek aid from supporters of the black movement.[32]

The growth of support for NWRO was also aided by the emergence toward the late 1960s of a "welfare crisis." One form which

---

[32] All observers agree that NWRO's membership was almost entirely black. Martin, for example, estimates that 85 percent of the membership was black, 10 percent white, and 5 percent Latin (2, fn.1, and Appendix C., Table 44) .

governmental responsiveness toward the black movement in America had taken was to allow the welfare rolls to expand, and the expansion was rapid after 1965. In our terms this meant that defiance of the prohibition against the dole was escalating, partly as a result of the activities of the antipoverty program. Tens of thousands of welfare rights brochures were being distributed from storefront offices; thousands of VISTA and other antipoverty staff members were helping people to establish their eligibility; scores of legal services attorneys were initiating litigation against the welfare system. It also seems reasonable to believe that the many who were successful in getting on the rolls encouraged others to make the attempt. The very density of the welfare populations which had by this time built up in the cities suggested the likelihood of such a cumulative effect. A survey of slum families in ten central city neighborhoods in late 1966 revealed that almost half—47 percent— of the surveyed families reported income in the previous year from welfare or other non-job sources.[33] In the words of a report prepared by the Urban Coalition in 1969, "The welfare system continues to be the major growth industry of the slums and ghettos. . . ."

In late 1967 Congress enacted a series of amendments to the Social Security Act intended to slow the rise in the rolls. The states were required to establish work training and referral programs for recipients defined as employable. Participation in these programs was made compulsory, a condition of receiving assistance. (However, local welfare administrators did not enforce these new measures; they feared the political repercussions in the ghettos of large-scale efforts to force mothers and children off the rolls.) To insure that the states would exert themselves to cut the rolls, Congress also enacted a "freeze" on AFDC reimbursements. Under the freeze each state was to receive future federal reimbursements only in an amount calculated by a formula fixed at the ratio of AFDC children to the total population of children in the state as of January 1967. In other words a state with a rising ratio of children in impoverished female-headed families would, whatever the causes, nevertheless in future years be obliged either to reject new applicants, to lower grant levels and spread the same money among a larger number of cases, or to

---

[33] *Congressional Quarterly Weekly Report*, No. 36, September 8, 1967 (Washington, D.C., Congressional Quarterly Service), p. 1729.

raise more revenues to pay the entire cost of the increased caseloads. (However, after Congress enacted the freeze, state and local officials protested vigorously, with the result that the Johnson Administration postponed the effective date of the freeze, and the Nixon Administration did the same, until it was forgotten.)

A variety of more comprehensive proposals to deal with the welfare crisis were also put forward in this period. President Johnson, in his Economic Message of January 1967, promised to establish a Commission on Income Maintenance Programs (which he later did, and when the commission reported in the fall of 1969, it called for a national minimum income standard of $2,400 for a family of four). In March 1967, on the occasion of the one-hundredth anniversary of the New York State Board of Social Welfare, the cream of America's corporate leadership was summoned to an Arden House conference by Governor Rockefeller to consider remedies for the welfare crisis. The participants debated various income reforms—such as children's allowances, uniform national standards in AFDC payments, and a negative income tax—finding merit in them all.

Professionals in greater number and with greater vigor also began to advocate income maintenance reforms. As Congress debated a variety of restrictive measures and enacted some in 1967, OEO funded a negative income tax experiment among a sample of poor people in New Jersey, and not many months later, the Social and Rehabilitation Service of HEW allocated funds for similar experiments. In the spring of 1968 some 1,200 prominent economists signed a joint statement calling on Congress "to adopt this year a national system of income guarantees and supplements." When the report of the National Advisory Commission on Civil Disorders appeared in March 1968 it too called for a "National System of Income Supplementation" which would provide a minimum income for all families on welfare as well as for the working poor.

Moreover, the issue of income maintenance found its way into the presidential campaign of 1968. The Democratic platform stated that: "To support family incomes of the working poor a number of new program proposals have recently been developed. A thorough evaluation of the relative advantages of such proposals deserves the highest priority attention by the next administration. This we pledge to do." Eugene McCarthy, in the course of the Democratic primary contests, argued that the federal government had a responsibility to "determine a minimum income which it will assure for all Americans." And only days before his election, Richard Nixon, noting the great disparities in welfare payment levels from one state to another, which ostensibly encouraged migration from South to North, advocated the adoption of "national standards." The rising welfare rolls, in short, inexorably forced the question of welfare reform onto the national political agenda.

NWRO could capitalize on this development because many people —from members of the press to public officials—had reached the incorrect conclusion that "NWRO was largely responsible for raising the number of people on welfare in six years from less than [1 million families to over 3 million], and in quadrupling appropriations made to Aid to Dependent Children families. Friends and enemies alike credited NWRO with a major role in this explosion of welfare aid" (Meier and Rudwick, x). Consequently three kinds of resources became available to NWRO.

First, legitimacy came to be conferred upon the welfare rights struggle itself. The rise of a black movement (especially rioting) in the North had helped to focus attention on the economic plight of the black masses. Given the persistence of black unemployment and underemployment, some modestly influential groups began to reach the conclusion that government had a responsibility to provide income to the poor. One result of this shift in attitudes was increasing approval by these groups of the idea that people had a "right" to welfare. To the extent that NWRO was publicly defined as leading the fight to make this right a reality, it gradually came to enjoy the support of these groups—notably, small foundations which generally supported the civil rights struggle, the leadership of several national religious denominations, segments of the social welfare community, some civil rights leaders, political leaders identified with the "struggle against hunger," and a small number of wealthy individuals.

To say that the welfare rights struggle enjoyed some legitimacy is not to say that it enjoyed much. Welfare rights never became ennobled by the honor of its cause. With a few exceptions, powerful and prestigious figures, whether black or white, did not flock to its demonstrations (as they had to those of the civil rights movement in the South), nor did they contribute money to finance organizing, nor lend their influence to further welfare rights demands. This was to remain a movement of paupers, of a pariah class. The civil rights movement was widely extolled as a force strengthening the American character and American values by furthering the highest democratic ideals; the welfare rights movement was widely denounced as a force weakening the American character by undermining the most cherished value of self-reliance. Such legitimacy as it enjoyed—and it was meager at best—was due less to recognition of the injustices perpetrated by economic arrangements and by the welfare system than to the widespread sympathy which "the black cause" in general had aroused in American society during the 1960s. Still, as the welfare crisis ballooned, NWRO did receive a measure of recognition and that was important in sustaining the organization for a brief time.[34]

A second form of support was financial. In this later period civil rights groups, religious institutions,[35] social welfare organizations, and various foundations began to make money available to NWRO in larger amounts. For the first two years NWRO had struggled to find funds to sustain its operations; deficits ran into the tens of thousands of dollars; the payment of salaries in the national office often lagged behind by several months. By 1968, however, funds became available; the national operating budget rose to more than

---

[34] In the first year or two after NWRO formed, little support came from established black leaders and organizations. In part this merely reflected competitive strains for constituencies and resources. But it also reflected deep ambivalence about welfare. Generally speaking, black leaders felt that welfare was something blacks ought to get off of, not on to. The enlarging number of blacks on the welfare rolls was a source of acute embarrassment to them. When we approached one prominent black leader for help in gaining access to funds, he probably expressed the sentiments of most when he said that getting one black female a job as an airline stewardess was more important than getting fifty impoverished female-headed families on the welfare rolls. As a national debate over poverty, unemployment, and the rising welfare rolls broke out, however, a number of black leaders became more sympathetic. Among other things they began to condemn current welfare practices and to call for the establishment of some kind of national minimum income program.

[35] The private institution that probably provided the most assistance to NWRO was the church. Some churchmen, having been deeply involved in and affected by the southern civil rights movement, were likely to have an understanding of the depths of race and class oppression to which blacks had been subjected. These churchmen sometimes turned out to be the most ardent advocates and organizers of welfare rights groups. At the local level churches expressed their support by providing some money, office space, telephones, and access to equipment for the reproduction of welfare rights literature and fliers. Many clergymen throughout the country joined demonstrations, a number organized welfare rights groups, and some local confederations of churches sponsored a clergyman to organize on a fulltime basis. At the national level several major denominations funnelled hundreds of thousands of dollars to NWRO or its affiliates over the years, they provided forums for the discussion of welfare rights goals and policies, and denominational leaders joined in coalitional efforts to influence political leaders regarding welfare issues. The participation of clergymen was an important source of reassurance to welfare recipients. It helped them to deal with their sense of shame by giving them the feeling that what they were demanding—in effect, dependency with dignity—found some justification in moral and religious principles.

"dependency with dignity" — the death of the organizational problem was, indeed, immense

$250,000 annually in 1969. These monies made possible frequent regional and national meetings of recipient leaders and organizers, and the hiring of a large national staff.

Some money, it should be noted, came directly from government. The occasion for the largest grant arose from the enactment in 1967 of the amendments to the Social Security Act which required the states to establish vocational training and placement programs for AFDC mothers in the hope of reducing welfare costs. Suspecting that HEW would not implement this program as fervently as its sponsors wished, Congress assigned the task to the Department of Labor. That department, in turn, anticipated the possibility that considerable trouble might be provoked in the urban ghettos if the state employment agencies began forcing women off the relief rolls and into the labor market on a large scale. When NWRO proposed that it be commissioned and funded to hire a staff to monitor local employment programs, the better to ensure the willing participation in the program by AFDC mothers, the Labor Department quickly agreed. NWRO leaders publicly justified the arrangement as a way of ensuring that the rights of AFDC mothers would be respected, but privately they viewed it as a way of greatly expanding the national staff. A larger staff, they felt, even one tied to the federal agencies, would support and stimulate the growth of local affiliates. And so a grant of more than $400,000 was accepted from the outgoing Johnson Administration. Robert Michels would have found Gilbert Steiner's defense of this arrangement rather naïve:

> If the government can buy the support and the outreach efforts of the organized welfare leadership elite for half a million dollars, it will be a great bargain. If Wiley can sustain his organization with a great bloc of federal money, he can live to fight another fight. . . . There is no reason why Wiley should have rejected the federal gold. Claims of the Philadelphia WRO chapter that the contract involved selling out to the Establishment have more emotional than rational appeal. . . . The money means more to [Wiley] than to the Department of Labor, and the high-level recognition of NWRO's importance facilitates organizing (294).

The third resource which various groups provided NWRO was political status—the appearance of possessing conventional political influence. As the welfare crisis mushroomed, organizations of various kinds became responsive to NWRO, with the result that NWRO's leaders and organizers became confident that the opportunity for the welfare poor to win concessions by lobbying had finally presented itself. And there was certain evidence that this was so. The welfare crisis led to the proliferation of hearings, forums, conferences, and meetings devoted to the subject of relief giving. Some were convened by private groups, others by public and political figures, but all were devoted to debate over welfare reform. Each of these occasions appeared to be an opportunity for the welfare recipient's point of view to be heard. Although NWRO frequently crashed meetings to which it had not been formally invited, the late 1960s brought an increasing volume of formal invitations for the leadership to appear. Public officials faced with the problem of holding back angry taxpayers nevertheless also tended to try to be responsive to NWRO, for they had the problem of restoring civil order in the cities. Consequently they too reached out to recipient groups to establish relationships and to initiate dialogue. As a matter of fact NWRO's recipient leadership found itself being invited to international conferences:

> Leaders are involved in conferences and meetings to the point where they have been known to find themselves with conflicting conference dates. Mrs. Tillmon, the national chairman, was unable to make NWRO's 1968 National conference held in Lake Forest, Illinois, because she was a delegate representing poor people to the International Conference of Social Welfare in Helsinki, Finland, meeting at the same time. In a "memorandum to all affiliated groups," which sounded bureaucratic enough to have come out of HEW itself, Mrs. Tillmon delegated authority and announced appointments to committees of the conference (Steiner, 289).

Attendance at these foreign meetings was even justified to the NWRO membership on the grounds that a "new international welfare rights organization" was being talked about:

> I've been out of the country [to attend peace conferences] three times—in 1967 to Paris, in 1968 to Stockholm, in 1970 to Bogota. I just got back from Bogota. . . . These things I go to are important and they are for NWRO—for you, all of you, not me. In Bogota, they talked about setting up a new international welfare rights organization. This would mean NWRO would be in all kinds of different countries and would have a lot more power. This is the kind of thing I'm doing, working for you and trying to make your organization something (Martin, 109).

Superficially, these symbols of recognition suggested that NWRO had become something of a political force. Gilbert Steiner, for example, read the signs that way:

> Objectively, it can be noted that the welfare clients' organization has weathered its theoretical and practical problems to the point where its director is known, recognized, and consulted by the secretary of health, education, and welfare and resented at other high levels in that department; its chairman, an AFDC mother, sits with bureaucrats, scholars, and lobbyists in all-day conferences to plan welfare changes . . . (285).

But the truth was quite different. As NWRO's integration with other groups progressed, the political beliefs of those in the leadership stratum became more conventional, the militancy of the tactics they advocated weakened, and the professed goal of membership expansion receded. We will first describe these effects at the national level, and then at the local level, for the way in which external incentives shaped the orientation and direction of the national and local organizations varied somewhat.

THE IMPACT OF EXTERNAL INCENTIVES ON THE NATIONAL ORGANIZATION

NWRO was rapidly transformed as relationships with political figures and various private groups developed. Its efforts to influence administrators, legislators, political leaders, and private groups soon overwhelmed investments in all other areas. For all practical purposes NWRO became a lobbying organization.

The emphasis on lobbying progressed in stages. NWRO first entered state and national legislative arenas; it then began to build a "welfare coalition" consisting of a variety of national organizations that shared its perspectives on welfare reform; finally, it entered the arena of Democratic Party politics. The process began in 1967 with the welfare amendments then before the Congress as the major target. A modest demonstration was called in Washington in September and NWRO's top leadership testified before Congress and staged a sit-in in the chambers of a congressional committee (the first in history, it is said). This was the much-publicized occasion on which Senator Long (Democrat, Louisiana), chairman of the

powerful Senate Finance Committee, denounced AFDC mothers
as "brood mares."

From this beginning NWRO began to seek relationships with a
variety of organizations in the hope of developing support for its
legislative efforts. One of the early occasions for coalition was provided by SCLC's "Poor People's Campaign" in the spring and summer of 1968. NWRO launched the first demonstration—a Mother's
March on May 12 (Mother's Day)—during which George and Coretta
King led some 5,000 demonstrators through the still-charred ruins
of that section of Washington where rioting and burning had broken
out following the assassination of Martin Luther King. During the
ensuing months, until SCLC's poor people's campaign finally became mired in the mud and in the complexities of the federal
bureaucracies, NWRO coordinated many of its lobbying activities
with those of SCLC.

Another highly visible occasion to broaden its external support
presented itself in the fall of 1968 when the president convened a
White House Conference on Hunger and Malnutrition. The NWRO
leadership was so successful in presenting its case to the participants
that a resolution was passed calling for a guaranteed annual minimum income of $5,500 for a family of four, much to the embarrass-
ment of the president.

The antiwar movement was a logical locus for coalition-building.
NWRO quickly became a prominent constituent of the antiwar
movement, not because it could muster many demonstrators for
national or local rallies, but because NWRO's presence enabled
antiwar groups to link the issues of imperialism and war abroad with
the government's failure to deal with poverty and injustices at home.
Most major antiwar demonstrations featured one or more NWRO
leaders on the speaker's platform and some local WROs sent a few
delegates.

Militancy, as might have been expected, declined as a result of
this heavy investment in coalition-building and lobbying. By 1970
recipient leaders who had begun their careers storming relief centers
could hardly keep pace with their speaking schedules in one local,
state, or national forum after another. They had become celebrities
and they behaved accordingly. Here is a striking but not atypical
example:

The Massachusetts Conference on Social Welfare, a private social
work-oriented organization, made it a practice to select the chair-

man of the MWRO to serve on the Board of Directors. When the governor of Massachusetts decided to institute a "flat grant" welfare system, he chose a meeting of the Massachusetts Conference on Social Welfare to make his announcement. The chairman of the MWRO chose to sit on stage near the podium from which the governor spoke rather than lead a group of her members to that podium to disrupt the speech (Bailis, 73).

THE IMPACT OF EXTERNAL INCENTIVES ON LOCAL ORGANIZATIONS

The forces that shaped the orientation and direction of the national leadership were also at work at the local level. Local WROs also received resources that shaped their beliefs and tactics. Sympathetic individuals and organizations publicly identified themselves with the welfare rights struggle, yielding a measure of legitimacy. Anti-poverty agencies, churches, settlement houses and other organizations, including a few unions,[36] provided meeting rooms, organizers, access to printing supplies and machines, and money.

However, the most important integrative relationships at the local level were those formed with the welfare system itself. These relationships were a powerful force in transforming WROs from protest to lobbying and service organizations. Welfare officials reached out to protesters in the hope of restoring calm, and protest leaders reached out to government officials in the hope of achieving reforms. Thus as groups of recipients caused repeated disruptions of welfare procedures by picketing, and by sit-ins and demonstrations, welfare officials began to search out organizers and recipient leaders to initiate "dialogue" and, as often as not, organizers or recipient leaders demanded dialogue. The result, everywhere in the country, was the development of procedures for the negotiation of grievances. Many welfare departments established advisory councils composed of recipients; sometimes recipients were appointed to policymaking boards.

If some local WROs were wary of these arrangements (at least at first) and therefore chose to maintain a certain distance from govern-

---

[36] In New York City, for example, District Council 37 was extremely helpful.

ment, then welfare officials sometimes formed independent recipient organizations to which they tried to attract the leadership of the WROs. The most elaborate development of this kind occurred in New York City. The department of welfare established a division of "Community Relations" staffed by "community coordinators" or "community organizers" (who were usually young black or Latin graduates of schools of social work). These staff members then went into the slums, ghettos, and barrios to organize "client advisory committees" which met monthly to discuss grievances and advise welfare officials on policy changes. The welfare department organizers also assiduously cultivated the leaders of existing WROs throughout the city, hoping to get them to join as well, and over time they succeeded in winning over a number of recipient leaders. The kinds of political attitudes which were acquired or reinforced through this process are exemplified in the following excerpts from the remarks of a client advisory committee member as quoted in a monthly newsletter:

> I feel there are obviously two ways to work—either to be adamantly demanding, issuing ultimatums, making use of opportunism and perhaps exaggeration in order to press a point—or the slower, admittedly, but perhaps more effective eventually, way of using the techniques of gathering together, speaking frankly, continuing to ask, to question, to discuss, to learn, bringing faith and belief in each other and high hopes in our hearts that we will be fairly heard—and our recommendations and proposals, when found to be valid, acted upon.

The dawning of this new era of mutuality and exchange was signaled by the appearance of articles in leading professional journals extolling the beginning of free and open communication between giver and receiver. And just as it had done in the 1930s, the Commonwealth of Pennsylvania negotiated a model agreement with welfare recipients as a result of a hearing in October 1968. It stipulated that:[37]

> The Executive Director of each county shall instruct the supervisor of each District Office to make available upon request by the County Welfare Rights Organization:

---

[37] Stipulation between the Commonwealth of Pennsylvania, *Department of Public Welfare* v. *Philadelphia Welfare Rights Organization*, West District, October 17, 1968, issued by Elias S. Cohen, Commissioner.

   a. Space when available in the reception or waiting area and a table and several chairs to accommodate members of the Welfare Rights Organization in reasonable number.

   b. A pay telephone in the reception or waiting area convenient to the use of Public Assistance applicants and recipients and members of the Welfare Rights Organization, and designated by a clearly visible sign for their specific use.

   c. One complete current copy of the Pennsylvania Public Assistance Manual for the specific use of Public Assistance applicants and recipients and members of the Welfare Rights Organization.

   d. Members of the Welfare Rights Organization of the County are entitled to access in reasonable numbers to the District Office to occupy the table, to maintain on and near the table signs identifying them and announcing their availability to assist applicants and recipients, to pass out in the reception or waiting area literature and leaflets announcing their availability and function, and to accompany any applicant or recipient who requests assistance in any dealings with Public Assistance personnel.

   e. No Public Assistance personnel shall refuse or delay interviews or otherwise differently treat any applicant or recipient who is assisted by a member of the Welfare Rights Organization, but rather, all Public Assistance personnel shall cooperate with members of the Welfare Rights Organization and shall recognize them as representatives of the client whenever the client so wishes.

Such agreements, whether formalized in writing or not, became well-nigh universal.

The development of these grievance procedures had a large influence on the political beliefs that dominated the local WROs, for these arrangements went far toward reaffirming for leaders and organizers the conviction that they represented a powerful organization. It was not remarkable that welfare officials, confronted by turbulent interference with the operation of their programs, moved to grant the disrupters a symbolic role in the system, for it was a time-honored method of restoring calm. What was remarkable was the ease with which the method worked. Each such "victory" was the occasion for self-congratulations among recipient leaders who, upon reading in the press of their appointments to advisory committees or upon receiving written invitations to negotiating sessions or upon being invited to testify at legislative hearings, envisaged the emergence of a new period of justice for the welfare poor. To be listened to by the powerful conveyed a sense that they were at last wielding a measure of influence, that progress was being made, that reforms would follow.

Another consequence of these arrangements was a decline in militancy. Government officials agreed to deal with the WROs but they exacted a price. Sometimes the price was so subtle as to make it appear that none was being asked. It may merely have consisted in an implicit understanding, all too readily acknowledged by recipient leaders and organizers, that the proper path to welfare reform was through negotiation by leaders and not protest by unruly mobs. Sometimes the terms were more explicit and included the understanding that the welfare rights organization would desist from abrasive actions. The agreement reached in Pennsylvania, which was mentioned earlier, provides a good case in point. Groups were not simply given open access to the welfare offices and to welfare officials; they were expected in exchange to do nothing to disrupt office routines or to interfere with the "rights" of clients to be left alone:

Courtesy and Behavior

It is suggested that agreements with the welfare rights organizations recognize that there are obligations with reference to behavior incumbent upon public assistance personnel and welfare rights organization representatives. Welfare rights organization representatives are expected to take no steps designed to intimidate, harass, embarrass or threaten public assistance personnel. . . . As representatives of clients, they are being provided with certain prerogatives, but these are not unbounded.

Solicitation of Applicants and Recipients

It is appropriate for county boards to reach agreements about the limits of welfare rights organization representatives accosting, interrupting, or importuning applicants or clients.

Settlement of Disputes

It is suggested that county executives may wish to reach agreement with welfare rights organization groups on the immediate settlement of a dispute which threatens or which has disrupted work to the point where staff cannot reasonably continue to work.[38]

---

[38] Commonwealth of Pennsylvania, Department of Public Welfare, Harrisburg, Pa., Public Assistance Memorandum No. 968, Supplement No. 1, March 11, 1969.

As WROs became enmeshed in arrangements of this kind, the demonstrations, picketing, and sit-ins which had dominated the birth of WROs were gradually abandoned. Even the militancy of the rhetoric deescalated. Association with government officials who were "sympathetic" and "reasonable" and "oriented toward the problems of recipients" produced a large number of recipient leaders and organizers who came to affirm the efficacy of persuasion and negotiation. In early 1970, for example, a group of organizers and recipient leaders decided to attempt to revive direct action in New York, and began one morning in the crowded waiting room of a Harlem welfare center. The best-known figure in the group was a recipient who held a national office in NWRO. Upon learning that she was present, the director of the center offered to conduct her on a personal tour of the entire operation. It is a measure of the extent to which leaders had come to be controlled by such gestures that she accepted and was not seen again for several hours.

Integrative relationships of this kind not only blunted militancy, they also interfered with the expansion of membership and even weakened the ties of existing members to the group. Negotiations absorbed the energy and time of leaders and organizers. The more the investment in these procedures, the less the investment in enlisting new members. Moreover formal relationships with welfare officials had the effect of making membership superfluous. Before such relationships became the rule it was not unusual for fifty or one hundred recipients to burst into a welfare center and demand that their grievances be settled on the spot. This tactic often worked and when it did, it was the *group* that had proved its strength; everyone depended upon everyone else. But once grievances came to be dealt with through negotiations between welfare rights leaders and welfare officials, group action no longer seemed necessary, and group consciousness disintegrated. The sense of participation in something larger than oneself, the sense of belonging to a movement, was gradually lost.

And now a final but crucial point. As NWRO and its local affiliates moved into the maze of legislative and bureaucratic politics, the failure to sustain, much less to expand, the membership base among the poor was obscured. For as the membership base dwindled and became less militant, the resources which NWRO secured continued to enlarge. In effect it became possible for NWRO to function without a mass base, without a broad constituency. The sympathy and fear generated by the black movement, together with the emerging crisis over welfare, enabled NWRO to present itself to elites as the representative of a large segment of the black poor and thus to obtain the legitimation and money required for the maintenance of its organizational structure. *In effect, external resources became a substitute for a mass base.*[39]

But the availability of external resources upon which the organization depended was not a response to organization; it was a response to widespread black unrest. Once unrest began to subside, these external resources were withdrawn. The result was organizational collapse, as we shall now see.

The Ebbing of Black Unrest

If the developments already described had not caused the decline of NWRO, the decline of black unrest would have. As it was, the ebbing of black unrest dealt the death blow to an organization that was already greatly weakened.

Toward the late 1960s the black movement which began in the South in the mid-fifties subsided, and the movement organizations it had spawned were dying if not already dead. For one thing much of the leadership of the black movement (as we noted in chapter four) was being absorbed into electoral politics, into government bureaucracies, into the universities, and into business and industry; correlatively the ideology of protest was repudiated and the efficacy of electoral politics was affirmed. As a result the cadres of organizers dwindled, their ranks diminished by the concessions won.

While there is no way of marking the exact time when the tide of unrest turned, the year 1968 might be considered such a point. It was the last year of major urban rioting (in the wake of Martin Luther King's assassination); it was also the year that the presidency passed from a liberal to a conservative leadership. With Nixon's

---

[39] Bailis' description of the Massachusetts Welfare Rights Organization perfectly fits our general observation: "Perhaps the final phase in the developing rifts between lay leaders and staff came when some local lay leaders began to realize that they did not need strong groups to play an important role in MWRO statewide politics, and the MWRO Executive Board began to reach the parallel conclusion that the honors and respect they were receiving from politicians, welfare administrators, and leaders of the social welfare community did not really require a functioning state wide grassroots organization at all" (73).

accession to power the class and racial injustices that had figured so
prominently in the rhetoric and action of earlier administrations,
and that had encouraged protest among the black poor, gave way to
rhetoric and action emphasizing law-and-order and self-reliance, with
the effect of rekindling shame and fear among the black masses. A
white backlash against black gains had developed and conservative
leaders acted to stimulate it all the more as a means of building
support. By the election of 1972 this rhetoric reached a crescendo,
much of it focused specifically on the last vestige of black defiance—
the still rising welfare rolls. In the presidential campaign of 1972
Republican-sponsored television advertisements warned the American people that if McGovern won the election he would put half of
the population on welfare. Nixon exhorted Americans in his in-
augural address not to ask what government could do for them,
but what they could do for themselves, and then he rapidly popularized the slogan "Workfare not Welfare." A mobilization against
the black poor was occurring, with the welfare poor a particular
target.

THE END OF WELFARE LIBERALISM

Not all was simply rhetoric. Acting through its various executive
departments the Nixon Administration also cut the flow of resources
to ghetto organizations and reversed earlier policies which had
yielded concessions to the poor. The Office of Economic Opportunity came under siege from the administration. Within a year or two
the Department of Health, Education, and Welfare began to issue
more restrictive policies and regulations in an effort to squash the
substantive and procedural rights which welfare recipients had won
through protest or that antipoverty attorneys had won through litigation. One of the most significant steps it subsequently took—a step
unmistakably signaling the end of an era of welfare liberalism—
was to introduce a system of substantial financial penalties to be
imposed upon states when "quality control" studies showed that
more than 3 percent of those receiving welfare were "ineligible."
As those familiar with the welfare system maze know, low ineligibility levels can be achieved only at the price of keeping much larger
proportions of eligible families off the rolls.

Political leaders at other levels of government joined in, either because new officials had come to power with a social philosophy which resonated with the new mood of the times or because continued incumbency by existing leaders demanded accommodation to that mood. Governor Rockefeller had already perhaps outdone them all with his bizarre proposals to refuse welfare benefits to any newcomer to New York State who could not find decent housing or health care, followed by highly publicized investigations of "welfare fraud" conducted by a newly created office of Inspector General (headed by a millionaire of inherited wealth who despised the welfare poor). In California Governor Reagan garnered a national reputation by mounting similar anti-welfare campaigns. (New York and California, it should be noted, contained more than half of the nation's welfare recipients.) One of the most celebrated anti-welfare events of the period occurred in Nevada, where the Department of Welfare launched a major campaign against "welfare cheaters." On January 1, 1972, 21 percent of Nevada's welfare population did not receive their welfare checks and 28 percent more received reduced checks. This came about because the welfare department decided to deal with the "welfare crisis" by conducting an "audit," consisting of mobilizing virtually the entire work force of the department to interview employers and neighbors of the poor and to study the records of the social security and unemployment compensation agencies for any evidence of unreported income in the preceding five or more years. For most recipients the first notice of the audit was the failure of their checks to arrive, or the arrival of checks for smaller amounts. The reason given, in subsequent notices to recipients, was simply "overpayment" or "ineligibility."[40] Many other

---

40 NWRO quickly decided to try to make an "example" of Nevada, hoping thereby to deter other states from instituting similar "reforms." George also hoped that a mass mobilization in Nevada would bolster NWRO's flagging fund-raising efforts and otherwise boost morale in the organization.

Within weeks NWRO had "Operation Nevada" under way. A "Lawyer's Brigade," consisting of some forty lawyers and seventy law students led by Edward Sparer (NWRO's chief counsel), stormed the courts of Nevada, while NWRO's national staff as well as organizers from various parts of the country flew in to mobilize marches and demonstrations on the famous Las Vegas "Strip." Notables also joined the demonstrations, including Ralph Abernathy, David Dellinger, Jane Fonda, and Sammy Davis, Jr.

The most effective remedies were achieved through the courts. On March 20 the Federal District Court issued an order reinstating everyone who had been terminated or who had received reduced grants, and retroactive payments were ordered. The court

states cut welfare payment levels or introduced eligibility restrictions between 1970 and 1972, although not on such a large scale.

One immediate consequence of this changing political climate was to dry up many of the resources—especially government resources—upon which local WROs had drawn. As funds for the Great Society programs were cut (and diverted into "revenue sharing," for example), the ranks of organizers were decimated. The welfare rights organizers who remained found that local administrators of the Great Society programs had become fearful and would no longer support organizing efforts.

Under these influences the militancy of the welfare poor all but vanished. As we noted earlier, most local groups across the United States had been formed by grievance work. But by the early seventies the few organizers who remained found that welfare administrations were stiffening their resistance to demands by organized recipient groups. The new national rhetoric diminished their responsiveness to the poor and the passing of rioting and other forms of mass protest diminished their fear of the poor. If once welfare officials had been oriented toward the great turbulence in the streets beyond their office doors, now they were oriented to the growing signs of restrictiveness contained in regulations being issued from Washington and from their respective state capitals. Given both of these conditions local recipient groups won less and less, and the fewer the victories the more difficult it became to sustain participation by even the more committed and loyal recipients. Month by month the belief grew that the fight was being lost—even, perhaps, that it was no longer worth being fought. Consequently more organizers and recipients drifted away.

It was also true that many local WRO members themselves had lost whatever inclination they might once have had to help other poor people. Their special relationship to the welfare system still sometimes served their individual needs, aiding them in solving

---

found that "as a result of the precipitous action described, the Administrator and his staff ran roughshod over the constitutional rights of eligible and ineligible recipients alike." The Department of Welfare, in short, had acted too flagrantly, too blatantly. There were more subtle ways of curbing welfare growth and of inducing terminations; other states were slowly developing them.

Operation Nevada was a victory for NWRO, but it was the last. Indeed it was probably the last national demonstration of black people employing mass marches and civil disobedience coupled with supporting litigation in the courts. It was the end of the era that had begun almost two decades earlier in Montgomery, Alabama.

their own problems and even in obtaining special grants. In a rapidly changing political climate, especially with public welfare expenditures becoming a target of public ire, these remaining members became fearful and drew inward, trying to protect their privileged access. The narrowest possible self-interest and the ideological justification for it thus came to dominate the few fragmented groups that survived.

Under these circumstances, it would have taken a strenuous, devoted, and resourceful program by the national leadership to try to buttress failing morale at the local level. In truth there is no reason to believe that the effort could have succeeded. The fires of protest had died out and organizers probably could not have rekindled them. The endless debates over the best means of building a mass-based permanent organization no longer mattered: whether by single- versus multi-issue organizing, or by single- versus multi-constituency organizing, or by decentralized versus centralized staffing patterns, or by placing less emphasis on material incentives in attracting members versus placing more emphasis on "educating" and "radicalizing" the membership. The fact is that an era of protest had inexorably come to a close.

But it was not an analysis of the forces making for the probable futility of local organizing by 1970 that turned the national leadership away from the membership base. It was the promise of "welfare reform" and of the organizational and leadership rewards which would become available in the course of a struggle for reform.

Welfare Backlash and Welfare Reform

In a nationwide radio and television address on August 8, 1969, President Nixon announced a series of proposals for welfare reorganization. The Nixon proposals—known as the Family Assistance Plan (FAP)—called for the elimination of the AFDC program and its replacement with a program that would have guaranteed every family an annual minimum income at the level of $1,600 for a family of four, to be paid for by the federal government. Moreover, the proposed program included the working poor (i.e., two-parent families) who would be made eligible for wage supplementation by a formula that disregarded the first $720 of earned income for purposes of determining eligibility, and imposed a tax rate thereafter of 50 percent, until the family of four had a total income from wages and welfare of $3,920, at which point supplementation would be discontinued.[41]

The proposals created a considerable stir. The main features appeared liberal, and in some ways were. The proposal for a federal minimum income standard and for wage supplementation would have mitigated some of the worst poverty in the South. The proposal would also have relieved states and localities of at least some of the fiscal burden of the rising rolls.[42] These were the aspects of the overall plan which tended to be featured in the press, and it was these aspects which attracted liberal support for FAP.

In other major respects the plan was not liberal but regressive, and the longer-term implications of the more regressive provisions were less apparent to most observers. The plan would have wiped out the procedural rights which recipients had won through protest and litigation in the 1960s—for example, the right to a hearing if terminated from the rolls. It also contained provisions to enforce work among those deemed "suitable" for employment and would have required these "employable" recipients to take jobs at less than the minimum wage.

The most urgent and the most straightforward political problem with which Nixon was trying to deal in proposing relief reform was the clamor among local officials for fiscal relief, a clamor generated by rising budgets in the states, counties, and cities. Pressure for reform was a direct consequence of the fact that the American poor had made a modest income gain through the welfare system in the 1960s. Enormous political pressure had built up at the state and local levels in response to the resulting fiscal strains; in his televised address, the president acknowledged that the rising rolls were "bringing states and cities to the brink of financial disaster."

Two broad constituencies had developed around this issue: those

---

[41] Detailed discussions of the FAP proposal and of the ensuing congressional struggle can be found in Moynihan; Burke and Burke; and Bowler. Bowler's study contains exceptionally lucid explanations of the complex details of both the existing and proposed welfare programs.

[42] Since most states provided welfare grants at levels far higher than $1,600 for a family of four, states would still have had to supplement the federal payment, and more liberal states would have had to bear heavier costs than restrictive states, an arrangement not very different from that which existed under the old grant-in-aid formula. Nevertheless all states were assured of realizing at least some savings under the Nixon plan.

who simply wanted to cut back the gains made by the poor by slashing both the rolls and grant levels, and those who wanted to see the
burden of paying for relief costs shifted to the federal government.
The latter constituency was by far the more powerful; it contained
the bulk of the nation's mayors, county officials, and governors. They
wished to be spared the politically onerous and potentially dangerous
necessity of cutting back welfare. Thus "the explosion in family
benefit recipients put welfare, a subject typically shunned by the
White House, on the agenda of President-elect Nixon," according to
two journalists, Burke and Burke, who covered these events. "Republican governors wanted relief from Washington and from their
party's president-to-be" (41). Referring to the long congressional
struggle which then ensued over the proposals, these same authors
go on to note:

> The only strong and unqualified pressure for H.R. 1 came from
> those who wanted welfare change not for reasons of philosophy, but
> rather for the promise of fiscal relief. These were many of the
> nation's governors and county officials. To these men, frustrated by
> ever-rising welfare budgets, the structural reforms of H.R. 1 were
> relatively unimportant. What they wanted was money, and H.R. 1's
> federal floor for current welfare recipients would supply it (179).

But while FAP would have provided some fiscal relief for states
and localities, that objective, taken by itself, could have been
achieved in any number of ways. The federal government might
simply have arranged to pay relief costs, for example, while leaving
the system otherwise intact. As it turned out, something like that
happened. When relief reform failed, Congress enacted instead a
multibillion dollar program of general "revenue sharing." In other
words the clamor of state and local officials clearly dictated a federal
response to the fiscal crisis, but it did not dictate the specific changes
in the welfare system proposed under FAP.

In point of fact the FAP proposals were not designed mainly to
ease fiscal strains. They were mainly designed to halt the growth
of the AFDC rolls. Internal memoranda prepared for the president
predicted a continuing steep climb in the rolls unless the system was
redesigned. Stated another way, the growing dependency of the
American underclass was defined as having its roots in the welfare
system. There were two ways in which welfare practices were thought
to produce this condition.

First, it was argued that existing relief policies provided a disincentive for self-reliance since recipients who worked were required to report their earnings which were then deducted from monthly grants. The conventional wisdom held that this "100% tax" discouraged recipients from working their way off the rolls, generating perpetual dependency. Second, the rising rolls were considered to be a problem not only because they discouraged work, but because the ready availability of benefits presumably undermined the family system of the poor. Fathers were believed to be deserting in order to make mothers and children eligible for relief. "Fiscal abandonment," some called it, and the president was advised that this circumstance generated a continuous stream of new relief applicants.

Various "pathologies" among the poor—mainly crime and civil disorder—were also attributed to welfare. Daniel Patrick Moynihan, a presidential advisor, played a large role in promulgating this diagnosis to the larger public and apparently he persuaded the president as well. The family assistance plan, he said, "was made . . . as part of an over-riding short-term strategy to bring down the level of internal violence" (12). The chain of reasoning was that crime, civil disorder, and other social pathologies exhibited by the poor had their roots in worklessness and family instability which, in turn, had their roots in welfare permissiveness. This chain of reasoning is vividly revealed in a summary of the views expressed by a group of "administrators, academicians and intellectuals" with whom Moynihan met to discuss the welfare crisis in the big cities, New York City being the particular focus of attention:

> The social fabric of New York City is coming to pieces. It isn't just "strained" and it isn't just "frayed"; but like a sheet of rotten canvas, it is beginning to rip, and it won't be too long until even a moderate force will be capable of leaving it in shreds and tatters. . . . Among a large and growing lower class, self-reliance, self-discipline, and industry are waning; a radical disproportion is arising between reality and expectations concerning job, living standard, and so on; unemployment is high but a lively demand for unskilled labor remains unmet; illegitimacy is increasing; families are more and more matrifocal and atomized; crime and disorder are sharply on the rise. There is, in short, a progressive disorganization of society, a growing pattern of frustration and mistrust. . . . This general pathology, moreover, appears to be infecting the Puerto Rican community as well as the Negro. A large segment of the population is becoming incompetent and destructive. Growing parasitism, both legal and illegal, is the result; so,

also, is violence. (*It is a stirring, if generally unrecognized, demonstration of the power of our welfare machine.*) (Moynihan, 76; emphasis added.)

As for this "stirring . . . demonstration of the power of our welfare machine" going "unrecognized," that was, of course, far from being true. Everyone believed that relief-giving destroys the poor. Conservatives said it; middle-of-the-roaders said it; and liberals said it. The well-off said it and the bulk of the poor would have said it had they been asked. On this point there was unanimity.

Armed with this analysis, relief reformers set out to rehabilitate the culture of the poor. The key to reducing "parasitism" was to redesign relief arrangements so as to enforce work. Moreover, by restoring the discipline of work, family stability would also be reinforced and various social pathologies curbed. This was the overarching objective of FAP and, given the analysis on which it was based, one can understand why a deeply conservative president confronted by extraordinary manifestations of social and civil disorder as he assumed office might have been led to embrace welfare reform.

In fact the objectives underlying this effort at relief reform bore a striking resemblance to the objectives underlying earlier periods of relief reform. The fundamental conditions that gave rise to the reform impulse were also historically familiar. The periodic expansion of relief-giving in western industrial countries has frequently been associated with agricultural transformations that uprooted the peasantry and drove them into the cities and towns where many languished without work. With people loosened from traditional controls and not enmeshed in new institutional patterns, social disorder worsened and took form finally in the widespread civil disorder that forced elites to create relief arrangements or to allow an existing system to expand. Then, with quiescence restored, the "social pathologies" of the poor were redefined as having their cause in overly permissive relief arrangements, not in defective socioeconomic arrangements.

As often as not this social theory has led to the poor being expelled from the relief rolls on the ground that by no other means can they be forced to overcome the habit of idleness. Nixon would ostensibly have done it differently. FAP provided a variety of measures intended to buttress work motivation. On one side, as we said earlier, there were incentives—a modest income disregard of $720 annually, coupled with a tax rate allowing half of additional earned income to be retained to a maximum of $3,920 for a family of four. On the other side, there were sanctions—the denial of benefits to those who declined to work. Moreover, to insure the absorption of the poor into the labor force, the bill provided that recipients could be compelled to work at jobs significantly below the minimum wage. Through these measures the state would have intervened in the secondary labor market, subsidizing low-wage employers and insuring a disciplined supply of workers.

Over time these arrangements might well have come to be used to force the poor to take any work at sub-minimum wages, one way of stemming the projected rise in the rolls which so troubled Nixon and his advisors. And that brings us to a crucial question: How harshly would the work requirements be administered once the turbulence of the 1960s had passed and with it the fear of the poor? On this question there was ample reason to be concerned, particularly after Nixon's first year or two in office.

There was, first, the evidence of Nixon's orientation toward the existing welfare system. Even as the congressional struggle over welfare reform was beginning, Nixon's appointees in HEW proceeded without fanfare to institute a host of new rules and regulations designed to make relief benefits more difficult to obtain and to keep. As time passed these regulations became increasingly restrictive, and the preoccupation was unmistakably one of reducing the rolls.

There was, further, the evidence of the Nixon Administration's economic policies. An administration concerned about the condition of the poor would not have initiated the policy of allowing unemployment to rise as a counter to inflation. By the end of 1970, the first year of debate over welfare reform, the nation had been plunged into the worst recession since World War II. And while the recession deepened, Moynihan wrote: "It cannot be too often stated that the issue of welfare reform is not what it costs those who provide it, but what it costs those who receive it" (18). It was a curious point to make during a period of rapidly rising unemployment; one might rather have called for an easing of relief restrictiveness in order to enable the poor to survive the impact of Nixon's anti-inflation policies. This general callousness toward unemployment, coupled with restrictive relief policies, suggests strongly that Nixon asked for welfare reform in the belief that a system of government coercion could succeed in driving the rolls down.

Finally, there was the gradually evolving evidence of Nixon's own conduct during the prolonged debate in Congress over welfare reform. With the passage of time he abandoned his proposed method of reducing the rolls in favor of a much more politically popular method, namely, to inflame public opposition to the welfare system and to let others (governors, county officials, and mayors) respond to the uproar by slashing the rolls. As he shifted from the one method to the other he withdrew support for his own plan even though victory in Congress was at hand.

To be sure, there was considerable congressional opposition to FAP, not because the plan was restrictive but because it was not restrictive enough, particularly as it would have applied to the South. Support for the plan came largely from the industrial states in the North which had suffered the brunt of the rising rolls. Southern representatives tended to prefer to see the relief rolls slashed, for the South still relied on the lowest paid labor supply in the nation, despite the out-migration of many of its displaced poor. Even an income standard as low as $1,600 for a family of four would have undermined the southern wage structure. Accordingly southerners played the leading role in defeating the plan, using their considerable power in the congressional committee structure to work for its defeat.[43]

However, the opposition of the South could have been overcome had the president persevered, but he did not. Publicly Nixon appeared to give continued support; in the day-to-day dealings between his administration and Congress, however, it progressively became clear that his commitment to the plan was weakening. At critical junctures, when compromises between liberals (led by Abraham Ribicoff, the Democratic senator from Connecticut) and con-

---

[43] When we wrote "A Strategy to End Poverty," we failed to foresee the full extent of southern opposition to a national minimum income system, an opposition rooted in a concern for preserving the extremely low wages which still prevail in parts of the South. One lesson from the debate over welfare reorganization is that a national minimum income standard, if it is enacted, will be very low in deference to the variations in wage levels associated with the different regional economies in the United States.

One large reform that did result from the great rise in the relief rolls was the federalizing of the so-called adult categories—those for the disabled, blind, and aged. These categories were taken over by the federal government and absorbed into a new system called Supplemental Security Income (SSI). As a result there is now a national minimum standard for these groups, and that is an advance for these poor in many states. Furthermore, many more people applied for benefits than had previously been the case, for SSI is administered by the Social Security system and is not therefore felt to be as stigmatizing as the older relief programs. This substantial advance would not have occurred except for the fiscal crisis and the resulting political strains caused by the welfare explosion. The "strategy of crisis" had been partly right, but not quite in the way we had expected.

servatives seemed possible—compromises that would have raised the annual minimum income by a few hundred dollars and softened the work provisions—the president refused to sanction them.

The last and the most illuminating of these events occurred in June 1972. An option paper had been prepared for the president by the Office of Management and Budget, the Departments of Labor and of Health, Education, and Welfare, and the staff of the Domestic Council. "Three choices were analyzed: (A) stand pat with H.R. 1; (B) compromise with Long; and (C) compromise with Ribicoff" (Burke and Burke, 184). The option paper went on to note that option (C) is "the only possible strategy which can get us a bill." At this juncture most observers agree that the president could have won the day had he compromised with Ribicoff and the liberals. However he chose not to win. "President Nixon announced his decision on June 22, 1972, five days after the Watergate break-in. Nixon told a news conference that he would stay by his 'middle position' in support of the House-passed H.R.1," for which the option paper said only twenty Senate votes could be won (Burke and Burke, 185). Through a parliamentary maneuver, the Ribicoff compromise plan did come before the full Senate on October 4, 1972, but without presidential support it was defeated 52 to 34.

By this juncture the president had discovered that there was political capital in the welfare issue, and probably more capital in the issue itself than in the legislation he had introduced. By the unrelenting emphasis on the "pathology-generating" features of relief-giving, Nixon and Moynihan had played to the growing climate of relief-restrictiveness, if they had not done much to create it. As he previewed his 1972 presidential election campaign Nixon thus decided "that it would be wiser to have an issue than an enacted plan" (Burke and Burke, 185).

The lack of genuine support by the White House for a compromise welfare reform bill, together with the president's exploitation of the welfare issue to garner votes in the presidential campaign, angered and dismayed many liberals who had supported welfare reform. They, too, came to distrust Nixon's motives. One of them was Hyman Bookbinder, Washington Representative of the American Jewish Committee, who wrote Moynihan on November 14, 1972:

> I knew that HR-1 was dead about six months ago. It was clear that the Administration felt it could not be saddled with a welfare program during an election year . . . but my continuing participa-

tion in the support effort persuaded me that the bill *never* had the *hearty* backing it required from Pennsylvania Avenue. The several generalized Presidential pronouncements were welcome but they were made less than credible because of administrative inflexibility and intransigence on modest improvements that were being proposed. . . .

But now, Pat, I come to the real purpose of this letter. While I do not approve of the catering to anti-welfare prejudices that are engaged in for political advantage, I can at least understand them. There are subtle considerations of timing and emphasis in any legislative effort. But what concerns me is that these anti-welfare prejudices have become so ingrained and so widespread that no real progress may be possible. And, above all, my reading [of the President's remarks] persuades me that he is himself the victim of some of the harshest prejudices and misinformation . . . (emphasis in original).[44]

Given all of these factors, there was reason to believe that FAP, had it been enacted, would have been administered in keeping with other Nixon policies, all of which were antagonistic to the poor. Stated in simplest terms, it was the relief explosion of the 1960s that had precipitated official efforts at reform. As a result of that expansion millions of people had come to receive benefits. Poverty in the United States had been substantially reduced and a step toward something like a national minimum income had in fact been taken. It was these gains that were the object of "reform."

NWRO Lobbies Against Welfare "Reform"

In the interim between the introduction of FAP in 1970 and its final defeat in 1972 the issue of welfare reorganization was high on the national political agenda. Despite the furor we advised George that NWRO should not plunge into the congressional maelstrom. We thought NWRO continually overestimated its effectiveness in the lobbying process. At the time NWRO had virtually no grassroots base left; far from remedying that circumstance (if it could have been remedied), the congressional struggle over the president's proposals would surely be a long and exhausting one, and just as surely it

---

[44] Quoted with permission of Hyman Bookbinder.

would divert the whole of NWRO's resources away from its base. Instead we thought that NWRO should turn back to the streets and welfare centers, with the aged and the working poor as new targets. The barrage of publicity over Nixon's proposals to supplement low wages might give a new legitimacy to campaigns to mobilize the working poor to obtain supplements through general assistance programs in the northern states.

As before, we argued our view by pointing to the continued defiance among the *unorganized* poor themselves. While the black movement as a whole was ebbing in this period, applications for public assistance remained high, and approval levels were still high as well. Although *organized* recipient groups were beginning to encounter resistance from welfare administrators in the changed political climate following Nixon's election, the eligibility process still remained relatively open. The impact of years of protest on policies and practices would take time to be reversed. Significant cases dealing with eligibility restrictions were reaching the Supreme Court in this period and the decisions being handed down were still favorable. HEW could not implement restrictive policies all at once. In fact, under the impact of the Nixon recession, the rolls were rising even more rapidly than before.

But George decided otherwise. In reaching this decision he was constrained by a number of organizational problems. He was not, to begin with, unaware of the diminishing membership base and of the weakening militancy of local groups. It was therefore far from clear that an infrastructure existed that could develop organizing campaigns among new groups; it was also not clear that a sufficient grassroots base remained to mount resistance campaigns against the rising tide of welfare restrictiveness. To have announced either kind of campaign, only to have it fail, would have revealed NWRO's weakness at its base. In any case he could not turn the organization toward multi-constituency organizing (e.g., toward the aged or the working poor)—not, that is, without the killing internal struggle with the established recipient leadership that had prevented such a turn at earlier points.

On the other hand, there were strong inducements to join the fray over welfare reform. NWRO had a large national office staff by this time. The operation was expensive to maintain, especially in a political climate that made fund-raising increasingly difficult. The congressional struggle over welfare reform promised to give NWRO high visibility, thus enhancing its ability to raise funds.

Finally, the interest of many groups and of the press in the issue of welfare reorganization promised to give extraordinary visibility to the representatives of a relief recipients' organization who joined in the lobbying process. The opportunity to achieve a large measure of national recognition for NWRO's top leadership was at hand and that was a powerful incentive. The decision, then, was to lobby.

One measure of the lure of recognition and of organizational rewards which the pending debate over welfare reorganization held for NWRO is the fact that there was, at the outset, considerable uncertainty among the leadership as to whether the family assistance proposals should be supported or opposed. However, that did not matter as much as the chance to lobby mattered. The NWRO intended to seize the opportunity to enhance its waning visibility; the substance of its position could be developed over time.

A somewhat uncertain decision was first reached to support the bill. The objective was to improve it: to raise the minimum payment level ("UP THE NIXON PLAN!"), to eliminate workfare penalties, and to introduce various substantive and procedural rights. By the summer of 1970, however, NWRO turned against FAP and tried to defeat it ("ZAP FAP!").[45] Thereafter it worked assiduously to produce analyses of the veritable mélange of alternative bills and amendments that were placed before Congress, and it distributed these analyses widely through its newsletter and other mailings; it lobbied incessantly with individual congressmen; it helped organize anti-FAP caucuses within Congress; and, finally, it tried to rally local WROs across the country to devote themselves to lobbying activities, such as buttonholing their local congressmen and participating in various demonstrations in the nation's capital. From the fall of 1969 onward, in short, NWRO devoted a substantial part of its resources to trying to shape the course of welfare legislation in Congress.

How effective was NWRO's campaign against welfare reform? The answer to this question is obviously central to the argument of this book. NWRO itself took generous, if not full, credit for the defeat of the bill. But the facts lead to the opposite conclusion; its influence was negligible.

The only point at which NWRO had some, but hardly critical, influence on an important outcome occurred in the vote of the Senate

---

45 For a discussion of NWRO's shifting position on FAP, see Burke and Burke (159–165).

Finance Committee in November 1970, after the House had first passed the bill. The Senate Finance Committee defeated the plan 10 to 6, and the majority included three liberal Democrats who might have been expected to support the bill (Eugene McCarthy, Minnesota; Fred Harris, Oklahoma; and Albert Gore, Tennessee). NWRO lobbyists claim that they influenced the votes of both Harris and McCarthy, and judging from other forms of support which these particular senators gave NWRO over the years, this claim is reasonable. However, Gore's vote was not influenced by NWRO. He had just been defeated after thirty-two years in the Senate, in part because he had been a special target of Republican midterm campaign strategists; his vote was retaliation against the Nixon Administration.[46] Therefore, were it not for NWRO, that early and important committee vote might have been 8 to 8. Under the rules of the committee, however, a tie vote is a losing vote, and thus the bill would not have been reported out, whether NWRO had lobbied or not.[47]

In June 1971 the House (by a smaller margin) again enacted a version of the bill. Once more the crucial struggle was played out in the Senate where Long's committee bottled up the bill. NWRO's role during this period was chiefly to weaken liberal proponents of the bill by dividing and confusing them. If blacks were seemingly opposed to the bill, it became more difficult for some white liberals to support it. Nevertheless a liberal coalition formed under the leadership of Abraham Ribicoff, whom NWRO denounced. At several junctures this coalition managed to negotiate compromises with conservatives and with administration representatives. By this time, however, the president was backing away from his own bill and would not sanction the compromises.

Moreover these particular events were of no great significance, *taken by themselves*. Chairman Long and others had made it abundantly clear that they would organize a filibuster should the bill ever

---

[46] Moynihan claims that another negative vote—Anderson (N.M.)—was influenced by Harris, and thus indirectly by NWRO (533). Burke and Burke do not confirm this claim; nor does Mitchell I. Ginsberg, the New York City Human Resources Administrator and the most active lobbyist for FAP.

[47] One member of the committee, Hartke from Indiana, was absent from this crucial vote. A liberal, Hartke had just barely survived the midterm election. Burke and Burke are silent on the question of how he might have voted had he been present. Moynihan also gives no clue, and Ginsberg also finds it difficult to say what his vote would have been. In any event there is no evidence that he was influenced by NWRO, nor did NWRO's lobbyists make such a claim.

reach the floor of the Senate. In the judgment of various persons close to the congressional struggle, such as Mitchell I. Ginsberg, it would have been impossible to find the votes to invoke cloture. And even if one grants the extremely remote assumption that cloture might have been invoked, the opponents of the bill would have had many other chances to destroy it through repeal, or to emasculate it by crippling amendments. The point is that the test of a lobbying strategy is not merely momentary success, if even that can be achieved; the test is the capacity to sustain influence year after year in the face of a continuing and determined opposition.

NWRO's ineffectiveness in the Congress is further illustrated by another incident. During the course of the welfare debate Congress enacted an extremely restrictive amendment to the Social Security Act. It will be recalled that congressional concern over the welfare rises had begun to be expressed some years earlier, as marked by the enactment of training and employment programs in 1967. Under the original "Work Incentives Now" program, welfare files were presumably to be combed for people eligible for training and work, who were then to be registered as "ready for employment." In the late 1960s welfare administrators implemented this program laxly for fear of the possible repercussions in the ghettos. But in late 1971 Congress acted to put teeth into the program with an amendment specifying that any state which failed to refer to employment at least 15 percent of the average number of individuals registered during the year as "ready for employment" would be penalized by the subtraction of one percentage point from its matching funds for each percent by which referrals fell below 15 percent. The amendment was passed in the Senate *without a single dissenting vote* despite the fact that NWRO's lobbying presence was at its peak during this period (Burke and Burke, 164).

But NWRO did not lobby simply to be effective in the legislative process. NWRO and its leadership obtained enormous visibility and substantial resources in the course of the struggle over welfare reorganization, thus reinforcing the illusion of its influence. Consistent with this illusion NWRO's leadership determined to make its presence felt as the Democratic and Republican parties formulated their campaign platforms in the spring and summer of 1972. These events indicate just how invested NWRO had become in electoral politics and in an image of itself as being influential in electoral politics. This turn had been signaled by George at the convention in 1970 when he announced: "We've got to get into lobbying, political organization, and ward and precinct politics" (Martin, 131). With that rallying cry a welfare recipients' organization which no longer had a constituency capable of storming a welfare center anywhere in the country issued a call through its newsletter in November 1971 to storm the American electoral system. This statement by Beulah Sanders, who was elected chairman of the National Coordinating Committee in 1971, deserves to be quoted completely if only to convey the full measure of the unreality which had come to dominate the organization:

> At the last NWRO Convention, there was a clear mandate from the membership that NWRO take a major role in the various political arenas all across this country. In keeping with that mandate your chairman consented to testify both in Boston and New York before the New Democratic Coalition's regional platform hearings.
>
> NWRO also has played a significant role in the building of the National Women's Political Caucus and we are helping to build similar caucuses in several states. The upcoming year is going to be most active politically for the entire country and a very significant one (politically) for WRO's across the country. So with the slogan of Bread, Justice and Dignity, let's unite all our brothers and sisters in the struggle and hard fight ahead.
>
> For it is our intent to develop a large welfare rights caucus at the Democratic convention. We must begin on local levels to make sure that our members are registered to vote, and that we begin as early as possible to vote for the various delegate seats by demanding that there be equal representation for our members. We must begin to link up with other organizations and run candidates for the various local, state, and national offices. Politics has in the past been a very dirty and closed business in this country.
>
> We must be about changing that. For we have seen in the past what has happened to candidates who have gotten the support of the people but decide that the old line party powers are who they need to be beholden to. So the burden is going to be on us to pick and support candidates for office whom we can trust.
>
> It is going to be very important for us to know what is happening in your local areas so that we can work from a national level to develop our plans for the coming year. So begin now: get together with other groups, especially women's groups, to discuss your strategies. As welfare recipients who represent a major portion of the poor in this country, the burden is ours to keep the goal of "adequate income" in the forefront as the most vital issue in any and all of our campaigns. "Welfare Reform" will be a vital issue

in '72, but we must not get caught up in that trap, as so many of the liberal candidates and organizations have, for we are about more than just "Welfare Reform." We are about a "Guaranteed Adequate Income" for all Americans; and that means a true redistribution of this country's resources in such a way as to guarantee the right to a decent life to all Americans, be they man, woman, child, black, white or red, working or non-working.

In June 1972 the NWRO leadership announced to its membership: "We will go to the Democratic National Convention in the same manner we have always dealt with an unjust system—with representation on the inside, but our real strength on the outside, in the streets." A major demonstration was planned, and at a huge financial cost to the organization and its affiliates about 500 leaders, members, and organizers actually attended. Given the extraordinary delegate composition of that particular Democratic convention, NWRO obtained 1,000 votes (about 1,600 were needed) supporting a plank calling for a guaranteed income of $6,500 for a family of four. It was heady stuff. "We lost," NWRO announced in a post-convention newsletter, "but in a spiritual sense, we had won." (Just how great a spiritual victory had been won was to be revealed in November when in part because of McGovern's advocacy, at least in the early months of the campaign, of a guaranteed income of $4,000 for a family of four, he was obliterated by the voters.) As for the Republican convention, there was no spiritual victory; it was, NWRO proclaimed, "No place for the poor."

The Demise of the National Welfare
Rights Organization

A good number of local organizers had come in this period to think that there was "no place for the poor" in NWRO's national office, either. NWRO's national convention in 1971 was the setting for a revolt led by some of the senior organizers who objected to the fact that they were being provided with so little assistance from the national office at a time when local organizing was foundering. Local organizers were intent on expanding their membership so they could lobby at the state and local level against welfare cuts of various kinds, and they wanted resources from the national office to aid in that process. From their perspective the national office, because of its emphasis on national lobbying, had come to give the building of local membership a low priority. They were also concerned about the adverse effect on local organizing of NWRO's repeated calls for demonstrations in the nation's capital (and later at the presidential nominating conventions). These demonstrations drew local recipient leaders away from local organizing activities and the travel costs depleted local treasuries, already nearly empty.

The character of the 1971 convention itself helped to trigger discontents among organizers. It was staged to dramatize NWRO's lobbying and coalitional role. The featured speaker was Senator George McGovern, who was then preparing to run for the Democratic presidential nomination but who had not yet been overwhelmed with speaking invitations. McGovern had agreed to introduce (but not to endorse) a guaranteed income bill which had been drafted by NWRO, and the leadership hoped by his presence at the conference to give their bill national prominence. Other notables, such as Shirley Chisholm and Gloria Steinem, also graced the speaker's platform. The organizers pointed out that no one was talking about organizing and that was very troubling to them.

Moreover the structure of NWRO and of the conventions had by this time effectively separated organizers and recipient leaders. The recipient leaders met separately with a few members of the national staff, presumably to set policy; organizers were not consulted. In this sense, it was truly a poor people's organization, and organizers had developed a certain resentment about their exclusion (although the organizational structure was one which they had themselves created). As a practical matter most of the recipient delegates from local groups had little more than the most formalistic role in policymaking; the influentials were the state representatives who comprised the National Coordinating Committee and the Executive Committee. These women had become so famous and so intimidating to the typical local recipient leader that they dominated the convention platforms and the policymaking process. It was left for the delegates simply to ratify what their leadership recommended. For all practical purposes, the conventions in the 1970s were arranged to benefit the national leaders. Organizers and most delegates felt left out, shunted aside by the sweep of NWRO's large legislative objectives, its visiting dignitaries, its press conferences, its prearranged agendas.

And they were bewildered and bored by the hours devoted to passing amendments to NWRO's intricate constitution and debating resolutions regarding legislative programs which seemed remote from the everyday realities of their existence. The anger was gone, the spontaneity was gone, and the sense of community, solidarity, and militancy were gone. All had given way to the preoccupation with the maintenance of organizational structure and lobbying activities.

The organizers' complaints, however, met with little response from either the national staff or the National Coordinating Committee. In the continuing contest over resources and priorities the national leadership consistently won, mainly because of their superior capacity to attract money and their superior capacity to attract publicity, even when the publicity was generated by the activities of local welfare rights groups. Consequently many organizers, especially the more experienced ones, turned away from NWRO following the convention in 1971. Until that time they had shown great loyalty, and could be depended upon to abide by the decisions of the national leadership. But no longer. NWRO had first lost its membership base; it then lost the allegiance of many of its senior organizers.

One measure of how little importance, in practice, was assigned to the grassroots in these years is revealed by the distribution of NWRO's national budget. In the early years a modest proportion had gone to support the salaries and other expenses of some local organizers, and another part of the budget paid for national staff whose main function at that time was to provide services to local groups. But in the 1970s virtually all of the funds raised went to support national office operations. NWRO had a rather sizable budget in those years, usually well in excess of $250,000 per year. But precious little of it found its way to the local level. A large bureaucracy, as these things go, had developed in Washington; the staff on payroll ranged from thirty to fifty persons. The periodic meetings of the Executive Committee and of the National Coordinating Committee were expensive. The research, writing, and publication activities associated with lobbying were expensive. National demonstrations were extremely costly; the planning and execution of the Children's March for Survival, for example, is estimated to have cost more than one hundred thousand dollars alone. In other words, local groups, despite their much inferior fund-raising capabilities, were largely left to fend for themselves.

Many more complaints were voiced by the remaining local organizers and recipients at the convention of 1973. Faith Evans, who was then acting executive director of NWRO, told a reporter for the *Washington Post* after the convention that

> NWRO spent its $300,000 budget (in 1972) fighting President Nixon's welfare reform plan in Washington and fighting for more political representation for the poor at the Democratic and Republican Presidential conventions. At the NWRO convention, folks kept telling me for the past two years National has sort of withdrawn and drained resources from us and we've been struggling out here and we didn't get nothing back. If we get $100,000 in the next six months, I anticipate spending 80 percent in the field.

And in a postconvention newsletter, the NWRO leadership announced:

> There was a mandate put on the National Office by the delegates at the Convention for us to reorient our priorities and begin redeveloping our field operation, so that we can provide continuing build-up and support to local organizing groups. It has been our intention in the National Office for some time now since the end of the FAP fight to begin that process. The National Office has now committed itself to providing most of its resources to help local people organize in their communities.

But it was too late. The chance to organize the grassroots had passed, not least because black unrest had passed. And with the demise of the black movement, there were no resources to be had for organizing. Private elites, like government before them, had begun to withdraw support for organizing among the urban black poor. As one funding source after another put it, "We are no longer emphasizing poverty." Consequently NWRO rapidly fell deeply into debt. In the fall of 1974 Johnnie Tillmon (NWRO's first national chairman), who had succeeded George as permanent executive director after his resignation in December 1972, issued a "Master Plan for Fund-Raising for the National Welfare Rights Organization." The fundraising goal was $1 million annually for six years and it called mainly upon the poor to send in contributions. But there was no response—not from the poor nor from anyone else. Several months later NWRO went bankrupt and the national office was closed.

NWRO failed to achieve its own objective—to build an enduring mass organization through which the poor could exert influence. Certainly NWRO did not endure; it survived a mere six or seven years, then collapsed. Just as certainly, it did not attract a mass base: at its peak, the national membership count did not exceed 25,000 adults. And it is our opinion that it had relatively little influence in the lobbying process to which it progressively devoted most of its resources.

But in the final analysis we do not judge NWRO a failure for these reasons. We ourselves did not expect that NWRO would endure or that it would attract a mass base or become influential in the lobbying process. Rather, we judge it by another criterion: whether it exploited the momentary unrest among the poor to obtain the maximum concessions possible in return for the restoration of quiescence. It is by that criterion that it failed.

NWRO had a slogan—"Bread and Justice"—and NWRO understood that for the people at the bottom a little bread is a little justice. Had it pursued a mobilizing strategy, encouraging more and more of the poor to demand welfare, NWRO could perhaps have left a legacy of another million families on the rolls. Millions of potentially eligible families had still not applied for aid, especially among the aged and working poor, and hundreds of thousands of potential AFDC recipients were still being denied relief in local centers. To have mobilized these poor, however, NWRO's leaders would have had to evacuate the legislative halls and presidential delegate caucuses, and reoccupy the relief centers; they would have had to relinquish testifying and lobbying, and resume agitating. They did not and an opportunity to obtain "bread and justice" for more of the poor was forfeited.

The parallel with the relief movement in the Great Depression is striking. Poor people exerted influence just as long as they mobilized to disrupt local welfare practices and to demand relief, at once forcing concessions from welfare departments and generating pressure for federal concessions as well. Except for widespread disorder and deepening local fiscal strains, the Roosevelt Administration would hardly have ventured into the emergency relief business. Organizers, however, soon turned to developing intricate national, state, and local structures as well as to cultivating regular relationships with public officials. Its leaders were soon converted from agitators to lobbyists, its followers became progressively inert, and the capacity to capitalize on instability to secure economic concessions for the poor was lost. Finally, with the passing of mass unrest, the Workers' Alliance collapsed. The relief organization of the 1960s met the same fate, and by the same processes.

A Closing Note on the Postwar Black Movement

By the close of the 1960s, the black movement which began in the postwar period had made some modest economic gains. A large proportion of the unemployed and impoverished masses in the cities were receiving welfare grants. Others had benefitted from the expansion of municipal payrolls, an expansion stimulated in part by the federal programs inaugurated during the Great Society years. The economic boom in the late 1960s also enabled more blacks to gain employment in the private sector. Taken together, enlarged public and private employment had somewhat diminished the overall rate of nonwhite unemployment.

By the mid–1970s, all of these gains had been substantially eroded. There were several reasons. For one, as black protest subsided, federal concessions were withdrawn. With the ascent to the presidency of Richard Nixon, the administration of welfare by states and localities became more restrictive, partly in response to threatening rhetoric and restrictive regulations promulgated by the federal government. At the same time, the Great Society programs that had provided resources and justification for black protest were stifled, their activities curbed, and their funds curtailed or eliminated in favor of new revenue-sharing or black grant programs. Whatever else the new revenue-sharing formulas meant, they slowly redirected monies away from the older cities to richer cities, suburbs, and towns, while within each locality some of the monies which had previously provided jobs and services in the ghettos were spent to fund police departments and to reduce taxes.

Meanwhile, as federal policies curtailed the public programs which had given aid to the urban poor, the persisting recession and rampant inflation that characterized the 1970s caused a sharp reduction in the standard of living of already depressed groups. Unemployment rates were, as usual, much higher among blacks; and inflation rapidly destroyed the purchasing power of welfare grants, which, in the hostile political climate of the seventies, were rarely increased, and were surely not increased to keep pace with the rising cost of living. By the mid–1970s, the real income of welfare recipients in many states had been cut by as much as half.

These were national trends. Most of the minority poor were located in the older northern cities, where the impact of the eco-

nomic trends of the 1970s was even more severe and where the effects
of inflation and recession were exacerbated by related political developments. The so-called "urban fiscal crisis" of the 1970s signaled a
concerted effort by political and economic elites to reduce the real
income of the bottom stratum of the American working class, largely
by slashing the benefits they had won from the public sector.

The processes underlying the fiscal crisis of the cities had been
under way for at least two decades. In the years after World War II,
the manufacturing base of many older cities weakened. The decline
in central-city manufacturing had a number of causes. In part, it
resulted from the movement of both older plants and new capital
to the South and abroad in search of cheaper labor. In part, it was
the result of the movement of plants to the suburban ring, where
labor costs were not necessarily cheaper but where federal investments in highways, housing, and other service systems reduced the
costs of doing business in various other ways. In part, it was the
result of the pattern of federal investments in defense and space
exploration which bypassed the older manufacturing cities for the
new cities of the South and West. These trends in manufacturing
were intertwined with the flight of commerce and of the more affluent
classes from the older central cities to the suburban rings and to the
"southern rim" of the nation. (Meanwhile, with the aid of federal
urban-renewal subsidies, the downtown areas of many of these cities
were redeveloped with huge office towers and luxury apartment
complexes to house the increasingly complex administrative apparatus
and the managerial personnel of national and international corporations whose plants had come to be located elsewhere.)

It was, of course, during this same period that large numbers of
black and Hispanic people migrated to the cities. By the mid–1960s,
these displaced and chronically impoverished people had become
rebellious. In turn, their demands helped to trigger greater demands
by other groups, such as municipal employees. As mayors struggled
to appease these insurgent urban groups with jobs, benefits, and
services, municipal budgets rose precipitately. But so long as the
cities were in turmoil the political price exacted by the insurgents
had to be paid in order to restore order. Accordingly, municipalities
raised tax rates despite their weakening economies, and state governments and the federal government increased grants-in-aid to
municipalities. By these means, the cities stayed afloat fiscally, and
they stayed afloat politically as well. Over all, the share of the

American national product channeled into the public sector rose dramatically in the 1960s, and the largest part of that rise was due to mounting municipal and state budgets.

By the early 1970s, urban strife had subsided; a degree of political stability had been restored, in no small part as a result of the concessions granted in the 1960s. At the same time, however, the disparity between expenditures and revenues in the older cities widened dramatically, for the long-term economic trends that were undercutting the manufacturing base of these cities worsened rapidly under the impact of the recessionary policies of the Nixon–Ford administrations. As unemployment rates rose in the central cities, municipal revenues declined, for much of these revenues was earned through sales and income taxes. Moreover, once the turmoil of the 1960s ebbed, the federal and state governments could and did reduce grants-in-aid to the older central cities, thereby widening the disparities in the city budgets even more. The situation thus became ripe for a mobilization of national and local business interests to bring expenditures into line with revenues by cutting the cost of the populist politics in the cities.

The trigger for this mobilization was the threat of a default by New York City in 1975. Banks with large holdings of New York City securities became unnerved over the rapid increase in short-term borrowing, and refused to float loans until the city "put its house in order." Whatever the bankers intended, their action precipitated the theatrical spectacular of a New York City default. The city did not default, but the drama made it possible to impose entirely new definitions of the urban fiscal situation upon the populations of the cities across the nation. There simply was no money, it was said; municipal budgets had to be balanced. In the face of that definition, urban pressure groups became frightened, confused, and helpless, and were transformed into passive witnesses to a municipal politics in which they had been active participants only a short time earlier.

With the threat of default as the justification, locally based business interests (who historically have often operated under the aegis of municipal reform groups) moved to restructure urban policies. On the one hand, they insisted upon slashes in payrolls, wages, and benefits and in services to neighborhoods. On the other hand, they argued that to bolster declining city revenues, states and municipalities would have to make new and larger concessions to business: reduced taxes, improved services, enlarged subsidies, and a relaxation of public regulation in matters such as environmental pollution. And while New York City's plight captured the headlines, it was only the exemplary case, the means that was used to instruct poor and working-class groups in other cities not to resist similar and even more drastic cost-cutting campaigns by local elites.

Nor, appearances aside, did the federal government remain aloof from these urban fiscal troubles. The crisis provided legitimation for the imposition of a national economic policy to reduce public-sector expenditures in the United States, a policy much in accord with national corporate interests, which claimed that American industry was suffering from a severe shortage of capital. The gradual reduction of federal grants-in-aid to the older central cities, combined with the federal government's refusal to aid cities on the verge of bankruptcy, combined to bring about a shift in the balance between public and private sectors in the United States. Since state and local budgets accounted for two-thirds of total government expenditures, they bore the brunt of the cuts. Whatever position one takes on the seriousness of the capital crisis in the United States, there is not much question that this method of solving the problem of capital formation places the heaviest burden on the lowest income stratum of the population (the very groups that are also least likely to benefit if the position of American capital subsequently strengthens and a period of prosperity ensues). Under the guise of the urban fiscal crisis, in short, local and national business interests joined to reassert control over the municipal level of the state apparatus, for it was on the municipal level that popular struggles by working-class groups had forced some concessions in the 1960s.

The impact of these political developments on urban minorities was clear from the outset. Services to neighborhoods were reduced, and much more so in impoverished neighborhoods than in better-off ones. Municipal workers were laid off in large numbers, and the overwhelming impact of these layoffs was felt by the minority people who were hired during and after the turmoil of the 1960s. In New York City, for example, two-fifths of the blacks on the city's work force (and half of the Hispanics) were fired at the same time as recession-induced unemployment reached near-depression levels. For many of the unemployed, welfare eventually became the only possible recourse, a fact that lent the growing welfare restrictiveness of the period a special cruelty. The urban crisis, in short, had become the rationale for a mobilization against the urban working class, and especially against its enlarging minority segment.

Finally, and much to the point of this book, blacks were assaulted in another way as well. The events of the urban fiscal crisis deprived them even of the limited influence in urban politics ordinarily wielded by the vote. As the fiscal crisis deepened, with the result that financial and business leaders effectively took control of municipal budget decisions, the elected political stratum of the older northern cities was supplanted. Such gains in city and state electoral representation as blacks had made during the sixties were clearly of little consequence in resisting the slashing of municipal budgets when bankers and businessmen were, for all practical purposes, making the budget decisions.

The possibilities for reversing this campaign against the urban poor through ordinary political processes would not have been bright under any circumstances. As financial and business leaders took control, however, efforts by groups to lobby with city and state elected officials to save their services or their jobs became fatuous, simply because the events of the crisis deprived these officials of whatever authority they had once had. City and state governments have always been in large measure dependent for their revenues on locally raised taxes, which in turn hinge on business prosperity. They have also been dependent for debt financing on private credit markets. These arrangements meant that state and local officials were always ultimately vulnerable to those who made investment and lending decisions. Enlarging fiscal discrepancies in the municipal and state budgets made this vulnerability acute and the dependency of elected officials blatant. (Indeed, in New York City, businessmen and bankers used the crisis to formally restructure municipal political authority, depriving elected officials of even their customary formal budgetary powers.)

Still, the new black leaders, including the black city politicians who were caught in the fiscal crisis, continued to rely upon electoral politics to moderate the impact of the cutbacks on the ghettos. But this strategy was bound to fail.

This is not to say that mass protest was clearly possible in the mid–1970s. One can never predict with certainty when the "heavings and rumblings of the social foundations" will force up large-scale defiance, although changes of great magnitude were at work. Who, after all, could have predicted the extraordinary mobilization of black people beginning in 1955? Nor can one calculate with certainty the responses of elites to mass disruption. There are no blueprints to guide movements of the poor. But if organizers and leaders want to help those movements emerge, they must always proceed as if protest were possible. They may fail. The time may not be right. But then, they may sometimes succeed.

References

Bailis, Lawrence Neil. *Bread or Justice*. Lexington, Mass.: D. C. Heath and Co., 1974.

Betz, Michael. "Riots and Welfare: Are They Related?" *Social Policy* 21 (1974).

Birnbaum, Ezra, and Gilman, David. Unpublished paper on the minimum standards campaigns, New York City, January 1968, mimeographed.

Bowler, Kenneth M. *The Nixon Guaranteed Income Proposal*. Cambridge: Ballinger Publishing Co., 1974.

Burke, Vincent J., and Burke, Vee. *Nixon's Good Deed: Welfare Reform*. New York: Columbia University Press, 1974.

Cloward, Richard A., and Piven, Frances Fox. *The Politics of Turmoil: Essays on Poverty, Race, and the Urban Crisis*. New York: Pantheon Books, 1974.

Donovan, John C. *The Politics of Poverty*. 2nd ed. New York: Pegasus Books, 1973.

Durbin, Elizabeth. *Welfare and Employment*. New York: Praeger Publishers, 1969.

Evans, Rowland, and Novak, Robert. *Lyndon B. Johnson: The Exercise of Power*. New York: The New American Library, 1966.

Fiske, Mary Ann. "The Politics of the Claiming Minority: Social Protest Strategies to End Poverty." Unpublished master's thesis, College of Human Ecology, Cornell University, September 1971.

Gelb, Joyce, and Sardell, Alice, "Strategies for the Powerless: The Welfare Rights Movement in New York City." Unpublished paper prepared for delivery at a meeting of the American Political Science Association in New Orleans, 1973, mimeographed.

Jackson, Larry R., and Johnson, William A. *Protest by the Poor*. Lexington, Mass.: D. C. Heath and Co., 1974.

King, Martin Luther, Jr. *Why We Can't Wait*. New York: The New American Library, 1963.

Kurzman, Paul, ed. *The Mississippi Experience: Strategies for Welfare Rights Action*. New York: Association Press, 1971.

Levens, Helene. "Organizational Affiliation and Powerlessness." *Social Problems* 16 (Summer 1968) .

Martin, George T., Jr. "The Emergence and Development of a Social Movement Organization Among the Underclass: A Case Study of the National Welfare Rights Organization." Unpublished Ph.D. dissertation, Department of Sociology, University of Chicago, September 1972.

Meier, August, and Rudwick, Elliott. *CORE: A Study in the Civil Rights Movement, 1942–1968*. Urbana: The University of Illinois Press, 1975.

Michels, Robert. *Political Parties: A Sociological Study of the Oligarchical Tendencies of Modern Democracy*. Glencoe: The Free Press, 1949.

Miller, Herman P. *Rich Man Poor Man*. New York: Signet Books, 1964.

Milwaukee County Welfare Rights Organization. *Welfare Mothers Speak Out: We Ain't Gonna Shuffle Anymore*. New York: W. W. Norton and Co., 1972.

Moynihan, Daniel P. *The Politics of a Guaranteed Income*. New York: Random House, 1973.

Piven, Frances Fox, and Cloward, Richard A. *Regulating the Poor: The Functions of Public Welfare*. New York: Pantheon Books, 1971.

Rabagliati, Mary, and Birnbaum, Ezra. "Organization of Welfare Clients." In *Community Development in the Mobilization for Youth Experience*, edited by Harold H. Weissman. New York: Association Press, 1969.

Rothman, Gene H. "Welfare Rights Groups of the 1930's and 1960's." Unpublished master's thesis, Department of Sociology, Columbia University, 1969.

Sardell, Alice. "The Minimum Standards Campaign: A Case of Protest Politics." Unpublished master's thesis, Graduate Division of the College of Arts and Sciences, City College of the City University of New York, September 1972.

Schlesinger, Arthur M., Jr. *A Thousand Days*. Boston: Houghton Mifflin Co., 1965.

Stein, Herman D., ed. *The Crisis in Welfare in Cleveland: Report of the Mayor's Commission*. Cleveland: Case Western Reserve University, 1969.

Steiner, Gilbert. *The State of Welfare*. Washington, D. C.: Brookings Institution, 1971.

Sorensen, Theodore C. *Kennedy*. New York: Harper and Row, 1965.

U. S. Department of Health, Education, and Welfare, *Social Security Bulletin* 34 (August 1971).

U. S. Department of Labor. *Manpower Report to the President* and *A Report on Manpower Requirements, Resources, Utilization, and Training.* Washington, D.C.: U.S. Government Printing Office, 1964.

U. S. Department of Labor, Bureau of Labor Statistics. *Recent Trends in Social and Economic Conditions of Negroes in the United States, July 1968.* Washington, D.C.: U.S. Government Printing Office, 1969 (BLS Report No. 347).

U. S. National Advisory Commission on Rural Poverty. *The People Left Behind.* Washington, D.C.: U.S. Government Printing Office, 1967.

U. S. President's National Advisory Commission on Civil Disorders. *Report of the National Advisory Commission on Civil Disorders.* New York: Bantam Books, 1968.

Van Til, Jon. "On Overcoming Barriers to the Organization of the Welfare Poor." Paper presented at a meeting of the Society for the Study of Social Problems, New Orleans, August 28, 1972, mimeographed.

Weissman, Harold H. "Problems in Maintaining Stability in Low-Income Social Action Organizations." In *Community Development in the Mobilization for Youth Experience,* edited by Harold H. Weissman. New York: Association Press, 1969.

Whitaker, William H. "The Determinants of Social Movement Success: A Study of the National Welfare Rights Organization." Unpublished Ph.D. dissertation, Florence Heller School for Advanced Studies in Social Welfare, Brandeis University, 1970.

Wilson, James Q. "The Strategy of Protest: Problems of Negro Civic Action." *Journal of Conflict Resolution* 5 (September 1961).

———. *Political Organizations.* New York: Basic Books, 1973.

Index

Abbott, Edith, 54n.
Abernathy, Ralph, 333n.
aged, programs for, 31, 266 n.
Agricultural Adjustment Act, 110
agriculture: labor, 184, 185, 187, 189–193, 205n., 269; New Deal and, 110, 190, 196–7; southern, 182–93, 196–197; World War I, 189–90; World War II, 190–1. *See also* farmers
Agriculture Department, 192n.
Aid to Families with Dependent Children (AFDC), 264, 266–7, 273, 274n., 302–4, 322, 325, 335, 353
aircraft industry, 166, 171–2
Akron, Ohio, 118; Central Labor Union, 134; rubber industry, 133–5, 136, 146, 148–9
Alabama, 182n.; civil rights, 199, 208–211, 226, 238–46, 248–52, 256; textile strike, 125. *See also place names*
Alabama, University of, 238–9
Alaska, 252
Albany (Ga.) Movement, 235–8, 240–1
Alcorn, James L., 225
Alexander, Will W., 197, 214
Allen, Robert L., 182n.
Allis-Chalmers, 166
Amalgamated Association of Iron, Tin and Steel Workers, 117–18, 148n., 158n.
Amalgamated Clothing Workers of America, 114, 163n.

American Association of Social Workers, 84n.
American Civil Liberties Union, 55n.
American Federation of Labor (AFL), 111–13, 115–16, 119, 134, 136, 146, 152, 154; Buildings and Metal Trades Dept., 117, 118; and communists, 151–2; craft vs. industrial unions, 116–18, 133, 149; electoral system and, 163; membership, 116, 154, 168; no-strike pledge, wartime, 166; strikebreaking, 115, 117, 149n.; and unemployed, 70, 72n. *See also names of persons, unions*
American Labor Party, 162, 163n.
American Legion, 109
American Liberty League, 130, 132
"American Plan," 120n.
American Public Welfare Association, 57
American Railway Union, 104, 148n.
American Workers Party, 75n.
American Workers Union, 76
Amsterdam News, 58
Anaconda Copper Mine Co., 118
Anderson, Clinton P., 346n.
Anderson, Gusta E., 30n.
Anderson, John, 136
Anderson, Nels, 86
antiwar movements, 22, 323, 325
arbitration, 157–8. *See also* mediation
Aristotle, 6
Arizona, 246

363

opportunities, social structure and, 3, 6–14; political impact, 27–32, 146–7; power system, 2–3, 146; reforms, residual, 34–6; repression, forceful, 102–5, 189; social location and forms of, 18–22; spontaneity, 27; by unemployed, *see* unemployed.

Prothro, James W., 215, 224, 233*n.*

Proudfoot, Merrill, 222*n.*

Provisional National Committee, 75

Public Health Service, U.S., 48

public opinion: antipoverty programs, 270, 292, 293; pro–civil rights, 183, 198, 199, 210–11, 225, 239–40, 250, 253; reforms and backlash, 34, 84–5, 337–9; repression and conciliation and, 27–32; strikes, 122, 172–3

Public Resolution No. 44, 132

public works programs, 47, 66, 82–5, 147; grievance procedures, 80; lobbying, by Workers' Alliance, 85–90; number employed, 83; strikes, 80, 88n. *See also specific programs*

Public Works Administration, 66, 147

Pullman strike, 103, 148*n.*

Rabagliati, Mary, 301*n.*

racism, 181ff; industry and, 190–4; in North, 188, 203–4; as political issue, 195–202, 214; Supreme Court and (*see also* Supreme Court), 207. *See also* blacks; civil rights.

radicalism, 151, 163*n.*; red baiting and purges, 123, 164–6, 168–9. *See also* persons, groups

Radosh, Ronald, 173*n.*

railroads, 108, 112, 159, 168, 169*n.*; strikes, 27, 103, 104, 148*n.*, 168

Railway Brotherhoods, 112

Railway Labor Act, 112, 131*n.*

Randolph, A. Phillip, 196, 204–5, 245

Raskob, John J., 65

Ratchford, B. U., 190*n.*

Raybeck, Joseph G., 102, 108, 113, 119, 120 *and n.*, 128*n.*, 131, 142, 143, 147, 154, 162, 164, 166

Reading, Pa., 75, 103

Reagan, Ronald, 333

Reconstruction, 185–7, 252

Reconstruction Finance Corporation, 59, 64*n.*

Reddick, L. D., 208*n.*

Reeb, Rev. James, 250

Rees, Goronwy, 109, 109*n.*

Reese, Jessie, 141–2

reforms: conciliation and repression, 27–32; lobbying for by Workers' Alliance, 85–92; New Deal, 85–6, 146–7; public opinion backlash and, 34, 84–5, 337–9; reintegration of disaffected, 32–6; residual, 34–6; southern political, 182ff., welfare, 335–49

Reich, Michael, 21*n.*, 99*n.*, 105, 107

relief, 41–4; for agricultural labor, 196–197; for blacks (*see* also welfare), 58, 204, 264–5, 268–9; contraction of, 82–6; federal, 64, 66–8, 76–7, 81–3, 268; fiscal breakdowns, 60–4; lobbying for, by Workers' Alliance, 85–92; numbers on dole, 67–8, 91–2, 268; protests, 30, 56–60, 67, 76–82, 84–5, 88, 88*n.*; southern economy and, 196–7. *See also* public works programs; welfare

rent: evictions and protests, 53–5, 71; strike, 23*n.*, 269

repression and conciliation, 27–32

Republic Steel, 143, 144

Republican Party, 184*n.*, 188; blacks and civil rights, 195, 197, 198, 201, 213–14, 217, 220, 221, 225–7, 246, 251; and racism, 186*n.*; and South, 195, 197, 198, 201, 213–14, 252, 254; and unemployed, 269*n.*; voting patterns (*see also* elections), 16–17, 65, 110; and welfare, 332. *See also* Congress

Reuther, Victor, 138*n.*

Reuther, Walter, 139, 162, 289

Rhode Island, 125

Rhodes, James Allen, 291

Ribicoff, Abraham, 341–2, 346

Rich, Marvin, 223, 224

right-to-work laws, 169, 170

Riot Commission, 273

riots: blacks (*see also* violence, racial), 206, 248, 265, 272–3, 325, 331; rent, 53–5; welfare, 274–5, 305

Rochester, N.Y., 248, 272

Rockefeller, Nelson, 248*n.*, 319, 333

Rodman, Selden, 88

Rogers, William P., 221

Rogg, Nathan, 75*n.*

ABOUT THE AUTHORS

Frances Fox Piven is Professor of Political Science at Boston University, and is also vice-president of the Society for the Study of Social Problems (SSSP). Richard A. Cloward is a sociologist and social worker on the faculty of Columbia University, and a member of the board of directors of the New York Civil Liberties Union. Together they have written extensively on urban politics and social movements. Their articles in *The Nation* are widely credited with stimulating the formation of the National Welfare Rights Organization (NWRO), a grass-roots protest movement of welfare recipients.

Their book on the welfare system, *Regulating the Poor,* also published by Pantheon, won the C. Wright Mills Award of the Society for the Study of Social Problems in 1971. A collection of their essays, *The Politics of Turmoil,* was published by Pantheon in 1974. Professor Cloward's book, written with Lloyd E. Ohlin, on the origins of gang delinquency won the Dennis Carroll Award of the International Society of Criminology in 1965.